W9-CFB-723

THIRTEEN SOLDIERS

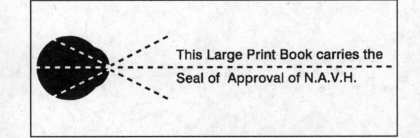
This Large Print Book carries the
Seal of Approval of N.A.V.H.

Thirteen Soldiers

A PERSONAL HISTORY OF AMERICANS AT WAR

John McCain
and Mark Salter

THORNDIKE PRESS
A part of Gale, Cengage Learning

GALE
CENGAGE Learning

Farmington Hills, Mich • San Francisco • New York • Waterville, Maine
Meriden, Conn • Mason, Ohio • Chicago

GALE
CENGAGE Learning®

ALL RIGHTS RESERVED
Thorndike Press® Large Print Nonfiction.
The text of this Large Print edition is unabridged.
Other aspects of the book may vary from the original edition.
Set in 16 pt. Plantin.

LIBRARY OF CONGRESS CATALOGING-IN-PUBLICATION DATA

McCain, John, 1936-
    Thirteen soldiers : a personal history of Americans at war / by John McCain and Mark Salter.
    pages cm — (Thorndike press large print nonfiction)
    Includes bibliographical references.
    ISBN 978-1-4104-7565-7 (hardcover) — ISBN 1-4104-7565-4 (hardcover)
    1. Soldiers—United States—Biography 2. United States. Army—Biography. 3. Military biography—United States. I. Salter, Mark. II. Title.
U52.M39 2014b
355.0092'273—dc23   2014036273

Published in 2014 by arrangement with Simon & Schuster, Inc.

Printed in the United States of America
1 2 3 4 5 6 7 18 17 16 15 14

*To the memory of Colonel
George "Bud" Day, USAF;
General James Robinson Risner, USAF;
Admiral Jeremiah A. Denton, USN;
and Captain Edwin A. Schuman, USN.*

It was a privilege, gentlemen.

What battles have in common is human: the behaviors of men struggling to reconcile their instinct for self-preservation, their sense of honor and the achievement of some aim over which other men are ready to kill them. The study of battle is therefore always a study of fear and usually of courage; always of leadership, usually of obedience; always of compulsion, sometimes of insubordination; always of anxiety, sometimes of elation or catharsis; always of uncertainty and doubt, misinformation and misapprehension, usually also of faith and sometimes of vision; always of violence, sometimes also of cruelty, self-sacrifice, compassion; above all, it is always a study of solidarity.

John Keegan,
The Face of Battle

CONTENTS

INTRODUCTION

Every Memorial Day at Arlington National Cemetery, soldiers from the 3rd U.S. Infantry Brigade place small American flags at the headstones of more than three hundred thousand graves. The headstones bear the names of people of every ethnic origin. They mark the final resting places of professional soldiers and conscripts; of rich and poor; Christian, Jew, and Muslim; believer and nonbeliever; descendants of *Mayflower* pilgrims and immigrants who had barely arrived in the country before they took up arms to defend her; dark-skinned and white; city dwellers and people from small towns and farms; teachers and machinists; businessmen and day laborers; poets and presidents. People of impeccable character rest here. Scoundrels do too. Most were brave; some may not have been. Some of the dead were celebrated successes in their lifetimes, and some obscure failures. Many here

11

perished in war and never had the opportunity to pursue peaceful ambitions; others died in ripe old age, rich in blessings. Some sacrificed willingly, others resentfully. But all of them sacrificed. And families from every place in America have wept at a graveside here.

War might be a great leveler while it is being experienced, but the millions upon millions of Americans who have gone to war are the most diverse population the country could produce. There is no other profession in all of human endeavor as varied as the profession of arms.

This book recalls the experiences of a single American soldier, sailor, airman, or marine in each of the thirteen major wars our country has fought. We did not attempt to identify the prototypical soldier. No such prototype exists. Not one of the subjects is much like the others. Rather the stories were chosen to represent a particular attribute of their service or condition in their experience of war. Obviously there is some arbitrariness at work here. The conditions illustrated are only a few features in the nature of soldiers and wars. We had only thirteen stories to tell. The intent was to write about things most soldiers in combat will have experienced or witnessed, but even then it is a very incomplete catalogue of commonly shared emotions and experiences.

The subjects hail from different walks of life, though most of them had modest origins, like most soldiers today and in the past. We wanted to represent all four branches of the armed services, as the experience of war can vary from one service to another, though many sensations and situations are common to all.

Many were chosen because they left accounts of their experiences that have survived to the present. Some kept diaries or wrote books or spoke publicly about their wars. A few subjects left little or no record of their service. One subject especially is mostly lost to history; we know where he served and a few incidents from his life and have tried to reconstruct his story informed by the few facts we do know and the experiences of others in the same or very similar circumstances.

We were not looking for thirteen stories of supermen or superwomen. We wanted to write straightforward, honest accounts of ordinary people in extraordinary circumstances. All thirteen soldiers were brave and sacrificed for our country. There are Medal of Honor recipients among them, and others distinguished by high decorations for valor. Some wore no decoration more proudly than their combat infantry badge. They are not perfectly virtuous. The readers will admire some of our subjects more than others, although all have earned admiration. Soldiers come in all types, from righteous, God-fearing human beings to wantonly cruel scoundrels. None of the stories we elected to recount features a soldier who belongs in the latter category, though one of them identified himself as a rogue and possessed some less than admirable qualities.

Soldiers in combat share a genuine and powerful bond, so powerful that they are willing to die for one another. The paradox that makes that bond so unique is that in their lives before war they might not have chosen to associate with each other. They might not have liked each other. They might not even like each other while they serve together, and yet they will fight for each other, and often die for each other.

Every war occasions heroism and nobility. Every war has its corruptions, which is what makes it a thing worth avoiding if possible. There is compassion and savagery in these stories, terror and valor, confusion and acuity, obedience and insubordination, self-aggrandizement and humility, brotherhood and individuality, triumph and loss, and in all of them, sacrifice for something greater than self.

Each of these stories is also a story of change. Rare is the soldier who is not changed by war. Some are changed for the better and some for the worse, but all are changed in some way and forever. It is a surpassing irony that war, for all its horrors, provides the combatant every conceivable human experience. Experiences that usually take a lifetime to know are all felt — and felt intensely — in one brief moment of life. Anyone who loses a loved one knows what great sorrow feels like. Anyone who gives life to a child knows what great joy feels like. The veteran knows what great joy and great loss feel like when they occur in the same moment, in the same experience. Such an experience is transforming. Some come home and struggle to recover their balance, which war had upset. For those who came home whole in spirit if not in body, civilian life will seldom threaten their equanimity. They have known the worst terrors the world holds and have seen acts of compassion and love that no evil can destroy. They have seen mankind at its most dehumanized and its most noble. No other experience will ever surpass its effect on their lives, and they can never forget it.

Here are the stories of eleven men and two women who went to war for our country, who risked their lives and suffered, and should not be forgotten.

Soldiers of the Revolution and their Commander-in-Chief at Valley Forge.

CHAPTER ONE:
SOLDIER OF THE REVOLUTION

Joseph Plumb Martin joined the Revolutionary War at fifteen and fought from Long Island to Yorktown.

Two days after John Hancock affixed his extravagant signature to the Declaration of Independence, an intelligent, spirited boy of fifteen pretended to write his name on an order for a six-month enlistment in the Connecticut militia: "I took up the pen, loaded it with the fatal charge, made several mimic imitations of writing my name but took especial care not to touch the paper."

Someone standing behind him, probably a recruiting officer, reached over his shoulder and forced his hand. The pen scratched the paper. The helpful agent declared, "The boy has made his mark." "Well, thought I, I may as well go through with the business now as not. So I wrote my name fairly upon the indentures. And now I was a soldier, in name at least, if not in practice."

Joseph Plumb Martin would remain a soldier for the duration of the revolution. He first saw action as part of Washington's outnumbered army on Long Island. Five years and many hardships later he witnessed the British surrender at Yorktown. He lived the remainder of his life in obscurity and poverty. He received little compensation for his service, not even, at least in his lifetime, the reverence of his countrymen that was his due as one of the patriots to whom they owed their liberty.

Major General George Washington's self-control, maintained in its severest trials by a supreme exertion of will, seldom failed conspicuously. But in the instances when it did, the effect was spectacular. Those who witnessed Washington's temper were stunned by its ferocity and left accounts of the experience that imagination need hardly embellish.

Around noon on September 15, 1776, after galloping the four miles from his command post at New York's Harlem Heights, General Washington beheld five hundred or so shell-shocked Connecticut militia fleeing from hastily constructed defensive works on the East River at Kip's Bay. As they ran from British and Hessian bayonets, he urged them to turn and retake the ground they had surrendered without a fight. They flooded past him.

Washington's physical bearing appeared no less striking, and perhaps more so, for his loss of composure. He wheeled his white charger amid the noise and confusion, his powerful legs gripped the animal firmly, his broad-shouldered, six-foot-two-inch frame sat erect in the saddle. Enraged, he cursed and threatened officers and men alike and struck at a few with his riding crop. Then he drew his sword and pistol and charged toward the enemy within range of their muskets, seeking to impart courage by his example.

It was all to no avail, as the terrified farmers and shopkeepers, boys and men, some having lost or abandoned their muskets, others armed only with pikes, found more to fear from the glittering bayonets of the enemy than the violent anger of their commander in chief. He threw his hat to the ground and groaned, "Are these the men with which I am to defend America?" At last the great man's frantic aides convinced him to ride to safety.

Private Joseph Martin must have made his escape that day by a route that avoided proximity to the raging Washington. Had he witnessed the unforgettable sight, he would surely have recounted it in his remarkable memoir, which includes a characteristically candid and ironic account of "the famous Kip's Bay affair, which has been criticized so much by the historians of the Revolution."

The British commander in chief, General William Howe, had waited more than two weeks to pursue the rebel army after Washington ordered its evacuation from Long Island to Manhattan on August 29. In the interim Washington and his officers had decided to abandon New York City, recognizing it was indefensible while the British fleet commanded its rivers and harbor. The American forces were widely scattered: four thousand men under General Israel Putnam garrisoned the city in lower Manhattan; nine thousand men under Major General William Heath protected the army's escape route in the north from Harlem to Westchester County; dispersed widely across the center of Manhattan were General Nathanael Greene's several thousand men, including the Connecticut militia under the command of the experienced Colonel William Douglas.

Washington was unsure where the British

invasion would make landfall. He feared they would try to block his outnumbered army's escape by attacking at Harlem, where he made his headquarters and where his largest force was deployed. On September 13 four large warships (by Martin's account, although most historical accounts put the number at five) sailed into Kip's Bay, a small cove that offered a deep-water anchorage on the East River's west bank.

Half of Private Martin's regiment was deployed to Kip's Bay that night to, in his words, "man something that were called 'lines,' although they were nothing more than a ditch dug along the bank of the river with the dirt thrown out toward the water." They returned to camp in the morning, and the following night the other half of the regiment, including Martin, were ordered to take their place in the lines. Sentinels were posted along the river for several miles and passed the watchword "All is well" on the half hour. "We will alter your tune before tomorrow night," Martin remembered the British on their warships retorting. "They were as good as their word for once."

He awoke that Sunday morning tired — and, as he would be throughout most of the war, starving — and saw the warships anchored within musket range of his regiment's crude defensive line. Although the ships' crews appeared to be busy with preparations, nothing happened until mid-morning. "We lay very quiet in our ditch waiting their motions," he recalled. By ten o'clock he could see scores of flatboats embark from Newton's Creek on the Long Island shore, ferrying four thousand British and Hessian soldiers across the river. They formed their boats into a line and continued "to augment their forces . . . until they appeared like a large clover field in full bloom." By late afternoon another nine thousand would join them.

Martin was idly investigating an old warehouse near their lines when, at eleven o'clock, he heard the first roar of ships' cannon, which, by his account, constituted over a hundred guns. He dove into the ditch and "lay as still as I possibly could" until British guns leveled the militia's breastworks, burying men in blasted earth. At that point, realizing they were completely exposed to enemy fire, their officers neither possessing nor issuing orders to continue their futile resistance, to the dismay of their commander in chief, the Connecticut men ran for their lives.

"In retreating we had to cross a level clear spot of ground 40 or 50 rods wide," Martin wrote, "exposed to the whole of the enemy's fire; and they gave it to us in prime order. The grapeshot and lagrange flew merrily, which served to quicken our motions."

Martin was separated from his regiment in the melee. He spent the long, dangerous, oppressively hot day searching for them with a neighbor from home. They made their way to the American lines in Harlem while trying to avoid, not always successfully, encounters with the enemy. Their progress was slow. His Connecticut neighbor became ill and dispirited, and Martin had considerable trouble convincing him to continue. At one point, after nearly stumbling into contact with a company of British soldiers, he quit the road they were traveling on and hid in a bog. When the enemy passed by after coming so close to him that he "could see the buttons on their coats," Martin emerged from his hiding place and discovered that his sick friend had vanished. He found him later, resting with a group of rebels in the shade of a tree. Martin pleaded with him to continue the march north but was rebuffed. "No, I must die here," his friend despaired. "At length with more persuasion and some force I succeeded in getting him on his feet again and moving on."

Martin and his companion had not eaten

anything in more than a day. They had slept hardly at all the previous night. They were thinly clothed, starving, and exhausted. Twice they spotted American forces in the distance only to watch them be overtaken by British or Hessians and flee in terror. "Our people were all militia," he explained, "and the demons of fear and disorder seemed to take full possession of all and everything on that day."

It began to rain, and as sundown approached, the hot day turned cool. "We were as wet as water could make us," Martin remembered, and he began to fear his sick friend would succumb to the chill. They came upon a large body of Americans preparing to make a stand with a few artillery fieldpieces. An officer ordered them to remain there. Martin argued that they were trying to rejoin their regiment, which he believed was located a short distance ahead. The officer didn't believe him and again ordered them to take a place in the line. Martin pleaded for his sick comrade, who would die of exposure if he spent the night in the cold air.

"Well, if he dies the country will be rid of one who can do it no good," the officer coolly replied.

"When a man has got his bane in his

country's cause," wrote Martin, who was still appalled by the cruel remark a half century later, "let him die like an old horse or dog, because he can do no more."

A drunk and distracted sentinel guarding the road north gave Martin and his friend an opportunity to escape. Not long afterward they found their regiment, which had joined Washington's lines at Harlem Heights, "resting themselves on the cold ground after the fatigues of the day." They were warmly received by their fellows, who had assumed they had been captured, as many others had, including the regiment's major, or killed.

Martin closed his reminiscence of the "Kip's Bay affair" by mocking the much publicized story of a soldier who claimed to have been sitting by the highway when Washington rode by and asked him why he sat there. "I would rather be killed than trodden to death by cowards," the soldier was purported to reply. Martin doubted whether the soldier had taken part in the fighting on September 15 and attributed the day's humiliation to the conspicuous absence of officers to lead them. "Every man that I saw was endeavoring by all sober means to escape death or captivity," he recalled. "The men were confused being without officers to command them. I do not recollect of seeing a commissioned officer from the time I left the lines on the banks of the East River in the morning until met with the *gentlemanly* one [the artillery officer who had insulted his ailing friend] in the evening."

What luck Washington's army had that day appeared in the cautiousness of the dilatory General Howe. After the British made quick work of the American defenders at Kip's Bay, Howe halted their advance to wait for reinforcements when they reached a small rise, now known as Murray Hill, less than a half mile from the landing. General Putnam, fearing his four thousand men would be cut off and trapped in lower Manhattan, rode to Kip's Bay to consult with Washington, who was futilely exhorting his soldiers to fight. Washington agreed that Putnam's position was hopeless and authorized his retreat to Harlem, which Putnam managed with astonishing speed, leaving his supplies and more than fifty cannon behind.

Had Howe ordered his troops to continue their advance west they would have encountered little resistance and reached the Hudson shoreline long before Putnam could escape, dooming a third of Washington's army and possibly ending the war. But he didn't. He held his forces at Murray Hill until five o'clock, and halted them again at nightfall. Putnam's rapid march north reached Harlem that night, with only the last of his line having been inconvenienced by the musket fire of the late-arriving British.

American casualties, while not light, with nearly fifty killed and four hundred captured, were not determinative either. Washington's army, tired, bedraggled, and outnumbered though it was, remained intact. The next morning, in the Battle of Harlem Heights, the Americans proved themselves capable of more than a retreat. Martin's regiment gave a good account of themselves that, if it didn't erase the memory of their disgrace at Kip's Bay, certainly improved their morale.

Just after daybreak a British force was spotted advancing north, and Washington dispatched a reconnaissance party under the command of Colonel Thomas Knowlton from Connecticut. They were soon skirmishing with advance elements of British light infantry, with little advantage gained by either. The Americans retreated in good order when superior British numbers began to press them. As the British followed, their buglers played "Gone Away," a tune familiar to fox hunt enthusiasts like Washington, signaling the fox was in flight from the hounds. The insult enraged the Americans, except for Washington, who ignored it while he conceived a plan for a counterattack.

When Knowlton's rangers reached the American lines, Washington reinforced them and ordered them to flank the British right while another party of volunteers staged a diversionary attack. The British escaped the trap and retreated some distance before turning to fight. Knowlton was killed early in the ensuing battle, as was his second-in-command, Major Andrew Leitch of Virginia. Martin had known Knowlton in Connecticut and regarded him as "a brave man and excellent citizen." But his loss didn't dispirit the Americans, who pushed the British back repeatedly.

Martin's regiment was ordered to take the field after Knowlton fell and the British were retreating into nearby woods. They remained in the battle until Washington called off the chase that afternoon, when the retreating British had reached the protection of their ships' cannon. Both sides had suffered heavy casualties, though British losses were greater. Martin recollected his regiment had lost eight to ten men, and their commander, Colonel James Arnold, had been wounded and would not return to the army. But the British had left the field. For the first time in the young war, Washington had stopped a British advance and won a battle. And the men of the 5th Connecticut, including young Joseph Martin, had played their part in the victory bravely.

During the battle a sergeant from one of the Connecticut regiments had been sent to find ammunition. An officer, a general's aide, stopped him and accused him of desertion. The sergeant explained his purpose, but the officer ordered him to return to his regiment. The sergeant refused, protesting that his mission was urgent. The officer drew his sword and threatened to kill him on the spot if he didn't obey. The sergeant drew and cocked his musket in response and was arrested, tried for mutiny, convicted, and, with Washington's approval, sentenced to death.

The Connecticut troops were ordered to witness his execution, and Martin's account of the incident claims they were on the verge of mutiny over the injustice. At the last moment the sergeant was granted a reprieve. "It was well that he was," Martin remembered, "for his blood would have not been the only blood that would have been spilt."

Martin's regiment also took part in the Battle of White Plains in late October, where they "lost in killed and wounded a considerable number." After the British left White Plains, many of the Connecticut men, including Martin, having had little or nothing to eat for days and being poorly clad for the wet autumn weather, became ill. They were sent to convalesce in Norwalk, Connecticut, quartering with local, mostly Tory residents, and returned to camp in New York a few weeks later. He remained in the militia until Christmas, when his enlistment expired. "I had learned something of a soldier's life," he wrote, "enough I thought to keep me at home for the future." The sixteen-year-old veteran bid his comrades farewell and walked home to his grandparents' farm in Milford, Connecticut.

He did not remain there long. By spring he would again take up arms, this time as a regular soldier, a private in the new Continental Army.

Fifty years after he helped America win its independence, Joseph Martin, at the age of seventy, anonymously published a memoir of his service in the war. *A Narrative of Some of the Adventures, Danger and Suffering of a Revolutionary Soldier, Interspersed with*

Anecdotes of Incident that Occurred Within His Own Observation did not sell well in the author's lifetime, and the aged veteran died a pauper at ninety. Many who did happen to read it were offended by its tone and content. Rediscovered a century later, it has become a highly valued primary source for historians of the revolution, and Martin has finally received the acclaim he never received in his lifetime.

Martin's is not a story of glorious triumph over adversity but a chronicle of privation, misery, confusion, blunder, near mutiny, endurance, humiliation, and resentment. He warns his readers not to expect an account of "great transactions," of martial conquests won by great men daring to change the course of history. "No Alpine wonders thunder through my tale," he wrote in the book's preface, quoting a British poem written at the turn of the nineteenth century. His was merely an anecdotal account of the "common transactions of one of the lowest in station in an army, a private soldier."

His narrative is outspoken, acerbic, self-deprecating, irreverent, humorous — often darkly so — sarcastic, ironic, poignant, and at times embittered. He doesn't trumpet his or anyone's heroism. He doesn't expound eloquently on the meaning of the revolution

33

and the ideals of the glorious cause. His patriotism sprang from a simpler under- standing of the purposes for which the founding fathers pledged their lives and sacred honor. He shows rather than pro- fesses his love of country and her cause by his endurance in a terrible trial of body and mind. And his claim is made more powerful by the honesty and humility of his testi- mony.

He admired Washington and other cel- ebrated heroes of the revolution. Some offi- cers he served under received his praise and others his contempt. He reserved his great- est respect for the men like him, the mostly poor and young regulars of Washington's army, the weary, hungry, aggrieved survivors of shell, shot, ball, and bayonet, of deadly winters and lost battles, of harsh discipline and their countrymen's indifference.

His father was an itinerant and impover- ished preacher, who sent young Martin to be raised by his maternal grandparents on their farm near Milford. They were exacting guardians, who put him to work on the farm at an early age. They were caring and gener- ous as well. He remembers his childhood with fondness and parting from his grand- parents with sadness.

Martin rarely interrupts the account of

his life with a discourse on the ideals of the revolution. Patriotic sentiments are scarce and written matter-of-factly. "I collected pretty correct ideas of the contest between this country and the mother country," he wrote about his decision to enlist in the militia. "I thought I was as warm a patriot as the best of them."

His grandparents opposed his enlistment. Even he didn't warm to the idea until his friends and neighbors began enlisting. He recalled the passions aroused by the Stamp Act and the Boston Tea Party and confessed they had not stirred him to militancy. His grandfather described to him the hardships and savagery of the French and Indian War, and Martin felt then that "nothing should induce me to get caught in the toils of an army. 'I am well, so I'll keep,' was my motto then, and it would have been well for [me] if I had ever retained it."

His attitude changed when war came. Enthused by the spectacle of neighbors marching off to Boston, excited by the talk of soldiers who had been briefly billeted on his grandparents' farm, and having become tired of farm work, he resolved to "go a so-gering." But his grandparents refused their permission. He spent 1775 resenting his fate, envying the adventures of his friends, and working up the nerve to defy his grand-parents. They finally relented early the following year, after he threatened to run off to sea. But his enthusiasm for "sogering" dimmed when he discovered that enlistment in the militia obligated him to give a year's service. "I wished only to take a priming," he explained, "before I took upon the whole coat of paint for a soldier."

His opportunity arrived when the army, facing daunting odds against a numerically superior British in New York and desperate for troops, cut the enlistment period to six months. So he made his mark and went to war as many young men have, harboring misgivings and expressing bravado. He confessed his determination was at times "almost overset" by the knowledge that once he enlisted there would be no turning back: "I must stick to it; there will be no receding." And yet when he heard the British were being reinforced by another fifteen thousand troops, he claimed, "I did not care if there had been 15 times 15,000. . . . The Americans were invincible in my opinion."

His opinion soon changed. He sailed for New York City, where he joined his regiment and began brief and improvised training in the practices of soldiering. His regiment was ordered into action not long after the start of the Battle of Long Island. They were ferried to Brooklyn and marched to a plain, where he first encountered soldiers wounded in battle, the sight of which "a little daunted me and made me think of home." A battle raged nearby, and a young lieutenant lost control of his emotions, "sniveling and blubbering" and begging the men in his company to forgive any injuries he had done them.

Martin saw his first action the next afternoon, when some men of his regiment, making for a cornfield in search of something to eat, chanced upon an equal number of British soldiers. The advantage shifted back and forth as both sides reinforced, until most of Martin's regiment was engaged and the British were driven off. The battle for Long Island ended the next night. Surrounded by the British and facing the prospect of complete annihilation, Washington ordered his army's evacuation after a valiant stand by Maryland troops had temporarily delayed its destruction. Martin's regiment marched back to Brooklyn as quietly as it could manage and joined the rest of the army waiting on the wharves to be ferried to Manhattan. In the morning the British discovered the rebels had escaped.

Then came the disgrace at Kip's Bay and

the regiment's partial redemption in Harlem, the retreat from White Plains and Martin's return home, a bloodied, hard-worn veteran, still possessing the boyish sense of humor he would never lose but not the swagger that had been the first casualty of his war.

In his telling Martin went to war the first time for adventure, the second time for money. After his defeat at Fort Washington in November, Washington took his main army to New Jersey and across the Delaware River into Pennsylvania, where, a month later, he would recross the Delaware and surprise a Hessian garrison at Trenton and a British garrison at Princeton. The Continental Congress, heeding Washington's urgent pleas, had finally recognized the need to field and train an army that would not be in constant danger of disintegration due to the prevalence of short-term enlistments and poorly trained, independent-minded militia. It authorized a new standing army of seventy-five thousand men who would enlist for three years or the duration of the war. Each of the thirteen states was given a recruitment quota it was to fill by whatever means it deemed necessary.

Notwithstanding the morale-boosting victories at Trenton and Princeton, the size and success of the British offensive dampened the patriotic fervor for the war that had characterized the initial response to Concord and Lexington. States had a difficult time meeting their quotas and instituted drafts, or schemes that were not quite drafts but that obligated towns to recruit the service of a specific number of citizens. In Connecticut, townships divided men into separate groups, and each group was required to procure one soldier for the army either by finding a volunteer or paying for a substitute. If they failed to produce a volunteer or substitute, one of their number would be drafted.

In the spring of 1777 Martin was entreated to reenlist by a friend who had taken a lieutenant's commission. He was slowly warming to the idea, and eventually decided to put his name forward as a substitute, and was happily accepted by his peers. "I thought, as I must go, I might as well get as much for my skin as I could," he explained. He didn't remember the sum he was paid but doubted it was more than the amount he spent enjoying his last few days of freedom. He marched off to war for the second time with greater misgivings than he had the first time and none of the bravado. His sense of humor, however, remained intact. "That little insignificant monosyllable — No — was the hardest word in the language for me to pronounce," he recalled, "especially when solicited to do a thing which was in the least degree indifferent to me; I could say Yes, with half the trouble."

He joined his new regiment, the 8th Connecticut, in May in Newtown, New York, and shortly thereafter marched to Peekskill, New York. He remained in the Hudson highlands most of that summer as part of an undermanned force that was expected to prevent the British from gaining control of the entire Hudson and severing New England from the other colonies.

But rather than challenge the Americans' hold on the highlands, General Howe believed he could end the rebellion by occupying the rebel capital, Philadelphia. In late August he landed a force of fifteen thousand men at the northern reach of the Chesapeake Bay and two weeks later defeated the Americans at Brandywine Creek, after which he marched triumphantly into Philadelphia. Martin's regiment was one of several ordered to reinforce the battered main army after the Brandywine defeat.

Martin had injured his ankle some days before and was left to guard the regiment's baggage train as it made its way to Bethlehem, Pennsylvania. But he chafed at the duty. He had for some time been under the command of officers who were not from his regiment, and he didn't like it. "Soldiers always like to be under the command of their own officers," he explained. "They are generally bad enough, but strangers are worse." As soon as the baggage reached Bethlehem, he asked for permission to rejoin his regiment. He returned in time to limp along with the 8th Connecticut as it marched through the night to Germantown, where Americans and British were about to clash again. The regiment arrived not long before the tide of battle turned. The Americans fought well in the beginning and seemed to have the advantage. But Washington had conceived a complicated battle plan involving four separate columns, and in the gun smoke and low-lying fog their lines became entangled. Americans began to fire on each other, precipitating another disorderly retreat.

The Battle of Germantown inaugurated what Martin would remember as the period that encompassed his worst experiences in the war, including a brutal siege of a small island fort in the Delaware River, but also a more comfortable winter than that experienced by soldiers who bore the awful deprivations of Valley Forge — hardships that Martin witnessed but, for the most part, did not share.

He begins his account with reference to the deprivation that plagued him the worst throughout the war: the constant want of food. He makes his first complaint about hunger days after entering the army. From there to the end of his narrative all the experiences he recounts, the battles won and lost, the long marches and near escapes, the many mishaps and few occasions of unexpected good fortune, all the wounds and exhaustion and heat and cold he and his comrades endured, never figure so prominently in his story as does the subject to which he always returns: starvation. Every few pages there appears another account of it. Sometimes, most times he recalls it humorously, just as he does the improvised feasts he rarely enjoyed. Nothing in the war seems to have lodged so firmly in his memory as the experience of marching, fighting, freezing, and boiling without enough to eat.

When the army reorganized after their rout at Germantown, Martin recalls "marching and countermarching, starving and freezing, nothing else happened, although that was enough," until they encamped at White Marsh north of Philadelphia, and he went to sleep having had nothing to eat since noon the previous day. Soon afterward he wandered into a place where cattle had recently been slaughtered and happened upon an ox spleen, which he took back to camp, roasted, and hastily consumed. "I had not had it long in my stomach," he recalled, "when it began to make strong remonstrances and to manifest a great inclination to be set at liberty again . . . and with eyes overflowing with tears at parting with what I had thought to be a friend, I gave it a discharge."

Shortly after his brief bout with the ox spleen, his regiment joined a detachment ordered to scatter a British force encampment on the other side of the Schuylkill River. They carried few provisions and nothing edible. They waded across the freezing river that night before their officers ordered them to halt. For the remainder of the night they stayed in place, shivering, forbidden to light fires to warm themselves and dry their clothes. Near daybreak they were made to ford the river again and backtrack to a place they had reached the previous day to wait for reinforcements. That next night, after reinforcements arrived, they forded the Schuylkill again. Wet, cold, and starving, they arrived the next morning where the British were believed to be camped. But the British had left.

They marched back to White Marsh slowly, pausing for an hour's rest near a walnut tree, where nuts lay on the ground in abundance. Martin grabbed a few handfuls and cracked and ate them. They crossed the river again at sunset at a ford where the cold water was deeper. On the other side they were met by quartermasters who had brought no nourishment other than barrels of whiskey. Their intention was to give the men a small measure to warm them, but the tired and hungry marchers tried to revive themselves by consuming more than their allotment, and empty stomachs ensured the effect was immediate and noticeable. Resuming the march, the inebriates encountered a fence they had to climb over. "Here was fun," Martin remembered. The men "would pile themselves up on each side of the fence, swearing and hallooing, some losing their arms, some their hats, some their shoes, and some themselves." Once over they stumbled on and reached camp at midnight. "I had been nearly 30 hours without a mouthful of anything to eat, excepting the walnuts, having been the whole time on my feet (unless I happened to fall over the fence, which I do not remember to have done) and wading in and being wet with the water. . . . I rolled myself up in my innocency, lay down on the leaves and forgot my misery till morning."

As winter approached, General Howe increasingly turned his attention to opening secure supply routes from New York to occupied Philadelphia. At present the British were landing supplies at Head of Elk, Maryland, and marching them fifty miles to Philadelphia, a route vulnerable to American raids. A safer alternative was to bring British supply ships up the Delaware River. But the Americans had established a network of forts along the Delaware to make it impassable to British ships. Howe resolved to destroy it.

British forces had captured the southernmost fort on the New Jersey side of the Delaware, and British land and naval batteries had laid siege throughout October to the two most important forts, Fort Mercer in Red Bank and Fort Mifflin, on an island in the Delaware, just below its confluence with the Schuylkill River (where Philadelphia International Airport is located today). Washington dispatched two Connecticut regiments, including Martin's, to reinforce them.

They marched through the night, as they were often made to, barefoot, poorly clothed, tired, hungry, and cold, until they "could proceed no further from sheer hunger and fatigue." They crossed the Delaware at Bristol, Pennsylvania. At the end of a three days' march, having eaten meals of rotten beef one night and a goose wing the next, Martin arrived at the army's encampment in the village of Woodbury, New Jersey. From there, in the last week of October, he and the other able-bodied soldiers of the two Connecticut regiments deployed to Fort Mifflin, which lay on an island surrounded by a swamp that Martin describes as "nothing more than a mudflat."

The fort itself was hardly picturesque. In a colorful description of its wretchedness and vulnerability to British artillery, Martin disparaged "the pen I was confined in," a "fort it could not with propriety be called." The historian Thomas McGuire called it "a hodgepodge of stone and mud; of logs and ship's spars and pine rafts set in mud; of ramparts and dikes filled with more mud."

The history of the American Revolution often seems to abound in improbable coincidences. Built before the revolution by a British Army engineer, Captain John Montresor, Fort Mifflin's fate was again in its creator's hands, for Montresor had been assigned the duty of destroying it.

The defense of Fort Mifflin was Martin's worst experience in the war. He devotes more pages of his narrative to his sufferings there than he does to any other battle. Fifty years later the memory of it still embittered him. "In the cold month of November," he begins, "without provisions, without clothing, not a scrap of either shoes or stockings to my feet or legs, and in this condition to endure a siege in such a place as that, was appalling in the highest degree."

The siege had begun on September 26 and didn't end until November 15, two weeks after Martin's regiment reinforced its beleaguered defenders, who throughout the siege never numbered more than five hundred. Martin mistakenly remembered the first attack on Mifflin he experienced beginning on the night of October 22. It was actually an attack on Mercer by a Hessian force of two thousand infantry and an artillery battalion. It was repulsed with staggering losses by the fort's two hundred American defenders and the entangling, at times impenetrable network of sharpened tree branches they had constructed, called "abatis." Two British warships, the *Augusta* and the *Merlin,* were also lost in the failed attack, caught in the chevaux-de-frise, a marine abatis of long wooden poles with sharp metal tips, and destroyed in the morning by cannons from both Mercer and Mifflin. Martin recalled the fate of the *Augusta* being the result of a failed attack on Mifflin.

The attack on Mifflin was an ongoing affair, a daily bombardment of shell and shot, with little shelter available to its defenders. Martin describes the barracks at Mifflin being particularly dangerous: "It was as much as a man's life was worth to enter them, the enemy often directing their shot at them in particular." The men slept little if at all. Martin claims he never slept a minute through the entire siege. There were those who were so fatigued they went into the barracks to sleep a little, but "it seldom happened they all came out again alive."

The soldiers worked through the night rebuilding the works the British batteries leveled during the day, steeling themselves for the rain of grapeshot from British mortars. The only place Martin recalls being safe enough to grab a few moments' rest was a ditch between the fort's eastern wall and a palisade facing away from the British batteries. But the fort's engineer, a French officer named Fleury, "a very austere man," kept them at their labors. When they tried to slip away to their hiding place, Martin sadly recounts, Colonel Fleury would "come to the entrance and call us out. He had always his cane in his hand, and woe betided him he could get a stroke at."

Martin counted five British batteries with six heavy guns each on the Jersey shore, as well as three mortar batteries, and another battery of heavy guns higher up the river, all of them hammering away at Mifflin night and day. Soldiers can become inured to ceaseless terrors, and some will acquire a sort of shell-shocked indifference to their circumstances. The Americans had one 32-pound cannon in the fort but no shot for it. The British also had a 32-pounder, with an ample supply of solid shot, which they regularly fired at the fort's parade ground. The fort's artillery officers decreed that any soldier who managed somehow to get hold of one of the fired cannonballs would receive a slug of rum. "I have seen 20 to 50 men standing on the parade waiting with impatience the coming of the shot, which would often be seized before its motion had fully ceased," Martin recalled, "and conveyed off to our gun to be sent back to its former owners. When the lucky fellow had swallowed his rum, he would return to wait for another."

At dawn on November 14 the British commenced a final daylong artillery barrage in preparation for storming the fort. In addition to their seven land-based gun batteries and three mortars, Martin counted nine British ships bringing their guns to bear on Mifflin, including six sixty-four-gun ships of the line and a thirty-six-gun frigate. If his memory is correct, a total of 480 land and naval guns, as well as the three mortars, fired on Fort Mifflin in a single day. Some officers tried to count how many guns were fired every minute, "but it was impossible; the fire was incessant." Mifflin had become a hell that would disturb the sleep of its survivors for the rest of their lives.

The soldiers manned their posts on the palisades, "ordered to defend to the last extremity." Martin saw one man, who had climbed a flagstaff to raise a signal flag, cut in half as he descended. He saw five men manning one cannon "cut down by a single shot." Others were "split like fish to be broiled." The dead and wounded were too numerous to count. "Our men were cut down like cornstalks," he remembered.

By that afternoon all the fort's guns had been silenced despite a brief decrease in the volume of British fire as their ships battled several American ships that had attempted to come to Mifflin's rescue. "If ever destruction was complete, it was here," Martin wrote. The fort's grounds were "as completely ploughed as a field," all its buildings "hanging in broken fragments." At sundown the cannonade ceased, and the Americans, having little left to defend and no guns to defend it with, prepared their escape before the British stormed the fort. As the survivors made their way to the wharves, Martin looked for his closest friend in the army and found him "lying in a long line of dead men."

After most of the defenders took what supplies could be carried and abandoned the fort, Martin stayed behind as one of a party of soldiers ordered to torch anything left that would burn. As he was working, some of the British ships were near enough that he could hear soldiers saying they would "give it to the damned rebels in the morning." After the last of Mifflin's defenders had trooped to the wharves, where flatboats waited to ferry them across the river, the mounting flames consuming the battered fort so illuminated the river that Martin and his comrades could be plainly seen by the British, who immediately fired their guns at them. Miraculously they made it across unharmed. Five days later Fort Mercer was destroyed, and the Delaware was opened to British supply ships.

Martin ends his account "of as hard and fatiguing job . . . as occurred during the Revolutionary War" with an observation that has appeared in many histories of the war. It is a lament common to soldiers of every nation in every war and quite likely the inspiration for his book.

> I was at the siege and capture of Lord Cornwallis, and the hardships of that were no more to be compared with this than the sting of a bee is to the bite of a rattlesnake. But there has been but little notice taken of it; the reason of which is there was no Washington, Putnam or Wayne there. Had there been, the affair would have been extolled to the skies. No, it was only a few officers and soldiers who accomplished it in a remote quarter of the army. Such circumstances and such troops generally get but little notice taken of them, do what they will.

What is it soldiers expect from those whose lives and liberty they defend? Not fame and no more in the way of material compensation than the modest benefits they are promised. Few veterans of the Revolutionary War would receive in their lifetime the acclaim or compensation they deserved. But they must have had hopes that their countrymen would make good on that most basic obligation to them: a simple understanding of their sacrifice and appreciation of its contribution to the character of their country and the history of their times. Yet in that expectation too, as Martin's complaint makes clear, they were often disappointed.

After the loss of the Delaware forts, Martin's regiment rejoined the main army as it marched and countermarched to little effect in the weeks before it encamped for the winter. As winter came on, the soldiers' accumulating miseries left them, in Martin's words, "as starved and as cross and ill-natured as curs." He writes of envying a squirrel he watched starve to death: "He got rid of his misery soon. He did not live to starve piecemeal six or seven years." He mocks a Thanksgiving meal decreed by Congress that followed two or three days without any rations and amounted to nothing more than a small portion of rice and vinegar. "The army was not only starved but naked," he complains. "The greatest part were not only shirtless and barefoot but destitute of all other clothing, especially blankets." It is in this condition that they entered winter quarters at Valley Forge.

Martin arrived at Valley Forge on December 18 having had little or nothing to eat for days and "perishing with thirst." He couldn't find water in the camp, hadn't the strength to build a shelter, and worried that the entire army would freeze to death. He feared that were the British to attack then, the revolution would be finished. "But a kind and holy Providence took more notice and better care of us than did the country in whose service we were wearing away our lives."

He had been there for two nights with nothing more to eat than half a small pumpkin, when he was warned that in the morning he would be ordered to march again. "I never heard a summons to duty with so much disgust before or since as I did that." But the summons proved to be fortuitous. He was ordered to join a foraging party that scoured the Pennsylvania countryside for the army's provisions that terrible winter. The duty wasn't onerous. They were headquartered in a little village and were comfortably sheltered and fed well. When Martin wasn't hunting and collecting provisions, he was at liberty to come and go as he pleased. "I had had enough to eat and been under no restraint," he recalled. "I had picked up a few articles of comfortable summer clothing. . . . Our lieutenant had never concerned himself about us."

He remained in these comparatively pleasant circumstances until late April 1778, when he rejoined his regiment at Valley Forge. Nearly a quarter of the eleven thousand soldiers encamped there had perished during the worst suffering that winter. Martin returned in time to join the Continentals as they learned the drills, tactics, and exacting discipline of the Prussian military system under the tutelage of Baron Friedrich Wilhelm von Steuben, who was turning the ragtag, wasted remnant of a fighting force into a professional army.

In May Martin marched across the Schuylkill River to within twelve miles of Philadelphia with three thousand soldiers under the command of the Marquis de Lafayette. The British, having got wind of the advance, marched out to meet them and nearly trapped the Americans. But Lafayette recognized their vulnerability and skillfully got his force safely away, earning the praise of Martin, who wasn't normally given to complimenting the officers he served under. The young general "knew what he was about," Martin wrote. "He was not deficient in either courage or conduct."

That year's summer would be remembered as especially warm. In late June, as Martin marched through New Jersey to Monmouth Courthouse (where the town of Freehold is located today), oppressive heat with temperatures reaching 100 degrees was added to the usual miseries of hunger and fatigue. General Howe had asked to be relieved of command that winter and had been replaced by Sir Henry Clinton. The new British commander in chief was ordered to evacuate Philadelphia. His troops started to move in the third week of June, as fatigued by the miserable heat as were the Americans. Washington determined to strike them as they slowly progressed to New York.

Martin marched with an advance guard of Continentals, ordered to harass General Clinton's retreating columns while Washington and his generals decided where and whether to force a major engagement. The officer who argued most insistently against bringing the British to battle was General Charles Lee, a surly, eccentric though experienced officer. Lee had served as a soldier of fortune for several European monarchs and was notorious for his wanton lifestyle and his temper. He was convinced there was not another officer of his caliber in the Continental Army, including Washington. He argued that it was foolhardy to confront the British in New Jersey. He thought it foolhardy ever to risk a major engagement with the British, believing Americans were incapable of winning a set battle despite their recently acquired, well-drilled professionalism at the hands of von Steuben.

Despite Lee's reservations and arrogance, Washington gave him command of a force of five thousand men, including Martin's detachment, and ordered him to attack the rear of the British force and keep it engaged until Washington could bring up the rest of the army.

Dipping again into the meager supply of praise he reserved for officers, Martin recalled having been inspired on the eve of battle by the officer who commanded his "platoon," a captain in a Rhode Island regiment, who told them they had "been wanting to fight. Now you shall have fighting enough before the night." Even the sick and injured were stirred by their captain's call to arms and refused to remain behind. Remembering with pride the excitement he felt in that moment, Martin called the captain "a fine brave man. . . . He feared nobody nor nothing."

The attack began on June 28, and it would soon be clear that General Lee feared somebody. The morning broke hotter and more humid than the previous day. Men on foot and horseback stripped to the waist for relief from the roasting sun. Before the day ended many men and horses, British and American, who had survived musket ball and bayonet would perish from heatstroke. Martin's company was working its way through a dense wood late in the morning toward the sound of cannon and musket fire. They came into the clear onto a field that was a "trifle hotter" than a "heated oven" and fell back to the woods because "it was almost impossible to breathe." A moment later they were ordered to retreat.

They hadn't gone far when Washington himself rode by and demanded to know who had ordered them to retreat. "General Lee," he was informed. "Damn him," Washington exclaimed. "It was certainly very unlike him," Martin writes, "but he seemed in the instant to be in a very great passion."

That he was.

Lee had given his officers hardly any orders, much less a battle plan, before Americans struck the British in an uncoordinated attack, with some units fighting and others unengaged. General Clinton had anticipated the attack and detached forces from his column to reinforce his rearguard, commanded by General Charles Cornwallis. Confusion overtook the American ranks. Not knowing whether to advance or retreat, they prudently chose the latter. Lee did nothing to impose order on his soldiers, and their retreat turned into a rout.

The scene Washington surveyed as he rode up beside his diffident subordinate shocked him. Seeing his ranks completely broken, he demanded of Lee, "What is the meaning of this, sir? I desire to know the meaning of this disorder and confusion!"

"The troops," Lee replied, "would not stand the British bayonets."

"You damn poltroon," Washington countered, "you never tried them."

Washington did as much violence to Lee as words could do. According to an eyewitness, he "swore on that day until the leaves shook on the trees." The situation was desperate, however, and he couldn't give any more attention to the insufferable Lee, whom he ordered to leave the field.

He spurred his white charger into the thick of retreating soldiers, shouting at them, "Stand fast . . . and receive your enemy. The [army] is advancing to support you." While British cannonballs tore up the earth all around him, he was everywhere at once, ordering, frightening, and inspiring his soldiers to turn and fight. His horse collapsed from exhaustion, but he quickly mounted another, impervious to the enveloping danger. He was as magnificent on that day as on any day of the long war for independence. "Never have I beheld such a superb man," Lafayette remembered.

He rode back to where Martin and the New England troops had stopped their retreat and ordered them to make a stand behind a fence and keep the advancing British busy until the artillery formed a line. This they did, retreating only after what seemed to Martin to be the entire British force had charged them. Martin claimed they had been ordered by their officers to withdraw. The British brought their cannon to bear on the American artillery, but the Americans won the duel, leaving the British guns "mostly disabled" and forcing the British to fall back. During the cannonade Martin saw Mary McCauley, the famous Molly Pitcher, help man one of the guns, and admired her pluck when, after a British cannonball passed between her legs and tore away her petticoat, she appeared unconcerned by the near miss. Martin remembered her remarking only that it was "a good thing it did not pass a little higher, for in that case it might have carried away something else."

Some of the outgunned British sought shelter from the heat in an orchard. Martin and his fellow New Englanders were ordered to charge their position. "You are the boys I want to assist in driving those rascals from yon orchard," a New Hampshire colonel informed them. The British began retreating before the Americans could reach them. The same New Hampshire colonel ordered some of the troops, including Martin, to chase after them and keep them engaged until the rest of the New Englanders could catch them. "We overtook the enemy just as they were entering a meadow," Martin recalled. "They were retreating in line, though in some disorder." Martin singled out a British soldier "and took my aim directly between his shoulders." It is the only time in his narrative that he mentions trying to kill someone, and fifty years later he seemed to regret it. "He was a good mark; being a broad-shouldered fellow. What became of him I know not; the fire and smoke hid him from my sight. One thing I know . . . I took as deliberate aim at him as ever I did any game in my life. But after all I hope I did not kill him, although I intended to at the time."

When the retreating British reached a defensible position they turned and began exchanging fire with the pursuing New Englanders. Martin watched as a British cannonball cleaved an American officer's leg at the thigh. Soon, though, the British were forced to resume their retreat. The Americans fired a final volley, and the engagement ended. "We then laid ourselves down under the fences and bushes to take a breath," Martin wrote, "for we had need of it; I presume everyone has heard of the heat that day, but none can realize it that did not experience it."

Martin helped carry the captain who had lost his leg to the field surgeon. His part in the battle of Monmouth Courthouse ended there, although the battle continued throughout the day and "the troops re-mained on the field all night with the Com-mander in Chief." Darkness ended the fighting with both sides still on the field. But the British withdrew during the night, while the Americans remained with the man who had prevented their defeat and inspired them to fight the British to a standstill. Both sides had suffered heavy casualties, but the

British had lost more men. Evidence of the Continental Army's newly acquired discipline, ability, and resolve was plain for both sides to see.

Monmouth Courthouse was the last major battle of the war in the north. The British concentrated their efforts thereafter on conquering the south. But in that last major engagement, Joseph Martin and his Continentals, malnourished and exhausted though they were, had fought to a draw the best the British Empire could field. The next morning each of them received a drink of rum as a reward, though nothing to eat.

Washington followed the British and moved the main army back to New York. The Americans crossed the Hudson River at King's Ferry and marched on to White Plains, where Martin's regiment had fought two years earlier. Revisiting the battlefield, Martin was surprised to discover the skeletal remains of Hessians who had fallen at White Plains littering the ground, having been dug up, he assumed, by rooting dogs and wild hogs. The sad sight prompted him to offer a succinct and especially affecting definition of the cause for which he fought. There are more elaborate explanations of what liberty meant to the men who fought in the revolution, but never one that conveyed its essence more sensitively than the one Martin provides as he contemplates the inglorious fate of his fallen foes:

> Poor fellows! They were left unburied in a foreign land; they had, perhaps, as near and dear friends to lament their sad destiny as the Americans who lay buried near them. But they should have kept home; we should then never have gone after them to kill them in their own country. But, the reader will say, they were forced to come and be killed here; forced by their rulers who have absolute power and death over their subjects. Well then, reader, bless a kind Providence that has made such a distinction between your condition and theirs. And be careful too that you do not allow yourself ever to be brought to such an abject, servile and debased condition.

Martin was not yet eighteen years old. He suffered a worse fate in the winter of 1779 than he had the previous winter, when he was excused from the agonies of Valley Forge. The winter at Morristown was the worst of the war, with the coldest temperatures of the century and heavy snowfalls; food, adequate clothing, and warm shelter extremely scarce; and the men, as usual, denied the pay they were promised. "We were absolutely, literally starved," he recalled. He was reduced to eating birch bark, and others to roasting their shoes, if they had any.

By the spring of 1780, before the fighting season resumed, they began to mutiny. They had been pushed beyond endurance. With Congress insensible to their situation and a lack of support from too many of their countrymen whose hearts were hardened to their plight, they "saw no other alternative," in Martin's words, "but to starve to death or break up the army. . . . We had borne as long as human nature could endure." There were only three major mutinies in the Continental Army during eight years of war. The Connecticut line mutiny of May 25, 1780, in which Martin participated, was the first.

During an evening roll call, grumbling in Martin's regiment swelled to insubordination and then to open revolt when an officer traded abuse with one of the men. The men refused to leave the parade ground and, with their arms shouldered, formed into lines. Another regiment joined them. Though they had no clear plan of how they would proceed, they marched to where two other regiments were camped a couple hundred yards away to enlist them in their demonstration.

The officers of the two Connecticut regiments that were now mustering on their parade grounds tried to prevent their men from taking their arms with them. In an ensuing scuffle the officer in command of the 6th Connecticut, Colonel Return Jonathan Meigs, was stabbed with a bayonet and severely wounded. Martin, who admired Meigs, believed the wound was an accident. Accidental or not, the colonel's misfortune may have served to cool somewhat the passions of the rebellious regiments.

Martin's regiment started to return to their camp when one of the men shouted for them to stop. Some officers dragged the hothead out of the ranks, but before they could abuse him further they were forced at bayonet point to release him. When the men reached camp they re-formed lines. An officer tried to plead and coax them into dispersing, falsely promising them at one point that the army had just that day received a large herd of cattle. A lieutenant colonel in the 4th Connecticut gave the order for his ranks to shoulder arms. He was ignored, which caused him, in Martin's description, to fall into "a violent passion" before storming back to his quarters. Eventually the officers gave up and returned to their huts.

Most of the men remained on the parade ground. They were approached by a colonel from the Pennsylvania line whom they all admired and who mollified them a little by reminding them that their officers shared their privations. He "had not a sixpence," he told them, "to purchase a partridge that was offered me the other day." Eventually the mutiny, if it could fairly be called that since the Connecticut troops never formed a clear plan to do anything more than demonstrate their anger and desperation, subsided. Martin summed up their plight with the dark humor at which he was so adept: "We therefore still kept upon the parade in groups, venting our spleen at our country and government, then at our officers, and then at ourselves for our imbecility in staying there and starving in detail for an ungrateful people who did not care what became of us, so they could enjoy themselves while we were keeping a cruel enemy from them."

But as ill used and aggrieved as they were, they remained "unwilling to desert the cause of our country." This hard-pressed loyalty, more than battles won or lost or individual heroics, was the proof of their patriotism, a more durable and honest patriotism than most possess. It cannot be diminished by their complaints and resentment, not even by insubordination and near mutiny. It is a patriotism supported by the rarest of resolves: they would not betray their country's cause even when they believed their country had betrayed them.

Martin's service would continue until the war officially ended with the signing of the Treaty of Paris in 1783. The hardships and dangers he endured did not abate until after the Battle of Yorktown. He fought in other battles. He survived various illnesses, including frequent bouts of dysentery caused by rotten meat he consumed. He starved year after year. He froze in the winters and boiled in the summers. He watched close friends die. He never saw his grandparents again; when he returned home for a short leave early in 1781, he found his grandmother had died and his grandfather had moved away to live with one of his sons.

He was nearly killed while exchanging insults across the Harlem River with some British cavalry, when an enemy soldier in a nearby house fired a shot at him. He saw the musket flash and instinctively dropped to the ground, and the ball passed just over him. The British thought they had killed him, but he jumped to his feet, slapped his backside at the enemy, and took off. Had he not moved when he did, "the ball would have gone directly through my body," he recalled. "But 'a miss is as good as a mile' as the proverb says." That same afternoon he was talking with a few other soldiers when a British sniper took a shot at them: "[The] ball passed between our noses which were not more than a foot apart."

Not many days later he received his first and only wound of the war when a dozen Continentals were surprised by a larger party of loyalist troops. The two sides traded fire until the patriots ran off with the loyalists on their heels. They came to a fence made of fallen trees. Martin was the last to climb over it and caught his foot in one of the trees. He was still struggling to free himself when the enemy reached him. The loyalist commander drew his sword and slashed him below the knee, "which laid the bone bare." Martin gave his foot one last desperate tug and managed to get free, leaving behind his shoe. He heard the loyalist who had cut him call him by name and urge him to surrender. He was a childhood friend who had served in Martin's first regiment and had deserted early in the war. None of the loyalists fired their muskets at him as he ran, though he was within their range. Martin was never sure if their forbearance was an act of mercy from his former friend or if they just didn't have time to reload their muskets before he ran out of range.

Martin left his Connecticut regiment in 1780, when he was selected to join a newly formed corps of miners and sappers and promoted to the rank of sergeant, an assignment that reflected the high regard his officers had for him. It was in this capacity that he found himself in Philadelphia in early September 1781, where he received his wages for the first time since 1776, with gold borrowed from the French after some soldiers refused to leave the rebel capital until they had been paid. He boarded a schooner there and sailed down the Delaware River, past the remnants of Fort Mifflin, where he had suffered two terrifying weeks in 1777, to Wilmington, Delaware. From there he marched overland to the north end of the Chesapeake Bay. During a brief halt in their march, he and his sergeant major sat on a fence that stood atop a steep bank. Their company's captain, whom Martin disliked, sat on the other end. Noticing the fence's flimsy construction, the sergeant major winked at Martin and both men began to wiggle the fence until it collapsed, tumbling the officer down the bank.

When they reached the Chesapeake they boarded another ship and sailed to the James River and then on to Williamsburg, Virginia. There they joined a corps under the command of Lafayette and marched for Yorktown, a tobacco port named for the river that ran beneath its bluffs. General Clinton had ordered Lord Cornwallis to construct defensible fortifications for his nearly eight thousand British and Hessian troops along the deep-water port, from where, if need be, the British fleet could evacuate them.

But on September 5 that fleet was defeated and chased back to New York by a French fleet commanded by the Comte de Grasse, recently arrived from the West Indies. By the last week of the month the British were surrounded on water by de Grasse's fleet and on land by eight thousand Continentals, an equal number of French troops commanded by the Comte de Rochambeau, and over three thousand militia.

Rather than suffer heavy casualties by storming the British fortifications, Washington resolved to bombard the British into submission and ordered a series of parallel trenches dug where he could bring up his artillery and lay siege. Martin and his fellow miners and sappers were given the assignment. "We had holed him," Martin wrote, referring to the British, "and now nothing remained but to dig him out."

As they were about their work one dark, rainy night, they were approached by a tall man in a long overcoat, who "talked familiarly with us a few minutes." Before he left, he warned the men that were they captured by the enemy, not to tell them who they were. The British would treat them like spies and refuse them quarter. The stranger returned a short time later with a company of engineers, who addressed him as "Your Excellency," and Martin and his comrades discovered they had just been amiably chatting with their commander in chief.

Their work was undiscovered until the first line of trenches was nearly finished; too late the British began firing at them. The batteries were brought up at noon the following day, and the guns all fired at once. "It was a warm day for the British," as Martin described it. The bombardment lasted several days, until the enemy's forward guns were destroyed, after which Martin and his fellow sappers began work on a second, parallel line of trenches.

Under fire from British redoubts one night, the Americans decided to storm them, and four hundred soldiers commanded by Lieutenant Colonel Alexander Hamilton made the assault. Martin's company was supplied with hatchets to cut away the abatis that lay in their way. A brief but bloody battle ensued, and Martin was exposed to a fierce barrage of British shells and grenades, his friends falling dead or seriously wounded at his side. Having cleared the abatis, he joined the assault on one of the redoubts armed with his hatchet.

By the time Martin and his sappers finished the second line of trenches, Cornwallis asked for a cease-fire to negotiate the terms of his surrender. A day later the American army stood at attention and watched as the British army marched out of their fortifications and stacked their arms.

After the surrender the French force remained at Yorktown, and the Continental Army returned to New York. Martin's corps remained behind for a few weeks as winter approached and cold rains fell. Lacking tents or any shelter they slept in the elements. Eventually they boarded schooners and sailed north, disembarked in Maryland, and marched overland from there. They stayed two weeks in Philadelphia before marching to Burlington, New Jersey, where they quartered for the winter in a "large, elegant house."

With the war for independence effectively won, Martin looked forward to a more comfortable winter than he had spent since the war began.

Nearly two years would pass before the Treaty of Paris was signed and the war officially ended. Martin had more adventures before him, and more hardships too. He was ordered to leave winter headquarters and take two men with him to find and bring back a deserter. He took his time and never did manage to locate the fugitive, but he spent a number of nights enjoying the hospitality of families residing in the various towns he passed through, marveling at the change in civilian attitudes now that the country's independence was in sight. During previous encounters the Continentals had often been treated with disdain, suspicion, and sometimes outright hostility by people whose rights they were fighting to secure. They were begrudged food and other provisions, and often had to take it by force. They were given shelter reluctantly, usually only when demanded, accompanied by meager if any hospitality to underscore how greatly private citizens resented the army's demands and how broadly they distrusted standing armies, be they British or American.

Now Martin and his friends were plied with food and drink, regaled with stories, and comfortably bedded in one household after another. They were conquering heroes. However, this benefaction too would prove temporary as the old prejudice against a standing army returned to the new republic in the years of peace ahead.

He contracted yellow fever that winter, and it nearly killed him. He was placed in a hospital with a number of sick and dying men, and he lost all his hair. There were no army physicians available to attend them, and "the apothecary's stores in the Revolutionary army were as ill furnished as any others." A local doctor treated him, and Martin credited his care and compassion with saving his life.

He recovered in the spring, and after walking ninety miles in two days without provisions he caught up with his corps as it was about to cross the Hudson River. Shortly after he arrived, he and nine other men were ordered to hunt down two more deserters. They traveled another ninety miles in twenty-four hours without finding the fugitives, who, as it turned out, had been hiding only a few miles from camp.

He spent the summer on an island in the Hudson quarrying rock to use in repairing the army's fortifications at West Point. The officious captain he had tumbled into a ditch the previous fall was still in command and still hated by his men. Martin discovered that some soldiers were planning to make a bomb in a canteen, filling it with gunpowder and attaching a fuse. They said they intended only to frighten the officer. Martin believed it would have killed him and was barely able to persuade the men to drop their plan.

He spent another hard winter in New York waiting anxiously for peace to be declared. Sent on a detail one day to cut wood for the barracks, he walked downriver five miles, where he was caught in a sudden blizzard and had to return by a circuitous route of ten miles in a bitterly cold wind and snow eighteen inches deep. His right ear was frostbitten and he was sick for several days. Accustomed to suffering, he dismissed the incident, explaining, "Afflictions always attended the poor soldiers." A friend of his, of the same age, was showing off with his musket one day to amuse Martin, tossing it overhead and catching it, when he lost control and his bayonet stabbed him in the leg. "An ignoramus boy of a surgeon" dressed the wound. A few days later his friend complained that his neck and back hurt. Martin informed the captain, who had the boy taken to a hospital in Newburgh, where he was seized with lockjaw and died.

When spring came the men watched to see if the great chain the Americans stretched across the Hudson in navigable months to impede British ships would be laid down again. If it were not, they reasoned, then peace must be at hand. It wasn't. On April 19, 1783, they learned that Congress had preliminarily approved the terms of the Treaty of Paris, which wouldn't be formally concluded until September. Martin described the men as exultant when they heard the news, but worried about the condition in which they would return to their homes. They were "starved, ragged, and meager," he wrote, with "not a cent to help themselves with."

On June 11 their captain entered their barracks and informed them that, though they were not formally discharged from service, they could all return home and would be recalled if circumstances required it. If they weren't recalled, their furloughs would be considered honorable discharges when the war's end was officially declared. The joy they had expected to feel when the end arrived was little in evidence; sorrow was the more common emotion. They had lived so long together, shared so much suffering together, "bearing each other's burdens" and concealing "each other's faults," it was hard to part. "Ah, it was a serious time," Martin remembered.

They were allowed to keep their muskets and take some ammunition with them. That and the clothes on their backs were all they possessed. They were to receive certificates for the years of back wages owed them and were told their discharges could later be used to claim the hundred acres of land in the Ohio country they had been promised when they enlisted. Many of the men set off immediately for home. Martin and others stayed at West Point, waiting for their "settlement certificates" for back pay. It wasn't clear when the certificates would be provided, so Martin volunteered to serve the final few months of a friend's enlistment while he waited for his money. He was honorably discharged less than two months later and received his certificates, some of which he sold for a little money to buy some clothes.

He never went home. He stayed in New

York for the year and taught school for a time. In the summer of 1784 he left New York for what is now the state of Maine, where he had heard rumors of free land being granted to veterans. He settled in a little town on Penobscot Bay where the water narrows into a river. He never received his hundred acres of Ohio land. Instead he worked a hundred acres of Maine farmland, to which he did not possess title; as many veterans did, he simply claimed a parcel of unused land and tried to make a life for himself. He married Lucy Clewley, and they had a daughter and a son, who was mentally disabled.

The famous Henry Knox, who had been Washington's general of artillery, had acquired something called the Waldo Patent, a land grant giving him title to a vast swath of Maine, which encompassed many veterans' farms, including Martin's. He demanded payment for them and evicted the veterans who couldn't pay. Martin could not pay.

"I throw myself and my family wholly at the feet of your Honor's mercy," he wrote Knox, "earnestly hoping that your Honor will think of some way, in your wisdom, that may be beneficial to your Honor and save a poor family from distress." Knox never replied, and Martin lost his farm. He is believed to be one of a party of veterans who fired their muskets one day at some of Knox's surveyors.

He served as his town's clerk and a select-man and was a captain of the Maine militia. He managed somehow to obtain another, smaller holding and farmed it. He wrote poetry and hymns, and he painted. He was well liked by his neighbors. And he was always poor and often nearly destitute.

In the first decade of the new century, a national debate began over the question of providing pensions to Revolutionary War veterans. The idea was not universally popular; far from it. Most Americans, and many of their elected representatives, were still suspicious of standing armies. Reflecting that suspicion was the popular belief that it had never really been necessary to create the Continental Army, that militias could have won independence with more regard for the nation's republican character. Nevertheless a federal law was enacted in 1818 granting a $96 annual pension, approximately $1,800 in today's dollars, to any male who had served for more than nine months. A year later the law was amended to restrict pensions to those veterans who could prove they were living in poverty. The law didn't make any provision for women who had served or for the thousands of African Americans who had fought for the country's independence. In the end only a little more than three thousand veterans actually received compensation. Martin was one of them, and in a petition he filed to claim his pension he claimed his net worth to be negligible. He had "no real nor personal estate, nor any income whatever, my necessary bedding and wearing apparel excepted, except two cows, six sheep, one pig."

A more generous law was adopted in 1832 that included many veterans who had been denied a pension previously. At the time Martin wrote his narrative, the debate over what the Continentals deserved from their country still continued, and many Americans resented even the modest compensation veterans received under the terms of the 1818 law. Martin saved the last few pages of his narrative to address the controversy, not bothering to conceal his contempt for those who questioned the honor and worth of the men who had liberated the nation and done so without demanding anything from the ungrateful people who now dismissed their sacrifices.

He began by cataloguing everything they

were promised when they enlisted and the very little they actually received, even basic commitments of food and clothing. He recalled their terrible suffering: "Almost every one had heard of the soldiers of the Revolution being tracked by the blood of their feet on the frozen ground. This is literally true; and the thousandth part of their sufferings has not, nor ever will be told."

They had fought exhausted, naked, and starved, he reminded his readers, and were kept in that condition in winter quarters, when marching, and on the battlefield. He allowed that many militia had served bravely and well, a fact he could testify to personally as he had served alongside them. But he argued that militia had not and could not have won the war. That had been accomplished by a standing army, well trained and serving for the duration of the war because, he explained, militia "would not have endured the sufferings the army did; they would have considered themselves (as in reality they were and are) free citizens, not bound by any cords that were not of their own manufacturing."

To those who resented veterans for receiving pensions, he wrote, "The only wish I would bestow upon such hardhearted wretches is, that they might be compelled to go through just such suffering and privations as that army did." He closes his tirade by assuring any readers for whom the old veterans were "an eyesore, a grief of mind," that they need only wait a little while to be relieved from their offense. "A few years longer will put [the veterans] all beyond the power of troubling them, for they will soon be 'where the wicked cease from troubling, and the weary are at rest.' "

Joseph Plumb Martin would take a little longer to go to his rest, likely showing a spirited obstinacy to the end. He died twenty years later, in 1850, at age ninety. His narrative deserves an honored place in the archives of the revolution among our most famous founding documents.

Martin would be the last person to begrudge the appellation "the father of his country" to the great man he served under and esteemed. But a nation doesn't have a single parent; our history identifies a whole class of founding fathers. The men who fought, suffered, and died to achieve the independence the founders declared surely deserve a share of the distinction, though for their part, they thought it honor enough to be described as just who they were.

Joseph Martin's final resting place is in a small cemetery in Stockton Springs just a few paces from U.S. 1, which in summer is often choked with traffic as throngs of vacationers make their way to the pretty harbor towns of the Maine coast. If any of them happen to spot the small marble monument that decorates his grave, not one in ten thousand will know who it memorializes or read the simple inscription it bears:

PRIVATE JOSEPH PLUMB MARTIN
SOLDIER OF THE REVOLUTION

CHAPTER TWO:
BROTHERS-IN-ARMS

Charles Black, a freeborn African American sailor, risked his liberty and life for his country and comrades in the War of 1812.

On the first day of August 1842, a thousand members of the Young Men's Vigilant Association marched along Lombard Street in what is today Society Hill, the tony Philadelphia neighborhood of gracious streets lined by brick townhouses and streetlights made to look like nineteenth-century gas lamps. It was a humbler address in 1842, home to the city's growing population of free African Americans and fugitive slaves. The marchers had staged the parade to celebrate the eighth anniversary of the British Empire's abolition of slavery in the West Indies.

Philadelphia's African American community had increased by 50 percent over the previous two decades, and the modest economic and social progress that accompanied their growing numbers was perceived as a threat by another expanding community nearby. Rural, uneducated, and poor Irish immigrants competed with African Americans for subsistence work and housing. The Irish occupied the last rung of the economic ladder and resented the success of African Americans, who just barely grasped the rung above them. Freed black males in Philadelphia had even briefly possessed the right to vote until 1838, when it was stripped from them.

Both communities had reasons to fear for their security, of course, in a country that had little respect for the rights and dignity of either. The Irish, beset not only by desperate poverty but by the bigotry and violence of anti-Irish, anti-Catholic nativists, and who understandably held the British Empire in low regard, blamed the city's other victims of prejudice for their wretched circumstances.

They had clashed before, but never as violently as on this day, when an Irish mob attacked the marchers as they passed Mother Bethel Church, one of the first African American churches in the country. The marchers fought back, further enraging their assailants. The ensuing riot lasted for three days.

The mob made for the home of a leader of the black community and outspoken abolitionist, who had armed himself in preparation for the confrontation. A Catholic priest dissuaded the rioters from attacking him and burning his house, but they burned and looted a great many other places, scores of homes, the Second African Presbyterian Church, and Smith's Hall, a well-known meeting place for abolitionists. Blacks were dragged from their homes and savagely beaten. Hundreds were injured, the number killed unrecorded but presumably many. Firemen were attacked as they fought the blazes. Philadelphia's mayor and police did little to quell the violence until the riot began to subside on the third day and the local militia was called in to restore order.

The African American abolitionist and historian William Cooper Nell, in his history of African Americans who had served in the Revolutionary War and the War of 1812, quoted a "local philanthropist" describing the fate of one of the riot's victims:

A Colored man, whom I visited in the hospitals, called to see me to-day. He had just got out. He looked very pitiful. His head was bent down. He said he could not get it erect, his neck was so injured.

87

He is a very intelligent man, and can read and write. I will give you his story.

Charles Black, over fifty, resides in Lombard Street. Was at home with his little boy unconscious of what was transpiring without. Suddenly, the mob rushed into his room, dragged him down stairs, and beat him so unmercifully that he would have been killed, had not some humane individuals interposed, and prevented further violence.

Charles Black had known more than his share of misfortunes before he was set upon by the mob that day. He had lived for a time within the walls of one of the most notorious prisons in the world. He had braved the fire of cannon and musket and heard the terrible ring of cutlass striking cutlass. He bore wounds inflicted by one or more of those arms, though the scant information we have about his life doesn't specify which weapon — grapeshot, ball, or blade — drew his blood.

Black was a sailor. His father had fought at Bunker Hill, and his grandfather in the French and Indian War. When the War of 1812 began he was impressed as a seaman in the British Navy who refused to fight against his country and, eventually, fought for her.

There is little more recorded about his life before he was dragged from his home by an angry mob and savagely beaten. But we can imagine it by recalling the experiences of other African Americans who served in the navy during the wars that preceded the war that would end slavery.

It was a hard life that followed the day he felt, as had thousands of other men from the lower orders of their societies, "a damp, drizzly November in my soul" and went down to the sea to seek opportunities unavailable to him elsewhere. It would have been an unpredictable life, much of it spent in miserable living conditions, an often dangerous life and subject to violent discipline. But for however much of his life was spent under sail, Black would have known what it was like to live as a rough equal among white men.

Racial prejudices and tensions didn't entirely disappear at sea, but most ships were integrated. There was a social hierarchy at sea, of course, and those on the top held absolute power over those beneath them. But the caste system at sea had much less to do with racial prejudice than did the one on shore.

Fifteen to twenty percent of sailors in the U.S. Navy during the War of 1812 were African Americans. They constituted anywhere from 12 to 25 percent and in some cases 50 percent of a single ship's company. The percentage was the same or higher on privateers during the war as it had been on American merchant ships before the war.

The War of 1812 was fought primarily for "free trade and sailors' rights," for the freedom of American seaborne commerce and in opposition to the British practice of impressment. More of the war's turning points were the result of naval engagements than land battles. When it was over, neither side had acquired new territory, but the British blockade and seizure of American merchant ships and the impressment of American sailors was finished.

During the Napoleonic wars Great Britain imposed economic sanctions called the Orders in Council to curtail American trade with Britain's enemies. The British Navy was ordered to stop and search neutral ships and confiscate those that were carrying contraband goods to or from enemy ports. Britain had expanded its navy to more than six hundred ships, and it couldn't meet its manpower needs by press-ganging only men residing in the British Isles. So His Majesty's ships were authorized to abduct sailors on American privateers. Ostensibly only British-born sailors were to be impressed, even if they had acquired U.S. citizenship. But in practice British captains had quotas to fill, and they weren't overly scrupulous about establishing the national origins of the sailors they seized. Thousands of American sailors, British and native-born, were impressed, and there was little the small U.S. Navy could do to prevent it.

The harm to America's economy caused by the obstruction of her maritime trade was severe. The injury done to national honor by the seizure of American ships and sailors outraged the American public. One incident in 1807 lit the fuse for the war that would erupt in 1812.

"Give a ship an unlucky name," wrote the nineteenth-century naval historian James Barnes, "and it will last throughout the whole of her career." The superstitions of sailors ought not to be taken lightly. The unfortunate career of the American frigate *Chesapeake* is a case in point.

Barnes records that the *Chesapeake* was stuck in her slipway at her launch and the following day ran onto a sandbar. She didn't handle well at sea either. Improvements were made to her, and she eventually sailed more gracefully, "yet her bad name stuck to her, as bad names will." It never stuck faster than on June 22, 1807, when the HMS *Leopard* cut across the bow of the *Chesapeake* about fifty miles off Norfolk, Virginia, and hailed the American ship's captain, Commodore James Barron.

In the spring of 1807 two French ships that had been damaged in a hurricane limped into Hampton Roads, Virginia, for repairs. British ships were stationed off shore to block their escape. During the blockade three impressed seamen from HMS *Melampus,* Daniel Martin, William Ware, and John Strachan, and another from HMS *Halifax,* Jenkins Ratford, a British native, took advantage of the opportunity and escaped to Portsmouth, where they were seen on shore by some of their officers. To avoid being taken back into service, all four enlisted on the *Chesapeake* as she was taking on stores and crew for a voyage to the Mediterranean.

Vice Admiral George Berkeley, commander of the British North American Station in Halifax, Nova Scotia, wrote the U.S. secretary of the navy, Robert Smith, to demand the runaways' return. Smith wrote to Commodore Barron, who investigated the matter and reported that three of the four were native-born Americans: Strachan and Ware were from Maryland, and Martin was a native of Massachusetts. Barron wasn't certain about Ratford, who had enlisted under an alias. Smith dutifully informed Admiral Berkeley the men were American citizens and would not be returned. An infuriated Berkeley issued orders to his fleet, instructing his captains to stop the *Chesapeake* once she put to sea and recover the deserters by force if necessary, which is what the *Leopard* intended when she hailed the *Chesapeake*.

The *Chesapeake*'s captain wasn't expecting a battle that day, nor was he prepared for one. Many of his crew were new recruits; his stores had yet to be secured below decks. Two women were aboard, traveling to Europe with a party of civilians, and were standing on deck chatting with some of the officers.

The *Leopard*'s captain, Salisbury Humphreys, sent a lieutenant to the *Chesapeake* with a search warrant. Barron explained that he had investigated the matter and determined they were U.S. citizens who had been wrongly impressed into British service. The lieutenant asked for a private word in the captain's cabin, where he made clear to Barron that they would search the ship and apprehend the deserters with or without his permission. Barron refused again and didn't appear to take the warning seriously. He sent the officer back to the *Leopard* bearing a letter assuring Humphreys that no British sailors were aboard the *Chesapeake.* When Barron's officers asked him if they should prepare the ship's guns for action, he dismissed the idea and conversed with the two female passengers before returning to his cabin.

The *Leopard,* with Humphreys's emissary back on board, fired a shot across the *Chesapeake*'s bow, followed quickly by a full broadside. The ladies were rushed below deck. Commodore Barron emerged from his cabin shouting, "To quarters!" Three of her crew lay dead on her decks, and another eighteen had been wounded. The *Chesapeake* managed to fire only a single gun in retaliation before Barron ordered her colors struck and surrendered. The *Leopard* refused the surrender. Humphreys boarded her, arrested the four men, and sailed for Halifax.

The *Chesapeake* returned to Norfolk in disgrace. Barron was court-martialed and suspended from service. Jenkins Ratford was tried for desertion and hanged from a yardarm in Halifax. Americans seethed over the violation of American sovereignty and clamored for war. A diplomatic crisis ensued. The British government disavowed the action and relieved Admiral Berkeley. It was also prepared to release the three Americans and to pay an indemnity to the wounded and the families of the dead. But Britain refused to discontinue the practice of impressment.

To avert war, President Thomas Jefferson resorted to economic sanctions to compel both Britain and France to respect American neutrality. But the Embargo Act of 1807 hurt American commerce more than it did the two belligerents and was repealed a little more than a year later. Two of the three Americans were eventually returned to the United States; the third had died from disease while in custody. By the time they reached their native soil, the War of 1812 had already begun, caused in part by British injustice to the two surviving Americans, Martin and Ware, who were of African descent.

Well before the turn of the eighteenth century, black sailors on American whaling and merchant ships were a common sight in the world's ports. A life at sea offered freedom and mobility to people who were marginalized in their societies. African Americans, primarily from northern coastal communities, were drawn to the maritime industry in disproportionate numbers. They earned decent pay and had opportunities for advancement that were unavailable to them elsewhere, as did white sailors from disadvantaged backgrounds. Life at sea promised adventure and the chance to escape poverty, and for black sailors at least a partial escape from the racial prejudice that prevented them from improving their lives on land. But it was dangerous, arduous employment in harsh conditions with long absences from home, which seldom attracted people who had better options. Thus, of necessity, it was obtainable by men of any race.

The cramped, isolated, and practical world of a ship at sea shaped a social order that, while not free of racial prejudice, placed a higher value on attributes other than skin color. Men worked side by side at the same tasks and relied on each other for their success and safety. They were usually paid the same, shared the same food and quarters, endured the same hardships, suffered the same illnesses, braved the same risks, and died at the same rate. When serving on privateers, they received a fair share of captured prizes. Sailors' manner of dress, their vernacular, and the rhythm and lyrics of the shanties they sang were the products of their various ethnic traditions, not the least of which were African American traditions. A sailor's skills and industry influenced his shipmates' opinions more than his race and won him advancement. As the historian Gerald Afton notes, "Black seamen who persevered for multiple voyages and gained the necessary experience and skills were promoted, and white sailors were subject to the orders of black officers and petty officers." Some African Americans even managed to become ship's captains, and a few earned enough to purchase their own ship.

"Atlantic maritime culture," writes the historian Jeffrey Bolster, "included strong egalitarian impulses that frequently confounded the strict racial etiquette of slave societies." To illustrate his point, Bolster uses the example of three white sailors who were befriended by a Georgia slave, whom they thanked and shook by the hand, "a gesture unthinkable to most white Americans."

African Americans in bondage also went to sea, the property of ship owners and captains or owners who hired them out and took their wages. Fugitive slaves found opportunities in the maritime industry as well, using their earnings to purchase their freedom or seizing it by jumping ship when anchored in a free port. There was also among sailors white and black a sense of shared bondage: they were subject to the same deprivations and harsh discipline, including flogging, and expected to pay the same strict obedience to orders on voyages that could last for years. White and black also shared the fear of being taken from their ship and forced into service in the British Navy.

Thus race had nothing to do with the fact that sailors had the most cause to resent British policies that threatened equally their livelihood and liberty. So it is hardly a surprise that when those policies precipitated a war, African American sailors rushed to enlist in their country's service. The rough equality they experienced in the unique subculture of a ship at sea would be fortified by the most important quality in the unique subculture of men at war: solidarity.

Veterans from every war have the same reasons for enduring all they endured. First, they wanted to get the damn thing over with so they could go home. Second, they didn't want to let their buddies down.

Much has been written about the camaraderie of soldiers and the practical and psychological reasons that nurture it. I (McCain) can testify to its uniqueness. The bonds I had with men I served with in war have never been replicated in friendships I have made in civilian life, even with my closest friends. It's not just a difference of intensity; it's an entirely different species of relationship that simply doesn't exist outside of war. It is a bond with people with whom you might have little and sometimes nothing else in common beyond the experience of war, some of whom you might not have liked in civilian life, whom you might even have actively disliked. And yet it is a bond that thousands upon thousands of soldiers have honored with their lives. It involves total reliance on each other, a trust that breeds virtues up and down the line, not the least of which is the courage it takes to withstand bullets, fear, and even death if it comes. And with that trust comes the insistent, overwhelming desire not to be found wanting by the men to your right and left when your courage is put to the test.

The retired general and war hero Hal Moore commanded a battalion of the 7th Cavalry Regiment at the Battle of Ia Drang

Valley in Vietnam. In the movie based on his memoir of the battle, *We Were Soldiers,* Moore (played by Mel Gibson) makes the point eloquently as he addresses his battalion on the day before they deploy to Vietnam:

In the 7th Cavalry, we've got a captain from the Ukraine; another from Puerto Rico. We've got Japanese, Chinese, Blacks, Hispanics, Cherokee Indians, Jews and Gentiles. All Americans. Now here in the states, some of you in this unit may have experienced discrimination because of race or creed. But for you and me now, all that is gone. We're moving into the valley of the shadow of death, where you will watch the back of the man next to you, as he will watch yours. And you won't care what color he is or by what name he calls God. They say we're leaving home. We're going to what home is supposed to be.

The navy in which African Americans enlisted in 1812 certainly wasn't free of racial prejudice. It wasn't what home was supposed to be if you observed the social mores of the time. And it wasn't a test-tube culture simulating a genuine brotherhood of man. The cruelties and other corruptions of war are antithetical to the virtues of just societies. Their service in that war, as it would be in other wars, was a practical necessity to the government that welcomed and armed them. And the brotherhood they entered was nothing more, but certainly nothing less, than a society of rough men with rough ways, encountering extreme adversity together, suffering sickness and injury together, killing and dying together, being terrified and brave and relieved and destroyed together, and discovering that all they had in that weird, vicious, and scary world was each other.

At the start of the War of 1812 African Americans were officially barred from service in the army, although the war's growing manpower needs would eventually cause the army to change its policy. Before the war blacks were also officially excluded from naval service, but that policy had always been more or less ignored. After war was declared, African Americans were welcomed in the navy by an act of Congress. They had suffered no less than white sailors at the hands of the British. They had pride in their seamanship, and a desire to prove their value to their country, which they hoped would improve their race's position in American society after the war. So they went to war for America, for "free trade and sailors' rights."

The U.S. Navy in 1812 was considerably smaller than the enemy's, but not necessarily outclassed. American warships were well built and well handled. American frigates were heavier and carried more cannon than their British counterparts. Many of their captains were aggressive and resourceful, and their crews skilled and brave under fire. Moreover most of the Royal Navy's six hundred ships along with most of the British Army were still engaged in the war with Napoleon and wouldn't be available for the war with America until Napoleon's abdication and exile in April 1814.

American victories in the early stages of the war were won on the sea, beginning with a brief but decisive battle off the coast of Newfoundland. The three-masted, forty-four-gun heavy frigate USS *Constitution,* named by George Washington, was launched in 1797 and is still afloat today at the Charlestown Navy Yard in Boston. On August 19, 1812, she was searching the North Atlantic for British frigates to fight, when one of her crew spotted the sails of HMS *Guerriere.* Two hours later the British frigate was burning to the waterline.

The *Guerriere* fired the first shot. The *Constitution*'s experienced captain, Isaac Hull, a Connecticut native and lifelong mariner, deftly maneuvered her alongside the *Guerriere* within pistol range and fired a double-loaded broadside of grapeshot and shell, battering her severely. The British ship lost her mizzenmast, and her bowsprit became caught in the *Constitution*'s rigging. The crews of the entangled ships exchanged musket fire, with marksmen firing from the mast tops to deadly effect. Casualties were heavy on both sides, but when the *Guerriere* finally broke free her other two masts collapsed. She was dead in the water and surrendered. Hull took the British survivors on board, ordered the *Guerriere* torched, and sailed the *Constitution* back to her home port, Boston, and to the huzzahs of its citizens. Her sailors recalled British shot bouncing off the *Constitution*'s thick hull and christened her "Old Ironsides," the nickname she is still called today.

African Americans constituted at least a tenth and probably more of the *Constitution*'s crew. However many they were, they left little doubt of their ability and courage. Of them Hull wrote later, "I never had any better fighters. . . . They stripped to the

103

waist and fought like devils, sir, seeming to be utterly insensible to danger and to be possessed with a determination to outfight the white sailors."

Americans won several other naval engagements that first year. Black sailors fought with distinction in every one of them, as they did in most and likely all the naval battles of the war. Accounts of their individual heroism are scarce, but enough testimonies exist to conclude that race had little bearing on whether a sailor could prove himself in combat. In combat men don't kill and die for their race; your only enemy is the man trying to kill you and those who stand with you. Men die because they were brave or foolish or slow or unlucky; they live because they were brave or smart or resourceful or lucky. The survivors share the same fatigue and grief, and the dead are buried in the same indifferent sea.

However, prejudices that were ignored or held in check in the non-discriminating realities of war were usually only held in abeyance aboard ship. When warships sailed into port to replenish their stores and wait for new orders, African Americans were often granted only restricted liberty and were sometimes denied permission to leave the ship at all. When the war was finished, the society they returned to and had risked everything for remained as bigoted as it had been before the war.

Even African Americans who were taken prisoner during the war found prison life as segregated as civilian society. The British built a prison in 1809 on a remote, wind-swept moor in Devonshire to hold French soldiers during the Napoleonic wars. Sixty-five hundred Americans would be imprisoned at Dartmoor over the course of the War of 1812, most of them taken from captured privateers and a smaller number from navy warships. The proportion of African American prisoners was the same as in the general population of American seamen, between 15 and 20 percent.

Dartmoor was an immense stone fortress with two concentric walls. The outside wall was a mile in circumference, enclosing nearly fifteen acres. Prisoners passed through five separate gates as they were brought to one of seven stone prison blocks, each constructed to hold a thousand in-mates. The blocks were unheated and freez-ing in the winter. There were no beds or other furniture; prisoners slept in ham-mocks or on the floor, with many forced to accept the latter as the number of prisoners interned in each block eventually grew to as

105

many as fifteen hundred. The nearest city was Plymouth, where the prisoners were landed and then marched seventeen miles at bayonet point over the freezing moor, poorly clothed and often shoeless. Situated in a desolate, unforgiving wilderness and guarded by two thousand British militia, Dartmoor made escape nearly impossible.

Discipline was harsh, living conditions were miserable, the food was rotten, disease was rampant, and prisoners suffered constant exposure to the elements. Something like three hundred of the thousands of Americans crowded there would never leave. They were buried in a shallow, unconsecrated mass grave outside the prison walls, where decades later ceaseless wind and rooting animals would disinter them, leaving their bones bleaching on the moors.

As soon as Americans arrived at Dartmoor they segregated themselves by race. The integration African Americans had become accustomed to at sea was spurned by the white prisoners, who had recently fought beside them, had suffered and celebrated and buried their dead together, and now insisted on reclaiming racial superiority. Most of the African American inmates were crowded into No. 4 Block, which had been designated as quarters for the prison population's "undesirables."

Although British muskets kept them captive and imposed discipline, the prisoners themselves ran the place. Most captured officers were either paroled to live in relative comfort in nearby villages, as long as they promised not to escape, or interned in buildings just outside the prison's walls. White seamen were free to organize their ranks, which they did more or less democratically. They elected committees to adjudicate disputes and punish wrongdoing and to operate businesses and markets, laundries, churches, and various entertainments.

The British allowed black inmates to administrate their prison block as well, which they did by decidedly less democratic methods. No. 4 Block was ruled by a monarch, Richard Crafus, a native of Maryland, known to his subjects and to all Americans at Dartmoor as "King Dick." Wearing a grenadier's bearskin cap and standing six feet three inches, he was a fierce brawler and natural autocrat, enforcing his will with the large club he carried at all times, in the company of two handsome white sailors he employed as his retinue. He patrolled his kingdom daily, threatening and beating prisoners who violated the rules or offended his sense of decorum. He intimidated white prisoners as much as he did his own subjects.

Unsurprisingly, then, under King Dick's regime, No. 4 Block contained a more orderly society than the democratically run white cell blocks. It was cleaner, less troubled by petty crimes, and apparently a more congenial place as well. The entertainment on offer — gambling, theatrical performances, boxing matches — was generally acknowledged to be superior to the amusements staged in the other blocks. Consequently white prisoners frequently went to No. 4 to trade or take in a play or bet on a sporting match. Small numbers even chose to live there. Troublemaking prisoners known as "rough allies" were usually transferred to No. 4, where they temporarily reformed themselves enough not to disturb the peace noticeably and face the King's justice.

At some point in 1812 Charles Black was interned at Dartmoor. He was an ordinary seaman on a captured American merchant ship when he was pressed into service on a British warship. When the war began, he refused to continue serving the Royal Navy, was made to forfeit the nine hundred dollars he was owed as his share of captured prizes, and was sent in chains to Dartmoor, along with other impressed sailors who refused to fight against their country.

There are no detailed accounts of his experiences there, but it is safe to assume they were as miserable as everyone else's. The overcrowding would have been worse than the cramped quarters aboard ship. The discipline was probably harsher and the food more likely to poison him. He might have slept on a cold, stone floor. He might have been whipped severely for some small infraction. He surely would have yearned for relief from bitter winter winds. He might not have risked death in combat, but had he challenged his captors he could count on being flogged or shot, and he likely had to brawl from time to time to discourage thieves or defend his person and honor from assault. He would have run a greater risk of death by illness than he faced at sea once the remedy for scurvy had been discovered. King Dick might have been a more benevolent dictator than some ship's captains he had known, but Black could very well have resented being the subject of an absolute monarch who made his own rules and likely enforced them capriciously. And he would surely have been discouraged by the discovery that men like those he had lived with on long sea voyages, whose respect and even friendship he had enjoyed, now considered him an inferior human being.

Accounts of how Black managed to get out of Dartmoor also lack details. All that is known is that he was released at some point during the war, possibly as part of a prisoner exchange, but was brought back to Dartmoor before he left England. He was released again, and this time he managed to make his way back to America, where he promptly enlisted in the navy. The historian David Fitz-Enz, in his account of the Battle of Plattsburgh, New York, described Black as having "a particular hatred of two things: one was digging holes and the other was the English who first impressed him and then imprisoned him in the hell hole of Dartmoor."

Americans were still stuck in that hellhole well after the Treaty of Ghent was ratified in February 1815. On April 6, 1815, Dartmoor's guards fired indiscriminately at prisoners they believed were about to riot, killing seven and wounding many more. Blacks were among the last Americans to leave. Some historians believe they preferred to remain in prison to await passage on ships bound for northern ports rather than board those sailing to southern slave ports. King Dick got on board a ship bound for Boston, where he would exchange the robes of monarchy for the smiles and glad-handing of a popular leader of the city's African American community.

While Charles Black spent his first discouraging weeks in Dartmoor, African Americans on privateers and navy ships helped win more victories on the high seas and Great Lakes, which shocked the British. During the same period British soldiers and their Indian allies won a succession of victories on land, which discouraged Americans. Sailors preferred serving on privateers because of the prospect of shared profits from captured prizes. Privateers filled their rolls quickly, which put a strain on the manpower available for service on navy ships, particularly those that sailed the remote Great Lakes, where there was little chance of booty and no lively port cities in the frontier wilderness in which to spend it.

Much of the war was fought near the U.S.-Canadian border. The British had stationed fleets in the lakes to transport men and matériel to their armies in the north. Americans had to catch up quickly, so hastily built frigates were launched, requisitioned merchant vessels were converted to warships, and higher pay was offered to induce sailors to crew them. By the second year of the war, U.S. Navy squadrons were patrolling inland lakes with large numbers of African American sailors.

The most famous American naval battle in the War of 1812 is Commodore Oliver Hazard Perry's victory over a British squadron of six ships in the Battle of Lake Erie on September 10, 1813. After British broadsides had disabled her guns and killed or wounded four-fifths of her crew, Perry was forced to abandon his battered flagship, the USS *Lawrence*. He and his battle flag were rowed a half mile under gunfire to another ship, the *Niagara*. An immense oil painting of the scene looms over a landing on the U.S. Senate's east staircase. Ships are clustered together in a haze of smoke, fire belching from their gun ports. Dead men and flotsam drift in the roiling water. Perry is standing heroically in the bow of a rowboat, pointing toward the *Niagara,* while a young midshipman, believed to be his brother, tugs at the fool's coat to get him to sit down. Six oarsmen row furiously through the maelstrom; only one of them is black. His is the only expression that suggests an emotion other than steely determination: he looks terrified.

The Battle of Lake Erie was a fiercely fought, narrowly won contest, and certainly a victory that earned its fame, giving Americans control of Lake Erie and bringing relief to Major General William Henry Harrison's struggling army in Ohio. It lasted nearly four hours. Perry's guns had a shorter range than those of the British, so he had to maneuver in light winds to get close to the enemy while the enemy's longer range guns pounded his flagship. Furious broadsides were exchanged, and sailors hanging in the rigging fired muskets at targets close enough to hear their cries. Dead and wounded littered the decks.

When the *Lawrence* was destroyed the British expected Perry to surrender. But he had the *Niagara* sailed straight to the center of the action, firing both larboard and starboard guns, and in less than half an hour the British had struck their colors and surrendered. After the battle Perry sent his famous dispatch to Harrison: "Dear Genl: We have met the enemy, and they are ours."

As important as Perry's daring and skill was on that day, just as important were the bravery and sacrifices of his sailors and marines, many of whom were African Americans. Unlike their representation in the painting, if they were terrified — and who wouldn't have been? — they were not incapacitated by fear. They fought fiercely, resourcefully, and determinedly, earning the respect and gratitude of their commander, who had once doubted their fitness to serve.

Commodore Isaac Chauncey, who commanded the American fleet on Lake Ontario, was Perry's commanding officer. Perry had been desperately short of men to crew the flotilla he was assembling in Lake Erie. He had little more than a hundred men and needed as many as seven hundred. He begged Chauncey for reinforcements, but Chauncey, who, as commander of all Great Lakes naval operations, had serious manpower issues of his own, was unresponsive. Perry went over his head and wrote directly to the secretary of the navy, infuriating Chauncey, who nevertheless felt compelled then to come to Perry's aid. He sent Perry 150 men. They were African American, and many of them had served on the *Constitution*.

When Perry saw them, he immediately wrote to Chauncey to complain:

Sir, I have this moment received . . . the enclosed letter from General Harrison. If I had officers and men . . . I could fight the enemy, and proceed up the lake; but having no one to command the "Niagara," and only one commissioned lieutenant and two acting lieutenants, whatever my wishes may be, going out is out of the question. The men who came by Mr. Champlin are a motley set, — blacks, soldiers, and boys. I cannot think you saw them after they were selected. I am, however, pleased to see any thing in the shape of a man.

Perry's tactless complaint, added to what Chauncey considered his earlier insubordination, was received with considerable indignation. We can feel the heat of Chauncey's anger in his written response:

Sir, . . . I regret that you are not pleased with the men sent you by Mssrs Champlin and Forest; for, to my knowledge, a part of them are not surpassed by any seamen we have in the fleet: and I have yet to learn that the color of the skin, or the cut and trimmings of the coat, can effect a man's qualifications or usefulness. I have nearly fifty blacks on this ship, and many of them are among my best men; and those people you call soldiers have been to sea from two to seventeen years; and I presume you will find them as good and useful as any men on board of your vessel.

Chauncey's prediction was proved accurate. After the battle Perry wrote the secretary of the navy and Chauncey, praising the "bravery and good conduct of his negroes."

When Perry left the *Lawrence,* he took with him his personal pennant, which bore the famous dying words, "Don't Give Up the Ship," of the man for whom his flagship was named, Perry's close friend, Captain James Lawrence. A lawyer by training, Lawrence joined the infant U.S. Navy in 1798, received a lieutenant's commission in 1802, and commanded several ships before and during the War of 1812. He first won renown as commander of the sloop of war USS *Hornet.* The *Hornet* had been cruising the Atlantic during the first four months of the war and had already distinguished herself by capturing a British privateer, blockading a British sloop off the coast of Brazil, and capturing a British packet ship, the *Resolution,* that was carrying a small fortune in gold and silver.

On February 24, 1813, while chasing another privateer into the mouth of a river off the coast of Guyana, the *Hornet* spotted a British man-of-war, the *Espiegle,* riding at anchor in the mouth of the Demerara River. As she was bearing down on the *Espiegle,* the *Hornet* was suddenly approached from the sea by the twenty-gun British sloop *Peacock,* commanded by William Peake. Lawrence brought the *Hornet* about, gaining the upwind advantage, beat to quarters, and cleared for action, leaving the *Espiegle* unmolested. At about 5:30 the two fast-closing sloops passed each other on opposite tacks within pistol range. Both fired broadsides, but the *Hornet* had more guns and better gunners, and while some of her crew were killed or wounded in the exchange, she inflicted far worse damage on the *Peacock.* Both ships made to come about, but the *Hornet* was faster. Lawrence brought her up to the *Peacock*'s defenseless stern, and his gunners destroyed the man-of-war in minutes. Commander Peake was killed, and his second-in-command ordered her colors struck.

Lawrence sent a crew to board the *Peacock,* but she couldn't be saved and quickly sank to the bottom. The survivors were brought on board the *Hornet.* Carrying too many men and too few provisions, she left the coast of South America and made for

Martha's Vineyard, where she could replenish her stores unmolested by British warships. Though they were desperately low on water, and the crew had been on reduced rations for a while, captain and crew treated their British prisoners generously, as the *Peacock*'s surviving officers publicly acknowledged when they reached the States.

In his after-action report to Secretary of the Navy William Jones, Lawrence praised "the cool and determined conduct of my officers and crew . . . and their almost unexampled exertions afterward entitle them to my warmest acknowledgements." Many of his men — half of them, according to one account — were African Americans, including many of the gunners whose skill had proved superior to the *Peacock*'s gunners.

Although the naval war hadn't gone well for the British, with Napoleon's abdication in April 1814, they could send additional regiments to North America and begin in earnest their plan to force America's capitulation. In August of that year, while British soldiers were marching on Washington and Baltimore, Lieutenant General Sir George Prevost left Montreal and invaded New York with an army of eleven thousand seasoned

British troops, many of them veterans of the Peninsular War. His object was control of Lake Champlain, from where he could eventually advance down the Hudson River Valley to New York City. He would have to take the lake from a small force of fifteen hundred American regulars and two thousand mostly untrained militia under the command of Brigadier General Alexander Macomb at Plattsburgh on the lake's Cumberland Bay.

The resulting Battle of Plattsburgh — or Battle of Lake Champlain, depending on which service's perspective you share, the army's or navy's — proved to be hugely consequential. But its importance has always been overshadowed by the hard-won American victory at Baltimore, when Francis Scott Key hailed the oversized American flag waving over Fort McHenry at dawn on September 14. The battle on the shores of Lake Champlain ended the war in the north and, arguably, the entire conflict. British intransigence had stalled the peace negotiations at Ghent; London insisted on terms that would have created an Indian buffer state between Canada and the United States and banned the U.S. Navy from the Great Lakes. After the smoke cleared at Plattsburgh and word of the outcome reached

London, Britain was prepared to accept a treaty that recognized the antebellum status quo. Negotiations proceeded swiftly, and the Treaty of Ghent was signed in December. In the words of Winston Churchill, the Battle of Plattsburgh was "the most decisive engagement of the war."

In the lead-up to the engagement, General Macomb sent a force of fewer than five hundred soldiers to harass and slow the British. Master Commandant Thomas Macdonough, in command of U.S. naval forces on the lake, hastily finished assembling his fleet of fourteen ships, which included the recently constructed twenty-six-gun *Saratoga,* the fourteen-gun *Ticonderoga,* and the just completed twenty-gun brig USS *Eagle.* He faced a British squadron of sixteen ships commanded by Commodore George Downie, which boasted the newly built thirty-six-gun frigate HMS *Confiance.* Though Downie had more and better guns, Macdonough had the better battle plan.

General Prevost's army arrived at Plattsburgh on September 6 opposite the Saranac River from the American defenders, who occupied a ridge just south of the little town. Friction in the British ranks had weakened Prevost's command; soldiers who had served under the Duke of Wellington grumbled about Prevost's timidity and indecisiveness, despite enjoying a huge numerical advantage. He spent the first few days at Plattsburgh exchanging artillery fire with the Americans and launching minor attacks that were easily repulsed. When the British found a place to ford the Saranac three miles above the town, Prevost committed to a full assault on the American left flank. The attack was scheduled for September 10, to coincide with the arrival of Commodore Downie's squadron. It would begin with a diversionary attack on the American center to keep the defenders occupied, while the main British force forded the Saranac and bore down on their left and Downie destroyed Macdonough's squadron.

Macdonough's ships, anchored in Cumberland Bay, were responsible for protecting Macomb's right flank. Macdonough knew he was facing a formidable foe. None of his ships could match the firepower of a British frigate, and the British guns were longer range than his. He needed to erase Downie's advantage by enticing him to fight at close range. Cumberland Bay was only three miles wide, and with its hidden shoals and sandbars it could be treacherous to maneuver. It was ideal for a close fight. Macdonough decided to fight his ships at anchor, with his four biggest ships in a line north to south, their spring lines attached to their anchor cables so they could be turned from side to side, and the gunboats interspersed between them.

In the weeks before the battle Macdonough's biggest challenge had been finding sailors and marines for his fleet. He had to plead for soldiers from Major General George Izard, who commanded America's northern army. Izard sent him two hundred fifty men whom Macdonough quickly trained as marines and sailors. He still needed oarsmen for his gunboats and asked Macomb for some of his. But the badly outnumbered Macomb had no men to spare and agreed only to empty his stockade and have the prisoners man the oars. A few members of Macomb's regimental band volunteered to fight on the lake, as did an African American seaman, just arrived from Boston and recently an inmate in Dartmoor prison.

We don't know which ship Charles Black fought on that day. We know he fought bravely, and he fought alongside other brave men, black and white. They fought for the country each called home and for each other. Some knew their business, and some had never fought at sea before. They withstood the fire together. They killed together. They were wounded together. They died together. And they deserve equal credit for the victory that turned the tide of the war.

Around eight o'clock on the morning of September 11, a day later than Prevost planned, Macdonough saw Downie's flagship, the big frigate *Confiance,* her sails full, round Cumberland Head, two miles northeast of where his little fleet was anchored. Minutes later the other British ships appeared. The noise they made as they readied their guns for battle alerted Prevost and his officers that the Royal Navy had arrived and the battle was at hand. Prevost issued orders to begin executing his battle plan.

Prevost heard Downie's ships fire their first salvo and then gave the order to fire his six artillery batteries all at once at the American lines. A brigade marched in formation to the bridges over the Saranac as if readying a frontal assault and began firing their muskets at the Americans. The main body of Prevost's army marched north to the ford, while the noise from naval cannon and field artillery and the drifting gun smoke masked their movements.

Downie's plan was to cross Macdonough's line out of range of their guns. But as they sailed downwind toward the anchored

American fleet, with the *Confiance* leading the way, the wind fell off. The British ships, their sails luffing in the dying, shifting breeze, slowly drifted into harm's way and had to drop anchor a few hundred yards in front of the American line. The *Confiance* approached Macdonough's flagship, the *Saratoga.* On Macdonough's order the *Saratoga* fired first. A single cannonball hit the bow of the *Confiance,* and all at once American guns opened fire. British guns, loaded with double shot, replied. A British sloop, HMS *Chubb,* was quickly disabled. Her main boom destroyed and anchor cable severed, she drifted helplessly along the battle line, her decks crowded with dead and dying. Another British sloop ran aground on a sandbar. But HMS *Linnet* crossed in front of the *Eagle* and fired a full broadside at her before dropping anchor.

Macdonough held his fire while he let the *Confiance* drift closer to him. Before he could order another salvo, Downie dropped anchor and gave the *Saratoga* a tremendous battering with his starboard guns, killing or wounding nearly a fifth of her crew. Body parts, rigging, and all manner of debris were strewn across her deck. Macdonough was struck by falling timber and knocked briefly unconscious.

All hands cleared decks, carried the wounded below, and manned the guns as the two naval lines pounded each other. Macdonough himself manned a gun. So did his counterpart, Commodore Downie. Charles Black, an experienced seaman, likely manned one as well. Gunners fired at will. No orders, no battle plans directed the action now, just desperate broadsides exchanged every few minutes in the hope the enemy would be annihilated first. Hardly a mast in either fleet was undamaged. The *Ticonderoga* fought off attacks from a half dozen British gunboats. The battered *Eagle* cut her anchor lines in an attempt to escape complete destruction, exposing the *Saratoga* to the *Linnet*'s guns.

The *Saratoga*'s starboard guns were knocked out of action and her masts and rigging shot away. Macdonough had her hauled about on her spring line and brought his port guns into action, pounding the British frigate mercilessly, killing Downie and several other officers. The *Confiance* tried to come about but was stuck and couldn't return fire. Her stern exposed to the *Saratoga*'s guns, she struck her colors. Macdonough turned his guns on the *Linnet*, whose captain realized the hopelessness of his situation and surrendered. The British gunboats escaped, but all four of the fleet's big ships were now American prizes.

The battle had lasted two hours. A surviving midshipman from the *Confiance* wrote his mother to describe the carnage: "The havoc on both sides is dreadful. . . . Never was a shower of hail so thick as the shot whistling about our ears." One of the marines on board the *Confiance* had been a veteran of Trafalgar, which he called "a mere Flea-Bite in comparison with this." Casualties were high on both sides: fifty-seven British killed and seventy-two wounded; fifty-two Americans killed and fifty-eight wounded.

During the naval battle Prevost's main force had marched past the ford, but after discovering their mistake they turned around and belatedly crossed the Saranac. They were bearing down on Macomb's left flank when Prevost saw the British fleet surrender. Fearing he could not resupply his army with the lake in American hands, he halted the attack and, ignoring the protests of his officers, marched his soldiers back to Canada.

The exhausted survivors of the Battle of Lake Champlain, their clothes blackened with gun smoke and blood and shredded by grapeshot and flying debris, their ears deafened from the ceaseless cannonade, most of them bearing wounds, saw to the severely wounded and counted their dead. Macdonough refused the swords proffered by surrendering British officers and commended the gallantry of his defeated foes. He surveyed the damage to his ships and gave orders for the disposition of his captured prizes. He surely praised the courage and resolve of his makeshift crews and made note of those he would recommend be decorated for exceptional bravery.

Charles Black was one of them. He had been wounded in the battle but survived. He then drifted from history until nearly three decades later, when he became a victim of the Lombard Street riots. He was a decorated hero of the War of 1812 but denied a pension by his ungrateful country. For all he suffered before and after the war, he would have known what it was to be a man equal to the dangers and hardships of war, and equal in all things — courage, ability, honor, and dignity — to the men with whom he braved them.

James Lawrence was promoted to captain when he returned from South America in triumph. He had hoped to be given command of the *Constitution* in reward for his victory and was disappointed to learn he would command that unlucky frigate, the USS *Chesapeake,* instead. In May 1813 he was stuck in Boston Harbor with a green crew and a ship he didn't want, anxious to put to sea again and fight the enemy. Commodore Philip Broke, the captain of the British frigate HMS *Shannon,* part of the squadron then blockading Boston, was anxious to fight too. He wanted a one-on-one battle with an American frigate and sent an American prisoner to Lawrence bearing an insulting letter challenging him to a fight. Lawrence never received it. But that hardly mattered. The *Chesapeake* put to sea on September 1 with orders to sail to the Gulf of St. Lawrence to interdict British supply ships. As she got underway, Lawrence could see the *Shannon* tacking back and forth on her own in front of the harbor, spoiling for a fight. Lawrence accepted the challenge.

Fifteen minutes after the battle began the *Chesapeake* was disabled and captured and taken away to Halifax. The *Shannon* was the smaller ship, but her crew was more experienced and her gunnery superior. Lawrence had suffered a mortal wound from small arms fire in the battle's first moments. Taken below deck, he told his officers, "Don't give up the ship. Fight her till she sinks." He died three days later.

Just two months before Lawrence met his end, the USS *Hornet* sailed into New York Harbor with its full ship's company and the HMS *Leopard*'s captured officers on board. Before the men of the *Hornet* returned to war; before a regiment of African American troops distinguished themselves in the Battle of New Orleans, the last major battle of the war, earning the praise of Major General Andrew Jackson; before African Americans, who had fought for their country bravely, had returned to the society that degraded, ostracized, and enslaved them; before the navy discouraged their continued service; before they would come to their country's aid again in America's war in Mexico; before they fought in the war that would end slavery; before all the injustices and indignities afflicted on African Americans after the War of 1812; before Charles Black was dragged from his home and beaten nearly to death; before all that tragic history, for a brief moment on land the officers and crew of the USS *Hornet* were brothers-in-arms and the toast of New York City.

Lawrence and his officers were feted at a dinner in Washington Hall, given the "freedom of the city," and presented with a silver plate commemorating their victory. The *Hornet*'s petty officers, marines, and seamen were entertained in an adjoining ballroom. After the dinner the entire ship's company walked to a theater, where they had been invited to attend the performance of a popular play. Lawrence and his officers were seated in the theater's boxes, while the crew filled the entire pit. The audience stood to applaud the happy sailors, who "seemed to cheer everything" and "roused the house by their jollity and applause during the performance."

Probably few if any of the members of that audience had been to war or understood the bonds that are forged in war. They might have been somewhat taken aback by the boisterous camaraderie of the *Hornet*'s sailors. At least one eyewitness was astonished to see the sailors taking pleasure in each other's company. "The crew marched together into the pit," he observed, "and nearly one half of them were negroes."

Brevet Brigadier General Samuel Chamberlain, adventurer, painter, memoirist, and decorated veteran of two wars.

CHAPTER THREE:
ADVENTURE

Sam Chamberlain was a flawed hero of the Mexican-American War, whose tale inspired the novelist Cormac McCarthy.

Samuel Emory Chamberlain was a scoundrel in many people's opinion, including his own. He titled his rollicking, handwritten account of his experiences in the Mexican-American War and with the gang of cutthroats he said he rode with *My Confession: Recollections of a Rogue*. The self-deprecation is appropriate for an author who paints himself as a choirboy, a patriot, and a brave man but who was also a racist, a religious bigot, a braggart, a murderer, a serial seducer, and a deserter. He defended the honor of women whose virtue he gladly compromised. He protected from atrocities Mexican civilians he disparaged as "greasers." He clearly invented some of his adventures. Yet, allowing for creative exaggeration here and there, Chamberlain's descriptions of the horrors and thrills of war are convincing and compelling, as are the watercolors he painted that illustrate his manuscript. In the words of the military historian John Eisenhower, Chamberlain's *Confession* is "the most vivid recording of what a soldier would see and feel as he trudged down from San Antonio, Texas to Buena Vista, Mexico."

No scene in the book is more thrilling than Chamberlain's account of the harrowing urban combat of the Battle of Monterrey, Mexico. "Old Rough and Ready," General Zachary Taylor, had defeated the Mexican Army in the battles of Palo Alto and Resaca de la Palma in Texas. As word of his victories spread across the country, thousands of men from all parts of the United States responded to Taylor's call for volunteer regiments to join his army. Like Chamberlain, most were in their teens and early twenties. Many left home for the first time, some for a life immeasurably harsher, cruder, crazier than life at home. Many would have their first taste of liquor. Many would lose their virginity. Many would kill for the first time and watch their friends be killed. They joined the army anticipating thrills and triumphs, which they would find along with terror and hardships and brutality and boredom and disease and death. Disease would kill more of them than the enemy would, and often kill them more horribly. They would discover that war's thrills are indistinguishable from its terrors, and glory is usually a state of exhausted relief. But for some men, men such as Chamberlain, war, with all its horrors, is still the adventure of a lifetime.

General Taylor crossed the Rio Grande and entered the undefended city of Matamoros on May 18, 1846. His light, horsedrawn, or "flying," artillery had carried the day at Palo Alto and Resaca de la Palma. Transportation and supply problems kept him in Matamoros longer than planned, as did the time it took for new volunteers to muster into his army and for short-term enlistees to be transported home. He didn't begin to move west until late July and didn't reach Monterrey for another two months. Some of his army traveled by river on crowded steamers, and some made a long, dusty march in sweltering heat to the little town of Camargo on the mudflats of the lower Rio Grande, where Taylor established a supply base. There his soldiers, weakened by the heat and unsanitary conditions, became sick with malaria, yellow fever, and dysentery. As many as fifteen hundred of them would die from disease.

In the middle of August, Taylor organized over sixty-five hundred soldiers, roughly equal numbers of regulars and volunteers, into two columns and marched them to Monterrey, 120 miles to the south. He left seven thousand men behind, many of them too sick to fight. He left his heavy artillery behind too rather than haul it over the mountainous roads.

The Mexican Army of the North, under the command of General Pedro de Ampudia, had a combined strength of over six thousand regulars and three thousand militia. Monterrey was well situated on a vast flat plain, snug in a bend of the Rio Santa Catarina, with the towering Sierra Madre guarding its southern and western approaches. Ampudia had strengthened nature's defenses outside the city's walls. An unfinished cathedral with high, black stone walls, dubbed the Citadel, loomed over the northern road manned by several hundred Mexican defenders and artillery. An earthwork fort built on the site of an old tannery, La Tenería, guarded the northeastern corner of the city, with the river to its east and clear fields of fire to the north. Fort Diablo protected the eastern approach. On the western side two fortified hills, Independence and Federation, shadowed the road to Saltillo, Ampudia's resupply route. Taylor believed capturing the heights, with their forts and heavy cannon, was the key to the conquest of the city.

The American Army reached the northern approach to Monterrey on September 19. As Taylor surveyed the situation, cannons fired from the Citadel, and Mexican cavalry galloped onto the plain, hoping to entice the Americans to fight within range of the Citadel's guns. Instead the nonchalant Taylor moved his army to a campsite in a pecan grove on the banks of a creek, mistakenly named Walnut Springs, three miles northeast of the city. He ordered the city's defenses reconnoitered and made plans for an attack the following afternoon.

He would divide his force in two. Brigadier General William Jenkins Worth would lead one division, with another mounted division in support, in a sweeping hook to the west to attack Federation Hill, then the fortifications on Independence, and cut off the road to Saltillo. Taylor would lead the rest of his army in a diversionary attack on the city's east side.

Worth's division, twenty-seven hundred strong, marched out of Walnut Springs at two o'clock on the afternoon of September

20, hoping to hide his movement behind high ground. But enemy soldiers on the higher of the two hills, Independence, soon spotted the advance, and Ampudia ordered the hills reinforced. Worth's column made camp at six o'clock that night and resumed their march at dawn. A force of two hundred Mexican cavalry attacked the column as it approached the Saltillo Road around six in the morning. They were quickly rebuffed by a regiment of mounted riflemen from west Texas, known as Texas Rangers.

The Americans reached the foot of Federation Hill early that afternoon, and about eight hundred men, led again by Texas Rangers, made the steep ascent under fire. Five hundred Mexicans gave battle but were quickly routed and retreated in poor order to a fort on the eastern side of the hill. By day's end the defenders had abandoned Federation altogether for the higher elevation and stronger fortifications of Independence, leaving their artillery behind.

Events had not gone as well for General Taylor. He had launched his diversionary attack as soon as he heard Worth's guns open fire that morning, ordering two regiments to approach La Tenería and Diablo, which he expected would discourage Ampudia from reinforcing his defenders on the western hills. It didn't work. When Taylor realized the Mexicans weren't reacting to his ruse, he decided to make a genuine assault on the city's eastern defenses. To do so the two regiments commanded by Colonel John Garland had to cross five hundred yards of open ground, exposed to fire from the Mexican guns at the Citadel and La Tenería. As they rushed across the flat plain, concentrated fire from Tenería's guns and musket fire from the rooftops in the city devastated the column, inflicting heavy casualties and causing confusion and panic.

Things got even worse when, intending to take the tannery from the rear, the surviving attackers entered the city. Americans had no experience with urban combat, and the warren of narrow, twisting streets hid dangers behind every wall and on every rooftop. The Americans marched in tight column formation, crowded between rows of adjoining stone houses that obstructed their sightlines. They were easy targets for the Mexican rifles that opened up from above and in cross fires from windows. When they reached intersections, hidden artillery batteries tore into them. When Taylor reinforced them and sent a battery of flying artillery to their aid, it proved little use against the protected batteries and heavy stone walls that shielded the enemy.

By dusk, with his troops terrorized, bloodied, and exhausted, and some of his best officers among the many casualties, Taylor ordered a retreat. The Americans had managed to take Tenería in a frontal assault led by a Mississippi regiment commanded by Colonel Jefferson Davis, and they still held it after Taylor withdrew his battered force from the city to regroup.

The next morning Worth's division stormed Independence Hill and by late afternoon had captured the last and strongest fortification, a former bishop's palace known as the Obispado. The rout convinced General Ampudia to pull back his men from other defensive positions outside the city to reinforce defenders within the city. The final assault on Monterrey began just after dawn the following day, September 23. Worth's column attacked from the west, and Taylor's forces again entered the city from the east. They now had bitter experience with urban combat, and, as American soldiers can always be relied on to do, they had adapted their tactics. They wouldn't march again in tightly squeezed formations or rely on maneuvering their flying artillery down Monterrey's treacherous streets. They advanced from house to house, battering down adjoining walls to rout out defenders with rifle, bayonet, and bowie knife. It was slow, wearying, hand-to-hand fighting, and it worked. At midnight Ampudia signaled that he wished to negotiate his surrender. By the following afternoon the Battle for Monterrey was over.

It had been a bloody affair for both sides. Americans had suffered five hundred casualties, the Mexicans a little fewer than four hundred. Among the Americans who survived the fierce fight for Monterrey were men who would figure prominently in the history of America's Civil War, serving on both sides of the fratricide: Jefferson Davis, Ulysses S. Grant, Albert Sidney Johnston, George Meade, James Longstreet, Joseph Hooker, Braxton Bragg, and a dozen or more other distinguished commanders.

Although his would not become as prominent a name as these, Sam Chamberlain would also prove himself a brave and capable commander in the Civil War. Among his brother officers and enemies at Monterrey, he left the most vivid account of their bloody experience. In Chamberlain's telling, after taking Independence Hill and the Obispado, he and the Texas Rangers found ourselves in a hornet's nest; every house was a fort that belched forth a hurricane of ball; the flat roofs surmounted by breastworks of sand bags were covered with soldiers who could pour down a distructive fire in safety, the windows of iron barred "Rejas" [grilles] were each vomiting forth fire and death. On we went at a run, stung to madness at not being able to retaliate on our hidden foes, we gained a large square, the "Plaza de la Capella," when artillery opened on us with canester! The heavy stone wall of a churchyard was embrasured for their guns, while a scaffold was erected from which infantry were posted who kept up a constant fire. Our men were falling fast, and not a Mexican hit; they were all under cover, our fire was only waisted on their stone walls. I was close to Col. [Samuel H.] Walker when a column of Mexican Infantry came round the corner of the church and at double quick charged us with the bayonet. We were in a tight fix, not twenty rangers were in the square. Fortunately our arms were all loaded and we made every shot tell, but we were compelled to give ground.

Riveting stuff, despite the poor spelling,

and a very convincing account of the action, as are Chamberlain's paintings of the battle. That's quite an accomplishment, considering Chamberlain was about three hundred miles away when the battle occurred. He would fight in other battles in the war, most notably at Buena Vista, and there is evidence to corroborate many of his other war stories. But it's no small part of his roguish charm and the pleasure of his extraordinary book that the reader can never be certain which accounts are his own, which are based on the record of other people's experiences, and which he made up entirely.

His account of his adolescence is only slightly less brash, pugnacious, and immodest than his account of his wartime experiences, and shows him no less vain about his looks, physical prowess, and irresistibility to the opposite sex. Chamberlain was born in New Hampshire in 1829, and his family moved to Boston when he was seven. Raised a devout Baptist, he sang in the choir of the Bowdoin Square Baptist Church. At a local gymnasium he learned to fight and fence and acquired what he called a "muscular Christianity." He fell under the spell of the novels of Sir Walter Scott and "longed to emulate its heros." He confessed "without egotism" to being the favorite of the prettiest girls at his church, inciting both the jealousy of his male contemporaries and the dislike of his minister.

His devotion to a certain young lady, "a splendid Brunette, with magnificent black eyes and hair," required him to defend her against their choirmaster's criticism. When the choirmaster attempted to eject Chamberlain from the premises, young Sam gave him a thrashing that left the offender "prostrate, bleeding, almost annihilated." Not long afterward he was expelled from the church, denounced by his minister as "worse than the Devil." Then he fell in with a more worldly crowd associated with the National Theater. The National's scene painter, Bob Jones, probably taught Chamberlain to paint. He was even closer friends with Jones's attractive daughter, Fanny, and, in his telling, was the darling of all the ladies of the National. That was to be expected considering he was a "boy of a man's proportion, muscles like steel, not bad looking, and very modest."

Those attributes apparently came in handy when Chamberlain's father died. Lacking a place in polite Boston society — and much in the way of prospects — the penniless fifteen-year-old left home to seek his fortune in the West. His journey to an uncle's farm near Alton, Illinois, was the first of many wild adventures, each a tale of high drama, hardship, heroism, and romance. In this one the dangers and privations of winter travel by stagecoach and steamboat were relieved by occasional brawls and several amorous encounters, including an affair with a U.S. senator's daughter, the persistent attentions of an infatuated boardinghouse landlady, and a near escape from a houseful of malarial farmer's daughters.

He didn't get on well with his uncle and cousins. The uncle treated him unkindly and refused to pay him a debt owed to his father. His cousins resented the attention he received from the residents of a nearby girls' boarding school. According to Chamberlain, his eldest cousin, enraged with jealousy, started a fight. When Chamberlain knocked the boy down, his uncle attacked him with an ax. Seizing the weapon, Chamberlain nearly buried it in the old man's head before the screams of several witnesses from the boarding school brought him back to his senses. He left Alton the next day for St. Louis, and a few weeks later for New Orleans, where he "indulged all kinds of dissipation." He found work in Baton Rouge and remained there some months, until his affair with the young wife of an elderly Creole planter came to her vengeful husband's attention, and he caught a steamboat to St. Louis and from there back to Alton.

The war with Mexico had begun by then, and in June 1846 Chamberlain joined a local volunteer company of river town toughs, the Alton Guards. By his account he was the most capable and well-liked soldier in the company and would have been elected captain had not a self-professed killer of a local abolitionist promised to spend a hundred dollars on whiskey and taken the honor from him. In the months before the Alton Guards departed Illinois for Texas, Chamberlain helped put down a mutiny, came to the favorable attention of his commanding general, and tried manfully but ultimately unsuccessfully to resist the proffered intimacies of a pretty girl engaged to another soldier.

The company embarked for New Orleans and then on to San Antonio. By the time Chamberlain arrived in Texas, he had been attacked, robbed, and nearly killed by a fellow soldier, briefly resumed a love affair with an acquaintance in New Orleans, nearly died of malaria contracted while aboard ship in the Gulf of Mexico, and suffered terribly on the overland march to San

Antonio. Too ill for service, he was mustered out of the army and given money to return to Alton.

He remained in San Antonio instead, fell in with a very rough crowd, and hung out in a gambling den, where he watched a Texas Ranger, John Glanton, kill another Ranger with a bowie knife. After witnessing its deadly effectiveness, Chamberlain bought a bowie knife for his own use, and during a quarrel over money stabbed a friend with it. He was thrown in San Antonio's "Old Spanish Jail," where he spent several unpleasant days. He later wrote, "The wretches incarcerated with me, their horrid bestial orgies too revolting for belief, drove me in my weak state insane."

His friend recovered from his wound and gallantly declined to press charges, and Chamberlain was released from jail sick with fever and delirious. He recovered thanks to the care of a local doctor, whose kindness Chamberlain repaid by resisting the advances of his amorous sister.

After his convalescence he reenlisted, this time in a cavalry regiment of the regular army, the 1st Dragoons, part of General John Wool's army, stationed in San Antonio. They were still in San Antonio when Old Rough and Ready's army took Monterrey.

Two days after Monterrey fell, Wool, with orders to take to the city of Chihuahua in northwestern Mexico, marched his army south, and Sam Chamberlain finally went to war.

After he crossed the Rio Grande, Wool determined that Chihuahua, which would have entailed several hundred miles of desert marching to reach, was an impossible objective and proposed to Taylor that they join armies. Chamberlain claims he was one of six dragoons in a scouting party commanded by a Lieutenant Carlton that carried Wool's dispatch to Taylor. Here he reports his first taste of battle. It was a brief one, a surprise encounter with a "crowd of fierce Gurillars [guerrillas]." The lieutenant ordered a charge with sabers drawn. Chamberlain confesses his heart was "in my throat choking me," but he gave a good account of himself. "I parried a lance thrust," he recalls, "a black savage face was before me for an instant, my horse crushed another, and another under foot, then another, and I came out of the dust surprised to find myself alive and unhurt."

The entire party of dragoons was unscathed, though the same could not be said for the "Gurillars." Separating fact from fiction in Chamberlain's recollections can be a tricky business, though there's no evidence to suggest he fabricated this story or his role in the scouting party that made contact with Taylor's forces. The late historian William Goetzmann, who edited the definitive edition of *My Confession* and is the leading authority on our colorful hero, believes history corroborates more of Chamberlain's account than it disproves. That Chamberlain describes his "maiden charge" as a more frightening than thrilling experience recommends its honesty, but skepticism is always warranted when evaluating his war stories.

Wool's army had reached the city of Monclova, 120 miles northwest of Monterrey, when he sent his proposal to Taylor. The dispatch reached Taylor on November 8, 1846, just as Taylor decided to move his part of his army south to Saltillo. He welcomed the additional troops. He would need them.

President James K. Polk was angry with Taylor for offering the Mexicans terms at Monterrey that were more in the nature of a truce than a surrender. He also considered Taylor, correctly, a political rival. (The general would be elected Polk's successor in the next presidential election.) He offered a new command in Mexico to Major General

Winfield Scott, who would land an army at Veracruz on the central coast in March and move on Mexico City. Nearly two-thirds of Taylor's army would be transferred to Scott's command.

Taylor opposed not only the reduction of his army but the strategy of conquering all of Mexico. He believed the occupation of northern Mexico would eventually convince the Mexican government to agree to American peace terms and territorial demands. He divided his army to garrison various northern cities, including Saltillo, where he had sent General Worth's division. Wool proposed to occupy Parras, ninety miles west of Saltillo, and his army entered the city unopposed on December 8.

Chamberlain enjoyed his time in Parras. He found the climate and the beauty of the city's young women to his liking, and, as he frequently observes, they found the six-foot-two, handsome young man with the long, flowing blond hair irresistible. That's not to say, however, that his sex appeal was always sufficient to discourage local treachery. He writes of his romance with twin sisters in Parras, whom he believed were as smitten with him as he was with them. But he found them sharing a bed one morning with Antonio, a local "renegade" the Americans employed as a guide. The discovery resulted in a swordfight between the two rivals, while the twins encouraged Antonio to "stick the foreigner and come back to bed." "But I did not lose heart," Chamberlain reassures us, "and finally succeeded in giving my antagonist an ugly slash across one of his bare legs, causing him to drop his knife, when I gave him a point in a part, that made him howl with agony, and would cause him to lose the regards of the 'dos margaritas.' "

While Taylor established a chain of strongholds in the north, the self-styled Napoleon of the West, General Antonio López de Santa Anna, who had returned to Mexico from exile in Cuba in the summer of 1846 and seized power again, had begun assembling an army of twenty thousand in San Luis Potosí, three hundred miles to the south. When Taylor received word in December that Santa Anna's army was preparing to march north, he decided to concentrate his forces in Saltillo. Wool's division made the 130-mile march to Agua Nueva, twenty miles south of Saltillo, in three days, which in Chamberlain's estimation was "an achievement unparalleled in history." Taylor joined Wool in Agua Nueva in January, while Worth's division remained in Saltillo for the winter.

In late January Chamberlain and a small party of dragoons were escorting Wool to a meeting with Worth, when Wool ordered them to investigate the gunfire they had heard as they rode by a mountain ridge. They climbed to the top of the ridge and discovered "a greaser, shot and scalped, laying on the ground yet alive," feebly trying to fend off vultures. They could hear the shouts and cries of women and children emanating from a cave some distance away, and they ran toward it.

Inside they found a "den of horrors." A hundred or more notoriously undisciplined and brutal Arkansas volunteers, or "Rackansackers," as they were called, were "yelling like fiends" as they butchered men, women, and children. Chamberlain counted more than twenty dead and described the survivors "clinging to the knees of their murderers and shrieking for mercy." He and the other regulars took positions outside the cave and aimed their carbines at the entrance as their sergeant ordered the Rackansackers to surrender, which they did grudgingly. The dragoons marched the murderers down the mountain at gunpoint and then returned to the cave with the division's surgeons. Chamberlain reports that no one was ever punished for the atrocity.

Earlier that month a young lieutenant carrying orders from General Scott transferring most of Taylor's army to his command had been in an encounter with a Mexican patrol. His killers had confiscated Scott's missive and delivered it to Santa Anna, who was delighted to learn his enemy's intentions and that Taylor would soon be left with an army a quarter the size of his own and comprising mostly volunteers. Of course, knowing that Scott intended to land a large army at Veracruz and march on the Mexican capital, Santa Anna should have focused his attention there rather than on Saltillo. But the chance of an easy victory that would enhance his political stature proved irresistible to Mexico's Napoleon.

Scott had also ordered Taylor to withdraw from Saltillo and pull back to Monterrey the remains of his army of occupation. Taylor, angry about the loss of much of his command and confident that Santa Anna would attend the greater threat from Scott's army, disregarded the instruction. Advance units of Santa Anna's army left San Luis Potosí on January 28, 1847. By February 2 the entire force was headed north. It was a long, miserable march over mountains and desert. Santa Anna lost as many as five thousand of his twenty thousand soldiers to desertion, illness, and death. Despite their losses, however, the Mexicans still vastly outnumbered Taylor's army, which now mustered fewer than five thousand.

Santa Anna's lead division reached Encarnación, thirty miles south of Agua Nueva, on February 17, and a few days later the rest of his army assembled there. Reports from a deserter that Santa Anna's army was nearby reached Taylor, and at daylight on February 20 he sent out a reconnaissance party of four hundred cavalry, including the 1st Dragoons and a company of Texas Rangers. Chamberlain's squadron was the advance guard.

The squadron reached the crest of a hill and looked across a plain to a ranch house situated at the base of a mesa, where Chamberlain could see a few Mexicans milling about. He also saw an immense dust cloud rolling along the top of the mesa, which he attributed to the movement of a large army. The dragoons seized the ranch house and placed the Mexicans there under guard. Chamberlain was posted as a lookout on top of the ranch's tallest structure, where he kept a worried vigil on the progress of the dust cloud. The rest of the American column soon reached them. Their commander, Colonel Charles May, whom Chamberlain despised, climbed up to the lookout and dismissed the dust cloud as most likely raised by a cattle herd. Chamberlain argued it was more likely "caused by the march of troops." Colonel May ridiculed the assertion but nevertheless sent search parties to investigate.

It would turn out to be a detachment of Mexican cavalry. Santa Anna's army was still concentrated at Encarnación, though not for long. But that wasn't known when, just after May dismissed the possibility, Mexican horsemen became visible on the mesa and "the setting sun glittered on a long line of lance blades." In Chamberlain's telling, May lost his head, yelled and cursed and countermanded his own orders as they prepared to defend the ranch. At ten o'clock, after all but one of the scouting parties had returned, they decided to abandon the ranch and make a run for Agua Nueva, chased by a column of enemy cavalry. They reached camp at dawn, having ridden eighty miles in twenty-four hours and been fired on, fortunately to no effect, by their own picket lines. May reported to Taylor, and Chamberlain and his comrades retired to their tents for a few hours' sleep.

They were roused by bugle call at nine o'clock and fell in with the rest of the army as it marched out onto the plain in front of Agua Nueva. Major Benjamin McCulloch, who commanded a company of Texas Rangers and had led the scouting party that hadn't returned with the rest of the column, had just returned. He had slipped into Santa Anna's camp and now reported that the Mexican Army was no more than a day's march away. Taylor proposed to meet them on a broad, flat plain, ground that would play to the enemy's advantage and where the Mexicans could flank and envelop the outnumbered Americans. Fortunately Wool persuaded a reluctant Taylor to fall back twelve miles to a more defensible position in a mountain pass called La Angostura (the Narrows), the entrance to Hacienda Buena Vista, a vast cattle ranch. The narrow pass and very rough ground in front of it would offset some of the attackers' advantage. The army moved out at midday. Chamberlain's squadron brought up the rear of the column. An Arkansas cavalry regiment remained behind to transport the army's supplies.

Not long after they arrived at La Angostura, Chamberlain and his comrades were ordered back to Agua Nueva, where, he reports, they found the Rackansackers gathered around campfires, "some sleeping, others playing cards, none at work." The dragoons quickly loaded twenty wagons with supplies and sent them to the rear just as they came under fire from Mexican cavalry. The Arkansans panicked and fled. The dragoons, according to Chamberlain, kept their cool, torched the remaining depots, and retreated in good order.

Santa Anna arrived at Agua Nueva the next morning, February 22, found it evacuated, and pushed on to La Angostura. Taylor, who had spent the night in Saltillo, returned to the field at noon. He reminded his soldiers it was George Washington's birthday and told them to give a good account of themselves that day to honor the father of the nation. "The men cheerd," Chamberlain recalled, "hats were thrown up and all seemed 'eager for the fray.' Poor fellows, one fourth never left the ground alive."

At one o'clock the vanguard of the Mexican Army came into view. At three an enemy officer approached the American lines under a flag of truce. He presented Taylor with a letter from Santa Anna, courteously recommending an American surrender to avert a "catastrophe." Taylor declined the offer. According to Chamberlain, who claimed to have witnessed the exchange, Taylor told his chief of staff to "tell Santa Anna to go to hell," but the aide drafted a more diplomatic refusal.

Diplomatically expressed or not, it's unlikely Taylor's obduracy greatly disappointed Santa Anna, who enjoyed a three-to-one numerical advantage. It would take him the rest of the day, however, to arrange the disposition of his forces, who were exhausted from marching sixty miles in two days. Taylor, realizing that Santa Anna wasn't quite ready to fight, returned again to Saltillo for the night. Other than an inconclusive exchange of fire that afternoon, the Battle of Buena Vista, the bloodiest and most consequential battle of the war, wouldn't begin until the following morning.

Both armies spent a miserable night in freezing rain, but with dawn came pageantry, excitement, and dreams of glory, followed inevitably by terror, confusion, and death. "I doubt if the Sun of Austerlitz shone on a more brilliant spectacle than the one before us," Chamberlain writes, referring to the site of Napoleon's victory over the empires of Russia and Austria. The enemy was magnificently arrayed, with fine new uniforms, burnished brass, plumed helmets, six thousand cavalry horses stamping and snorting, glittering lances, and a procession of priests bestowing final blessings on kneeling soldiers. Then "smoke arose from a battery a mile and a half off, and a thirty-two pound solid shot plumped into the road near the pass and the conflict commenced."

Santa Anna's battle plan called for a simultaneous attack. One division advanced down the main road to Saltillo to attack the Americans defending the Narrows, the forty-foot-wide mountain pass. The main attack, however, occurred east of the Narrows on a flat plain fifty feet above the road called the Plateau, where Santa Anna's three best divisions advanced east to west on the thinly stretched American left. The attack on the Narrows was repulsed easily enough by Taylor's artillery, but the attack on the Plateau looked like it might become a rout.

The enemy had gained the Plateau under cover of a ravine, and the lead division, four thousand strong, smashed into the center of the American lines, defended by fewer than four hundred men of the 2nd Indiana Regiment. The regiment's commander, Colonel William Bowles, panicked and ordered retreat. His men broke and ran to the rear. A second Mexican division poured over the ravine, and the combined enemy force began pressing the regiments positioned to the right of the broken 2nd Indiana. At the base of a ridge on the far end of the American left, two dismounted cavalry regiments, Arkansas and Kentucky Volunteers, broke under fire from a Mexican battery as a brigade commanded by General Ampudia, the loser at Monterrey, swept down on them.

"The panic was contagious," Chamberlain remembered, "men left the ranks in all the regiments, and soon our rear was a confused mass of fugitives, making for Buena Vista and Saltillo."

Wool shortened his lines and deployed more artillery to the Plateau. Chamberlain and the rest of the 1st Dragoons ran down fleeing soldiers and drove them back to the line. The American left flank was on the brink of collapse, but when enemy infantry attempted to sweep around it, American flying artillery once again saved the day, as concentrated fire from several guns checked the Mexican advance.

Taylor, fearing an attack in Saltillo, had spent the night there and returned to the field around nine o'clock with Colonel May's 2nd Dragoons and Colonel Davis's 1st Mississippi Rifles. By then as many as a thousand Americans had abandoned the Plateau. He ordered Davis's regiment, reinforced by another Indiana regiment and the returning remnants of the 2nd Indiana, to fill the gap in the center of the line. May's dragoons and two Arkansas cavalry companies stopped the Mexican cavalry from flanking the American left. More American batteries were hauled up the Plateau; they poured canister into the Mexican lines and checked the fire of the San Patricio Battalion, the infamous enemy artillery battalion comprising mostly Irish-American deserters. The American line held and regained some ground.

The situation was still desperate, but Santa Anna, his exhausted divisions on the Plateau disorganized and seriously bloodied by American artillery, decided to surround the Americans by using his last division to take the mountain ridge above the Plateau. Taylor ordered the 1st Mississippi and the 3rd Indiana to intercept them. They surprised the Mexicans who reached the high ground and with effective, concentrated fire managed to halt the advance of the enemy infantry. With the support of an artillery battery commanded by Braxton Bragg, the Mississippians and Indianans formed a V and held their fire until a column of Mexican cavalry swept around the right of the stalled infantry advance and charged the American lines. They were brought down in a hail of rifle fire and grapeshot and finished off with bowie knives. Chamberlain, who generally disliked southerners and particularly southern slaveholders, greatly admired the courage and élan of Davis and his regiment. He provides an eyewitness account of the scene as the Mississippi Rifles, in their distinctive red shirts and white pants and with eighteen-inch bowie knives, did their worst:

Davis' men, profiting by the confusion caused by their terrible fire, threw down their rifles, and with frightful cries dashed on the astonished horsemen who seemed helpless now their charge had failed. Catching the horses by the bits they backed them onto their haunches and knifed the stupefied riders, who as soon as they could turned and fled with shouts of Diablo Camisa colorados! [Devil Red Shirts!]

A sudden, passing thunderstorm resulted in a brief, unplanned cease-fire, and a feigned truce parley gave Santa Anna time to withdraw his battered division from the ridge. Taylor, overconfident in the wake of Davis's triumph, decided to rally his forces on the Plateau for an attack. They were still greatly outnumbered, and their disadvantage was made unmistakably clear when thousands of Mexican reserves poured over the top of a ravine and turned the attackers on their heels. A general assault along the entire line by Mexican infantry and cavalry began pushing the Americans off the Plateau.

The reversal would likely have been decisive but for Taylor's artillery advantage. Several batteries, including Bragg's, pounded the attackers and turned the advance. In the middle of the fight Taylor rode up to Bragg and barked, "Double-shot your guns and give them hell," although newspaper accounts and Chamberlain reported a more composed Taylor coolly instructing, "Give them a little more grape, Captain Bragg."

Chamberlain had been in several close scrapes that day, including a charge into the center of a Mexican cavalry column that had reached the Buena Vista ranch house. "Our column . . . gave a wild hurrah and charged the foe by the flank," he recounts. "They went down under our steed's rush, man and horse." He had also joined a charge on the St. Patrick Battalion, which had barely avoided catastrophe when at the last moment an alert bugler sounded the call, and the dragoons swung to the right before they charged into a ten-foot-wide chasm. Chamberlain claims to have witnessed the deaths of several gallant American officers that day, including Henry Clay Jr., whose famous Whig father was the nation's leading opponent of the war.

When the day ended and the guns fell mostly silent, the toll on both armies was steep. Americans had lost somewhere between six hundred and seven hundred; more than a thousand had deserted. Santa Anna had more than two thousand dead, wounded, or captured. The carnage was everywhere visible: dead bodies were strewn across the landscape, some tangled together in heaps and others lying individually at a lonely remove from the comfort of friends. The cries of dying men and horses rent the air. Neither side had gained a distinct advantage. The Americans still held the field but were desperately short of ammunition and far from certain they could repulse another attack.

An exhausted and complaining Chamberlain was ordered on picket duty that night. "It was a cold night," he recalled, "with clouds scudding across the moon, which threw a weird light on the dismal scene. The ground was strewn with ghastly corpses, most of which had been stripted by our foes. A picket line of Mexican Lancers on white horses, was stationed not over two hundred yards in my front."

Santa Anna wasn't sure his army could survive another battle either, and rather than see his command reduced further, he declared victory and left the field in the dead of night. At daylight a relieved Taylor and his army watched the last of the Mexican column disappear into the desert. The war in the north was effectively over. No other major engagements occurred there for the duration of the war; all the action was in the south, as Winfield Scott marched from Veracruz to Mexico City and became the last of several American generals to defeat the Napoleon of the West.

Though the Battle of Buena Vista ended in a stalemate, given the odds against the Americans it was rightly celebrated in the United States as a triumph, especially for Old Rough and Ready (whose contributions to the victory Chamberlain wrongly belittles). Taylor was elected president the following year, after a campaign for which

"Give them a little more grape, Captain Bragg" became an unofficial slogan. Jeff Davis would also win a presidency based in large part on his courage and skill at Buena Vista, where he had been painfully though not seriously wounded in the foot. Mississippi's governor appointed him to the U.S. Senate the following January, and in 1853 President Franklin Pierce made him secretary of war. He was elected president of the Confederate States of America in 1861, having seldom missed an opportunity to remind his fellow Confederates of the famous V, where he had destroyed the elite of Santa Anna's cavalry.

The army of occupation remained in northern Mexico under Taylor's command. So did Sam Chamberlain. But after Buena Vista his *Confession* offers no other accounts of historically significant battles. It becomes instead a chronicle of riotous living, of drinking, fighting, seducing, near escapes, desertion, and murder, frequently punctuated by close scrapes with "Gurillars" and occasionally by pangs of regret. He recounts most of it in an almost lighthearted tone before his story takes a decidedly darker turn. It is an amusing, offensive, ribald, exciting, and shocking tale. Some of it is probably true.

He rescues the three Traveinia sisters the first time while on patrol, when he hears their screams and jumps his horse over a courtyard wall of their hacienda. There he finds two "rough looking volunteers" from the 2nd Mississippi Rifles about to rape the sisters and their mother and murder their elderly servant. Drawing his saber, he runs the brutes off. Naturally their hero wins the instant devotion of the mother, daughters, and gray-haired retainer. He becomes a frequent guest in their home, where he enjoys the tender affections of two of the sisters, Franceita and Delorosa. Their mother implores him to marry either daughter and leave the army to live a life of wealth, ease, and beauty, but he regretfully declines the tantalizing offer. "Honor and my strong proclivity for a military life," he explains, "made me remain firm in my loyalty to my flag."

He had also become the object of Private William Crane's attention. "A powerful fellow with a bull dog's temper," Crane was the squadron bully. Chamberlain admits having been whipped several times in brawls with Crane and subsequently giving him a wide berth. One morning both men were ordered by their lieutenant to cut fodder for the regiment's horses in a cornfield near

Casa Blanca, the Traveinia family home, using machetes fashioned from sabers. When they arrived at the field, Crane disappeared with the wagon driver and left Chamberlain to cut the corn. As he was about his work, Delorosa appeared on the scene, and the young lovers passed an hour exchanging "loving endearments." Suddenly Crane returned, drunk on mescal, and threatened to force himself on Delorosa. Chamberlain claimed he tried to humor Crane and dissuade him from making good on his threat, alas, to no avail.

"Muerto! Muerto!" Delorosa shouted as the two men fought to the death. It was a fierce contest, with a drunken Crane attacking blindly and Chamberlain trying to avoid his blows until both men were exhausted. Crane thrust his blade a final time at Chamberlain, who turned it aside and stabbed Crane in the chest. "He fell with a cry more like a wild beast than a human being," Chamberlain writes, "and for a moment tore up the earth in an impotent fury, then black blood gushed from his mouth and my foe was dead."

He covered Crane with fodder, cleaned himself up, and rode back to camp. Fearing the body would be discovered, he returned to Casa Blanca only to find that the Traveinias' elderly servant, Francisco, had witnessed the fight and already disposed of the corpse. Crane was marked down as a deserter, and the killing was never discovered. Delorosa "was now in love with me more than ever," Chamberlain records. "There is something in the Spanish blood that causes the fair sex to admire gallants who show courage and kill." Killing Crane changed him. "My temper became more violent," he confesses. "I drank deeply, and was ready to take up the gauntlet in the least provocation."

He fought yet another duel for the Traveinia sisters, this time with someone he considered a friend, his jealous company sergeant. The fight ended with a superficial but sufficiently bloody wound to the sergeant's right forearm, at which point Francisco lassoed the wounded man around the neck and pulled him to the ground. Ten days later the sergeant and a party of dragoons arrested Chamberlain at Casa Blanca for taking unauthorized leave. A fight ensued. A trooper knocked Chamberlain to the ground with a blow to the head from his rifle butt. Francisco suffered a mortal wound from the sergeant's saber.

The company captain ordered Chamberlain taken to the guardhouse in chains. According to Chamberlain, he would surely have been executed for mutiny but for the Traveinias, who assiduously pressed their charms and his innocence on General Wool. Instead he was assigned the dangerous duty of carrying dispatches from Saltillo to Taylor's headquarters in Monterrey, during which he barely escaped death at the hands of determined guerrillas in a chase scene that rivals any Hollywood invention.

Chamberlain remained in northern Mexico after the war's end. The Traveinias eventually disappeared from the scene, but the "long flowing hair" that "excited their admiration" apparently mesmerized a succession of señoritas. The affairs, recalled with suspicious detail considering the years that elapsed before he writes of them, involved women of high and low station, but all were in love, all were treated gallantly by their brave and handsome lover, and more than a few were the cause or victim of misadventure. His great love, the woman who might have kept him in Mexico, Carmaleita, is murdered by a bandit, El Tuerto, whom Chamberlain had wounded in a fight one night in his favorite bordello. Add to these romances numerous fandangos, brawls, life-and-death struggles, insubordination, injustices avenged, atrocities, and various other adventures, and they made for quite an exciting time for our hero after Buena Vista, even as the war, or at least its major battles, occurred elsewhere.

He was promoted to corporal and soon after court-martialed for refusing to carry out an officer's order to flog a man. When the officer threatened to have Chamberlain flogged, he threatened to shoot the officer if he tried. According to Chamberlain, he was found guilty, but the court, presumably out of respect for his previous service, rejected the recommended sentence of death and instead had him incarcerated fastened to a ball and chain. He was pardoned two weeks later but would spend time in the guard-house occasionally for bouts of insubordination.

Wool's army didn't receive word of the war's end until June 1848. Many of the men of the 1st Cavalry, including Chamberlain, believed they had enlisted only for the duration of the war and expected to be mustered out now that peace had been declared. Most of them, however, ended up being transferred to the command of Major Lawrence Graham, who was to lead an expedition from Mexico. More than a few dragoons were incensed, but not Chamberlain. He claims he was looking for a new adventure, and an expedition to California fit the bill. He soon changed his mind, however. Graham was a drunk and a cruel and incompetent commander. He took an intense dislike to Chamberlain and abused him constantly, even stringing him up by the thumbs and nearly killing him.

Chamberlain's *Confession* descends into a netherworld of wickedness and terror when he deserts the army after Graham's expedition arrives in Tucson. He joined a notorious gang of scalp hunters led by John Glanton, the former Texas Ranger whom Chamberlain had seen kill a man in a San Antonio saloon, and the mysterious and malevolent Judge Holden. The gang slaughtered its way through Sonora and Arizona before most of its members were massacred by Yuma Indians. Chamberlain was among the few survivors. So was Judge Holden, who, among other depravities, molested and murdered children. The *Confession* ends with Chamberlain wandering the Mojave Desert chased by the devil incarnate, Holden. It's the end of the line for the Boston choirboy who went to war looking for adventure and lost his soul.

We'll leave that part of Chamberlain's story unexplored. The story of the Glanton Gang requires a book of it own. In fact, it has one, *Blood Meridian* by Cormac McCarthy, who based the novel on Chamberlain's account of the gang's exploits, and the character of the kid on Chamberlain himself. It is probably fiction based on fiction. Most likely Chamberlain didn't ride with the Glanton Gang but had read about them and incorporated (and no doubt embellished) their legend into his good-boy-gone-bad moral tale. He was determined to be an entertaining writer, even if he could not be a reliably honest one. " 'My Confession' is a form of history," Goetzmann writes, "an historical narrative that is so detailed and so plausible as to create its own reality." For all its embellishments and inventions, Chamberlain's "history" manages to convey a paradox of war: that it is an adventure unlike any other, an adventure that thrills and torments in equal measure.

We do know that for a time after the war Chamberlain prospected for gold in California. He later traveled across the Pacific and returned to Boston in 1854 at the age of twenty-three, engaged to Mary Keith, a Canadian he had met on his travels. They wed the following year and had three daughters, to whom he gave the misspelled names of three of his Mexican mistresses: Carmeleita, Dolorios, and Franceita. He worked at several undistinguished occupations until the outbreak of the Civil War, when he enlisted in the 1st Massachusetts Cavalry.

He was a good officer, brave and competent. He fought in dozens of battles, including Gettysburg. He was wounded several times, once quite severely. He was taken prisoner and exchanged. He was decorated for bravery, promoted to lieutenant colonel, colonel, and eventually brigadier general, and given command of the regiment. The aristocratic Charles Francis Adams Jr., grandson and great-grandson of presidents, called the lowborn, colorful Sam Chamberlain "the best officer the regiment ever had."

After the war he briefly commanded the 5th Massachusetts Volunteer Cavalry, an all-black regiment. He took them out west to Texas and the Rio Grande, where our hero had first taken up arms for his country and embarked on a tale worthy of Walter Scott's pen that he had imagined for himself.

In civilian life he was appointed warden of two Massachusetts prisons and a Connecticut prison, where he gained a reputation for brutality. He lived in Barre, Massachusetts, after he retired, collected Bibles and antique weapons, and was considered a devoted family man. He died in Worcester, Massachusetts, in 1907.

It took him most of the remainder of his life to handwrite and illustrate *My Confession,* producing four copies, one for himself and one for each of his daughters. He must have hoped it would bring him the renown he had risked and sacrificed much to earn. Alas, he would never be as famous or as admired as his cousin, Joshua Chamberlain, hero of Little Round Top, governor of Maine, and chancellor of Bowdoin College. But no veteran of any American war has ever left a record of his exploits quite like Sam Chamberlain's memoir.

He can claim another singular distinction as well: he is reported to have been the model for the Civil War monument on Cambridge Common.

Above a bronze sculpture of Abraham Lincoln by Augustus Saint-Gaudens, a young, good-looking rifleman with a handsome mustache stands erect, arms crossed, rifle in hand. He appears to be watching the horizon for his country's enemies or for whatever adventure the war would bring next. It might be just imagination, but there seems to be something about the pose and the soldier's features that suggest an attitude of resignation to his fate. Whatever approaches, pleasure or pain, life or death, our hero will play his role in the drama.

First Lieutenant Oliver Wendell Holmes Jr., 20th Massachusetts Volunteers, shortly before he left Boston for war.

CHAPTER FOUR:
TOUCHED WITH FIRE

Oliver Wendell Holmes Jr., an aristocratic idealist, was disillusioned and ennobled by the Civil War.

In September 1861 a young lieutenant in the 20th Massachusetts Volunteer Infantry scribbled a brief, cheerful note to his mother describing his journey. During an overnight stay in New York, en route from Boston to Washington, he had "dined with some of the fellows at Delmonico's" and eaten "breakfast next morning in Philadelphia." Although he complained that the regiment's progress had been slow and rest and nourishment were not as plentiful as he would have liked, he confessed he had "rather enjoyed" himself nevertheless. He laments the damage done to his trunk when a wagon wheel rolled over it, and the loss of a brandy flask. He is confident that having reached their destination, the officers of the

20th Massachusetts had "seen the worst in the way of hardships unless on special occasions."

By "special occasions" our correspondent presumably meant battles. Oliver Wendell Holmes Jr. would see plenty of those. The 20th Massachusetts was known as the "Harvard Regiment" in recognition of the number of Harvard men who served in it. By the time Holmes fought his last battle, his letters home were as altered in attitude and content as the man himself. The young idealist who, out of noblesse oblige, had volunteered as soon as shots on Fort Sumter were fired was changed by war, changed forever.

His father was famous. His family, particularly his mother's side, was an old and prominent one, if not the locus of eminence and wealth some have suggested. The poet Anne Bradstreet was an ancestor. Forebears had fought in the French and Indian and Revolutionary wars. The family lived comfortably, though not luxuriously, on Beacon Hill. Their friends were distinguished. Holmes Sr. was a physician and Harvard professor of anatomy, who became one of the most popular poets, essayists, and lecturers of his day. His collections of essays, *The Autocrat of the Breakfast Table* and

The Professor at the Breakfast Table, gained him an international reputation. His friends included Emerson (whom the Holmes children called "Uncle Waldo"), Longfellow, Hawthorne, and other leading transcendentalists. He cofounded the literary magazine *Atlantic Monthly.* He invented or at least popularized the term *Boston Brahmin* to describe that city's elite. He was garrulous and charming and accustomed to being the center of attention. Holmes Jr., Wendell to his family, lived much of his accomplished life as the less distinguished Holmes. Like many sons of famous fathers, he was both awed by his father and craved his own prominence, beyond the shadow of his father's reputation.

Wendell was a high-spirited and cheerful boy, when "the Boston of my youth was still half-Puritan," he recalled. Holmes Sr., although modern and liberal in outlook, still expected his son to conform to the manners and conventions of his half-Puritan society. Young Wendell read avidly, relying on Walter Scott's and others' tales of chivalry to inspire his imagination. He was spared much of the physical brutality commonly used to educate young children in those days, which his father had suffered at his age. His first school was a school for girls.

He was as talkative as his father, and as insistent, and the rivalry between father and son was conducted most often in conversation. Holmes's love and respect for his son is implicit in the enjoyment he took from engaging with him on equal terms. But he would tease him often, usually about one or another physical shortcoming, which seems to have at times stirred Wendell's resentment. Friends recalled a frequently noticeable tension between father and son and the son's reluctance to express openly his admiration for his father. Yet he began an autobiographical sketch for his Harvard senior yearbook with just a line identifying his date and place of birth before he summarized his father's life and detailed his genealogy. Near the end of the sketch he proclaimed, "The tendencies of the family and myself have a strong natural bent for literature."

His relationship with his mother, Amelia Lee Jackson Holmes, appears to have been warmer and uncomplicated. He was her acknowledged favorite; she doted on him and was a steady moral influence on the idealistic young man. Holmes Sr. was not an abolitionist, but his wife was. She enlisted Wendell in the cause and encouraged his admiration for Boston's leading radicals.

She communicated her expectation that the issue would be settled by war, and any man who paid attention to his conscience, including her son, would embrace his duty.

Harvard College in 1857, when Holmes enrolled there, was a small school run by Unitarian ministers. It enjoyed a national reputation, but there were fewer than a hundred students in Holmes's class. Most were from New England, but a number hailed from other regions, including southern states. Norwood Penrose Hallowell, a Philadelphia native, a Quaker, and a militant abolitionist (his family's summer home was a stop on the Underground Railroad), was Holmes's closest friend at Harvard. A widely admired member of his class, Hallowell was elected president of the Hasty Pudding Club, which Holmes served as secretary. Outspoken and assured in his convictions, he had enormous influence on Holmes, who was nearly two years his junior. For the rest of his life Holmes would consider "Pen" the most gallant man he had ever met.

As an underclassman, Holmes was socially successful, academically undistinguished, and occasionally unruly. He joined his father's dining club, the exclusive Porcellian, as well as the Hasty Pudding. He edited *Harvard Magazine* and was elected class poet. Few of his classes excited his interest, however, and while his grades were acceptable they were beneath his abilities. He improved his class standing by his junior year and wrote an essay on Plato his senior year that won a prize. But his conduct was wanting often enough that he stood fifty-fourth in his class by the time he graduated. In his final year he did manage to find a cause that excited not only his interest but his passion and chivalry: abolitionism. But in this instance it wasn't so much his mother's opinion that inspired him as it was the example of Pen Hallowell, who had become Holmes's beau ideal and who, Quaker or not, was ready in the spring of 1861 to kill for his ideals.

Their southern classmates did not return from winter holidays that year, and as one southern state after another announced its secession from the Union, Hallowell and Holmes left Harvard in April, before their final examinations. They joined the 4th Battalion of Massachusetts Volunteers, expecting to march south soon afterward as part of the commonwealth's contribution to the new Union Army. Instead they donned exotic Zouave uniforms, drilled regularly, and guarded Boston Harbor.

His mother approved of his decision. His father did not, but neither did he strenuously object. After it became clear the 4th Battalion wouldn't be leaving Boston, Holmes Sr. persuaded Harvard authorities to let Wendell, Hallowell, and others take their final exams and graduate. He also seems to have intervened with the governor to help Wendell secure a commission in a volunteer regiment that would join the Army of the Potomac. Holmes Sr. would later write, no doubt with his skinny, bookish son in mind (who as a child had often been teased by his father about his unimpressive physique), "Even our poor 'Brahmins' — pallid, undervitalized, shy, sensitive creatures, whose only birthright is an aptitude for learning . . . count as full men, if their courage is big enough for the uniform that hangs so loosely about their slender figures."

Young Holmes had no training and little native ability or physical prowess for the profession of arms. His intelligence would scorn the many absurdities of military life, the inadequacies of some commanders, and the long stretches of boring inactivity that are an inevitable part of war. But he would show courage too and self-sacrifice and the ability to command other men in extreme circumstances as death breathed down their necks.

Before he left Boston for Washington and the war, his father handed him a full bottle of laudanum and advised him to drink it all should he be mortally wounded to spare himself a lingering, painful death.

The 20th Massachusetts was organized in the summer of 1861 not by a Harvard graduate but by a West Pointer, Colonel William Raymond Lee, who had received an honorary degree from Harvard in 1851. His second-in-command, Lieutenant Colonel Francis Winthrop Palfrey, had a Harvard pedigree, Class of 1851. Other Harvard men and scions of venerable Massachusetts families received commissions in the 20th. Henry Livermore "Little" Abbott, whose snobbery made him implacably hostile to the cause of abolition, proved to be an exceptionally able officer, whose composure in battle became legendary. He would be promoted to major, serve briefly as second-in-command of the 20th, and die in the Battle of the Wilderness. Charles Cabot, F Company's captain, was killed at Fredericksburg. William Lowell Putnam died at Ball's Bluff. His cousin, James Jackson Lowell, was wounded in the same battle and killed in action the next year, at Frazier's farm. Edward Hutchinson Revere, grandson of Paul Revere and a surgeon in the 20th, was shot and killed at Antietam. His brother, Paul Joseph Revere, would eventually serve as the regiment's colonel and fall at Gettysburg. Their fates gave authority to the regiment's eventual sobriquet, "the Bloody 20th."

Most of the regiment's enlisted and noncommissioned officers were working-class German and Irish (two entire companies, officers and enlisted, were German speakers), but some Harvard men were found in the ranks as well. William Francis Bartlett, a handsome and popular member of the Class of 1862, had been sympathetic to the South's cause. Yet when the war came, he enlisted in the 4th Battalion as a private. Like Holmes and other Harvard contemporaries in the 4th, when it became clear the battalion would remain in Boston, Bartlett sought a commission in the 20th. He became one of the regiment's most admired officers. He lost his left leg in the Peninsular Campaign and returned to his studies at Harvard. After graduation he accepted command of a new regiment, the 49th Massachusetts Infantry, and went into battle mounted, on account of his missing leg, which made him an obvious target for

Confederate marksmen. He was wounded in the wrist and right ankle at the siege of Port Hudson in Louisiana and was shot in the head while commanding the 57th Massachusetts in the Battle of the Wilderness. When he recovered, he was given command of a brigade consisting of several Massachusetts regiments. While fighting in the deathtrap known as the Battle of the Crater at Petersburg, Virginia, his wooden leg was shot away and he was taken prisoner. He became gravely ill and nearly died while a prisoner, and although he was exchanged two months later, he didn't recover for many months. Bartlett survived the war, "a wreck of wounds," according to the historian Richard Miller, and his ruined health finally claimed his life in 1876.

Holmes was commissioned a first lieutenant in Company A in August 1861. His classmate, Charles Whittier, served as the company's second lieutenant. Hallowell had received his commission a month earlier, as first lieutenant in Company H. The regiment was encamped at Camp Massasoit, on a plain in Readville, a few miles outside Boston, where Colonel Lee, a distant cousin of Robert E. Lee, undertook, mostly successfully, to impose good order and discipline on a disparate, disorderly group of recruits — German and Irish immigrants, seamen from Nantucket, roughnecks from Boston's waterfront — who had pre–Civil War notions about the obedience they owed the inexperienced, young blue bloods who ordered them about.

Those blue bloods were advised by more experienced officers to disabuse themselves quickly of the conceit that the regiment was the property of their class. They would discover the wisdom of that advice on the battlefield. Decades later Holmes would tell a friend that one of the many lessons the war had taught him was "to know however fine a fellow I thought myself . . . there were situations . . . in which I was inferior to men I might have looked down upon had not experience taught me to look up."

The 20th was one of the last Massachusetts regiments to leave for the front. While they waited their turn, the Harvard men still dined well, enjoyed each other's company, kept a lively social calendar when off duty, and managed to learn the rudiments of their new profession. Holmes, aping British military custom, grew an enormous mustache, which he kept for the rest of his life. Most of the officers had personal servants, and he and Whittier shared a servant. The regiment finally received orders to join the

Army of the Potomac and on September 4 boarded cars on the Boston & Providence Railroad for Washington and war. The regiment's twenty-five-wagon baggage train carried, among other necessities, officers' bathtubs, bedsteads, and mattresses.

The 20th arrived in Washington on September 7, 1861, and after Colonel Lee had reported to General George B. McClellan, Commander of the Army of the Potomac, marched to Camp Kalorama in Georgetown, where a large part of the army was bivouacked. On September 12, abuzz with rumors that they were soon to go into action, the officers and men of the 20th began a three-day march to their new camp near Poolesville, Maryland, about thirty-five miles from Washington. Camp Benton was on high ground a mile east of a bend in the Potomac River. The 20th and 19th Massachusetts had joined to form a brigade under the command of Brigadier General Frederick Lander in a division under the command of General Charles Stone, headquartered at Poolesville.

The Army of the Potomac had suffered a disaster at Bull Run in July, and it was now seized with speculation that a large force of Confederates was planning to cross the river and attack Washington. McClellan had ordered General Stone's Corps of Observation at Poolesville to monitor Confederate activity on the other side of the river and oppose an enemy crossing, but to exercise great caution before taking offensive action. Three days after the 20th arrived at Camp Benton, General Lander ordered companies A and I, the latter commanded by William Bartlett, to stand a post upriver from a ford in the Potomac called Edwards Ferry and prepare for an enemy attack. The men arrived at night. When the sun came up they could see Confederates across the river. Holmes would write his mother another short letter describing his eventful week: "It seems so queer to see an encampment & twig through a glass & think they are our enemies & hear some of our pickets talking across & so on." He signed off, "Goodnight my loveliest and sweetest." His next letter to her would be less cheerful.

Companies A and I remained at their post for five days. After they were relieved and returned to Camp Benton, they waited a little less than a month before they finally saw their first action. It was hardly the kind of battle they expected.

Neither General McClellan nor Confederate General Joseph E. Johnston, Commander of the Army of Northern Virginia, was interested in launching an offensive that autumn. McClellan was ever cautious, habitually overestimated enemy numbers, and was still preoccupied with reorganizing the army. Johnston believed correctly that his army was outnumbered. On October 18 he consolidated his forces in Centerville, leaving one brigade and some cavalry in Leesburg, Virginia.

An important railroad terminus near several critical river crossings, Leesburg lay just across the Potomac from Poolesville. Although McClellan had initially instructed Stone to exercise great caution when considering an attack across the river, he now believed that with only a single enemy brigade in Leesburg, the town was too far from the main body of the Confederate Army and too close to the Army of the Potomac to remain in rebel hands. He thought the Confederates would quickly vacate it if pressed, and he ordered Stone to make "a slight demonstration" of his division's presence.

On the afternoon of October 20 most of the division took up positions at three river crossings: Edwards Ferry, Conrads Ferry, and Harrison Island. Stone ordered artillery to begin shelling Confederate pickets across from Edwards Ferry. The rebels withdrew, and three boats carrying about a hundred soldiers of the 1st Minnesota rowed to the Virginia bank. They met with no resistance and returned later that night to the Maryland side.

That could have sufficed for the small demonstration McClellan had ordered, but Stone ordered another small reconnaissance party, about twenty men from the 15th Massachusetts, to cross the Potomac at Harrison Island, four miles north of Edwards Ferry. They landed at the foot of Ball's Bluff, a steep, rocky, wooded height with a narrow switchback path. There were no enemy pickets there. No Confederate thought it likely the Federals would attack at a place where the river was too deep to ford and they would have to scale a hundred-foot bluff.

The scouting party reached the top of Ball's Bluff and took cover in the woods that surrounded a grassy field. Through the foggy moonlight the soldiers saw what they believed to be Confederate tents about a mile beyond their position. They returned to Harrison Island and reported their observations to their regimental commander, Colonel Charles Devens, who dispatched the information to General Stone. Stone ordered four companies from the 15th, around three hundred men, to attack the enemy encampment the next morning and either return to Harrison Island or hold ground in Virginia until reinforced. The 20th Massachusetts was to act in reserve on Harrison Island, while the remaining companies of the 15th Massachusetts and the 1st California were positioned on the Maryland bank across from the island.

In the predawn hours of October 21, with Colonel Devens in command, the raiding party crossed the hundred yards of swift-running river between the island and Ball's Bluff in three small boats, carrying about thirty men at a time, which took several hours. Once across they made the steep ascent unopposed. But when they came out of the woods onto the grassy field, they saw that the thirty or so Confederate tents the scouting party had reported were just trees in an apple orchard. Devens sent a dispatch to Stone asking for new orders, deployed his men in the tree line on the southern end of the field, and sent a scouting party toward Leesburg. A hundred men of the 20th had also crossed the river, with Colonel Lee in command, and were moving up the bluff.

After reading Devens's dispatch, Stone

instructed Colonel Edward D. Baker, commander of the 1st California, a sitting U.S. senator, and close friend of President Lincoln, to assume command of the force at Ball's Bluff. As he rode north, Baker encountered a Union lieutenant on his way to report that soldiers had stumbled upon pickets from the 17th Mississippi, a skirmish had ensued, and the small force of Federals in Virginia were now believed to be in trouble. The gunfire had alerted Confederate Brigadier General Nathan G. "Shanks" Evans in Leesburg that the enemy was on his side of the river. He sent a regiment and three troops of cavalry to meet them. Baker began ferrying the rest of the 15th and 20th and the Californians across the river as more skirmishing was heard on the bluff.

By three o'clock most of General Evans's brigade was on the scene, deployed along the west tree line and in the south and north woods. He ordered a general attack, planning to envelop the Federals. The 15th Massachusetts was deployed in a crowded front line along the northern tree line. Company H of the 20th, Pen Hallowell's company, anchored the right flank. It took the hardest hit in the early fighting; the company's commander was seriously wounded, and Hallowell assumed command. When the main action began the 20th was lying bunched tightly together near the edge of the bluff, their backs to the river. Company A, Holmes's company, formed the center of the line. Bartlett's Company I was on the right.

The Confederates had the advantage in numbers, position, and experience. The inexperience of the Federals quickly showed; their firing was random and often misdirected. The rebels' fire was concentrated, low, and deadly. The Union artillery hadn't any canister, only shells, which were nearly useless on such a small battlefield. But the Federals' courage was evident as well. The fire was so fierce it's a wonder such green troops, most of them never tried in battle, didn't break in the first bloody exchange. As the battle lengthened and casualties mounted, the Federals steadied somewhat, but their situation was hopeless. An hour and a half into the battle, Colonel Baker, who had shown immense courage, if not good sense, by constantly exposing himself to enemy fire, was shot in the head by a Confederate pistol at close range. When he struggled to his feet a volley of musket fire from the woods cut him down for good.

Around the time Baker fell, Colonel Lee ordered the reserve companies of the 20th to move forward. As soon as Holmes stood up a spent ball struck his stomach and knocked him down. Lee ordered him to the rear, but Holmes, realizing he was not seriously wounded, drew his sword and returned to the front. A second shot hit him in the chest. "I felt as if a horse had kicked me," he wrote. He was taken to the rear and laid down near the body of "poor Sergt Merchant . . . shot through the head and covered with blood."

Holmes started to spit up blood and remembered the bottle of laudanum his father had given him; he resolved to drink it when the pain became intolerable rather than suffer an agonizing death. He was carried down the bluff and ferried across the river with the other wounded to a field hospital on Harrison Island. The next morning he asked a surgeon if he would recover. "You may recover," came the reply. Holmes explained that he had bled "at the mouth" very freely through the night. "That means the chances are against me, doesn't it?" "Yes," the surgeon agreed, "the chances are against you."

The Federal lines contracted as their losses increased, making their encirclement more likely. A doomed if valiant attempt to cut their way through Confederate lines failed and demoralized the survivors. When the Confederates fixed bayonets and charged the weakened lines, some of the Union soldiers simply leaped off the edge of the bluff or tumbled down it onto the heads of soldiers making their way down the path in an orderly retreat. Those who reached the bank alive were pinned down by the rebels' fire while they waited for the wounded to be evacuated.

Most of the officers, many as inexperienced as their soldiers, kept their composure. None abandoned their men. Some, including Hallowell, bravely led skirmish lines to keep the Confederates at bay as the shattered Union forces tried to get back across the river. But their boats were too few and too small. Men tried to swim while rebels fired at them, and many drowned in the swift current. Others swarmed and overturned boats with the same result. Over five hundred Federals surrendered on the bank; over two hundred were killed and a roughly equal number wounded. The "butcher's bill" for the 20th, as Holmes called it, was forty killed and over forty wounded. Of the twenty-two officers of the 20th who fought at Ball's Bluff, thirteen were killed or seriously wounded. Colonel Lee and Major Paul Revere and his brother, the surgeon Edward Revere, were taken prisoner. It was the worst Union defeat since Bull Run, a poorly planned and ill-informed assault, broken up and routed by an enemy who knew his business better than they did — and the newspapers reported it that way. But on that bloody bank the officers and men of the 20th Massachusetts forged bonds of respect and trust that would see them through other, much worse battles in the years ahead.

Holmes seems to have drifted in and out of consciousness. He heard someone remark about the soldier lying next to him, "He was a beautiful boy," and he knew it must be his cousin and classmate, Willy Putnam. Putnam had been shot in the stomach and, knowing the wound was mortal, had refused the surgeon's assistance. He lingered a day in great pain.

Holmes stopped a surgeon from another regiment, gave him his address, and asked him, in the event of his death, to write his parents and tell them he had done his duty. "I was very anxious they know that," he recalled. When he confided that he intended to take a fatal dose of laudanum, the surgeon appears to have given him a nonlethal dose instead and confiscated the bottle. Holmes claimed his most vivid memory of the experience was fearing he was "en route for Hell" and debating with himself whether he should renounce his agnosticism. He decided at length that it would be cowardly to do other than "take a leap in the dark." Eventually he was ferried to the Maryland side of the river and taken by ambulance to the regimental hospital, where a "cockeyed Dutchman . . . bound me with an infernal bandage . . . having first rammed plugs of lint into the holes . . . and told me I should live."

Two days later he scrawled a letter to his mother: "Here I am flat on my back after our first engagement — wounded but pretty comfortable — I can't write an account now but I felt and acted very cool and did my duty I am sure."

By the end of the month the young combat veteran was at home in Boston recuperating from his wounds. He was visited and feted by the city's elite, enjoyed pleasant holidays, and reportedly held spellbound the young ladies for whom he recounted his brush with death at Ball's Bluff. As he grew stronger, the nights grew even longer for the hero of the hour. His social calendar was so crowded his physician wondered if he wouldn't be better off back with the regiment. He was well enough to rejoin the 20th just after New Year's, but recruiting duties kept him in Massachusetts until March.

Holmes returned to Poolesville late that month in time to join the Peninsular Campaign, McClellan's four-month failed attempt to slog his way from the tip of the Virginia peninsula through swampy low country to Richmond, the Confederate capital. It was a memorable failure for a number of reasons, not the least of which were the high cost in dead and wounded, McClellan's indecisiveness, and Johnston's wound at the Battle of Seven Pines (also known as the Battle of Fair Oaks), which resulted in the transfer of command of the Army of Northern Virginia to Robert E. Lee.

By the end of May 1862, after more than two months of excruciatingly slow progress, the Army of the Potomac was finally closing in on the rebel capital. McClellan had deployed his five corps north and south of the Chickahominy River just six miles from Richmond. Johnston, usually as cautious a commander as McClellan, decided to forestall a siege by attacking the two corps nearest his lines, south of the Chickahominy. Had it been better executed the attack might have resulted in the biggest northern disaster of the war to date. As it turned out, the battle, fought over two days, May 31 and June 1, was inconclusive. The Confederates suffered somewhat higher casualties and failed to destroy McClellan's two isolated corps, but the attack did stop the Union advance on Richmond.

It was also one of the bloodiest battles of the war to date, second only to Shiloh. The Federals lost more than five thousand killed and wounded; the rebels more than six thousand. The butcher's bill shook McClellan's confidence, but his curious combination of insecurity and vanity always made him as prone to doubts as he was to self-aggrandizement.

It seemed to also affect the temperament of Oliver Wendell Holmes Jr., the idealistic young veteran of Ball's Bluff and romantic hero of Boston salons. War was making him grimmer, wearier, and fatalistic. The 20th had fought well at Seven Pines, and Holmes had distinguished himself in his first battlefield command. He had recently been promoted to captain and given command of Company G. The company repulsed an attack at Seven Pines and drove the surviving enemy from the field. The day after the battle he sent his parents a brief account. In it he mentioned the "indifference one gets to look on the dead bodies in gray clothes wh. lie all around. . . . As you go through the woods you stumble constantly, and, if after dark, as last night on picket, perhaps tread on the swollen bodies already fly blown and decaying, of men shot in the head back and bowels." He closed the letter with the following request: "If I am killed you will find a Mem. [*sic*] on the back of a picture I carry wh. please attend to. I must sleep a few minutes I can hardly keep my eyelids raised."

General Lee spent several weeks after Seven Pines reorganizing the Army of Northern Virginia and planning a new offensive. The result was the Seven Days Battle, six battles over seven days, which drove the Union Army away from Richmond, effectively ending the campaign. Union casualties in the campaign approached twenty thousand. Included among the dead was James Jackson Lowell, Holmes's cousin.

Lincoln ordered the army's return to Washington in August. Confederate General Stonewall Jackson was marching north, threatening the Federal capital. The Army of Northern Virginia would inflict a second defeat on the Federals at Bull Run. Then Lee would launch his first invasion of the

North, and McClellan would have to chase him.

In the predawn hours of September 17, Holmes sent his parents a letter to let them know another battle was imminent:

> It's rank folly pulling a long mug every time one may fight or may be killed. Very probably we shall in a few days and if we do why I shall go into it not trying to shirk responsibility of my past life by a sort of death bed abjuration — I have lived on the track on which I expect to continue traveling if I get through — hoping always that though it may wind it will bring me up the hill once more with the deepest love.

He gave his address as "Beyond Boonsburg [Boonsboro]." The 20th was encamped for the night on a hill a few miles southwest of the little Maryland village and just east of a creek called Antietam. He noted that the regiment had "not been in any recent fight" but "may fight today," and assured his parents they would "lick 'em if we do." He would write them again the very next day.

The Battle of Antietam was really three battles fought in one long day along a five-mile front, beginning at a stand of oak called the North Woods and ending at

Burnside Bridge to the south. McClellan
had nearly twice the numbers Lee had at
Antietam, six infantry corps to Lee's two.
But as usual he feared he was at a disadvantage. The 20th Massachusetts was assigned
to Major General Edwin Sumner's II Corps,
as it had been during the Peninsular Campaign, and formed part of a brigade commanded by Brigadier General Napoleon J. T.
Dana. It was in reserve when the Battle of
Antietam began around 5:30 in the morning with an attack on Stonewall Jackson's
corps on the Confederate left flank by
General Joseph Hooker's I Corps, with
Brigadier General Joseph Mansfield's XII
Corps in support. Federals streamed out of
the North Woods into a cornfield and after
an intense artillery exchange met Confederate General John Hood's division. Confederates and Federals fought bayonet to
bayonet, hand to hand in hellish combat.
Possession of the Cornfield changed hands
over a dozen times.

A little after seven o'clock McClellan,
watching the battle from his headquarters a
mile away, concluded that Hooker and
Mansfield were in trouble. I Corps had been
repulsed and XII Corps looked as if it were
about to be overrun. Hooker had been
wounded, and Mansfield would be too,

mortally. McClellan ordered General Sumner to send two of his three divisions to woods west of the Cornfield. They moved in three columns, with General Dana's 3rd Brigade and 20th Massachusetts in the center, across Antietam and to the East Woods, where the columns formed into three battle lines crowded close together. Dana's brigade formed the second line, with the 20th on the left flank.

The 20th marched from the East Woods at the quick step, across a creek, through an open field in the teeth of rebel artillery fire, down a hill to the Hagerstown Pike, past the Dunker Church to the Cornfield. Wounded soldiers from I and XII Corps streamed past them, heading for the rear with a good number of able-bodied soldiers accompanying them. At the Cornfield they beheld the wreckage of the morning: dead and wounded littered the field, bodies intact and in pieces. The heaviest Confederate artillery fire of the morning commenced with canister and shell. Sumner had rashly pressed his lines so closely together — at some points only fifty feet or less separated them — that the barrage killed nearly as many in the second and third lines as in the first. At around nine o'clock the Federals reached the West Woods and charged through them.

The 20th halted near the western edge of the woods as the brigade battle lines tried to disentangle themselves. The front line climbed over a fence and into a field where several hundred rebel infantry and artillery batteries were waiting. The second and third lines could only watch the firestorm in their front even though they were being hit as well. They couldn't return fire without hitting the Massachusetts men in their front. Suddenly they began to take fire from their left and rear. Parts of five Confederate brigades had enveloped the Union lines unnoticed. Holmes was looking toward the action in the front when an Irish soldier standing next to him took a knee and started firing to the rear. Holmes called him a "damn fool" and struck him with the flat of his sword before realizing they were being shot at from behind.

Incessant fire poured down on the Federals from three sides. Survivors would remember the intensity of the fire and the immediate devastation it caused as the worst of the war. Some regiments broke instantly. Green regiments misdirected their fire on other Union soldiers. The 20th Massachusetts held its ground in the best order it could manage until Sumner ordered them to retreat. Colonel Palfrey, the regiment's second-in-command, was wounded, as was Lieutenant Colonel Revere, again. Pen Hallowell's left arm was shattered. Edward Revere, operating on a wounded soldier in the field, found himself suddenly at the front as the retreating Federals streamed past him; he was shot and killed. General Dana was wounded in the left leg as he tried to lead his brigade to safety and turned over his command to one of his regimental colonels. Most of the 20th emerged from the northern end of the West Woods in good order, regrouped, joined fresh reinforcements, and turned to face the pursuing Confederates. Federal artillery eventually managed to push the rebels back, and with that, the battle in the north at Antietam would end.

As soon as the order to retreat had been given, Holmes began to run with his company to the rear. A bullet struck him in the back of the neck, missed arteries and spine, exited the front of his throat, and knocked him unconscious. At some point he managed to get on his feet and walk several hundred yards to a log cabin known as the Nicodemus House, where Federal wounded had taken refuge. There he found his friend Hallowell and took a place beside him on the floor. Expecting he would die, he tore a piece of paper from his notebook and scribbled, "I am Captain O. W. Holmes 20th Mass. Son of Oliver Wendell Holmes, M.D. Boston." Then he waited for whatever would come.

Rebels came. Hallowell recounted in his memoir their arrival at the Nicodemus House as they advanced:

The first Confederate to make his appearance put his head through the window and said: "Yankee?" "Yes." "Would you like some water?" A wounded man always wants some water. He off with his canteen, threw it in the room, and then resumed his place in the skirmish line and his work of shooting retreating Yankees. In about fifteen minutes that good-hearted fellow came back to the window all out of breath, saying, "Hurry up there! Hand me my canteen! I'm on the double-quick myself now!" Someone twirled the canteen to him and away he went.

As the fighting moved elsewhere, a Union surgeon entered the house, briefly examined Holmes, told him the wound wasn't fatal, and made a splint for Hallowell's broken arm. Late in the afternoon both men were taken by ambulance to a Union hospital in the nearby town of Keedysville. Dana's brigade quartermaster, Captain William Le Duc, had taken charge of the wounded and called a surgeon over to attend to Holmes. But the busy physician refused, saying, "I've no time to waste on dead men." Le Duc asked what he could do for Holmes. The surgeon told him to clean off the blood, plug the hole with lint, and give him an opium pill. Le Duc did as instructed and managed to get Holmes out of the crowded hospital tent and into a private home.

Holmes wrote his parents on September 18, describing his wound and informing them the surgeon had "glanced hastily & said it wasn't fatal." But a telegram from Captain Le Duc reached Holmes Sr. before his son's letter did, and it left the question of his survival more ambiguous.

The butcher's bill at Antietam was staggering, the bloodiest single day of the war, with more than ten thousand Confederate casualties and over twelve thousand Federal. The fight was essentially a draw. But Lee could ill afford such heavy losses, and because his army withdrew from the field and from Maryland (unbothered by the ever cautious McClellan), the North could claim the victory. But it was costly and left many witnesses unable to find words to describe it. "No description I ever read begins to give one an idea of the slaughter," a young lieutenant in the 20th wrote. Few could survive such carnage and not be forever changed by the experience. Of the four hundred to five hundred men in the 20th Massachusetts who fought at Antietam, 150 had been killed or wounded or were missing.

"Capt. Holmes wounded shot through the neck," read the telegram from Le Duc to Holmes Sr., "thought not mortal at Keedysville." Knowing such a wound would likely cut arteries or spine and "ought to kill at once," Holmes Sr. feared that "not mortal" referred to his son and not the wound. He boarded a train that afternoon in the company of William Dwight, the father of another Bostonian wounded at Antietam, and set out "with a full and heavy heart" in search of his son. He would later write an account of his odyssey for the *Atlantic Monthly* entitled "My Hunt for the Captain."

He stopped in Philadelphia at the Hallowells' home, hoping Wendell would be there. He wasn't, but Pen Hallowell was, and Francis Palfrey, both recovering from their wounds, as was Pen's brother, Ned, who was sick with typhoid. A bed was waiting there for Wendell, but Pen had received no word from him since they had parted at Keedysville and didn't know where he was. A surgeon at Keedysville had managed to save Pen's wounded arm, at the cost of an inch or so in its length. He would recover and return to the war, but not to the 20th Massachusetts. He was promoted to lieutenant colonel and transferred to the first all-black regiment, the 54th Massachusetts, as second-in-command to another wounded Antietam veteran, Robert Gould Shaw. Ned would follow him.

Holmes Sr. and his party pressed on to Baltimore, where William Dwight received word his son had died and his body was en route to Baltimore. Holmes left for Frederick, Maryland, where he found Little Abbott in a hospital, prostrate with typhoid fever and grieving the death of his brother, who had been killed in action in August. He also encountered another young officer he knew, Henry Wilkins, who was preparing to escort Edward Revere's body home. Wilkins reported that he had heard Wendell's wound was not as serious as initially feared. But he added that he had more recently heard an unconfirmed rumor that Wendell had been killed.

With his heart made heavier by the worrying report, Holmes Sr. left by wagon for Middletown, Maryland. The road from Frederick "was filled with straggling and wounded soldiers," he wrote in the *Atlantic*.

> Through the streets of Frederick, through Crampton's Gap, over South Mountain, sweeping at last the hills and the woods that skirt the windings of the Antietam, the long battle had travelled, like one of those tornadoes which tear their path through our fields and villages. . . . It was a pitiable sight, truly pitiable, yet so vast, so far beyond the possibility of relief, that many single sorrows of small dimensions have wrought upon my feelings more than the sight of this great caravan of maimed pilgrims.

He searched for his son in hospitals, churches, and private homes in Middletown and Boonsboro to no avail. In Keedysville he found a doctor who directed him to the house where Le Duc had taken his son, only to learn from its owner that Wendell had left for Hagerstown by milk cart the day before. Holmes assumed Wendell would take the train from Hagerstown to Harrisburg and from there travel to Philadelphia and the Hallowells. So he decided to backtrack to Frederick and Baltimore, where he would catch the train for Philadelphia. On his way to Frederick he stopped at the battlefield, where the dead were still being buried. He stood in the infamous Cornfield, so fiercely contested in the battle's first fight. "The opposing tides of battle must have blended their waves at this point," he would write, "for portions of gray uniform were mingled with the 'garments rolled in blood' torn from our own dead and wounded soldiers."

In Hagerstown on September 20 a widow, Mrs. Howard Kennedy, watched wounded Union soldiers trudge by her gate and noticed Wendell with a "bandage around his neck . . . and walking very languidly." She asked if there was anything she could do for him. He thanked her and complained he was "suffering greatly." She invited him to remain in her home until he was strong enough to travel. She proved to be an excellent nurse, and her charge improved quickly. He was "a delightful guest," one of her children remembered, who flirted a little too boldly with a visiting cousin, "a very brilliant young woman" from Philadelphia.

Holmes Sr. reached Philadelphia on the 23rd and rushed to the Hallowells hoping to reunite with his son. But Wendell wasn't there. He had sent a letter to Boston from Hagerstown the day before explaining his circumstances and improved health: "Tho I am unheard from I am not yet dead." It wouldn't arrive for many days. No word had been received from him in Philadelphia, and Holmes Sr. worried Wendell's wounds had become infected or some other misfortune had befallen him. He set out the next day for Harrisburg, where he encountered a wounded officer from a Pennsylvania regiment who told him a group of Massachusetts men had passed through town that afternoon on the way to Philadelphia and one of them was a young captain with the name Holmes. The elder Holmes rejoiced and telegraphed the Hallowells, only to learn in reply that they had not seen or heard anything from Wendell.

Holmes Sr. remained in Harrisburg the next day. He received word from Philadelphia that Wendell was last seen in the care of a Hagerstown family, the Kennedys. He sent two telegrams to Mrs. Kennedy, and at last, late in the evening of the 25th, received a reply: "Captain H. still here leaves seven tomorrow for Harrisburg, Penna. Is doing well."

The following afternoon the father waited impatiently for the late-arriving train from

213

Hagerstown. When it finally pulled into the station, the anxious man composed himself to "walk calmly through the cars."

In the first car, on the fourth seat to the right, I saw my Captain; there saw I him, even my first-born, whom I had sought through many cities.
"How are you, Boy?"
"How are you, Dad?"

Decades later another account of the reunion surfaced in which Wendell replies, "Boy, nothing." It is considered a less reliable version than his father's, but it makes little difference really. Oliver Wendell Holmes Jr. wasn't a boy any longer. And he wasn't the man he might have been had he not gone to war. There was less of the romantic in him and less of the idealist. Hard use left him clearer-eyed and, at times, a grimmer, more cynical, and less trusting soul. As men fresh from combat often do, he could restrain expressions of positive emotions but could less easily suppress discouragement and resentment. The night before father and son left Philadelphia for Boston, they were having a drink with a friend of Holmes Sr. when "Wendell spoke with bitterness and gallows humor about the senseless battles and the mismanagement of the army."

When they reached Boston the following day, a letter was waiting for Wendell, which he kept among his papers for the rest of his life.

sir Captain Holmes i take the opportunity of writing these few lines to you hoping that this will find you recovering from your wound fast. . . .
Hayes in behalf of the Company.
Captain we would like to hear from you.

Wendell's stay in Boston was brief this time. He returned to Washington in November with Little Abbott, who had spent a few weeks recuperating at home. When they reached the capital they discovered their regiment had left for Virginia. They followed after it deep into hostile country and caught up on November 19 in the village of Falmouth, across the Rappahannock River from Fredericksburg. The Army of the Potomac was gathering there for another fight, under the command of Major General Ambrose Burnside, who had replaced the fired McClellan.

The 20th Massachusetts was under new leadership as well. General Dana did not return after he recovered, and Colonel Lee inherited formal command of the brigade. But Lee, who was greatly admired by the regiment, had been broken by his experiences, particularly the slaughter in the West Woods. He had disappeared after the battle; a young lieutenant found him two days later in a stable in Keedysville, drunk, filthy, and insensible. Colonel Palfrey, whose wound at Antietam left his arm permanently crippled, never returned to the field. Command of the 20th went to the senior company commander, Ferdinand Dreher, who had commanded one of the German companies. Dreher didn't like many of the Harvard officers, and they, including Holmes, disliked him for, among other reasons, not being one of them. They successfully conspired to have him removed from command and one of their own, George Nelson Macy (Class of 1860), made acting commander, with Little Abbott as his second-in-command. So it was that the 20th Massachusetts, depleted, distrustful, and weary, would lead the advance into Fredericksburg.

The army waited several weeks in the hills north of the town. Winter arrived. Snow fell. Temperatures were well below freezing as army engineers struggled to finish construction of pontoon bridges on December 11 while Confederate sharpshooters subjected them to withering fire. An intense Union artillery barrage failed to suppress their fire, and by midafternoon parts of two regiments crossed the river on pontoon boats, followed immediately by the 20th, to drive the rebel marksmen from their positions, an advance that would be recalled as suicidal. Holmes remained behind in the regiment's hospital, stricken with dysentery.

The last of the bridges was finished by late afternoon on December 11, but the bulk of the army wouldn't cross the river until the next day. Remnants of the 20th returned to camp the morning of the 12th, and Holmes learned the toll from the previous day's urban combat. His cousin, Charlie Cabot, had been shot in the head and killed. At least six others were killed or later died of their wounds, and many more were wounded, including Holmes's second lieutenant.

Holmes wrote his mother that afternoon, informing her of Cabot's death, and despairing of his situation: "I see for the first time the Regt. going to battle while I remain behind — a feeling worse than the anxiety of danger, I assure you — Weak as I was I couldn't restrain my tears."

The big fight started the next day, December 13, in thick fog that blinded both armies. It was a catastrophe for the Federals. Union assaults on Confederate lines were repeatedly repulsed south of the town and on Marye's Heights, where the bloodiest fighting occurred, in attacks that lasted into the night. Holmes watched the fighting from a distant hilltop. "We couldn't see the men, but we could see the battle," he wrote, "a terrible sight when your Regt. is in it but you are safe."

General Burnside wanted to launch another attack the next day, but his generals convinced him it would be as futile as the attacks of the previous day. The Federals collected their dead and wounded and slipped back across the river on December 15. The Army of the Potomac had suffered over twelve thousand killed, wounded, and missing. The Confederates lost fewer than half that number. The 20th Massachusetts, in front for much of the fighting, was commended for its "unflinching bravery" and paid a heavy price for the distinction, with dozens of dead and scores of wounded, including Ferdinand Dreher. The regiment remained in Falmouth for the winter, its morale as depleted as its numbers.

Brigade and division headquarters were in Falmouth as well, and Holmes came to be on familiar terms with the general staff. He was offered a staff position, as were Abbott and Henry Ropes (Class of 1862). All three chose to remain with the regiment. Pen Hallowell wrote to recruit Holmes to the new black regiment he had joined, but Holmes refused that offer too.

The Army of the Potomac got a new commander; Lincoln fired Burnside after Fredericksburg and replaced him with Hooker. The 20th Massachusetts had a new colonel as well. Colonel Revere had been serving on General Sumner's staff since recovering from his wounds at Antietam. When Sumner was relieved as commander of II Corps, Revere petitioned the governor of Massachusetts for the colonelcy of the 20th and received it, though he wouldn't assume command until May. His appointment forced out George Macy and spread dissension among many of the Harvard officers.

The Union Army began its spring offensive in the last week of April 1863. Three corps with nearly forty thousand men crossed the Rappahannock thirty miles north of Fredericksburg, and another three with sixty thousand men were on the march a mile or so south of the city. General Lee could see he was in danger of being flanked on both sides with a powerful Federal army between his army and Richmond. He withdrew most of his army from Fredericksburg and marched to meet his foe near the tiny village of Chancellorsville. The 20th Massachusetts remained in Falmouth as the Confederates left Marye's Heights. They had heard the sound of fighting in the west for two days when they at last received orders late on the night of May 2 to cross the river and join the battle.

Lee had left a strong rearguard on the Heights, and they poured down artillery fire on the Massachusetts men who entered the deserted streets of the town. Pinned down and prone as rebel guns found their range, Holmes was struck by shrapnel in his heel. Before the surgeon chloroformed him and extracted the shrapnel, the patient wrote his mother a note that he had been wounded. He didn't lose his foot, as he feared he would, but he had fought his last battle for a while.

The Battle of Chancellorsville was another disaster for the Union. At a critical moment Hooker halted his advance and took up defensive positions; that proved a costly decision. The next day Lee divided his army and flanked him. The Union lost a little more than seventeen thousand men at Chancellorsville; the rebels around thirteen thousand.

Holmes again went home to Boston to recuperate. Visitors remarked on his changed appearance and personality. Thin to the point of emaciation and wan, his former liveliness, or, as his father described it, his "nervous" disposition, was replaced by a detached air that seemed not to appreciate (and even at times to recoil from) the well-wishes of family and friends. He remained in Boston while Lee, flush with his second victory at Fredericksburg, invaded the North again. The 20th fought at Gettysburg, as always with distinction and at great cost. They were in the center of the Union line the second day of the battle after III Corps on the left flank had been overwhelmed. Holmes's first sergeant and friend, Gustave Magnitzky, was wounded; so was his classmate, Henry Patten, Company G's captain, and his first lieutenant, Charles Cowgill. All three would return to the line in time for the next day's battle.

The regiment had hunkered down on July 2 under a ferocious artillery barrage until General Winfield Scott Hancock arrived with reinforcements and turned back the Confederate advance. Colonel Revere acquitted himself bravely, walking among his prostrate men and officers, giving instruction and encouragement. Shrapnel from a rebel shell tore into him, and he died two days later. Macy reassumed command of the 20th with Abbott as his second in command.

The regiment bedded down that night expecting Lee to attack the Union center the next day. He did, and it cost the 20th dearly. Henry Ropes was the first casualty; a federal artillery shell prematurely detonated that morning and killed him. Abbott, his best friend, held his hand as he expired. At one o'clock that afternoon the greatest rebel artillery barrage of the war commenced on the Union center, firing every type of munitions, shell, shot, and case. Sheltering in a shallow trench behind a stone wall, the regiment held its position and managed to endure the bombardment with only a few casualties. At three o'clock the fire subsided, and the first line of Confederate Major General George Pickett's division emerged from the woods. "The moment I saw them," Abbott wrote later, "I knew we should give them Fredericksburg. So did everybody."

The 20th held its fire until the enemy was within a hundred yards of its line, and then opened up on them mercilessly. But the rebels managed to open up a gap by a copse of trees on the regiment's right. It reminded Abbott of the West Woods, when the Confederates had flanked and surprised them. He organized the regiment into a new line at a right angle, and the bloodiest work of the day commenced. Killing was done with rifle butt, pistol, sword, bayonet, and hand. When it was finished, the regiment had lost thirty-one killed, ninety-three wounded, and three missing. Ten officers were dead or injured. The casualties included Macy; knocked to the ground by shrapnel and struck by a bullet when he got back up, his left hand would be amputated. Sumner Paine, a young Harvard graduate who had just joined the regiment at Fredericksburg and had taken command of Company G in Holmes's absence, was struck by shrapnel in his ankle; kneeling, he continued to exhort his men to fight, until he was shot to death. Holmes tore accounts of the battle from the newspapers and put them in a scrapbook. He served as a pallbearer at Ropes's funeral.

The war was nearly over for Holmes: three times wounded in some of the fiercest fights of the war; repeatedly stricken with dysentery. The allure of glory or adventure or ideals or whatever had drawn Harvard's young men to war had expired in the mud, blood, misery, and terror that were its reality. He was, until Macy returned, senior man in the regiment, and after the New Year's holiday he left Boston for Virginia. But when he arrived he took a staff position in VI Corps as aide to General Horatio Wright. He planned to return to the 20th in time for the spring campaign with a promotion to lieutenant colonel. But he never did. He remained a staff officer in VI Corps in May, when the Army of the Potomac, now under the command of Ulysses S. Grant, marched for Richmond again.

On May 5 they met the Army of Northern Virginia in the woods near Chancellorsville that would come to be known as the Wilderness. The next day the 20th Massachusetts was ordered to make a suicidal charge on Confederate breastworks. A tremendous volley of musket fire cut down scores of men. Several officers were killed. Macy was wounded again, and Abbott assumed command. When they resumed the advance and reached the rebel line, they fought hand to hand. But another line of Confederates was advancing from the left, and the regiment was soon overwhelmed and forced to retreat. Little Abbott was shot in the stomach and died later that afternoon.

Years later a lieutenant in the 20th remembered the day bitterly: "We took into that charge five hundred and thirty-three men. It did not last over fifteen minutes and when the line reformed . . . we had only three or four officers and one hundred and ten men."

Abbott's death shocked and demoralized the regiment, and it seemed to have been the final blow for Holmes. After the Wilderness the two armies fought almost continuously, shedding blood on fields where blood had copiously flowed already. Relentlessly the Army of the Potomac kept pushing to the left, paying whatever price Lee extracted from them, until it reached Petersburg and dug in and then, finally, Richmond. Well before then Holmes had written his parents after weeks of incessant fighting: "By the time you get this you will know how immense the butcher's bill has been. . . . I have not been & am not likely to be in the mood for writing details. . . . Enough that these nearly two weeks have contained all of fatigue & horror that war can furnish. . . . Nearly every regimental off[icer] I knew or cared for is dead or wounded." He had decided to stay on staff and resign at the end of the campaign, he told them, "if I am not killed before."

He stayed with the army until July. Early that month the VI Corps was recalled to defend Washington from an attack by Lieutenant General Jubal Early. During the battle at Fort Stevens in northwestern Washington, Holmes is reported to have shouted at President Lincoln, who had come to observe the engagement and was standing up to get a better view, "Sit down, you damn fool."

He arrived home ten days later.

All wars change the men who fight them, but the Civil War was the most transformative conflict in the nation's history. Nothing on this scale had ever been seen before. The killing was so prodigious, yet the cause was so great and the outcome so consequential it was worth the human cost, staggering and sometimes senseless though it was. In its "new birth of freedom," America could become the just nation and the example to mankind our founding had promised and slavery had prevented. That future was worth every drop of blood spilled, every life claimed or shattered and changed forever.

Oliver Wendell Holmes Jr. became one of the most eminent jurists in the country's history, serving on the Massachusetts Supreme Court and then as associate justice on the U.S. Supreme Court for thirty years. He died in 1935 at the age of ninety-four, more famous than his celebrated father.

Family and close friends thought him dispirited, even embittered after he came home. He had surely been disillusioned. Most people who go to war return, if they return, without the illusions they had brought to it. What replaces those illusions determines how we are transformed. Wars don't change us once; they go on changing us, as we keep looking for meaning in the things that happened to us and the things we did.

For Holmes it was as Harvard's current president, Dr. Drew Gilpin Faust, wrote in her profound book, *The Republic of Suffering:* "The very purposelessness of sacrifice created its purpose."

Holmes gave a Memorial Day address in 1884 in Keene, New Hampshire, in which he touchingly recalled many of his fallen friends. He mentioned the Reveres and Charlie Cabot, who had a premonition of his death before Fredericksburg. He recalled "another youthful lieutenant in the Seven Days battle," referring to his cousin James Lowell. Right before the battle began, he said, "we caught each other's eye and saluted. When next I looked, he was gone." He described Little Abbott bravely leading his company through the firestorm at Fredericksburg: "If you had seen him with his indifferent carriage, and sword swinging from his finger like a cane, you would never have suspected that he was doing more than conducting a company drill on the camp parade ground."

These men, he said, though so "very near and dear to him," were no greater than other fallen heroes. "In the great democracy of self-devotion private and general stand side by side. Unmarshalled save by their own deeds, the army of the dead sweep before us, 'wearing their wounds like stars.' "

They had been transformed by war, he said, and by the suffering and loss that attended the transformation. He called it "our great good fortune" that "in our youth our hearts were touched with fire. It was given to us to learn at the outset that life is a profound and passionate thing."

Eleven years later he gave another Memorial Day tribute to the veterans of the Civil War, this time at Harvard. It was a shorter address than his earlier one, and he titled it "The Soldier's Faith." He talked again of the transformative power of the war. "We have shared the incommunicable experience of war," he told his fellow veterans, "we have felt, we still feel the passion of life to its top." Then he spoke of the meaning of their sacrifice, of finding purpose, shorn of illusions, for suffering and losses that could not be borne and yet were: "In the midst of doubt, in the collapse of creeds, there is one thing I do not doubt . . . that the faith is true and adorable which leads a soldier to throw away his life in obedience to a blindly accepted duty, in a cause which he little understands, in a plan of campaign of which he has little notion, under tactics of which he does not see the use."

He had lost illusions, ideals, and friends. He had been ill-used. He had been bored and exhilarated, brave and terrified, grateful and resentful. It was said that forever after he was a skeptical man in matters of jurisprudence and morality. And for the rest of his long life he carried his lunch in a tin ammunition box he had brought home from the war and preferred the address "Captain" over "Judge."

"War, when you are at it," he said, "is horrible and dull. It is only when time has passed that you see its message was divine," that man was, after all, "capable of miracle, able to lift himself by the might of his own soul."

Captain Edward L. Baker, Buffalo Soldier, officer in the 49th U.S. Volunteers, and recipient of the Medal of Honor for heroism in the Battle of San Juan Heights.

CHAPTER FIVE:
FOG

Edward Baker was a Buffalo Soldier whose courage and leadership under fire set an example for the Americans, white and black, who fought in Cuba.

All we know for certain about the sinking of the USS *Maine* is that five tons of gunpowder in her forward hold erupted in a sudden explosion at about nine thirty in the evening of February 15, 1898. She quickly sank to the bottom of Havana Harbor, and 266 men were killed. Most of the dead were enlisted; their sleeping quarters were in the forward part of the ship, where the explosion occurred. Officers were quartered aft, and most of them survived. A spontaneous fire is believed to have ignited the blast, but its cause was suspicious enough at the time that newspapers and politicians advocating a war with Spain could attribute it to a Spanish mine. Confusion, misunderstanding, and surprise, features of every war, were present at the very start of the Spanish-American War.

As wars go, it was a short one, at least that part of it fought on the island nation of Cuba, the theater that is this chapter's setting. The first American soldiers went ashore in Cuba on June 22, 1898, and the fighting was effectively finished with the surrender of Santiago on July 17. The first American troops embarked for home on August 7, fleeing a yellow fever epidemic.

The 9th U.S. Cavalry Regiment was left behind as a temporary occupying force. It was one of four "colored" regiments in the army, two cavalry and two infantry regiments in which the enlisted men were exclusively black and the officers exclusively white. All four regiments, the 9th and 10th Cavalry, and the 24th and 25th Infantry, were among the first American units ashore in Cuba. They boasted some of the most experienced fighters in the army, who had served in remote frontier forts fighting Indians and outlaws. In one of those "scientific" theories of the time that seem more social rationalization than rational explanation, African Americans were believed not to be susceptible to yellow fever, and the "colored" regiments were known in Cuba as the "Immunes." History remembers them by the name they were given by the Indians they had fought: Buffalo Soldiers.

The *New York Times* journalist Timothy Egan described the battles fought by the 1st U.S. Volunteer Cavalry — Teddy Roosevelt's famed "Rough Riders" — as "sharp, vicious crawls through jungle terrain in killing heat." Let's add the adjective *confusing* to Egan's description. Soldiers' uncertainty of their situation, what the great nineteenth-century strategist Carl von Clausewitz called "the fog of war," was as common in the brief war in Cuba as it was in other wars. The experience of the Rough Riders was shared by most of the regiments fighting in Cuba, including the Buffalo Soldiers, who advanced alongside them from the American landings at Daiquirí to the ascent up the San Juan Heights. And they deserve an equal share of the credit for the army's quick and complete victory in Cuba. History gives them a greater measure of it than their country gave them at the time. There is another kind of fog associated with war, the kind that changes a nation's way of looking at the world and itself. Unlike soldiers, a country can choose, at least for a time, not to see everyone's sacrifices equally.

The invasion of Cuba began with a two-hour naval bombardment on the village of Daiquirí, about fifteen miles east of Santiago. It succeeded in frightening off three hundred or so Spanish defenders, and the initial landing of V Corps, the army's invasion force, proceeded unopposed. Given the problems that attended the landing, had the Spanish soldiers opposed it instead of torching the village and fleeing, they might have turned the opening engagement of the invasion into a disaster for the Americans.

V Corps was commanded by Major General William Rufus Shafter, a corpulent, walrus-mustached, sixty-three-year-old veteran of the Civil War and Indian campaigns. He received his nickname, "Pecos Bill," during his service in the West, where he had commanded the 24th Colored Infantry Regiment and had hounded from service the first African American West Point graduate, Lieutenant Henry O. Flipper. Shafter proved to be overmatched by the Cuban assignment. Both the assembly of V Corps in Tampa, Florida, and the organization of its transport to Cuba was haphazard and slow. So too were the landings at Daiquirí.

It took two days to get all the troops ashore. The landing boats were small and too few, and there was no means to lower the troops into the boats; soldiers carrying full packs on their backs had to squeeze through portholes to reach them. The surf was exceptionally rough, and large breakers pounded the small beach. Several boats were smashed against rocks. Horses and pack mules were the biggest problem. All but one cavalry regiment fought dismounted, for there hadn't been room on the transport ships for their horses. The most senior cavalry officers were allowed to bring their mounts to Cuba, and one reserve brigade included a mounted regiment. But there was no means for conveying ashore the animals that did make the trip, so they were simply forced overboard in the hope they would swim ashore. Some didn't and drowned, but an alert trooper sounded "right wheel" on his bugle and succeeded in turning most of the horses toward the shore. Among the survivors was Little Texas, one of two mounts Teddy Roosevelt had brought to Tampa.

The troops were landed at an abandoned railroad pier, which required them to leap from their boats on the crest of a swelling wave. Some boats smashed against the pier's pilings. Two troopers from the 10th Cavalry, Corporal Edward Cobb and Trooper John English, missed the pier and sank in the turbulent waters below it. Rough Rider William "Buckey" O'Neill, whom Roosevelt called "the iron-nerved, iron-willed fighter from Arizona," jumped in and swam beneath the surface in a futile attempt to rescue them.

The 2nd Infantry Division, under the command of another Civil War veteran, Brigadier General Henry Lawton, was the first to disembark. It comprised three brigades, one of which, General Nelson Miles's 3rd Brigade, included the 25th Colored Infantry Regiment. The 2nd Division was followed by Major General "Fighting Joe" Wheeler's cavalry division, which included the 9th and 10th "colored" regiments and the Rough Riders' 1st Volunteer Cavalry. During the Civil War Wheeler had been a senior cavalry commander in the Confederate Army of Tennessee. Brigadier General Jacob Kent's 1st Infantry Division, which included General Shafter's old command, the 24th Infantry Regiment, would be the last to disembark, along with Shafter, who remained aboard ship, ostensibly directing the chaotic landings.

V Corps' main objective was Santiago, fifteen miles away. A Spanish fleet was anchored there, and a Spanish force of ten thousand defended it. The American fleet, commanded by Rear Admiral William

Sampson, prowled the waters waiting for its opportunity. Shafter ordered Lawton's 2nd Division to Siboney, ten miles west of Daiquirí, where he and Kent's division would go ashore in the morning. Wheeler's dismounted cavalry followed. The Americans made camp at Siboney just after nightfall as a tropical storm drenched them.

Shafter had ordered Wheeler to remain near Siboney until the rest of the army disembarked; they were not to initiate contact with the enemy if it could be helped. But Wheeler had other ideas. He ordered the Rough Riders, commanded by Colonel Leonard Wood with Lieutenant Colonel Theodore Roosevelt second-in-command, and a squadron of four troops each from the 1st and 10th regular cavalry regiments under the command of Brigadier General Samuel Young, about twelve hundred troopers in all, to march at first light on June 24 toward the town of Sevilla. His real objective was a Spanish rearguard of two thousand men that Cuban rebels reported were entrenched with artillery on a low ridge near a village called Las Guásimas.

General Young and the regulars proceeded in a column along the main road to Santiago, while Colonel Wood took the Rough Riders on a parallel, very narrow and steep trail to their left. Young's column reached the ridge first and waited for the Rough Riders to arrive before launching an attack on the front and right flank of the first Spanish line. General Wheeler rode up and waited with him. Young ordered his Hotchkiss field guns brought to the front and fired a couple rounds at a blockhouse on the ridge. The Spanish answered immediately with two 75 mm Krupp guns, and the battle commenced.

The 10th Regiment's Sergeant Major Edward Lee Baker Jr., a Buffalo Soldier with sixteen years of experience on the frontier, recorded in his diary the following summary of the Battle of Las Guásimas: "The advance guard was soon hotly engaged with them; after a very desperate fight of over an hour, the enemy was driven in confusion from their intrenchments. Our men were too exhausted to follow."

It was a desperate fight certainly, its length closer to two hours than one. The Spanish did eventually withdraw, but they were withdrawing to Santiago anyway. They hadn't been driven from their trenches. They hadn't been surprised. They had been waiting in ambush, and the results were very nearly a disaster for the Americans, particularly the 1st Volunteer Cavalry.

That's not to say the Rough Riders and the two regular cavalry regiments were found wanting that day. The Americans at Las Guásimas showed commendable courage, persistence, and resourcefulness. But what emerged from the fog of that first battle in Cuba was a story of a near calamity brought on by a commanding general's eagerness for a fight and of glory saved in the end by the valor of the Buffalo Soldiers and the tactics they had learned fighting Indians.

While the 10th was suddenly engaged at the center of the line, an advance party of Rough Riders led by Sergeant Hamilton Fish III, scion of the eminent New York family, had reached a junction in the trail where they found the body of a Spanish soldier killed by Cuban rebels in an engagement the day before. Fish passed word back to his troop captain, Allyn Capron Jr., and to Wood, who decided to split his column in two, placing a squadron under Major Alexander Brodie to the left of the trail and another under Roosevelt to the right. As they were getting into position the Spanish began to fire at the front of the column. Sergeant Fish was the first man to fall, followed by three troopers in his advance party. Captain Capron, whom Roosevelt later described as "the archetype of the fighting man" and "fitted to play his part to perfection," and whose father commanded an artillery battalion in Cuba, rushed with the rest of his troops to their fallen comrades' aid. He was shot in the chest and killed.

The American lines in the front and left were at an extreme disadvantage. They were fighting in dense jungle, hemmed in by barbed-wire fences in "undergrowth so thick and tall," Sergeant Major Baker described it, "scarcely any breeze could get to you." The Spanish had Mauser repeating rifles, superior to the Americans' Krag rifles, and pinned the Americans down with incessant volleys. They used smokeless gunpowder that didn't give away their positions. Rough Riders and Buffalo Soldiers alike struggled to find targets as they advanced to the base of the ridge.

The Rough Riders were soon in dire straits, exposed in a sunken road, trapped between wire and jungle and the heights from which enfilading fire poured down on them. They were stuck: they couldn't advance and wouldn't retreat. Both Major Brodie and Roosevelt conspicuously exposed themselves to fire, and Brodie was seriously wounded.

With smoke from their Hotchkiss gun giving away their position, troopers from the 10th fought to free the trapped Rough Riders by advancing on the enemy and drawing their fire, while their left flank struggled to reach the volunteers' lines. Roosevelt described the confused and desperate scene in his memoir, *Rough Riders,* when regulars from the 10th pushed forward:

The denseness of the jungle and the fact that they used absolutely smokeless powder, made it exceedingly difficult to place exactly where they were, and almost immediately Young, who always liked to get as close as possible to his enemy, began to push his troops forward. They were deployed on both sides of the road in such thick jungle that it was only here and there that they could possibly see ahead, and some confusion, of course, ensued, the support gradually getting mixed with the advance.

A troop of the 10th, braving intense fire and unable to return it as it was out of their carbines' range, made contact with the Rough Riders and cut holes in the barbed wire, freeing the volunteers to join the advance. B Troop had started up the ridge and managed to suppress some of the Spanish fire by aiming their Hotchkiss at the stone blockhouse from where much of it emanated. It was not easily done, as an African American surgeon for the 25th Infantry later recalled: "So hot was the fire directed at the men at the Hotchkiss gun that a head could not be raised, and men crawled on their stomachs like snakes loading and firing."

B Troop had become separated from their lieutenant, and troopers were led up the hill by two sergeants, John Buck and James Thompson. As the entire American line stoutly worked its way up the ridge and the Spanish began to drop back, General Wheeler is reported to have become momentarily lost in a reverie about battles in the previous war, when he most certainly did not command an advance led by African Americans. "C'mon men!" he urged. "We've got the damned Yankees on the run."

When the fight at Las Guásimas was finished and the casualties were being counted and official reports written, white officers praised the skill and courage of the troops engaged in the battle, regular and volunteer, black and white. But they didn't record the 10th Cavalry's heroics as fully as they deserved to be, at least on the subject of their assistance to the Rough Riders. That was left to other eyewitnesses, including a reporter for the Associated Press, who insisted, "If it had not been for the Negro cavalry, the Rough Riders would have been exterminated. I am not a Negro lover. My father fought with [the Confederate battalion] Mosby's Rangers and I was born in the South, but the Negroes saved that fight, and the day will come when General Shafter will give them credit for their bravery."

The regiment's young quartermaster, First Lieutenant John J. Pershing, who acquired the nickname "Black Jack" while serving in the 10th Cavalry, also commended the regulars for "relieving the Rough Riders from the volleys that were being poured into them."

Sixteen troopers were killed in the battle and fifty-four were wounded. Half the dead and thirty-four of the wounded were Rough Riders, who buried their dead in separate graves. Sergeant Major Baker superintended the burial of the regulars in one mass grave. He recorded their names in the diary he had been keeping since the regiment had boarded a south-bound train in Missoula, Montana, the previous April.

■ ■ ■ ■

Most of the Buffalo Soldiers in Cuba were veterans of the Indian wars, although it had been eight years since the last battle of those wars was fought, the shameful massacre at Wounded Knee. Congress had passed legislation in 1866 establishing the peacetime army and ordering the creation of two cavalry regiments and four infantry regiments "which shall be composed of colored men." The two cavalry regiments were the 9th and 10th. In 1869 the four infantry regiments were consolidated into two, the 24th and 25th.

The regiment was formed at Fort Leavenworth in Kansas in 1866 and treated with hostility by the fort's commander, who opposed the creation of black regiments, and by the white soldiers stationed there. But the 10th's stay at Leavenworth lasted only a short time before its first commander, Colonel Benjamin Grierson, arranged to have the regiment transferred to Fort Riley, Kansas. It was the first of many postings in Kansas and Oklahoma, and later ones in Texas, New Mexico, and Arizona, from which the Buffalo Soldiers of the 10th would distinguish themselves in action against Native Americans throughout the southern plains and Southwest. They crossed deserts, mountains, and plains in campaigns against the Southern Cheyenne, Comanche, and Arapaho. They chased the Apache Victorio into Mexico. They pursued Geronimo until he surrendered, and fought in the last battles of the Apache wars. They were given the name Buffalo Soldiers, a term of respect, by their Indian adversaries, reportedly because they were as hard to kill as buffalo and their hair resembled the animals' dark manes. The regiment left the Southwest in 1891 for the Department of Dakota, where it was stationed at various forts in the Dakotas and Montana.

Edward Baker was born on a wagon train in Wyoming in 1865 to an African American mother and a French father, who decided to remain in eastern Wyoming to raise their son. Growing up on the frontier, Baker acquired the skills he would use to advance in the cavalry. He was an excellent horseman and shot. He could rope as well as any cowboy. He could navigate plains and mountains. He was accustomed to the hardships of frontier life. He was also highly intelligent and decently educated. He could speak Spanish passably and French fluently. He enlisted in the 9th Cavalry as a bugler when he was just sixteen and transferred to the 10th five years later.

He would serve at posts in Arizona, Colorado, Kansas, Montana, Nebraska, New Mexico, Oklahoma, Texas, and Wyoming and usually enjoyed the favorable opinion of the officers he served under. He was married in 1887 to Mary Elizabeth Hawley and became regimental clerk in 1888. He was promoted to regimental quartermaster sergeant in 1891. The next year the regiment's colonel, Jacob Mizner, gave Baker the highest enlisted post in the regiment, sergeant major. He held that rank for the remainder of his time in the 10th, through six years in Montana and the war with Spain.

While in Montana in 1896 he applied to the prestigious French cavalry school, École d'application de cavalerie and asked the War Department for a one-year leave of absence, the first leave he had requested in fifteen years of service. Colonel Mizner, among others, endorsed the application, praising Baker as "a man of refinement, most excellent character, temper and disposition" and a "very capable and intelligent" soldier. Nevertheless the War Department refused the application without explanation. He reapplied the following year; this time the

War Department initially approved only to reverse their position a few weeks later.

Baker was still at Fort Assiniboine, Montana, when the *Maine* sank in Havana Harbor, and shortly afterward the 10th was ordered mobilized for war service. The West was certainly not free of the racism and bigotry of the age, but white settlers there had relied on African Americans to protect them from the Native Americans. In consequence many accorded the Buffalo Soldiers a degree of respect, even admiration, that was denied African Americans elsewhere in the country. Hard as life was, many lived with their families in isolated frontier communities that valued them, where they were assigned the same responsibilities as white troops and where they might have opportunities denied them in other regions of the country. It was no surprise, then, that most of the citizens of Missoula turned out to bid the 10th Cavalry farewell and that on their journey south they would encounter thousands of well-wishers along the way. "On April 19 we were off for Chickamauga Park," Baker wrote in his diary. "En route we were heartily greeted. Patriotism was at its height. Every little hamlet, even, had its offerings. To compare the journey to Caesar's march of triumph would be putting it mildly."

It was also no surprise that the regiment was unprepared for the very different treatment, the heartfelt and statutory racism they would encounter when they arrived in the Jim Crow South.

There was disagreement in 1898 within the African American press about whether black regiments should serve in the war. Some argued that as long as their officers were exclusively white, black soldiers shouldn't risk their lives for the country. Others believed that honorable service in the war would earn the respect and gratitude of the nation, which would lead to more just and equitable treatment of African Americans in general. The controversy didn't appear to affect the esprit of the Buffalo Soldiers. They went to war as enthusiastically as did volunteer regiments. The four segregated black regiments were possibly the finest regiments in the army, renowned for, among other attributes, their high morale.

It must have been something of a shock for the men of the 10th Cavalry to arrive at Chickamauga Park in Georgia and be greeted by the sheer astonishment of the locals, few of whom would have ever seen professional African American warriors, who carried themselves with the self-possession and dignity of veterans. Astonished ignorance quickly gave way to a hate common in the Jim Crow South. Sergeant Major Frank Pullen of the 25th Infantry, which had arrived in Georgia a week before the 10th, recalled their treatment: "Outside of the Park, it mattered not if we were soldiers of the United States, and going to fight for the honor of our country and the freedom of an oppressed and starving people, we were 'niggers,' as they called us, and treated us with contempt. . . . That is the kind of 'united country' we saw in the South."

The Buffalo Soldiers remained in Georgia only a few weeks. On May 14 the 10th relocated to a camp in Lakeland, Florida, thirty miles from Tampa, where they again encountered the contempt of white residents, who did not just require black soldiers to obey local segregation laws but, more often than not, angrily and crudely demanded it. The hostility became mutual and came to a head in a barbershop. A trooper from the 10th had asked for a shave and was purportedly threatened with a pistol while a crowd of angry whites hurled insults at a number of troopers, who responded by drawing their pistols and shooting up the barbershop, killing one of their abusers.

The 24th and 25th infantry regiments were camped in the city of Tampa, and they too were abused and threatened, and not just by the locals. Just before the regiments embarked for Cuba, a number of drunken Ohio volunteers used a two-year-old African American child for target practice. A bullet came so close to the boy that it went through his shirt-sleeve. When black soldiers learned of the outrage they retaliated by attacking white soldiers as well as some of the local businesses that refused service to "coloreds."

Sergeant Major Pullen from the 25th wrote that unlike white regiments waiting aboard ship, black soldiers "were not allowed to go ashore, unless an officer would take a whole company off to bathe and exercise." They were kept in the cramped quarters and stale air below decks for a week before setting sail for Cuba. Pullen noted that the main deck was reserved for the regiment's officers, where "no soldier was allowed to go abaft for any purpose, except to report to his superior officer." Once they were underway to Cuba on June 14, the brigade commander imposed a strict color line between the 25th Infantry and the white soldiers of the 14th Infantry Regiment, who were transported on the same ship, despite the fact the two regiments had served together in Montana and were, according to Pullen, "on the best of terms."

"All of these things were done seemingly to humiliate us and without a word of protest from our officers," Pullen remembered. "We suffered without complaint."

There are no reports that the segregated cavalry regiments were transported to Cuba in the same circumstances, although it's probably safe to assume the accommodations were less than comfortable for the ranks and only somewhat better for the officers. As mentioned earlier, they traveled without their horses, which would have seemed strange to a cavalry trooper going into battle. They also left almost a third of the regiment in Tampa, mostly new recruits, to care for the regiment's horses and supplies.

Fifty 10th Cavalry troopers and twenty-five Rough Riders were ordered on June 21 to escort weapons, ammunition, mules, and other supplies to Cuban rebels. Their first attempted landing, at Cienfuegos on June 29, was repulsed by the Spanish. Their next attempt, the following day, was at the mouth of a river called Tayabacoa by the Americans. It was calamitous. A party of thirty Cubans and American volunteers put ashore in rowboats to secure the landing site a few hundred yards from a Spanish fort that overlooked the beach. They were quickly discovered and engaged by the Spanish garrison and forced to retreat to the beach, where they discovered that their boats had been sunk by Spanish artillery. They were trapped. Survivors sought cover in a mangrove swamp. But seven of the party were wounded, two of them Americans, and were pinned down near the beach. The brother of the rebel commander, Emilio Núñez, was shot and killed. Their only protection was the guns of U.S. warships that had escorted the convoy, which were temporarily preventing the Spanish from capturing the stranded men.

The Cubans still aboard ship made four attempts to rescue their comrades, but each attempt was repulsed under heavy fire. Lieutenant George Johnson asked for volunteers from the 10th to make a last attempt after nightfall. A number offered their services, and Johnson chose five: his second lieutenant George Ahern, Sergeant William Thompkins, Corporal George Wanton, and Troopers Dennis Bell and Fitz Lee. While

Ahern and Thompkins were experienced soldiers, the three enlisted men were considerably less so, and Corporal Wanton had a troublesome reputation, having been court-martialed eight times for various offenses.

They made it ashore in a long boat and under withering fire helped the wounded into the boat and rowed back to the ship with no further casualties suffered, which, given the intensity of the Spanish volleys, seemed almost miraculous. The odds against the success of the rescue were considerable and the courage needed to undertake it immense. Once they were back aboard ship, Corporal Wanton volunteered to make another trip to the beach to recover the body of General Núñez's brother but was told he had done enough. All four troopers were awarded the Medal of Honor for their gallantry.

On the southeastern end of the island, General Shafter and his staff were making a reconnaissance of the outer defenses of Santiago. A ridgeline rose up from the jungle east of the city that featured two hill crests on a north-south axis, Kettle Hill and the larger San Juan Hill, and the village of El Caney three miles to the north. Lawton's division, which included the 25th Infantry Regiment, was given the assignment of assaulting the Spanish garrison at El Caney. The other three "colored" regiments would be part of the attack by Kent's 1st Infantry Division and Wheeler's dismounted cavalry on the Spanish entrenched on the San Juan Heights. However much the men of these regiments had been made to suffer the humiliation and injustice of segregation, whatever color lines they had been compelled to obey prior to this moment, the confused and chaotic fight they would join would be remembered as the most integrated battle of the nineteenth century, a battle that might have been lost but for them.

The battle of El Caney opened at dawn on July 1 with an American artillery barrage on a Spanish blockhouse, which was the only enemy position visible from the American lines below. General Lawton had estimated it would take his division two hours to overrun El Caney, and Shafter had ordered the attacks on the San Juan Heights to wait until Lawton's division had finished the assignment and joined the right flank for the assault on Kettle and San Juan.

Despite Lawton's optimism, it would take his division the entire day to drive the Spanish from El Caney. Two hours after American guns had opened fire on the blockhouse, an American artillery battery opened fire on San Juan Hill, the signal for the infantry and dismounted cavalry to begin moving into position. Spanish cannon immediately answered. Shafter had situated his artillery on a hill, El Pozo, opposite the Heights, where the clouds of black powder they belched with every salvo made them easy targets for the Spanish 77 mm Krupp guns. Spanish marksmen and skirmishers, using smokeless powder to conceal their positions, began killing and wounding Americans assembling in the jungle in advance of the attack on the Heights.

A gout-plagued Shafter returned to his headquarters, intending to direct the battle from there. General Wheeler had fallen ill as well and transferred command of the dismounted cavalry division to his brigade commander, General Samuel Sumner. Wheeler would return to the front early in the battle. General Young, 2nd Brigade commander, had become seriously ill just after Las Guásimas and had given command of the brigade to Wood, which left Roosevelt in command of the Rough Riders.

Kent's infantry held the left of the American line while Wheeler's cavalry division on

the right moved down jungle trails to a ford
in the San Juan River and formed lines on
the other side expecting to link up with
Lawton's infantry. 1st Cavalry Brigade,
commanded that day by Colonel Henry
Carroll, including the 9th Cavalry, crossed
the river first. The 2nd Brigade, with the
Rough Riders in the lead, followed. With
orders to act in support of Carroll's brigade
they held the extreme right of the line. The
10th Cavalry, to their left, was the only regiment that would join attacks on both hills.

As they waited for the signal to attack,
men felled by heat stroke added to the
casualties claimed by the rapid-firing Mausers and shrapnel from Spanish artillery
sweeping the jungle trails. Black gunpowder
smoke gave away their positions. Making
matters worse, as the cavalry were making
their way along the approaches to Kettle
Hill, a Signal Corps hot air observation balloon floated fifty feet above them and drew
what Sergeant Major Baker described as
"terrific converging fire from the blockhouse
and intrenchments in front and the works
further to the left" on the troopers scrambling to take cover in the tall grass. Baker,
who was constantly moving between the
regiment's command and the troops, found
himself pinned down beneath the balloon

on more than one occasion. "Every gun, both great and small, was playing on it," he remembered. Eventually shell shrapnel punctured the balloon and it dropped to earth — to the relief, one assumes, of every American on the scene except those who had been held aloft by it.

Roosevelt recalled in his memoir the dire situation the troopers were in as they splashed across the river at the crossing they would remember as "Bloody Ford" and waited three hours for the order to charge while bullets and shells rained down on them:

> While we were lying in reserve we were suffering nearly as much as afterward when we charged. I think that the bulk of the Spanish fire was practically unaimed, or at least not aimed at any particular man . . . but they swept the whole field of battle up to the edge of the river, and man after man in our ranks fell dead or wounded, although I had the troopers scattered out far apart, taking advantage of every scrap of cover.

One of the dead was Buckey O'Neill. According to Roosevelt, who deeply mourned the loss of "this wild and gallant soul,"

O'Neill had been conspicuously walking in front of his men, who were all lying prone. His company first sergeant had beseeched him to get down, but O'Neill replied, "Sergeant, the Spanish bullet isn't made that will kill me." Moments later just such a bullet struck him in the mouth and he fell dead.

Others were not as resolute in maintaining their positions under such duress. The 71st New York Volunteer Infantry, part of General Hamilton Hawkins's 1st Infantry Brigade, was ordered to the front. When the New Yorkers emerged from the jungle into massed rifle and artillery fire, they broke and fled back down the trail. Recalled one of them, "It seemed that if one stuck out his hand, the fingers would be clipped off. We huddled within ourselves and bent over to shield our bellies." Other calamities struck during the agonizing wait at the bottom of the hill. The 3rd Infantry Brigade's commander, Colonel Charles Wikoff, was shot and killed by a Spanish sniper, and his second- and third-in-command were wounded and carried from the field.

The 10th Cavalry's commander, Colonel Theodore Baldwin, was riding in the front of the regiment's lines when an artillery shell injured him and his horse. His sergeant major, Baker, ran to his side. Baldwin assured him he was all right and told him to return to the river crossing to hurry the rest of the men across. The observation balloon was still aloft at this point. Crouching troopers were pushing past dead bodies floating in the river when another raking volley of Mauser fire sent them scrambling for less exposed positions. Baker took cover in the bush with several other troopers, who attempted to return fire on their unseen enemies. "The atmosphere," Sergeant Jacob Clay Smith remembered, "seemed perfectly alive with flying missiles from bursting shells and musketry."

Baker was still crouched there when he heard the sound of a man in distress coming from the river. Private Lewis Thompson was wounded and floundering in the water, his heavy pack threatening to drown him. No one could do anything for him. The fire was so thick and constant at that point that anyone who put his head up was likely to have it shot off for his trouble. The fire was also "a trifle high," Baker remembered, so everyone near the ford was lying frozen on the ground. He described one trooper who let a poisonous snake "crawl over him while dodging a volley from the Spanish Mausers."

Nevertheless when Baker heard Thompson groaning, he got up and started toward him. The men nearest Baker tried to restrain him, but he wouldn't be dissuaded. He raced to the injured man as "another of those troublesome shells passed so close as to cause me to feel the heat." He was struck by shrapnel twice in his arm and shoulder. Somehow he managed to reach Thompson, drag him from the river, and help get him to the surgeon. When you read citations for decorated soldiers, the heroism described usually begins with something like "With little regard for his own safety." That's what "little regard" looks like. To the men who witnessed it, Baker's action was certain to get him killed. That it didn't they credited as miraculous. He would receive the Medal of Honor.

Minutes after Baker rescued Thompson, the observation balloon finally met its overdue fate, its occupants dazed but otherwise unhurt by their rapid descent. Baker, his wounds presumably dressed, helped Colonel Baldwin and another man cut breaches in the barbed wire strung along the base of the ridge. Then they waited for the order to charge. Just before they received it, Baldwin was wounded again and carried from the field, the first of many officers in the regiment who would be lost that day.

The Spanish had strongly fortified El Caney and now stoutly defended it with not much more than five hundred men to Lawton's sixty-five hundred. They were aided immensely by their Mausers' longer range, the difficulty of the terrain, the barbed wire stretched low to the ground that was instrumental in checking American advances, and the nearly constant exposure to fire their attackers faced. Americans remembered the scene as "Hell Caney." The first infantry assault, led by the 2nd Massachusetts Volunteers, was repulsed. Sergeant Major Pullen passed the defeated volunteers as the 25th Infantry made its way to the front. "They were completely whipped," he recalled, "and took occasion to warn us, saying: 'Boys, there is no use to go up there, you cannot see a thing; they are slaughtering our men!' "

But the 25th did go up there. After repeated attacks had buckled under devastating fire, the division's artillery battery, commanded by the fallen Captain Capron's father, had managed to breach a stone fort that was critical to the Spanish defenses. The 25th and the 12th U.S. Infantry were ordered to make the final assault. Pullen described the grim reality of their advance:

> This particular charge was a tough, hard climb, over sharp, rising ground, which, were a man in perfect physical strength, he would climb slowly. Part of the charge was made over soft, plowed ground, a part through a lot of prickly pineapple plants and barbed-wire entanglements. It was slow, hard work, under a blazing sun and a perfect hailstorm of bullets, which, thanks to the poor marksmanship of the Spaniards, "went high."

The charge may have been slow and fiercely resisted, but it was relentless. And it succeeded: they drove the Spanish from El Caney, albeit about seven hours behind schedule. Soldiers in the 25th were the first to enter the fort and capture the enemy's colors, though white soldiers of the 12th claimed the credit. The cost of the victory totaled eighty-one killed and 360 wounded.

Well before their triumph, Shafter had accepted that Lawton might not join the attack on the San Juan Heights. Casualties among infantry and cavalry, officers and men, were mounting, exceeding 5 percent, and not a single soldier had started up the hill yet. That number didn't include soldiers who lay prostrate in their wool and flannel uniforms, victims of heat stroke. Shafter's officers urged him to let them begin the assault rather than continue being shot to pieces while they waited in the sweltering heat. Continuing to hold their exposed positions or even retreating could prove almost as dangerous as a charge. Finally, sometime between noon and one that afternoon, Shafter ordered, "The Heights must be taken at all costs," and four Gatling guns began firing on the Spanish entrenchments as American infantry and cavalry shouted their approval.

As welcome a sound as the Gatlings were, Shafter still hadn't said when his corps would take the Heights, seemingly leaving it to his subordinate commanders to decide when to start. Everyone knew how it would have to be done, of course: an ascent over open ground and a frontal attack on the Spanish lines. But who would order it? Accounts of the Battle of San Juan Heights vary depending on which participant is reporting. Thirteen regular army regiments and two volunteer regiments were involved in the battle, each with a parochial regard for its own importance to the outcome. But there does seem to be a consensus about how the charge began.

A young lieutenant in General Hawkins's 1st Infantry Brigade, Jules Ord, is said to have volunteered to lead the charge. "I would not ask any man to volunteer," Hawkins is said to have replied. "Well, then, if you do not forbid it, I will start it," a presumably frustrated Ord replied. "I will not ask for volunteers, I will not give permission and I will not refuse it," Hawkins explained, underscoring his implicit approval with a "God Bless and good luck!" Ord, shirtless and brandishing his sword, gave the order to charge, and the soldiers of the 6th Infantry Regiment rose to their feet and followed him. The attack stirred other regiments into action. The 2nd and 10th Infantry advanced on the left. To the right the cavalry started up Kettle Hill, and Teddy Roosevelt dug his spurs into Little Texas and raced ahead of his men.

There was very little military order in the spontaneous general assault that commenced. Regiments that were already losing some of their cohesion in the long wait under constant fire became thoroughly mixed with each other. The Buffalo Soldiers of the 24th charged past regiments in front of them to join the attack on San Juan, sweeping along with them elements of the 9th and 13th Infantry and leaving behind the 71st New York Volunteers, still shell-shocked from their earlier exposure to combat. Buffalo Soldier Herschel Cashin remembered General Kent pleading with the New Yorkers to join the charge, "with tears streaming down his cheeks, begging, admonishing, persuading, and entreating," but to no avail. The New Yorkers remained in the rear, while the 24th, according to Cashin's description, "rushed . . . wildly across the open field, attracting the attention of the entire Spanish line and drawing concentrated fire."

Some troops in the 10th Cavalry joined the charge up San Juan with the 6th Infantry. The rest of the regiment "advanced rapidly" up Kettle Hill with the Rough Riders "under a galling, converging fire from the enemy's artillery and infantry," as Baker recalled. Troops from the 6th, 3rd, and 9th regiments in the 1st Brigade merged with each other and with the Rough Riders and other regiments in the 2nd Brigade as they navigated their way through barbed wire and the hailstorm of bullets and shells. Frank Knox, a Rough Rider and future secretary of the navy, found himself fighting in a troop of Buffalo Soldiers and later professed, "I never saw braver men anywhere."

Adding to the chaos was the confusion caused by casualties among the officers before and during the charge, which were many. Lieutenant Pershing, who was with the 10th during the charge, put their losses at "20 percent killed and wounded — 50 percent of the officers were lost, a fearful rate." The assault upon the San Juan Heights continued relentlessly in the teeth of fierce opposition, led as much by sergeants and corporals as lieutenants, captains, and colonels, white man and black man advancing over the steep, stony ground shoulder to shoulder. Buffalo Soldiers in G Troop of the 10th suddenly found themselves marching directly into the Spanish guns. Their sergeant, Saint Foster, suggested to Lieutenant W. H. Smith they take an alternative route up the hill. Smith abruptly rejected the advice. "All right, sir," Foster responded, "we'll go as far as you will." Seconds later Smith was killed. Foster took over command of G Troop and brought it to the crest without losing another man. He was commended in an after-action report for having "displayed remarkable intelligence and ability in handling the troop during the remainder of the day."

Pershing described the integrated cavalry charge that stormed Kettle Hill:

Each officer or soldier next in rank took charge of the line or group immediately in his front or rear and halting to fire at each good opportunity, taking reasonable advantage of cover, the entire command moved forward as coolly as though the buzzing of bullets was the humming of bees. White regiments, black regiments, regulars and Rough Riders, representing the young manhood of the North and the South, fought soldier to soldier, unmindful of race or color, unmindful of whether commanded by ex-Confederate or not and mindful only of their common duty as Americans.

The 3rd Cavalry's color bearer was shot and killed during the charge. The color sergeant for the 10th, George Berry, a thirty-year veteran of the regiment, saw him fall, retrieved his colors, and shouting "Dress on the colors, boys," carried both standards to the top of the hill, where he planted them.

Kettle Hill cost the cavalry thirty-five dead and several hundred wounded. Roosevelt was one of the first men to reach the top, but he wasn't *the* first. Some reports credit Color Sergeant Berry. Roosevelt was a conspicuously brave soldier that day, and an inspiration. But he wasn't the only one, although he adroitly managed — and we write this as his admirers — to make himself *the* hero of San Juan Hill. That was a disservice to the other Americans, black and white, who fought so heroically there.

After they drove the Spanish off Kettle Hill, the cavalry turned their attention to the Spanish on San Juan Hill, which had yet to be taken by Kent's infantry. Roosevelt ordered a charge, raced down the slope of Kettle under fire, and had just gotten over a barbed-wire fence and started up San Juan when he discovered only five men had followed him. Infuriated, he abandoned the idea and returned to his exhausted regiment. San Juan soon fell to the infantry. Lieutenant Ord, whose actions had triggered the advance of the American line, was one of the first men to reach the top, where he was shot and killed minutes later.

Two hundred five Americans died taking El Caney and the San Juan Heights, and almost twelve hundred men were wounded. Twenty-six of the dead were Buffalo Soldiers. Baker described their suffering and sacrifice:

Men shot and lacerated in every conceivable manner; some are expressionless;

268

some just as they appeared in life; while others are pinched and drawn and otherwise distorted, portraying agony in her most distressful state. Of the wounded, in their anguish, some are perfectly quiet; others are heard praying; some are calling for their mothers, while others are giving out patriotic utterances, urging their comrades on to victory, or bidding them farewell as they pass on to the front. July 1, in passing a wounded comrade, he told me that he could whip the cowardly Spaniard who shot him, in a fair fist fight.

The capture of the San Juan Heights and El Caney exposed Santiago to siege. The Spanish squadron anchored there attempted a breakout on July 3 and were destroyed in detail by Admiral Sampson's fleet. Though some intermittent skirmishing continued, the war in Cuba was effectively finished. Yellow fever and malaria drove most Americans home, including Roosevelt and the Rough Riders, leaving behind an occupying force under Colonel Wood. As he bade farewell to his regiment, Roosevelt had a few words of praise for the heroism of the Buffalo Soldiers:

Now, I want to say just a word more to

some of the men I see standing around not of your number. I refer to the colored regiments, who occupied the right and left flanks of us at Guásimas, the Ninth and Tenth cavalry regiments. The Spaniards called them "Smoked Yankees," but we found them to be an excellent breed of Yankees. I am sure that I speak the sentiments of officers and men in the assemblage when I say that between you and the other cavalry regiments there exists a tie which we trust will never be broken.

However, he took a different tack in his war memoir, faulting the resolve of some of the Buffalo Soldiers on Kettle Hill:

None of the white regulars or Rough Riders showed the slightest sign of weakening; but under the strain the colored infantrymen (who had none of their officers) began to get a little uneasy and to drift to the rear, either helping wounded men, or saying that they wished to find their own regiments. This I could not allow, as it was depleting my line, so I jumped up, and walking a few yards to the rear, drew my revolver, halted the retreating soldiers, and called out to them that I appreciated the gallantry with which they had fought and would be sorry to hurt them, but that I should shoot the first man who, on any pretense whatever, went to the rear.

In later press interviews Roosevelt suggested that while black troops would fight bravely, they couldn't be relied on without white officers commanding them.

A sergeant from the 10th, Presley Holliday, disputed Roosevelt's criticism in a lengthy letter to the *New York Age,* an African American–run newspaper. He reminded Roosevelt that at Las Guásimas and Kettle Hill, Buffalo Soldiers had come to the aid of the 1st and had led the final assault on El Caney after many of their officers had been killed or wounded or were missing. That black soldiers looked to return to their regiments after they reached the top of the hill did not necessarily make them shirkers. Their action was likely nothing more than an attempt to find order in chaos. He mentioned also that when Roosevelt drew his revolver, his own Rough Riders had defended the Buffalo Soldiers. "You won't have to shoot those men, Colonel," Holliday reports them saying. "We know those boys." He also alleges that Roosevelt apologized the next day to the men he threatened.

Holliday closed the letter by endorsing the demand to have black officers commissioned for black regiments: "Our motto for the future must be: No officers, no soldiers."

Some Buffalo Soldiers were given commissions after the war, but they were restricted to service in volunteer regiments. Baker was commissioned a first lieutenant in the 10th U.S. Volunteer Infantry, an all-black regiment recruited for war with Spain, although he spent the first months after he returned from Cuba at a quarantine camp in Montauk, New York, recovering from his wounds and illness. His old regiment, the 10th Cavalry, was posted briefly in Alabama and then at several camps in Texas. The "colored" regiments had received widespread praise in the newspapers for their heroics in Cuba. Yet that hadn't changed how they were treated in the Jim Crow South. Baker spent only a few months with the Volunteers in Macon, Georgia, before the regiment was mustered out. He returned to the 10th Cavalry in San Antonio, Texas, and his old rank, sergeant major.

In late 1899 he received another commission, a captaincy in the 49th Volunteer Infantry, one of two all-black volunteer regiments recruited to fight in the Philippines. He commanded Company L, with two other veteran Buffalo Soldiers serving as the company's first and second lieutenants. As usual his impeccable conduct made lasting impressions on his superiors, who frequently commended him in their reports. Major General Elwell Otis, military governor for the Philippines, recommended that forty-two black officers in the volunteer regiments serving in the war be given second lieutenant commissions in the regular army. His recommendation was ignored.

Baker anticipated that outcome, and after he returned to the States he petitioned for a commission in the Philippine Scouts, an indigenous army Congress created in 1901 to fight Philippine insurgents. He solicited several high-level endorsements, including one from the old rebel general Fighting Joe Wheeler. He also wrote directly to the president of the United States, Theodore Roosevelt.

He was commissioned a second lieutenant in the Scouts in 1902 and spent the next seven years in command of remote posts on the islands of Luzon and Samar. He never lived with his wife and children again, and something happened to him during those seven years of lonely and difficult frontier service. A soldier who in his more than two decades in the army had received only effusive praise from men who had served above and below him, whose admirers included the last commanding general of the army, Nelson Miles, and the incumbent president of the United States, a soldier who was routinely described as "sober," "intelligent," and "exemplary" became an alcoholic, and his superiors began to doubt his fitness for continued service. In 1909 he resigned his commission in the Scouts. In recognition of his many years of exemplary service, the army that could never bring itself to give him the commission he deserved allowed him to reenlist and retire in 1910 as a quartermaster sergeant.

He died alone in San Francisco three years later and was buried in Los Angeles, where his wife and children resided. His name slipped back into obscurity. His headstone made no mention of the fact that once, in a confused and terrible battle, where death was as likely as survival, he had commanded men with skill and courage and risked his life to save another. He did not receive his Medal of Honor until he had disappeared into the fog of another war. And the memory of what his regiment's colonel praised as a "fearlessness that was wonderful" was carried only in the hearts of those who witnessed it.

Major General Littleton Waller "Tony" Tazewell Waller, whom his protégé and Marine Corps legend Smedley Butler called "the greatest soldier I have ever known."

CHAPTER SIX:
A HOWLING WILDERNESS

Littleton Waller "Tony" Tazewell Waller, a court-martialed Marine officer, refused to massacre Filipino civilians.

In the first major battle of the Spanish-American War, in Manila Bay in the Philippines, Spain had lost a naval squadron. Now Admiral Pascual Cervera y Topete wished to avoid losing the Caribbean Squadron, which he had the honor to command. It was anchored in Santiago Bay, Cuba, protected by Spanish artillery from the American fleet that prowled the waters outside the harbor. Now that the Americans had taken the San Juan Heights, Santiago and its guns could no longer guarantee Cervera safe harbor. He attempted a breakout on Sunday morning, July 3, 1898. Rear Admiral William Sampson, commanding the American fleet, had taken his flagship with a torpedo boat as an escort to Siboney for a meeting with the V Corps commander, Major General William Shafter. That opened a small gap in the blockade line. Between nine thirty and ten o'clock, Spanish warships began steaming out of the bay in single file with Cervera's flagship, the *Infanta Maria Teresa,* in the lead.

Among the American warships waiting for them were the pride of the U.S. Navy, the newly built battleships *Iowa* and *Oregon,* and the oldest of their class, the USS *Indiana.* The cruiser USS *Brooklyn* signaled the fleet that enemy ships were leaving Santiago Harbor, and the *Indiana,* at the eastern end of the blockade, cleared for action. U.S. Marines manned her guns. They were commanded by Captain Littleton Waller Tazewell Waller, "Tony," to his family and friends. Waller had been an officer in the Marine Corps for nearly two decades and had been in a few overseas scraps, but this was his first real war and his first real naval battle. As soon as the *Maria Teresa* emerged from the harbor, the American line closed around her and marine gunners sent shells smashing into her hull. In less than an hour she struck her colors. In four hours the battle was over. Spain's Caribbean fleet was destroyed. Cervera had lost hundreds of men killed and wounded. Only one American sailor had died.

Spanish sailors jumped off the burning decks of their ships into shark-infested waters or huddled miserably on the beach while Cuban rebels took potshots at them. The *Indiana*'s skipper, Captain Henry Taylor, dispatched Waller and a party of marines with the ship's surgeon to rescue as many prisoners as they could. They worked all day and into the night, heroically, and in Waller's estimate managed to save 243 men and bring them aboard the *Indiana*. "We issued clothes to the naked men, and the officers gave up their clothes and beds to the Spanish officers," Waller recalled, adding that he had "received many tokens and letters . . . in grateful acknowledgement of the mercy shown." The navy gave him a medal.

With the destruction of Cervera's fleet, the war in Cuba drew to a close. The Spanish formerly surrendered Santiago two weeks later. On the other side of the world, Admiral George "You may fire when ready, Gridley" Dewey, hero of Manila Bay, welcomed Major General Wesley Merritt and an army expeditionary force to the Philippines. Emilio Aguinaldo, leader of the Philippine revolution, greeted Merritt's army warily, wondering whether its purpose was limited to driving the Spanish from the

Philippines or it intended to deny the national independence Aguinaldo and the insurgent army were fighting for. Dewey had brought Aguinaldo to the Philippines from exile in Hong Kong, provided arms to his rebel army, and formed at least an informal alliance with the Filipino leader against their common enemy. According to Aguinaldo, Dewey also promised him the Philippines would be independent once the Spanish were gone.

The Treaty of Paris, ending the Spanish-American War and ceding the Philippines to the United States for twenty million dollars, was signed in December 1898. The Philippine-American War began with the Second Battle of Manila on February 4, 1899, two days before the U.S. Senate ratified the treaty. It would last three years (and sporadic fighting would continue after that). Over four thousand Americans would be killed; five times that number of Filipino fighters would die. Many thousands of civilians would perish in the violence and from the famine and disease the war helped cause. And the Philippines wouldn't gain genuine independence until 1946.

Savagery occurs in all wars, from antiquity to the present; all belligerents are parties to it. But the Philippine-American War is remembered and was seen at the time as particularly brutal. Some Americans thought the rules of war, as changeable as they are, did not apply to any great extent in the Philippines. That attitude was derived in part from the feeling they were fighting "savages," not soldiers, and in part from American soldiers' alienation in such strange physical and moral circumstances from all they recognized as civilization. H. G. Wells, who reported from the Philippines for the *New York Evening Post,* quoted one soldier's succinct explanation of their transformation: "There is no question that our men do 'shoot niggers' somewhat in the sporting spirit, but that is because war and their environments have rubbed off the thin veneer of civilization."

That is the psychological and moral risk inherent in every war, including the wars Americans have fought in this century. Atrocities may not be as frequent or as easily overlooked as they were in past conflicts, but war can still rub off the "veneer of civilization" and the memory of the experience can still trouble a veteran's sleep long after he has come home.

Both sides committed atrocities in the Philippines. Filipino atrocities would inflame American public opinion, and the

American resort to concentration camps, torture, and summary executions would trouble its conscience. Ultimately America's dreams of empire that the triumph over Spain had encouraged would begin to subside in revulsion over the means used to build it.

Tony Waller was born on his father's tobacco plantation on the Virginia peninsula in 1856. His parents, Mary Waller Tazewell and Matthew Page Waller, were third cousins, hence the redundant name they gave their fourth child. The Wallers were an old and prominent Virginia family. Both sides of the family claimed generations of elected officeholders, eminent jurists, and respected professionals dating to the colonial period, but no tradition of military service.

Matthew Waller was a physician who practiced in Williamsburg, and later in Norfolk, where he moved his family in 1860. Tony learned to ride and hunt in the Virginia countryside, where he spent his first few years and many happy childhood days on the plantation. Years later his fellow marines would admire his superior marksmanship and dignified bearing in the saddle as well as the self-confidence and social graces he had acquired and the air of command he exuded that made him appear taller than the five feet four inches God had given him.

The pastoral pleasures of the young country squire gave way to the allure of international commerce in the port city of Norfolk. Tony's father died of typhoid in 1861, when the Confederacy still held the city. Not long afterward the Army of the Potomac occupied Norfolk, and held it until war's end. The Wallers remained there after the war, although, as with many planter families, in reduced circumstances. Tony did not go to college and had not found a profession that suited him until 1880, when he decided on a career in the Marine Corps.

Like the South's plantation aristocracy, the Marine Corps experienced a decline in its fortunes after the war. In the thirty-three years that passed between Appomattox and the sinking of the USS *Maine,* the country's only fights were on the frontier with Native Americans, and those were almost exclusively army shows. The marines were a very small, poorly funded, and insular service in those days, and advancement was exceptionally slow. Waller wouldn't rise much in the first two decades of his career, but he would steadily advance his reputation. His record would have blemishes, not the least of which were a couple of embarrassing incidents with alcohol and a reprimand for publicly insulting an assistant secretary of the navy. But by the turn of the century many knowledgeable observers would view him as a prospective Marine Corps commandant.

He first went to sea in 1881 on the flagship of the European Squadron, the USS *Lancaster,* as executive officer to the fleet marine officer, Henry Clay Cochrane, the distinguished Marine Corps veteran and reformer. After a year of port calls in various Mediterranean cities, Cochrane and Waller observed as the British Royal Navy bombarded Alexandria, the opening conflagration in Britain's suppression of an Egyptian nationalist rebellion. As commanding officer of a detachment of marines aboard the USS *Nipsic,* Waller returned to Alexandria in September 1882, when he got his first look at war with no quarter. He saw Arab cavalry parade the severed heads of captured Bengali Lancers on their spears. Every Arab horseman captured after that received the same fate.

Waller came home to the Marine Barracks in Norfolk in 1884. He married the following year and started a family that would ensure the Waller name's prominence in the country's armed forces. His three sons would all have illustrious careers in the military. His eldest, Littleton Jr., would retire a major general in the Marine Corps. Another son reached the rank of colonel, and another would be a navy rear admiral.

After returning to Norfolk Waller gained increasing recognition and respect over the next decade and a half for his demonstrated competence in various shore assignments and overseas deployments. He was promoted to captain two years before the war with Spain and returned from the war with the praise and respect of his superiors. He spent a dull year as a recruiter in Norfolk until, to his great relief, he was promoted to major and given command of a battalion of marines headed for the Philippines in November 1899.

The duty was barely more exciting at Cavite naval station in Manila Bay, where his battalion spent most of its time guarding a coal heap as tropical diseases thinned its numbers. Waller fell ill with malaria in March. By the time he recovered, Major General Elwell Otis, who had replaced General Merritt as military governor, had repeatedly asserted the rebellion was nearly finished after suffering several early defeats. Waller's battalion was ordered to the island of Guam.

Otis appears to have been a fool who

rarely left his palatial quarters in Manila to ascertain the war's progress firsthand. And his stubborn belligerence bore much of the responsibility for starting the war. He had rejected a peace proposal from Emilio Aguinaldo in the early days of the conflict, insisting that "fighting, having begun, must go on to the grim end." Otis seems to have disliked one of his division commanders, Henry Lawton, who had commanded the 2nd Division in Cuba and led the fight at El Caney. Lawton's early successes in the field, which drew praise from President William McKinley, and his popularity among Americans and Filipinos must have incited his superior's jealousy.

Unlike Lawton, Otis thought little about how to wage war in a manner that wouldn't make completely ironic McKinley's stated preference for the "benevolent assimilation" of Filipinos. He tolerated atrocities committed by American soldiers not just against the insurgents, or *insurrectos* as they were known, but against civilians as well. News of incidents of shocking brutality reached official Washington, and the government demanded that Otis punish the perpetrators and take measures to assure similar breakdowns in discipline wouldn't occur in the future. Otis dismissed the accusations and took steps to suppress information of other atrocities.

Despite his manifest failings, Otis's command of VIII Corps lasted nearly two years. The war, which had begun as a conventional conflict in a battle for the capital, became a guerrilla war, as the *insurrectos,* like guerrilla fighters before and after them, tried to outlast the patience of the colonial power. General Lawton might have succeeded Otis had he lived long enough. Lawton, who had commanded the cavalry troop that captured the Apache Geronimo, was killed in action in December 1899 in a firefight with insurgents commanded by a Filipino general also named Geronimo.

Just before he set sail for Guam, Waller received new orders instructing his battalion to join an international expeditionary force organized by eight world powers — Britain, France, Austria, Germany, Italy, Russia, Japan, and the United States — to "liberate" Peking from the Chinese Imperial Army and the fierce Chinese nationalists whom Western missionaries called Boxers for their mystical devotion to the martial arts.

A large foreign armada had gathered off Taku, China, as the Boxers conducted a bloody terror campaign, burning foreign diplomatic missions and Christian churches, murdering missionaries and converts. Waller's battalion came ashore at Taku on June 19, 1900, and set out the next day to relieve the besieged city of Tientsin. They joined a column of Russian infantry, and the combined force, numbering fewer than six hundred men, with Russians in the lead and marines in the rear, reached the outskirts of Tientsin on the morning of June 21. There they encountered a Chinese force three times their number. The Russians quickly fell back under fire, leaving the marines to bear the brunt of the attack. Waller's men fought into the afternoon, only to retreat in good order, repulsing repeated flanking attacks until they reached defensible positions. Four marines were killed in action and their bodies had to be left behind. The day was a temporary setback saved from being a complete disaster by the marines' steady professionalism and the cool competence of their commanding officer. Two days later the marines joined a larger allied force, this time composed mostly of British soldiers, and took Tientsin after an eight-hour battle.

Waller's marines distinguished themselves in a number of engagements in and around

Tientsin, gaining a reputation as one of the hardest fighting units in the allied force. In August they joined the allied march to Peking, fighting a series of battles along the way. Additional army and marine units had augmented the American force by then, which had been placed under the command of the recently arrived Major General Adna Chaffee, a hard-bitten Civil War veteran and Indian fighter, who suppressed restive native populations with more force than required. He liked to make a lasting impression. Advance elements of the allied force entered Peking on August 14. The city's foreign quarter was liberated that afternoon, and the Chinese Imperial Court fled the Forbidden City. By the afternoon of August 16 the battle for Peking was over, and so was the Boxer Rebellion.

The allies imposed a harsh peace, and the brutal reprisals that followed nurtured the resentment of Chinese nationalists for decades. Captured Boxers were usually executed without trial; some were beheaded and their heads impaled on the gates of foreign missions. Palaces were plundered and civilians killed indiscriminately. The worst of the atrocities was the work of other nations' soldiers, mostly Russians and Germans, although Americans appear to have participated in some of it and certainly in the widespread looting. Waller witnessed the mayhem, but there is no evidence his marines significantly contributed to it. Two years later he would have reason to recall the summary executions the allies ordered in China. Did that include orders by American commanders? Waller did not say. But he had not ordered any executions, and presumably his marines acted with however much restraint their commanding officer expected of them.

Waller left China in October 1900 with a brevet promotion to lieutenant colonel, the fulsome praise of his superior officers and allied commanders, his reputation ascendant, the commandant's office in prospect, and a lifelong friendship begun with a future Marine Corps legend, Smedley Butler, the massively tattooed, cockfight-loving, heavily decorated "Fighting Quaker." When he returned to the Philippines in 1901 Waller would add new successes to his reputation, and almost destroy it.

The Island of Samar lies in the middle of the Philippine archipelago just northeast of Leyte Island. Prior to the war Samar was the center of the Philippine hemp trade. In 1901 it became the center of hostilities.

There had been little fighting on the island the year before. Most of its interior was inaccessible; with few roads, dense jungles, and untracked mountains it was a safe haven for the local insurgents and their commander, Vicente Lukbán. American troops stationed on Samar were confined to coastal cities.

By the time General Chaffee, late of the China Relief Expedition, assumed command of VIII Corps in the Philippines, most Americans, including a recently reelected William McKinley and his vice president Theodore Roosevelt, believed the war was winding down. Emilio Aguinaldo had been captured in March 1901 and had declared his acceptance of American authority. On July 4 General Arthur MacArthur, father of Douglas, who had replaced the unlamented Otis in May 1900, transferred governing authority in the Philippines to a civilian administration headed by future president William Howard Taft and gave command of VIII Corps to Chaffee. Chaffee didn't share MacArthur and Taft's view that the insurrection was finished. He didn't care for either man, particularly Taft, whose advocacy of lenient tactics that wouldn't alienate the Filipinos Chaffee thought naïve and feckless. He set about pacifying with all necessary force provinces where insurgents still posed a threat or could pose one in the future. He sent two fellow cavalrymen from the Indian wars to Luzon Province, Brigadier General Franklin Bell and Colonel Jacob Hurd Smith. They would fight a counterinsurgency on Luzon using tactics they seldom troubled to hide from the press and that were anything but lenient, including summary executions, herding civilian populations into concentration camps, burning villages they suspected — with or without evidence — of having sympathy with the insurgents, and an interrogation practice called the "water cure," which is similar to waterboarding.

Insurrectos controlled the interiors of Samar and Leyte Island, mostly because of the expense and manpower it would require to establish American authority in the roadless wilderness that existed beyond the islands' coastlines. Chaffee would create a new military sector encompassing the two islands and allow the harshest pacification policies yet in what would prove to be the last campaign of the war.

In a prelude to that campaign American infantry was deployed to several of Samar's ports to interdict supplies intended for the insurgents. On August 11 the seventy-four soldiers of Company C of the 9th U.S. Infantry Regiment, most of them veterans of Cuba and China, disembarked from a coastal steamer and established a base in the town of Balangiga on the southern coast of Samar. They were commanded by a twenty-eight-year-old West Point graduate, Captain Thomas Connell. According to the letters some of the soldiers sent home, they were warmly welcomed by the local population.

The welcome lasted about a month, until the locals began to resent the treatment they received from the officers and men of Company C, which included forced labor, the confiscation of food stores, and the molestation of a young girl by two drunk soldiers. Relations became steadily more hostile, and Balingiga's outwardly friendly mayor, Pedro Abayan, and police chief, Valeriano Abanador, were soon conspiring with Vicente Lukbán's guerrillas.

Only four sentries were on duty in the early morning of Sunday, September 28. The rest of the men were unarmed, eating breakfast in mess tents. The company's officers, Captain Connell, his second-in-command, First Lieutenant Edward Bumpus, and the company surgeon, Major Richard Griswold, were still in their quarters in a convent. Women and children were nowhere evident, nor was the town priest; they had disappeared into the jungle. Men disguised as women carrying coffins they claimed held the bodies of children lost to a cholera epidemic had gained entry into the Catholic church the night before.

At 6:20, one of the sentries was crossing the town plaza on his way to his post when he encountered Police Chief Abanador, who suddenly wrenched his rifle away from him and slammed the butt into his head. As the sentry fell and Abanador shouted a signal, the church bells began tolling, and guerrillas armed with *bolos* (a long machetelike knife, the guerrilla's weapon of choice), which had been secreted in the otherwise empty coffins, poured out of the sanctuary and a contingent raced toward the convent. Men who had been pressed into work at various public works projects drew concealed weapons and set upon the soldiers. Others joining in the slaughter hastened to the plaza from barrios just outside town. Few of the soldiers were able to retrieve their rifles. Those who did had to fight off swarms of attackers and suffered multiple wounds to their extremities from slashing *bolos*.

After an hour of hand-to-hand fighting,

most soldiers having no other weapons than their fists or an iron pan or a chair leg they used for a club, the Americans who managed to retrieve their rifles and revolvers drove off their attackers, who got away with most of the company's weapons and ammunition. By then forty-four soldiers were dead or dying, twenty-two others were seriously wounded, and four men were missing. Their assailants had lost twenty-eight killed. The bodies of all three officers were found hacked to pieces. Two had been killed in their rooms. Captain Connell had managed to escape the convent but had died in the plaza. Only a few soldiers were able-bodied by the time they set off with the wounded in canoes. They paddled several hours until they reached Basey, another southern coast port, where Company G of the 9th Infantry was based.

The next day Company G's commander, Captain Edwin Bookmiller, led a party of volunteers back to Balangiga, hauling a Gatling gun and a Hotchkiss field artillery piece with them. They found the bodies of the fallen Americans strewn about the plaza. All had been mutilated. Captain Connell had been beheaded. The soldiers had interrupted a funeral in progress for the Filipino dead. Bookmiller had his soldiers round up twenty local men, who were ordered to haul the Filipino bodies out of the uncovered graves and replace them with the American dead. After presiding over a brief graveside service for the Americans, Bookmiller had the Filipino dead piled in a heap and burned. Then he ordered the town put to the torch and handed over the Filipino gravediggers to survivors of Company C, who shot them dead. Later that day Bookmiller wired a report to Manila: "Buried dead, burned town, returned Basey."

That was not sufficient retaliation, however, for Adna Chaffee. The 9th Infantry had served under him in China, and he meant to avenge it. He blamed the ambush on the "false humanitarianism" and "soft molly-coddling of treacherous natives" practiced by his predecessor, MacArthur, and Chaffee's civilian rival in Manila, Taft. Nor was it enough for most Americans, who regarded the massacre at Balangiga as the most notorious military disaster since the massacre at the Little Bighorn. Nor did it placate their new president, Roosevelt, sworn into office two weeks earlier after McKinley succumbed to the two gunshot wounds in his stomach he had received from the anarchist Leon Czolgosz. Roosevelt was close to Taft and might have shared at least some of Taft's concern that the harsh tactics advocated by Chaffee would prove counter-productive. But he couldn't afford to let the war he had been repeatedly assured was over drag on and claim more American casualties. He ordered Chaffee to employ "in unmistakable terms" the "most stern measures to pacify Samar," which Chaffee was prepared to do with celerity and with the help of his old friend Jacob Smith. Chaffee recalled Smith from Luzon, handed him his star as a newly promoted brigadier, and ordered him to Samar to "get the savage island under control."

According to some, "Hell Roaring Jake" Smith received his nickname for having a booming voice that could be heard over the din of the battlefield despite its owner's slight stature. Others claim it was bestowed to mock Smith's habitual bombast. Whatever its meaning, its owner doesn't seem to have objected to it. Smith had a long and checkered army career. He suffered a disabling wound at Shiloh, which kept him out of subsequent Civil War battles. For the balance of the war he served as a recruiting officer, in which occupation he enriched himself by pocketing the bounties paid for freed slaves he provided to fill recruitment quotas. Scandals seemed to follow him throughout his career, much of it spent in the West fighting Indians. (He is said to have been present at the Wounded Knee Massacre in 1890.) His persistent misconduct and notorious attempts to cover it up were often reprimanded, and on at least two occasions he was brought before courts-martial. Yet he had enough well-placed connections that he remained in uniform for forty years. He led a battalion into battle at the San Juan Heights and took a Spanish bullet in the chest. The wound wasn't fatal or disabling, and it won him a regimental command.

Smith made no secret of his intentions on Samar. In a notice sent to all post commanders in his sector and made known to the press, he declared that he intended to "wage war in the sharpest and most decisive manner": "Every native will henceforth be treated as an enemy until he has conclusively shown that he is a friend."

To help accomplish this task, Smith asked for a battalion of marines in addition to the two army battalions Chaffee had sent with him. The navy's commanding officer in the Philippines, Rear Admiral Fred Rogers, offered Colonel Waller's battalion. That was a fortuitous turn of events for Waller. He had spent much of his time since returning from

China in a peaceful and boring backwater of the war, the naval base at Subic Bay, where he seems to have gotten drunk one time too many. An admiral had pronounced him unfit for duty and suspended him for ten days. Samar was an opportunity to regain his good reputation.

Waller's battalion boarded the cruiser USS *New York* and arrived at Carbalogen on Samar's west coast on October 24. His new commanding officer was waiting there to brief him on his assignment. Smith told Waller the marines would be responsible for pacifying the southern half of the island, where Balangiga and Basey were located and where Smith seemed to consider the entire native population to be insurgents. Then Waller listened to an emphatic Smith order him to murder men, women, and children. "I want no prisoners," Smith explained. "I want you to kill and burn, the more you kill and burn the better it will please me. I want all persons killed who are capable of bearing arms in actual hostilities against the United States."

"I would like to know the limit of age to respect, sir," Waller queried in response.

"Ten years," Smith replied.

"Persons of ten years and older are those designated as being capable of bearing arms?" the marine asked incredulously.

"Yes," Smith confirmed.

As American columns swept around the island's coastline Smith's decrees were put into effect. Villages suspected of harboring enemy fighters were put to the torch, their food supplies destroyed, crops burned, and livestock shot. Suspected guerrillas were executed on the spot or tortured for information and then shot. Concentration camps were created for the dispossessed. To interdict the insurgents' food supplies, trade between Samar and Leyte was curtailed, and any native "found passing between these two islands . . . [was] fired upon and killed." Local officials in the south were given a week to turn over anyone who had participated in the Balangiga massacre and all captured arms or see their towns destroyed. No prisoners were taken in firefights with guerrillas. Of the thousands of Filipinos killed in the campaign, many, probably most, were noncombatants.

The slaughter of all natives over the age of ten did not occur, however, because most of Smith's subordinate officers ignored the order. After their conference aboard the *New York,* Smith traveled with Waller first to Basey, where Waller would make his headquarters, and then to Balangiga, where they were appalled to discover that hogs had dug up the graves of the American dead. A raging Smith turned to Waller and repeated his command to "kill and burn."

Waller left two companies of marines in Balangiga under the command of Captain David Porter. Before he returned to Basey with the nearly hysterical Smith, he took his subordinate aside and countermanded the order: "Porter, I've had instructions to kill everyone over ten years old. But we are not making war on women and children, only men capable of bearing arms. Keep that in mind no matter what other orders you receive."

Excluding women and children still allowed a wide scope for making war, however. Waller instructed his marines to "place no confidence in the natives and punish treachery with death."

The marines initially limited their patrols to clearing the jungle along the coast, and though they had little success locating and engaging many of the enemy, Waller could report that after eleven days they had burned "255 buildings, shot 13 carabaos [water buffalo] and killed 39 people." When they started probing the interior, skirmishes with the enemy were more frequent, and the marines picked up a trail to an enemy stronghold on the cliffs above the Sohoton River, where Lukbán had made his headquarters. Waller planned an attack using three columns. Porter led one column overland from Balangiga, Captain Hiram Bearss marched a second overland from Basey, and Waller led an amphibious assault team up the river, towing a raft that carried a cannon. The three columns were to rendezvous on November 16 and stage a combined water and land assault on the cliffs.

Porter and Bearss got there first. Waller's party was held up downriver by enemy defenses, and his two subordinate commanders decided to make the assault without him. Porter turned to Sergeant John Quick, who had received the Medal of Honor for his actions in Cuba, and told him to lay down covering fire with his Colt machine gun as marines scaled the two-hundred-foot cliffs. When they reached the top, they killed the guerrillas they could catch, estimated to be about thirty men, while the others fled into the jungle. The marines didn't suffer a single casualty. They destroyed the camp before fatigue and dwindling rations obliged them to make the difficult trek back to base.

The victory was impressive, but not as important as a boasting Smith and American newspapers made it out to be. It would take more than one successful battle for the Americans to pacify the island's forbidding interior. Both Smith and Waller recognized this. Smith's instructions to Waller, who was planning another expedition, sent by un-signed note, were to make the swamps, jungles, and mountains of Samar's interior "a howling wilderness."

The marines spent most of December working their way eastward along the south-ern coast, skirmishing occasionally with small bands of guerrillas and destroying vil-lages along the way. "Unless we meet some-thing much more serious than we have dur-ing this march," Waller reported to Smith, "I think it safe to say that the southern part of the island of Samar is as quiet as many parts of Luzon, where peace is supposed to reign." Smith wanted the marines to venture deeper into the interior and cut a trail from east to west across the island. Waller ap-peared eager to do it. His famed "March across Samar" began on December 28 at the army base in Lanang on Samar's east coast. The base commander, Captain James Pickering, tried and failed to dissuade him from making the march. Two previous at-tempts had been made, and both had turned back, daunted by the impenetrable terrain.

Waller brushed aside Pickering's pessimism. In bright sunshine after days of heavy rains, the party of six officers, including Captains Porter and Bearss, fifty enlisted marines led by the capable Sergeant Quick, two Filipino scouts called Slim and Smoke, and thirty-three cargadores (native bearers) set out in long canoes up the Lanang River.

Waller planned to travel by river as far as possible and then hope to find a trail the Spanish were thought to have blazed that would take them to a supply camp Waller had ordered established near the scene of the marines' earlier triumph, the Sohoton cliffs. From there they would travel by boat to Basey, where the expedition would end. They made seventeen miles on the river the first day while the weather held, although not many miles westward. They paddled another eight the next day before encountering rapids at the village of Lagitao. They camped there for the night and set out on foot the following morning. The rains returned and the terrain proved as daunting as Pickering had warned. The marines made little progress. They were forced repeatedly to ford the winding, swollen river, their uniforms constantly soaked and covered in leeches. There was no trail to speak of, Spanish or otherwise, and they had to hack their way through the dense undergrowth, which grabbed at their boots and tripped them as they climbed hills steeper than they had expected to encounter. It seemed they were forced to march several miles in every direction to progress a single mile westward. They encountered not a single guerrilla or any other human being.

Because they were far off schedule Waller cut their rations after the third day, and cut them again after the fourth. On New Year's Eve 1902 the rains prevented them from lighting cooking fires. By New Year's, the fifth day, all were exhausted and hungry. That day and the next they climbed one mountain after another. Their situation was dire, and Waller thought their survival in doubt. Starved, their wet uniforms in shreds, their boots destroyed and their feet bloodied, covered in sores and leech bites, the men were growing ill and despondent. Surprisingly, given he was the oldest man on the march, Waller was in better shape than most. He decided to proceed to Sohoton with two of the lieutenants and thirteen of the fittest marines. The rest of the company, under Captain Porter's command, would follow their trail at a slower pace. When Waller reached the supply camp he would send a relief party to them.

Accounts of what transpired next are somewhat confused. Some have it that, after discovering the way ahead was as difficult as the terrain they had already traversed, Waller sent word to Porter to build rafts and try to navigate the river back to Lanang. Others claim a feverish Porter despaired of ever reaching their destination and decided on his own to build the rafts; when they wouldn't float, he chose to march back to Lanang. All accounts agree, though, that Porter dispatched Captain Bearss and an enlisted man to catch up to Waller's column and inform him of his decision.

By the times Bearss reached them, Waller's party were enjoying their first bit of good fortune. They had wandered into a grove with sweet potatoes, bananas, and coconuts and were busy consuming their bounty. When Waller learned Porter was going to march his men back to Lanang, he sent one of his bearers, Victor, with a message not to attempt it. Instead Porter was to follow Waller's trail to the clearing, where they would find food, and remain there. Waller would press on to the Sohoton and return as quickly as possible with food, fresh uniforms, and boots. But Victor never delivered the message. He returned to the column as it made camp, claiming that he had encountered insurgents. That night Victor attempted to steal Waller's *bolo* as its suspicious owner pretended to be asleep. To Victor's surprise, Waller drew his revolver and had him placed under arrest.

Waller assumed Porter would change his mind about returning to Lanang once he had started back overland, so he continued on, expecting Porter would follow his trail. On January 5 the marines stumbled onto a hut inhibited by five Filipinos. They pressed into service a young boy who claimed he could take them to Basey. He led them across a river to the elusive Spanish trail, which they followed across another river and through a valley to a third river, the Cadacan, where, on the morning of the 6th, after ten days in hell, they encountered the resupply party coming up the river on a navy cutter. "The men," Waller recorded, "realizing that all was over and that they were safe once more near home, gave up. Some quietly wept; others laughed hysterically."

They reached Basey that afternoon, and a relief party was organized and sent off on the cutter back up the Cadacan. They made camp at the place where the marines had found the Filipinos' hut, and Waller joined them there on the 8th. For eight days they searched for Porter's column until, their rations depleted and Waller having succumbed to fever, they reluctantly returned to Basey.

Porter had not followed Waller's trail. He had taken the seven marines in the best shape, including Quick, and six bearers on what seemed a suicidal attempt to retrace their circuitous route back to Lanang. The rest of the marines were in too poor condition to make the march; they remained behind with thirteen bearers under the command of Lieutenant Alexander Williams.

Porter thought they might reach Lanang in four days; it took them eight. That they made it at all was a Shackleton-like feat of endurance, walking barefoot in constant rain with only what they could forage to sustain them, repeatedly crossing raging streams and dragging themselves over mountains. He had to leave four men at the place where the original column had left their boats; they were too weak to continue. The rest of the party reached Lanang on January 11.

Captain Pickering immediately assembled a rescue party commanded by a young army lieutenant, Kenneth Williams, but torrential rains prevented it from navigating the river for two days. Finally, on the morning of January 14, Williams, ten soldiers, an army

308

surgeon, and a number of Filipino porters set out to find the lost marines.

The other Lieutenant Williams and his party had followed after Porter as best they could, many so weak from hunger they were delirious. Ten men, one after another, dropped to the jungle floor and surrendered to their fate. The rest trudged on hopelessly, up and down mountains, with nothing to eat but a few wild tubers, while the most stouthearted encouraged them on. The marines suspected the bearers were hiding food and letting them die. Some of the Filipinos had refused to surrender their *bolos* at night, as they were required to do. And then three of them mutinied, refusing Williams's order to cut firewood. When Williams drew his revolver, one of them slashed his arm with a *bolo* before running off into the bush with the other two. A marine coming to Williams's rescue raised his carbine but was too weak to work the bolt. The ten remaining Filipinos, including the scout Slim, neither joined the mutiny nor intervened to stop it, and Williams feared greater treachery, which he would be too weak to prevent.

The army rescue party was battling through rapids on the morning of January 18 when they discovered ten marines, delirious and nearly naked, lying in a clearing next to the river. They had been sent ahead by Alexander Williams, who, along with the nine others, unable to walk, remained at the scene of the previous night's mutiny on the top of a nearby mountain. A few of the soldiers stayed with the ten marines at the river while the rest hacked their way up the mountain hoping to find the others in time. They did, and just barely: Williams and his group appeared to be within hours of death. But by nightfall the rescue party had got everyone back to Lanang. That night a barely conscious Williams reported the mutiny to Captain Porter, who had all ten Filipinos arrested.

Porter sent the bearers to Waller, who was still recovering at Basey. They were accompanied by Quick, who had had altercations with some of the bearers earlier in the expedition. Porter and Williams recommended they all be executed; so did Quick, who told Waller he "would shoot them all down like mad dogs," which is what Waller ordered done with no further adjudication other than a brief interrogation of the prisoners. That afternoon the ten, along with Victor, were shot to death by a firing squad. Their bodies were left to lie in the town square as a warning to the locals.

When recovered from his fever, Waller sent a telegram to Smith to inform him of what he had done. "It became necessary to expend eleven prisoners. Ten who were implicated in the attack on Lieutenant Williams and one who plotted against me."

Unfortunately for Waller and Smith, accounts of some of the atrocities committed on Samar and criticism of Smith's undisguised preference for cruel reprisals over winning hearts and minds had reached the American newspapers and were being used by prominent anti-imperialists to stoke opposition to the war. The Senate convened hearings and called Taft as a witness, who almost casually conceded that Americans had used torture and had shot some people who had not deserved it. In the uproar that followed the hearing, Roosevelt, Secretary of War Elihu Root, and Taft scrambled to counter the belief that American soldiers at the direction of senior commanders were systematically abusing the rules of war. The guerrillas were an especially treacherous enemy, but incidents of cruelty beyond the pale were punished, they assured the public. Reports of atrocities were still coming in, however, and the hearings continued and public outcry mounted.

In early March Secretary Root sent General Chaffee a cable instructing him to stop the torture and summary executions of Filipinos. Chaffee had already begun worrying that the savagery he had allowed and, one could argue, encouraged after Balangiga, and which the obtuse Smith had practically bragged about, had fallen out of official favor. He informed Root he had felt it necessary to investigate reports of unsanctioned executions on Samar, and he had made discoveries that obliged him reluctantly to order the arrest and court-martial of Major Littleton Waller.

Waller's battalion had been relieved on February 26 and returned to Cavite in Manila Bay to cheering crowds. Upon arrival Waller, still in his dress uniform, reported promptly to General Chaffee, who informed him he was under arrest for the murder of eleven men and asked for his sword. When the news broke, Waller became the number one target of the antiwar press. One headline called him the "Butcher of Samar," and all manner of atrocities, many of them pure invention, were attributed to him.

The court-martial, composed of seven army and six marine officers and presided over by Army Brigadier General William Bisbee, convened on March 17, 1902, and would last nearly a month. One of the marine officers was an old rival; two others were friends. Waller didn't know any of the army officers. It was probably for their benefit that he chose a West Pointer as one of his defense counsels. The judge advocate prosecuting the case was also a West Pointer, Major Henry Kingsbury.

Waller's counsels first argued that the army didn't have jurisdiction over the case since Waller was no longer subordinate to General Smith when he was arrested. General Bisbee, who appeared sympathetic to Waller, agreed the army probably didn't have jurisdiction but referred the final decision to General Chaffee, who consulted with Root before ordering the trial to proceed.

The prosecution maintained that the facts of the case were not in dispute. Waller had ordered the execution of the Filipinos without a trial or much of an investigation. He had not asked Smith for permission and had informed his superior of his action only after the fact. As evidence Waller had assumed authority he didn't lawfully possess, Major Kingsbury quoted from the instruction to punish "treachery with death" that Waller had sent his officers just after the battalion arrived in Samar. "Avenge our late comrades in North China, the murdered men of the 9th United States Infantry," he had added.

Waller claimed his actions were consistent with orders given him by Smith, although the defense didn't raise Smith's verbal directive to "kill and burn." They were also consistent with the authority granted to an area commander under General Orders Number 100, a Civil War measure signed by President Lincoln that permitted executions without trial of spies, saboteurs, and guerrillas when apprehended in the act of treachery. Captains Porter and Bearss appeared for the defense, as did a still recovering Alexander Williams, who dramatically recalled his ordeal for the court. Under cross-examination Porter conceded he had not believed the bearers were a threat when he left Williams. Bearss confirmed the unfortunate Victor had made an attempt on Waller's life, but all he could provide to substantiate the allegation was the fact that the Filipino had been apprehended in possession of Waller's *bolo.* The surviving scout, Smoke, was also called as a witness, and he testified that Victor had wanted to kill Waller and that the bearers had wanted to kill Williams and his men rather than share food with them.

Waller took the stand in his own defense and claimed he had issued his directive about punishing treachery with death only after conferring with Smith. But still he did not elaborate the details of their conversation. Nor would he have, it seems, had Smith not been called as a rebuttal witness and denied he had given his area commanders the authority to punish treachery with summary executions. "Did you ever indicate to Major Waller that 'he held power of life and death' over prisoners?" Kingsbury asked him. "No," Smith lied.

Waller returned to the stand the next day and revealed every detail of the seething Smith's instructions to him, including the order to kill every man, woman, and child over the age of ten, which Waller had ignored. The sensation his testimony caused was immediate and overwhelming. Explosive headlines appeared in newspapers across the United States: "KILL ALL"; "SAMAR TO BE MADE A HOWLING WILDERNESS. KILL AND BURN."

In testimony he gave the day after his shocking disclosures, Waller did not excuse his actions based on the ordeal his battalion had suffered, on the men he had lost, on his illness, or on any extenuating circumstance. Neither did he shift the entire responsibility to Smith. Rather he insisted he had acted lawfully irrespective of his superior's orders. His familiarity with the rules of war and his experiences in Samar and elsewhere convinced him he had acted properly to safeguard the marines under his command. "I do not beg for mercy or plead extenuation," he told the court. "I was either right or wrong. If I was wrong, give me the whole, full complete sentence required by the law. If I was right then I am entitled to the most honorable acquittal."

The "full complete sentence" for a murder conviction was death, of course. But Waller had little cause to be worried after his shocking disclosures that such a fate would be his. He was acquitted by a vote of eleven to two a half hour after Kingsbury's closing statement blamed the horrors and casualties suffered on the march across Samar on Waller's "foolhardiness" and poor planning, and not on the Filipino bearers, who had been cruelly denied the protections they were owed by the country they had served.

The Roosevelt administration, under pressure from growing numbers of war critics in the wake of Waller's damning testimony, ordered a "searching and exhaustive investigation" into army practices in the Philippines. The investigation resulted in Chaffee's referring charges against five officers, including Hell Roaring Jake Smith, who was found guilty of "conduct prejudicial to good order and discipline." He was sentenced to be reprimanded, but Roosevelt demanded his resignation. The army would have to manage without him somehow.

Littleton Waller Tazewell Waller served another two decades in the Marine Corps. He was never appointed commandant, as he once expected to be, and it seems likely his court-martial figured to some extent in that disappointment. But otherwise his career was not adversely affected by his experiences in the nasty little war in the Philippines. He held other important commands during America's comparatively brief history of empire building. He suppressed an uprising in Panama in 1904, where construction of the new canal had just begun. He commanded the occupation of Vera Cruz, Mexico, in 1914. A year later he put down a rebellion in Haiti. His old friend Smedley Butler served under him in all three actions and received Medals of Honor for heroism in Mexico and Haiti.

Waller was judged to be too old to serve in France, as were almost all officers of his generation, but all three of his sons served in the war. His oldest received the Navy

Cross and would rise in the Corps as far as his father had. Waller commanded a marine base at the Philadelphia Naval Yard during the war and retired a major general in 1920. As is often noted, during his forty-year career he served in almost every major engagement where marines were deployed and was proud to have avoided a desk assignment until the end of his career. He preferred to command marines in the field, and for the most part he did.

He suffered a stroke in 1923, and three years later the man Smedley Butler called "the greatest soldier I have ever known" died from pneumonia while on a visit to Atlantic City. A newspaper obituary paid tribute to his many qualities and achievements, noting near the end, almost as an afterthought, "The General was a disciplinarian. In 1902 . . . he was ordered before a court-martial to defend himself against the charge of executing Filipinos without trial, but was exonerated."

Corporal Elton Mackin, who fought in every major Marine Corps battle in World War I, in a portrait taken after the armistice.

CHAPTER SEVEN:
LOST, SCARED KIDS
A LONG WAY FROM HOME

Elton "Lucky" Mackin, a marine, survived one of the most dangerous assignments in the trenches of World War I.

It was now or never. With the collapse of the Russian army and the success of the Bolshevik coup d'état, the war in the East was finished. Germany could bring an additional fifty infantry divisions to the Western Front, almost three-quarters of a million men. The Kaiser now had 192 divisions in the West, giving Germany a considerable numerical advantage over the French and British. But that was all the Kaiser had. There were no more German reserves. And America had entered the war.

Major General John "Black Jack" Pershing and the first wave of the American Expeditionary Force, elements of the army's 1st Division, arrived in France in June 1917. To the despair of French and British commanders, Pershing insisted on taking the time to create an American field army rather than pour poorly trained battalions into depleted French and British ranks and see them fed piecemeal into the meat-grinder attacks across no-man's-land that had incited the French Army to mutiny that spring. The 1st Division did not arrive at the front until October. By early 1918 there were no more than four combat-ready American divisions in France. But thousands more soldiers were arriving every day, and with the institution of the draft in the United States, two million Americans would eventually serve in France. A million doughboys would be there by May. The German commander General Erich Ludendorff knew he had to press his advantage that spring or see it matched soon after and then be overwhelmed by a steady stream of inexperienced but very game and very many Americans. He knew he had to win the war before Pershing built his army.

The first of a series of German offensives, Operation Michael, commenced with a massive, five-hour artillery barrage and gas attack before dawn on March 31, 1918, along a fifty-mile front encompassing the old Somme battlefield that was defended by the weakest of Britain's armies, the Fifth.

The Germans had seventy-two divisions to the Fifth Army's twenty-six. The former swarmed out of their trenches with shock troops, called "Stormtroopers," in the vanguard in a massed, rapid thrust. They punched a hole in the British lines, a salient the Germans hoped to expand until they cut off the British from the French and pushed the former into the sea. The first day had been a rout, and bloody. Ten thousand German soldiers were killed, and three times that number were wounded. But by the end of the fourth day it appeared the onslaught might succeed in separating French and British armies. By April 4 the Germans were just a few miles outside of Amiens.

But the advance slowed. The Germans outran their supply lines and were no longer massed in one compact advance but were striking in three places. A final German attack aimed at taking Amiens failed. The next day the British mounted a successful counterattack. The first offensive had run its course, and Ludendorff called it off. While Operation Michael had captured over a thousand square miles and plunged twenty-five miles inside British lines, it hadn't achieved its strategic objectives. And it had cost Germany more than a quarter million dead and wounded, many of whom were from the Kaiser's elite assault divisions.

Ludendorff quickly launched a second strike, this time against the British lines in Flanders to the north, its objective to drive the British past Ypres to the English Channel. This advance too was initially successful. But the British defenses in that sector were stronger than those around the Somme, as strong as any sector in the Allied front. By the end of April Ludendorff had to concede the Flanders offensive had failed to achieve its objectives, and German casualties in the six weeks of fighting exceeded four hundred thousand.

Determined to press what remained of his advantage before it was lost for good, Ludendorff shifted his focus to the south, where the extreme right of the British line joined the extreme left of the French line. The Germans attacked south and west from positions they had occupied in their March advance. In their path were sixteen Allied divisions, including British divisions depleted and exhausted from the fighting in March and April. The objective was to open the road to Paris and lure enough British reserves to the front that defenses in the north were hollowed and the Germans could resume their advance to the Channel.

The Third Battle of the Aisne began on May 27 with the heaviest artillery barrage of the spring and another poison gas attack. The infantry attack that followed was swift and successful, advancing thirteen miles on the first day as battered British divisions and poorly led French forces from Soissons to Rheims virtually collapsed. The Germans obtained their initial objective: the capture of the Chemin des Dames ridge. But rather than consolidate their gains and wait for the attack in the north to resume, as originally planned, they kept going, and by the end of the first week Stormtroopers were within forty-five miles of the French capital. As they reached the Marne River, however, problems of resupply and replacements that had plagued the earlier offensives began slowing their advance.

The Allies staged counterattacks on the German salient but were careful not to overcommit their reserve forces, as Ludendorff expected them to do, a discretion they were able to exercise thanks to the U.S. divisions Pershing had finally sent to the front. The 1st Division had proven its worth by capturing the little village of Cantigny near Amiens on the second day of the offensive. The 2nd and 3rd divisions arrived on June 1 to stop forward elements of the German advance crossing the Marne. The 4th Marine Brigade, commanded by an army brigadier, James Harbord, constituted half of the 2nd Division and included the 5th and 6th marine regiments.

There were only fifteen thousand active-duty U.S. marines in 1917, and they were scattered around the globe. Honest commanders in all services, including Pershing, acknowledged them as the best American fighting force in existence. As marines in the 5th Regiment were digging in near the village of Lucy-le-Bocage on the afternoon of June 1, retreating French soldiers streamed past them. A French officer instructed a company commander, Captain Lloyd Williams, a Virginian who had served in Cuba and the Philippines, that the German advance was unstoppable and he had better take his men to the rear. "Retreat?" Williams answered in a response that has figured prominently in marine lore ever since. "Hell, we just got here." At the end of the marines' first major engagement in World War I, the German soldiers who fought them nicknamed them *Teufel Hunden,* Devil Dogs.

The Americans successfully counterattacked at the river town of Château-Thierry on June 3 and 4 and pushed the Germans back across the river. Two days later the 4th Marine Brigade drew a tougher assignment: they were ordered to take a two-hundred-acre, densely wooded hunting preserve five miles northwest of Château-Thierry. Belleau Wood was not much more than a mile in length and a thousand yards across at its widest point. The order to attack had come suddenly from a French corps commander, and there hadn't been a thorough reconnaissance of the area. The French reported the enemy was present in small numbers in the northeast section of the Wood. But since June 2 elite advance units of Germany's 347th Division from the army group officially commanded by the Kaiser's son, Crown Prince Wilhelm, were entrenched throughout Belleau Wood. They would fight tenaciously to hold it. In front of them a field of waist-high wheat rippled in the breeze. A little to the west, a small elevation, designated Hill 142, looked down on the Wood.

The Battle for Belleau Wood began before dawn on June 6 with an attack on Hill 142 by the 1st Battalion, 5th Marines led by Major Julius Turrill. At zero hour only two of the battalion's four rifle companies, the 67th and the 49th, were in position to make the attack on time. Bayonets fixed, they charged toward their objective in waves as German machine guns and artillery cut them down. They gained control of the Hill early that afternoon, turning back several German counterattacks, but Turrill's battalion was decimated in the effort, most of the officers and men of its four companies killed or wounded. "Our casualties are very heavy," one marine company commander reported to Turrill that morning. "We need medical aid badly. . . . Ammunition of all kinds is needed. . . . All my officers are gone."

A poorly coordinated frontal assault on the Wood proper began around five o'clock that afternoon and was even costlier. As marines from the 5th and 6th regiments lined up to make their assault on the southern end of the Wood and occupy a nearby village, they had to stand their ground while German artillery shells hit their positions with increasing accuracy and intensity. As they waded through the wheat field, German machine guns, positioned to bring the whole field under fire, swept it end to end. The 3rd Battalion, 5th Marines, which had to cover almost all eight hundred acres of the field, got the worst of it; by the end of the day it would list nearly 60 percent casualties. Entire companies seemed to sink beneath the waving grain. Reinforcements were chewed up in the murderous fire. As marines lay on the ground trying to make themselves invisible, a grizzled, forty-two-year-old first sergeant, Dan Daly, who had earned Medals of Honor in China and Haiti and would receive the Navy Cross for his heroism at Belleau Wood, shouted the line that would be the second exclamation of the battle to gain Marine Corps immortality: "C'mon, you sons of bitches, do you want to live forever?" The 3rd Battalion, 6th Marines didn't fare much better. They took the village of Bouresches by nightfall but had only forty or so marines able to fend off counterattacks through the night.

By nightfall the 5th Regiment had gained a foothold in the southern end of the Wood. As the fighting ended for the day and slipped into history and legend, casualties were the most suffered in Marine Corps history, nearly eleven hundred dead and wounded, more than those lost in all previous Marine Corps battles. And it was only the first day. It would take the marines three weeks to drive the Germans from Belleau Wood.

Replacements were rushed to the front, the 3rd Replacement Battalion among them. Two days earlier the battalion had been training for combat at a camp near the Swiss border. "We came across France in a hell of a hurry," one man remembered. Two decades later that marine, Private Elton Edward Mackin, would begin writing a memoir of his experiences in World War I that he would continue writing for many decades. In 1974 Mackin recorded an oral history that would augment his manuscript when it was published in 1993 as *Suddenly, We Didn't Want to Die,* a vivid, intimate, and often poetic account of the spectacle, suffering, and terror of war. "We heard the war scream and writhe and crash among the distant trees," he wrote of his green battalion as it approached the Marne. "The guns around us added to the din, and suddenly we didn't want to die."

His battalion arrived at the front on the afternoon of June 7. "Dark of night would have been welcome then," Mackin wrote, "so that a man might hide the terror in his eyes. The glare of sunlit day was hard to face with other fellows watching all your thoughts." They were ordered to replenish the decimated ranks of 67th Company, one of two companies that had led the attack on Hill 142 the day before. It had suffered appalling casualties, including the company's commanding officer. Only twenty-six of the

67th's original 250 men were still fit for duty, Mackin remembered. He was one of "sixty scared green kids" sent to "join the . . . survivors." They reached the lines at one o'clock on the morning of the 8th, having come through artillery and machine-gun fire to get there. He had already heard the "queer *zeep-zeep*" of machine-gun bullets, "like insects fleeing to the rear." He had seen one of the insects extinguish the life of his friend "little Purcell," who when he was hit had gazed up at Mackin with "the surprised look of a child hurt in play." Mackin wept in grief.

They were told to dig in. "The more we dug, the better we'd be because it was going to be hell at dawn, and it was." A German counterattack was coming, and German artillery pounded the marines in advance.

Entire batteries took up the chorus. The clatter of a machine gun joined in, then another, as the rising tide of sound merged into a crescendo that stifled thought and, for a moment, paralyzed all motion. Shrapnel rained upon the ridge. A running figure dashed along the line. Men sought shelter behind half-finished mounds of earth and hugged the ground. Whole trees crashed

331

down. . . . Fumes from the explosions became a blanket that crept over the forest floor like a pall. There were cries for "First aid, first aid!" Other cries — wordless, terrible cries — told of men in agony.

The company's first sergeant, gruff and profane John McCabe, steadied the new guys for the duty that was now before them: to kill or be killed. "Fix bayonets, and watch the goddamn wheat," he shouted.

"Are they coming?" Mackin managed to "croak from a throat that seemed to choke the words."

"Yeah, when the barrage lifts they'll come, and in numbers. . . . Shoot low and be ready to go meet them if they get too close."

Mackin, referring to himself in the third person, wrote that using and facing bayonets was his greatest terror: "The very thought left him weak."

The Germans attacked at dawn, "three massed lines of bayonets reflecting the first rays of the red sun." They reached the American lines twice, Mackin remembered: "I saw men beheaded within twenty feet of me." The enemy kept advancing as machine-gun fire swept their ranks but didn't stop them. Mackin fought the urge to flee as incredulity turned to panic. "That thin line must go back. Damn it . . . why won't it go back." He killed his first man in the first of four German attempts to retake the Hill that morning. So did other "scared kids" in their initiation under fire, "many of whom died before noon that day."

Scared kids. That is what combat mostly comes down to in the end. Scared kids fighting and killing other scared kids. The main objective of a soldier's training is to show him how to act while he is afraid, how to use a rifle and bayonet and his hands to kill a man he is afraid will kill him. A soldier's training is supposed to be intense and unpredictable and realistic so that even if actual combat isn't a familiar experience when you confront it — even though fear is choking your throat, even though your hands are shaking and your legs trembling, even though you are confused, shocked, terrorized, even though you want to run away — you still know how to fight, how to do your job, and you will still follow orders, you will still kill your enemy if you can.

Action is the most natural response to fear. Action might be running away from danger or running toward it. Though the latter seems counter-intuitive, it isn't. The exhilaration, the adrenaline rush of combat can suppress fear or at least hold it in check.

Fear is most debilitating when the soldier feels helpless. When he can only hunker down and endure an artillery barrage or when he gets lost or separated from his friends and must wait through the night to find his way back, a soldier's imagination will substitute for action and heighten his terror.

Mackin might have most dreaded a bayonet charge, but he would have been afraid long before he heard the order to fix bayonets. He and his fellow replacements would have felt fear intensely as soon as they arrived at the front, if not earlier. Rushed across France from the relative safety and comfort of a training camp and suddenly deposited in a place where the carnage and suffering of war were everywhere in evidence — villages in ruins, pitiable refugees streaming toward the rear, vacant-eyed, hungry children, the earth rent by shells, dead livestock rotting in muddy fields, field hospitals and walking wounded, burial details and stacks of corpses — they would have been shocked and scared by the stink, strangeness, and loudness of war, the "scream and writhe and crash among the distant trees" that Mackin described. Then they were shelled and shot at without being able to respond. They had to stand or crouch there and take it, close their eyes and pray. In such circumstances a lot of men break before they ever see an enemy coming at them with a bayonet.

Besides their training, soldiers' self-esteem is their best defense against succumbing to fear. You hold the soldiers you serve with in a special regard that, for the duration of your shared experience of war, is more important to you than any other relationship you formed before, with the exception of your children. Most soldiers cannot bear to be thought cowards by those they serve with. Being wounded, even killed can seem less objectionable than making your buddies' situation worse by not doing your job.

A soldier looks to his leaders, noncoms, and commissioned officers for instruction and for examples of how to behave under fire. Battles are the most confusing experiences a person will ever have. The leader who knows his business and gives direction, who sees what must be done and tells his soldiers what they need to do is invaluable in the chaos, terror, and din of a battle. Just his appearing purposeful and brave under fire is a powerful inspiration to men who look to him to make sense of the incomprehensible.

Combat veterans have the same effect on

the battlefield, impressing green soldiers with their composure and competency in dire situations. Most replacements will have to admire those attributes from a considerable psychological distance since most veterans treat replacements, whom they do not trust and whose lives they expect to end shortly, with disdain. "Any man who carried the notion that someone was responsible for guarding them from harm soon knew they were mistaken," Mackin explained, describing the experience of most replacements. "We who were to live awhile soon knew our way about, without a shepherd. There wasn't time for a proper initiation." Still replacements had role models present they could emulate, whether or not they could attain the same presence of mind and apparent (though not always genuine) indifference to the strain of combat the veteran evinced.

"We were too damned young and under fire too soon," Mackin wrote, to become as hardened as the "grizzled, graying men of many enlistments." Unlike them, teenage recruits who had been hurried to the front for a sudden, terrifying baptism of fire gained a "brittleness that was to mark all the remaining days of our lives." They might have looked to veterans in vain for instruction, but they could usually rely on them for an example of how to function when terror gripped them. "Their cocky bearing, their sneering self-confidence and almost utter disregard for danger," Mackin remembered, "coupled with a demand for absolute discipline, allowed us to follow them anywhere under any circumstances."

Veterans might very well have scorned Mackin and his fellow replacements. But so many veterans had been killed in that first day's fight for Belleau Wood that replacements would shoulder most of the fighting for the brigade from the second day there until the end of the war. And whether they liked it or not, replacements would determine whether the 4th Marine Brigade at Belleau Wood brought further renown or disrepute to the U.S. Marine Corps.

Mackin and four other replacements were ordered to guard the left flank of a platoon as it attacked a German outpost in the woods. They were too small a detail to be much help, Mackin wrote, but they were all that were available and, being replacements, more expendable than others. They crawled on their bellies into the wheat field, led by "a stony faced old timer," Sergeant Louis Peterson, who halted them at a drainage ditch that offered partial concealment. The old veteran told them to keep down and quiet as they listened to German machine guns trying and failing to turn back the Americans and occasionally sending a burst into the field near them.

The Germans made no attempt to turn the platoon's flank, so Mackin's squad never had to fire their weapons. After a while it became clear the marines had taken the outpost, and Mackin and the others "inch[ed] up to get a better view of things." The Germans fired a couple of machine-gun bursts their way that sent them sprawling back on their bellies. Mackin noted that Sergeant Peterson was the only one of them who hadn't ducked. "He was keeping a good watch. . . . Those fellows never seem to scare. Not like us green kids."

They remained prone and quiet for some time, while "the afternoon stretched into long shadows" and their sergeant was still silent on his watch. They became anxious about being left so far outside their lines as night fell. One of them called out, "Sarge?" and didn't hear an answer. They all looked to their quiet leader, who was lying outside the ditch. "His chin rested on his folded arms . . . his field glasses lay idle in front of him as he studied the lay of the land." At length the private who had called out to Peterson crawled to him, grabbed the old man's foot and shook it, calling again, "Sarge?" Again he didn't receive an answer, and he knew he never would. "We should not have left him there," Mackin regretted later, "but the evening star was glowing against the east and we were suddenly a bunch of lost, scared kids — a long way from home."

Home for Elton Mackin was Lewiston, New York, near Niagara Falls. He was six when his father died in a boating accident in the Niagara Rapids, and he was left in the care of attentive grandparents. In an interview Mackin suggests a permanent coolness developed between mother and son after she wrenched him away from his grandparents' home when she remarried. His mother and stepfather would have four children, whom Mackin would love. In the beginning he hated his stepfather for replacing his father, but in time he came to love him, hinting that he received from him affection that was lacking from his mother.

He had a high school education, a respectable achievement for a boy of his time and means. But he appears also to have been something of an autodidact, who, as his finely written memoir attests, absorbed not just information but a rhetorical style from the things he read. He said his paternal grandparents, his Irish family, were self-taught intellectuals though of modest means, and his grandda a "heavy drinking . . . mean, wild Irishman." They were caretakers of the village library and brought home books, newspapers, and the *Saturday Evening Post, Harper's,* and other magazines. They encouraged him "to read, read, read." His stepfather shared his interest in geography and history and "the world as a general thing." Mackin was an avid newspaper reader and so, "when WWI broke in 1914, my world exploded into headlines." He wanted to join the Canadian Army in 1916, but his mother refused to let him.

He reached a time in what he called his "bitter, bitter childhood" when he was obliged to leave home. This must be a comment on his relationship with his mother since he describes with affection every other person responsible for his care. "At the age of sixteen . . . without warning . . . I was simply ordered out of house and home at 4:30 of an afternoon in zero January weather." He stayed with his maternal grandparents and later with an aunt and uncle in Niagara Falls, where he found work. In 1917, missing his siblings and stepfather, he returned home and finished high school, graduating that spring. His mother still wouldn't let him go to France, even as friends and classmates began enlisting. Neither did the draft take him that year.

In December he went to Buffalo for a brief holiday. While there he read in the *Saturday Evening Post* that the 5th Marines had traveled to France with Pershing. "I threw the magazine across the room and I didn't quit until I walked into the recruiting station at Lafayette Square and enlisted in the Marine Corps."

The recruiters told him to make his goodbyes and report back in eleven days. There "was hell to pay" when he got home. His mother tried and failed to get him out of his enlistment. It must have been an unpleasant time. Mackin showed up in Buffalo again, five days early, and insisted on being shipped to basic training. He left for Parris Island that night. His memoir makes no mention of his training or any of his life before or after the war. It begins and ends in France. But in an interview he described his training tersely: "I lived through it."

He shipped overseas with the 3rd Replacement Battalion in April 1918, arriving in Brest, on the Brittany coast, on May 6. The

Great War would continue only six months more. Elton Mackin would participate in every major marine engagement, and his courage would earn him the respect of the veterans who had once awed him.

Mackin's education on the line was swift. He fought in or in support of attacks and counterattacks at Belleau Wood every day for several days until the bulk of the fighting shifted temporarily toward Château-Thierry. He had been shelled and shot at. He had known men who were killed. He had killed Germans. He caught a few minutes of sleep in a trench one afternoon while a German infiltrator wearing a purloined marine uniform pretended to stand watch next to him. Mackin's sergeant came over and, without explanation, casually apprehended the man and had him shot by firing squad. He drew burial detail one night, and a dead man's brains spilled onto his boots. Another night he spent in an outpost, where darkness and proximity to the enemy summoned new terrors of the night's "threat of stalking, creeping death," of "half seen shapes of trees at forest edge" that move and don't move, and eyes that "grow tired and conjure things": "It's good to feel a comrade's soldier then, to know that men like him don't run away. It's then you get the feel of soldiering."

He described how friendships formed in battle by writing about his close friendship with a private from Cleveland, Hiram Raymond Baldwin, "Baldy," who had spent a couple years at Ohio State University. An educated man suffered most in war, Mackin thought. It was easier for a man like him, without "too much family or education," to accept the stripping away of the veneer of civilization. An educated man was more reluctant to let it go. "They were pitiful sometimes," he recalled, "these men who took clean sportsmanship and decency to France."

One night the marines fired their Hotchkiss guns into the darkness to soften up an anticipated German counterattack. The Germans responded with greater force, a prolonged artillery barrage as well as machine-gun fire. Mackin and Baldy shared a rifle pit, and Mackin was supposed to get some sleep while Baldy stood the first watch. It's not easy to keep a good watch in the dark with shrapnel and machine-gun bullets flying all over the place. Baldy kept his head down when he needed to, but otherwise peered into the darkness for any sign of a German advance. Mackin, understandably, couldn't fall asleep with all the noise and anxiety the German rounds were causing. He stood up next to his friend and tried to keep watch too, as best he could. This restricted Baldy's freedom of movement to duck and dodge the flying ordnance. "Get down, you goddam fool!" Baldy shouted at him. "I'm watching out for us." But Mackin refused to sit down. They argued about it until Mackin confessed he didn't have "the nerve to stay down there and take it." If he was going to die, he wanted death to find him upright. He was afraid that a shell would hit the top of the trench and bury him alive.

Baldy understood the fear, and they shook hands. "Here was friendship formed and forming," Mackin wrote. "Not a friendship of the soft and slushy kind in which the best of us sometimes engage in time of trouble, but a friendship based on the realization of the little human fears we, man to man, try so hard to conceal."

The marines survived constant shelling, poison gas, multiple counterattacks, well-directed machine-gun fire, and sniping. They fought with bayonets and fists, proved themselves superior marksmen, and staged attacks at all times of the day and night. After eleven days they had gained control of a considerable part, though not all, of Belleau Wood and were relieved by the army and given a few days' rest in the rear. Mackin had eaten his first hot meal in a while, bathed in a nearby stream, and had just lain down in the shade when he was summoned by his platoon sergeant.

Gunnery Sergeant David McClain was respected by veteran and replacement alike. The former called him Uncle Dave, the latter Sergeant Mac, though no marine called him either name to his face. "We were glad to soldier under him," Mackin wrote. "He had a way of looking deep inside you, as though he read your very thoughts and fears, yet let you keep them hidden."

McClain told Mackin he had thought of him because they had the same nickname, and then proceeded to shoot the breeze, which puzzled the replacement since "gunnery sergeants don't ordinarily hold casual chats with recruits." As they talked, "the old soldier weighed and probed, making estimates," before finally revealing his purpose. "Battalion wants a new runner," he told Mackin. The prior occupant of the position, an unfortunate man called Itchy Fox, had been killed the night before.

Runners, Mackin explained, were always volunteers since the job was so dangerous.

"Runners didn't last. Everyone knew that." He could tell McClain he didn't want it, and that would be that, "no questions asked. Suicide squad. That's how the fellows spoke of it." Mackin said nothing at first, just looked at McClain. "The noncom's eyes were wells of patience," he recalled. "He let you fight it out with yourself."

"Want the job, son?"

"Sure, Sergeant. I'll take it." Mackin didn't want the old man to think him a coward. "There are some things a fellow can't admit. It makes for soldiering."

The marines returned to the line on June 22. The next night they began the final assault on the northern end of the Wood, which the Germans had recently reinforced. The first attack was a disaster, poorly planned and coordinated. Casualties were staggering: 140 marines were killed in machine-gun cross fires. Over two hundred ambulances were needed to evacuate the wounded. Very little ground was gained.

The next day, June 24, the marines let American and French artillery resume the battle. A fourteen-hour barrage ended with the last German-held section transformed into a wasteland of shattered trees and dead Germans. The 3rd Battalion, 5th Marines led the final attack the night of June 25.

The fighting lasted all night, but at daybreak the battalion commander, Major Maurice Shearer, could notify brigade headquarters, "Belleau Woods now U.S. Marine Corps entirely."

Over eighteen hundred marines lost their lives during the three weeks of fighting it took to drive the Germans from Belleau Wood, including Captain Lloyd Williams, who had derided the French order to retreat. Nearly eight thousand marines had been wounded. They had had to fight parts of five German divisions, some of the best soldiers the Kaiser had left. Every acre of the woods had been exposed to German machine guns and artillery. The attacks and counterattacks the marines staged were brave and determined but usually confused and poorly coordinated.

The price for Belleau Wood might have been steeper than it should have been, but the hard-won victory deserves its exalted place in Marine Corps history. It was the biggest battle the United States had ever fought against a foreign enemy, and it marked a turning point in the war. French and British troops that had been badly battered in the Spring Offensive felt the tide turn to their advantage. The Germans would launch one last-gasp offensive, but after that the Allies would send them reeling backward as the war drew to its inevitable close. The French knew the value of the marines' sacrifice. The brigade received the Croix de Guerre and forever after, Belleau Wood would be called the Boise de la Brigade de Marine.

Well before the last attack on Belleau Wood General Ludendorff accepted that his offensive, begun in May, had run its course, and he began to deliberate his next move. He decided on another offensive, against the French along the Marne, hoping still the German threat to Paris would draw enough British divisions into the fight that he could renew the advance in Flanders.

The final German offensive of the war, often referred to as the Second Battle of the Marne, began at midnight on July 14, 1918, with an artillery barrage that lasted through the night. In the morning all available German divisions advanced west and east of the city of Rheims. Germany's First and Third armies attacked east of the city, and the Seventh and Ninth west of it, hoping to split two French armies. Before it was over the Allies would have nine American divisions in the fight, which would prove critical to stemming the German tide.

The Germans east of Rheims were stopped on the first day, but the attack to the west made good progress initially. The German vanguard had crossed the Marne at multiple points between Épernay and Château-Thierry on July 15 and were still advancing, although their progress had been slowed by Allied resistance, most notably by the 3rd U.S. Infantry Division, which would be hailed afterward as the "Rock of the Marne."

The 4th Marine Brigade was located well to the rear on July 16, when it received orders to join other Allied forces in hurried night marches to the front and take up positions near the town of Soissons. The marines were to join the massive counterattack that Supreme Allied Commander Field Marshal Ferdinand Foch had been planning since Allied intelligence had reported German intentions before they launched their offensive. It began at daybreak on July 18 with the requisite artillery barrage, following which the 5th Marines and army infantry, supported by French tanks, swept the Germans from a forest, through wheat fields, and past ruined farms, driving them rapidly backward to lines west of the town of Vierzy, where they dug in. "One instant there was silence," Mackin recalled of the moments before the attack. "Then the world went mad in a smashing burst of sound." The 5th charged so far out in front of the Allied attack that it was exposed to horrific machine-gun fire on its flanks. The marines rested a bit before renewing the attack that afternoon, pushing the Germans west of Vierzy until, fatigued by two nights of marching in foul weather and a day of hard fighting, they could go no farther.

The 6th Marines renewed the attack the following day, paying a terrible price. German observer planes helped direct artillery and machine-gun fire, decimating the regiment as marines advanced over open fields. The entire brigade was taken off the line that night. Casualties in all American units involved in the fighting were the highest the American Expeditionary Force had yet suffered and on par with the staggering losses borne by the French and British in earlier battles. The Allies lost about 125,000 killed and wounded, of which twelve thousand were Americans. Germany suffered nearly 170,000 casualties.

By the end of the day on July 19 the Germans had been pushed back across the Marne. By August 3 they had been driven back to the lines they occupied before the Spring Offensive. The German offensives were finished. From that point on the initiative was with the Allies and would remain so until the armistice.

Though the job was every bit as dangerous as advertised, being a runner suited Mackin. He liked the independence it gave him. Wearing a red band that identified him (to friend and foe alike) as a runner, rushing orders and reports between battalion headquarters and company command posts by whatever route he deemed best, he could not be detained by noncoms or officers or even questioned. "You were a trusted man if you were a runner," he explained. "You didn't have to answer to a colonel, unless it was your own colonel." Despite potshots from snipers and other hazards, Mackin soon earned a reputation for being a resourceful runner and a new nickname, "Lucky," on account of his longevity in the job after coming through some of the worst scraps the marines experienced in France. He was one of four runners, "three Irish and an Ozark mountaineer," who called themselves the "Four Aces" and were, according to Mackin, "the favored ones of all our kind" because they escaped the fate of most runners. "Fate, death . . . passed us by, and in passing sometimes brushed us gently, warning us."

Fate in those parts was rarely gentle. During the fighting in the woods outside Soissons, Mackin was running a report from a company commander back to battalion past an overrun German position strewn with fallen timber and corpses, where he heard a voice cry out, *"Kamerad."* Fearing a trap, he ran wide of the spot and circled back carefully. He found a German with a shattered leg, "helpless, harmless, pitiful," lying in a foxhole. The wounded man motioned him for assistance, which Mackin refused. He "had a job to do," he explained, and left the German to his fate, whose cries of *"Kamerad"* "followed him a long, long way."

He saw a friend charged with marching a group of captured Germans to the rear shoot a prisoner who was too hurt and tired to continue. He heard a story of a runner, "an honest lad, too young . . . for war," shot by an officer of the "older military school" because he had failed to deliver a message to a company under intense artillery bombardment. He was darting through an abandoned German trench when he found a mortally wounded young German, who posed no threat. Struggling to his feet, the dying boy grasped Mackin's hand and made it known he needed assistance to reach another part of the trench, where his identical twin lay dead. Mackin did as he was asked and left after watching the boy drop "a hand in slow caress across the brow" of his dead brother.

He and the other Four Aces as well as the battalion clerks, who, like the runners, were armed only with pistols, were ordered by a visiting army colonel from division to join an undermanned assault on a German position at Vierzy. When their battalion commanding officer protested that they were just a few, barely armed runners and clerks, the colonel retorted, "I don't give a damn if you only got twenty of them, they are marines, . . . and I'm ordering you to take that goddamn town!" With that, Mackin observed, they knew their "old man would take us and our pistols into town."

After they formed their skirmish line and helped take the town, Mackin, armed with a German rifle, was put in charge of a party of captured Germans. Their captain started to approach Mackin, smiling, and announced in English that he was from Chicago. He had been in Germany on business when the war broke out, he explained, and been forced into the Kaiser's army. Mackin ordered him to halt, sensing the man had something other than a casual chat with a fellow Yank in mind. But the German from Chicago kept coming and smiling and talking and ignoring orders to stop until he made a grab for Mackin's weapon as the marine stepped back and slammed the butt of his rifle as hard as he could into the German's head. "Two of his lads came to drag him in," Mackin remembered. "I hope he didn't die. I liked the man."

In September 1918 Pershing had at last an American Army under his command ready to launch an offensive of its own against a bulge in French lines south of Verdun that the Germans had occupied since 1914. It was called the Saint-Mihiel salient. The American First Army that attacked it comprised four corps, including a French colonial corps. Two American corps, I and IV, led the attack on September 12. The 2nd Division, which included the marines, was part of I Corps and advanced on the right of the American lines.

The advance was swifter and easier than Pershing expected. By the end of the first day the Americans had exceeded their initial objectives and captured over thirteen thousand prisoners. Their success was due in part to the fact that the Germans had decided to abandon the salient and were in the process of retreating when the Americans attacked, which is probably why Mackin referred to the three-day battle as a sham. That's not to say it wasn't a real battle. The Allies suffered seven thousand casualties; the marines alone lost almost seven hundred men killed and wounded.

The offensive was notable too for the introduction of the first American tank corps, organized and commanded by a young army colonel, George S. Patton Jr. And despite Germany's cooperation in the attack's success, Pershing had established that Americans could fight as a single, powerful force, capable of beating the Germans without orders from French generals. But two weeks later the marines and the rest of the 2nd Division would find themselves again at the disposal of the French Fourth Army, assigned to take a white limestone ridge northeast of Rheims in the Champagne region that had been occupied by the Germans since the first year of the war.

The British were rolling back the Germans in Flanders and the American Expeditionary Force was advancing to the east in the first days of the Meuse-Argonne Offensive. For the French Fourth Army, in the center of the Western Front, the attempt to clear the enemy from the old Somme battlefield was blocked by a heavily fortified and entrenched German force atop Blanc Mont Ridge, which the French had tried and failed to dislodge over three days. Field Marshal Foch asked Pershing for help. He sent the 2nd Division, now commanded by a Marine Corps general, the legendary John Lejeune, and another infantry division in reserve, the 36th, composed mostly of green National Guard regiments.

On their way to the front, Mackin's company stopped to rest in a village, and an old woman approached him. One of the marines mocked, "Why didn't y' pay 'er las' night? Now she wants her franc." The *grandmère* hung around Mackin's neck a little crucifix on a piece of twine. "My son, you won't die," she said.

The attack jumped off at six o'clock on the morning of October 3, preceded by the largest Allied air attack of the war. Over two hundred planes bombed German trenches, machine-gun nests, and batteries on the ridgeline. When the planes finished, French and American artillery started in on them. Ten minutes later the 6th Marines poured out of their trenches and led the charge up the ridge, just behind the rolling artillery barrage, which now and again sent shrapnel flying into the American ranks. The marines advanced quickly and in good order by columns of battalions on a mile-long front. Their flanks were supposed to have been protected by supporting French columns, but the French had remained in their trenches, and German machine gunners and artillery tore into the exposed American columns. Despite heavy losses, the 6th Marines reached the crest of Blanc Mont a little more than two hours after the attack began, clearing German trenches at bayonet point but with their flanks still unguarded and Germans still in possession of the western side of the ridge.

The first German counterattack came from the west, a place called the Essen Hook, in what was supposed to have been the French sector of the attack, where a veritable thicket of German machine-gun nests poured enfilading fire into the marines. The 5th Marines, which had been in support of the 6th, rushed to close the gap and meet the counterattack. They would succeed, but after taking heavy casualties in fighting that was often hand to hand. The marines turned the Hook over to the French, who had to be summoned by a marine runner. But the Germans took it back with their next counterattack, and the French fell back again.

The next day was worse. October 4 is recorded as "the bitterest single day of fighting that the 5th Regiment experienced in the whole war." General Lejeune would later boast that the claim " 'I belonged to the 2nd Division, I fought with it at the Battle of Blanc Mont Ridge,' will be the highest honor that can come to any man."

But it was a debacle really. The 5th Marines led the attack that day, and they suffered severely. The French again were not where they were supposed to be. Crouched just below the crest waiting to renew the attack in trenches that had changed hands several times and where Mackin counted thirty-three French and German corpses, the marines of the 1st Battalion were "lashed down . . . by flailing whips of shrapnel, gas and heavy stuff that came as drumfire, killing them. . . . The fellows bunched against the fancied shelter of the larger trees in little close-packed knots, like storm-swept sheep, and died that way, in groups." Mackin and two of the other Four Aces were hunkered down in a shallow rifle pit in open ground and were about to seek the relative safety of a shell crater when a poison gas shell exploded close to them, severely wounding Gene, the "Ozark mountaineer." They were down to three Aces.

The 5th advanced so rapidly that day it started to lose cohesion, and some of the more scattered units of the line were nearest the strongest German positions. They had made their first charge after a hasty artillery barrage helped prepare the way, and succeeded in driving many Germans from their trenches. Yet German counterattacks would take back some of the ground they had gained. Mackin recalled watching one young marine, well ahead of the line, become hysterical and furiously attack two surrendering Germans who had their hands up, shooting one and stabbing the other in the belly with his bayonet. "He had not meant to do it" but had been lost to "bayonet lust," Mackin explained, and he would never be the same. "The charging line swept by, but the fight for him was done."

The Germans brought up Maxim machine guns on both sides of a stubbled wheat field and opened up a cross fire, killing many marines and trapping a good number of others. Mackin and most of the battalion's runners were stuck there. He could see the battalion's commanding officer, Major George Hamilton, a handsome, athletic marine whom Mackin described as a "huge Apollo of a man," standing on the ridge, looking down on their predicament. The marines in the field needed help, or at least more ammunition, so Mackin and one of the other remaining Aces, Bud, decided to risk a run across the field to reach the major. "Bud led the way, a frenzied, fleeing rush that took them halfway across the field before the guns swung down." Mackin reached the ridge. Bud didn't. He was cut down by two Maxim rounds to his spine.

Hamilton told Mackin and another runner to get word to the company commanders to stop advancing. Without cover from the missing French, they were walking into a trap. They did as they were told, at times running just past and even through German positions to reach the marine lines, and they had to kill a German officer and his orderly along the way. It was too late, though; the battalion had been lured into a narrow strip of woods, a salient that ran deep behind German lines down the western slope to the wheat field at the base of the ridge that Mackin had just crossed. "It was a good place to die," Mackin wrote, "exposed to fire from three sides, its line of communication cut off by enfilading Maxims firing from the flanks." The marines called it "the Box." There they would fight over the next two days, repulsing at great cost a German counterattack where the fighting was at close quarters and savage. Part of the battalion was nearly overrun. A lot of marines died in those woods. Mackin would later claim he was wounded there but stayed in the field. His old commander from the 67th Company, whom Mackin revered, was struck in the neck by shrapnel. He continued smoking a cigar and directing the company's activity while he dressed the wound himself.

The 5th Marines were relieved on the morning of October 6, and the 6th Marines finished taking the ridge that day. Two days later the division drove the enemy from the nearby village of Saint-Étienne, and the Champagne region was freed of Germans for the first time in the war. Nearly eight thousand soldiers and marines were killed or wounded taking Blanc Mont Ridge. Of the roughly one thousand 1st Battalion marines who had started up the ridge, Mackin counted only 134 who had come out of the woods on their feet. Only three of the battalion's sixteen runners survived the battle unscathed physically. Mackin was one of them. He had been certain he would die there and had run through hails of fire resigned to his fate. He received the Navy Cross, the Army Distinguished Service Cross, and two Silver Star citations for his service on Blanc Mont Ridge.

The last offensive of the war, the Meuse-Argonne Offensive, had begun on September 26 and would continue until the final hours of the war. Its main objective was the capture of the rail center in Sedan and severing the railroad lines that supplied the Kaiser's armies. The American sector west of the Meuse River included the densely wooded Argonne Forest, where a generation later Americans would again find themselves in a desperate fight with a German Army. It was the biggest American campaign of World War I. Over a million Americans fought in it; over a hundred thousand of them were killed or wounded. The 2nd Division, having earned a couple weeks' rest after the Battle of Blanc Mount, arrived at the front on October 30–31 and formed the center of the American line as part of V Corps in the final advance on Sedan.

V Corps was commanded by Major General Charles Pelot Summerall, "Old Charles P," Mackin called him, a determined, aggressive commander to some, to others a cold-hearted bastard who profligately wasted American lives. "An army general came on a beautiful black horse and lectured us," Mackin recalled, "telling combat men about the lay of the land ahead." He told them what he wanted done and how he wanted it done, slapping his riding crop against his boot for emphasis.

"Before you are twenty kilometers of machine guns. Go and get them.
"Way up north is a railroad. Go cut it for me.
"Before you there are three low ridges. Behind the third, the German artillery is parked. . . . Go and get them. Don't let them take away a single gun.
"On those ridges all your officers may be down, but you keep going. I want to sit back in my headquarters and hear you carried all your objectives on time.
"Go forward while you can still crawl. Top that third ridge. . . . Do it with rifle fire if you have nothing else, and . . . on those three ridges, take no prisoners, nor should you stop to bandage your best friend."

The marines moved out on the morning of November 1, on a line just south of the little village of Landres-et-Saint-Georges, following another immense artillery barrage. Their objectives, the ridges, formed the eastern section and hardest part of the Hindenburg Line, a stretch called the Kriemhilde-Stellung, that a historian later described as "a dense network of prepared killing grounds." Pershing considered it the key obstacle to a breakthrough. So did the Germans.

Two hours into the advance Major Hamilton, Mackin's battalion commander, reported heavy casualties and the loss of five officers. Mackin's pal Baldy died taking the first ridge, felled by a sniper's bullet. "He had long known he wasn't going home," Mackin observed. A stretcher carrier reached the body before Mackin did. "He stopped me with a look and shook his head twice. . . . We kept on going. The new men watched and learned as we had learned before." When they took the third ridge that day, shocked German commanders ordered their lines to withdraw. The 2nd Division marched through their abandoned positions and headed east to the Meuse.

On November 7 Mackin was at his battalion HQ preparing to report to Major Hamilton when he was delighted to see his old company commander, Frank Whitehead, who had been wounded and evacuated at Blanc Mont. The two men greeted each other warmly. "Haven't they killed you yet?" Whitehead joked. They had not, but

General Summerall intended to see to it that they would have another chance.

On the night of November 10 the 5th Marines were on the west bank of the Meuse River. Rumors had reached them that an armistice would be declared that night or the next day, but such speculation hadn't altered Summerall's plans. He ordered army engineers to build pontoon bridges across the river and sent his corps over them that night under intense fire from the Germans on the other side. Over a thousand more Americans would die or be wounded that last night of the war.

"They lied to us that night," Mackin wrote. The 1st Battalion marines had been told they needed only to bring ammunition to the army regiment that was constructing the bridges, but when the marines got to the river, they were ordered to cross and attack the Germans fighting on the other bank. Searching for the bridge, they passed many dead and wounded. "No one took the time to care for them."

Frantically they searched in the dark for the crossing. "Maxims on the far bank . . . found us and thinned our ranks." When they reached it, German flares illuminated the night and the slaughter going on below. Major Hamilton led the brigade over the bridge. "A stream of Maxim bullets churned up and down the river, searching. They rapped from time to time across the planks. . . . You felt their jarring shake all up your limbs and fought against the cramp of belly muscles knotted in fear. You watched men die in front of you."

The two men in front of Mackin fell. The first man "sank to his knees, twisting, and slid face first into the river." The second "staggered, unseen hammers driving him sideways." Mackin froze. His "shaking knees sagged in awful fear." He fought to keep on his feet. He took a step and stopped again. "The night belonged to bitter men," he wrote, "who long before had known there was no hope," who "thought they had conquered fear."

He spoke out once. "Oh, God!" Two words, a prayer. He moved toward a place of bullet-streaming death. The instant of it left a sense of guilt. He hadn't ever meant to pray again. Prayer was for men who carried faith, and most of them had died in other places.

The Maxims swung away to let him live.

The battalion had 350 men when it crossed the Meuse that night. Mackin didn't know how many of them made it across unhurt. If it hadn't been a foggy night, he believed none of them would have survived. Just after they crossed, German artillery took out the bridge. "I lost friends that night that I'd been with all the way from Belleau," Mackin grieved. "I lost guys that I loved."

They fought past daybreak on a skirmish line through a patch of woods. They found a drainage ditch just outside the woods, where they stopped. "I was so goddamn tired, weary, sick, and hungry, beat, whipped," Mackin recalled a few months before his death in 1974. "I got down on my knees in that drainage ditch. My rifle was sticking . . . under the fence through at the Germans. . . . I laid my head over on my rifle and went sound to sleep."

A few hours later, around noon, a pal shook him awake to tell him the war was over.

PFC Guy Louis Gabaldon poses with a Japanese family he saved from mass suicide on the island of Saipan.

CHAPTER EIGHT: LONE WOLF

Guy Gabaldon, alone and cave by cave, convinced as many as fifteen hundred Japanese on Saipan to surrender.

No one ever said he lacked guts or initiative. Private first class Guy Gabaldon was as brave as any marine on Saipan during World War II, and more enterprising than many. He had no shortage of bravado either, a common enough, if not universally admired, trait. Some marines felt his exploits were exaggerated and doubted he was quite the lone wolf he claimed to be. Many others believed he earned every bit of the acclaim he received. His company commander praised his courage unreservedly and credited his actions with shortening a campaign that was longer and bloodier than anyone had expected. He recommended Gabaldon for the Medal of Honor.

A marine sergeant on Saipan called

Gabaldon "a glory seeker," but then acknowledged, "The two traits often go together: bravery and glory seeking." So does the sort of enterprise Gabaldon possessed: daring, foolhardy, and individualistic to the point of insubordination. Courage was a common virtue in a three-week Saipan campaign where nearly fourteen thousand Americans would be killed or wounded. And many marines and soldiers who fought there showed initiative again and again in solving problems posed by difficult terrain and a tenacious, desperate enemy. The initiative Gabaldon took, at great peril to himself, helped spare even more lives, American and Japanese, from the prodigious killing that characterized the Battle of Saipan.

Gabaldon's war began and ended in the Marianas, a group of islands in the Pacific Ocean west of the Philippines. But to appreciate fully what he did there, and to understand the nature of the challenge Americans faced there, it is instructive to consider an earlier battle on a flyspeck of an island on the west side of a small atoll in the Gilbert Islands.

While General Douglas MacArthur's army slogged through northern New Guinea toward his rendezvous with destiny in the Philippines, Admiral Chester Nimitz opened the island-hopping campaign in the central Pacific that was the necessary prelude to the invasion of the Japanese home islands. In November 1943 Operation Galvanic, the invasion of Tarawa — specifically the invasion of an islet at Tarawa called Beito — was the first offensive of the campaign. Tarawa is shaped like a triangle, with a wide coral reef and thirty coral islets enclosing a lagoon. Beito is the largest of the islets, but still tiny at three miles in length and a half mile across at its widest point. It is hard to imagine such a small, unimposing place possessing strategic significance, but it did. Before the Allies could invade the home islands, they needed air bases in the northern Marianas, where they could base strategic bombers capable of reaching Japan. To take the Marianas they needed air and naval bases in the Marshall Islands. To take the Marshalls they had to invade Tarawa, from where the Japanese could threaten the sea routes from Hawaii to the Marshalls.

The Japanese likewise recognized Tarawa's strategic value. They built an airstrip on Beito and an elaborate network of trenches, concrete bunkers, and minefields connected by tunnels and defended by thirty-eight hundred soldiers and twelve hundred Korean slave laborers. The Japanese had fourteen big, eight-inch, coastal defense guns on Tarawa, forty field artillery pieces, and almost a hundred tanks. They would also adjust their tactics at Tarawa. Though they had fought their ground tenaciously, the Japanese defenders on Guadalcanal had offered only light resistance to the initial marine landings. Tarawa would be a fight to the death from the moment the first marine set foot on the beach.

The 2nd Marine Division, late of the Guadalcanal campaign, freshly reinforced and rested, and the army's 27th Infantry Division, roughly thirty-five thousand men in all, commanded by Marine Corps Major General Julius Smith, were given the assignment. They would arrive in an armada that included seventeen aircraft carriers and a dozen battleships under the command of Admiral Raymond Spruance. The invasion began before dawn on November 20, 1943, with a duel between the Japanese big guns and American battleships, followed by carrier aircraft strikes that dropped nine hundred tons of ordnance. After the planes finished their runs, the navy resumed its barrage, firing two thousand shells at the tiny island.

The barrage lifted at nine o'clock, and the first wave of marines were streaming toward their various landing zones on Beito's north shore when they encountered an unanticipated problem: the tide was too low for the landing craft to clear the reef. Only the armored tractors, amtracs, were able to get ashore. Most of the marines had to wade hundreds of yards through waist-high water. Japanese machine gunners who had survived the shelling fought from positions near the beach and mowed them down, and pinned down those who managed to reach the beach and huddle miserably among the corpses. Reinforcements were ferried into the battle throughout the morning, as were several tanks that enabled the marines to expand their precarious foothold and overrun the first Japanese lines by noon. Progress was costly and slow from there on out, but by the end of the day five thousand marines were ashore and were nearing the airstrip.

They took it the next morning and also succeeded that day in blocking and destroying a Japanese force that was trying to retreat to another islet. Heavy fighting continued for the next two days as more American reinforcements, tanks, and howitzers streamed ashore, killed the enemy in their bunkers and trenches, and pushed the survivors to the eastern end of the islet. The defenders, their commanding general already killed, attempted a counterattack the evening of November 22. It was repulsed. Before dawn the next day the last Japanese defenders launched a final banzai charge. When the killing was finished, only one Japanese officer and sixteen soldiers from a force of nearly four thousand were captured alive. Only 120 of the twelve hundred Korean laborers survived. Eleven hundred marines had been killed at Tarawa, and twice that number were wounded. In a little over three days on Tarawa, the marines had suffered casualties comparable to those lost in six months of fighting on Guadalcanal. The bones of half the American dead are still scattered in unmarked graves on Beito.

The American public was shocked by accounts of the bloody first day on Tarawa from correspondents who had come ashore with the marines and by descriptions of the awful toll paid by its defenders, who had fought, almost literally, to the last man. A correspondent who landed with the first wave of marines, Robert Sherrod of *Time* magazine, wrote, "No one who has not been there can imagine the overwhelming, inhuman smell of 5,000 dead who are piled and scattered in an area of less than one square mile." The marines learned important lessons at Tarawa they would put to use in bloodier battles to come. For as heavy as casualties were, they would not compare with casualties suffered in the island battles ahead, as the fanaticism of Japanese soldiers grew more extreme and deadlier the more desperate they became.

The invasion of the Marshall Islands was launched ten weeks after Tarawa, with the 4th Marine Division and the army's 7th Infantry Division in the lead. The 2nd Marine Division and the 27th Infantry Division had left the Gilberts several weeks earlier for a few days of rest and reinforcement in Hawaii before conducting amphibious landing exercises in preparation for their next assignment. After the Marshalls were secured, the 2nd Marines would join the 4th Marines in the first multidivisional landing of the Pacific war, and the army's 27th would follow them onto the island of Saipan.

A young, diminutive Mexican American would assault the beach with the 2nd Marines on D-Day in Saipan. It would be his first experience of combat. It wouldn't be his first fight, though. Guy Louis Gabaldon

375

had been in more scraps than he could remember. He took more than a few beatings too, and recounts some of them in the self-published autobiography he wrote decades after the war. He described himself as "the fightingest little Chicano." He was also resourceful and seems to have made his own way in the world from a very early age, even when his way was harder than it needed to be.

He was born in 1926, a descendant of Spanish settlers in New Mexico, and raised in poverty in the melting pot of East Los Angeles, one of seven children. He recalled his mother with affection, and two older brothers. He never mentions his father. At the age of ten he was hopping on the backs of streetcars and riding downtown to Skid Row, where he shined shoes. He hung out with derelicts and cowboys and with fighters from the Main Street Gym, who taught him how to spar. Bartenders on the Row and strippers from the burlesque houses looked after him; so did the beat cops. "Almost everyone on the Row was my friend," he claimed. It "was a place where you could get a fast education in life." With growing self-confidence, he began plying his trade all around Greater Los Angeles, from Chinatown and Little Tokyo to Hollywood and Santa Monica, Venice, and Long Beach.

Gabaldon seems not to have suffered much from racial prejudice as a boy. In East L.A. he fell in with the Moe Gang, named for the Three Stooges character. They were kids for whom neighborhood, not race, determined associations. Like East L.A. itself and Hollenbeck Junior High, where they went to school, the gang was a mix of Hispanics, Jews, Russians, Armenians, Italians, and Nisei, first-generation Japanese Americans. They occasionally got up to no good, but their antics were a far cry from the murder, mayhem, and drug trade associated with gangs today. They got in fights frequently, but Gabaldon is quick to explain that the only weapons used were their fists. But his inventory of the black eyes, broken noses, and perforated eardrums he suffered explains why his mother became so anxious about his welfare that she sent him to live with relatives in New Mexico.

His Manito relatives were self-reliant and proud people, and he returned to East L.A. a year later with newfound racial pride. But it didn't affect his friendships. He picked up where he had left off, he wrote, "fighting and raising hell," and he grew all the closer to his Nisei friends, Kakaro Mochinaga, Johnny Ito, Norman Shizumura, George Uno, and the Nakano twins, Lane and Lloyd. He was soon spending as much time living with the Nakanos, whom he considered his adoptive family, as he spent in his own home. To the end of his life, long after time and distance and differences had separated them, he would call his Nisei friends his brothers. They fought together, chased girls together, hopped freight trains and went on adventures together. They relied on each other. Gabaldon learned to speak a little colloquial Japanese and enjoyed Japanese food and customs. He admired Japanese culture too, especially Bushido, the code of the Samurai. Later, on Saipan, that admiration would turn to disdain and something close to hatred.

That happens in war. Among its many corruptions, war encourages hate. You work up an antipathy to your enemy that seems a necessary mind-set. Sometimes it is informed by your experiences of the enemy that have offended your customs and morals or that provoked in you a desire to avenge. Sometimes it appears racist. Sometimes you learn to hate because it just makes it easier to do the things you must do, to destroy, maim, and kill. My grandfather, a navy admiral who witnessed kamikaze attacks, once publicly recommended Americans "kill all the Japs, painfully." On Saipan Gabaldon would feel something very like that hatred. He would kill Japanese with little remorse, thirty-three of them by his own count. He would take their possessions for trophies. And for the rest of his life he harbored — and occasionally expressed — a lingering resentment toward the Japanese soldiers who had fought on Saipan and the nation that sent them there. He would describe them in terms considered offensive by most people and that likely would have offended the friends he called his brothers. But also on Saipan, to his everlasting credit, Guy Gabaldon risked his own life to spare the lives of the enemy he reviled.

He resented his own government for its actions after Pearl Harbor, when the Nakanos and Shizumuras, Itos and Unos, and all the Nisei of East Los Angeles were rounded up and sent to concentration camps so suddenly he didn't have a chance to say goodbye. He recalled the internment of Japanese Americans as "blatant racial discrimination, and an excuse to get their homes." Fifty years later you could still sense his shock and sense of betrayal: "The Federal Government had taken my adopted family and close friends and locked them up like animals. Their own country, the U.S.A., had uprooted them from their homes." Some of the victims would end up in uniform, serving the country that had treated them unjustly. The Nakano brothers joined the legendary 442nd Regimental Combat Team, the most decorated unit in the army. Gabaldon wouldn't see them again until long after the war.

Gabaldon had been sent to a high school for "incorrigibles," Andrew Jackson High. He dropped out after his sophomore year. His two older brothers had enlisted in the navy, and he wanted to join too. But he was only sixteen in 1942, and the navy wouldn't have him. He registered for the draft even though he was two years too young. He traveled to Seattle looking for work. Finding none, he saw an ad for jobs for boys over eighteen in fishing canneries in Alaska during salmon season. He showed the agents at the union hiring hall his draft card, was hired, and shipped out in steerage for a cannery in Tyee on an island in southeastern Alaska. He spent nine months working in Tyee, Ketchikan, and Juneau, mostly enjoying himself before returning to Los Angeles to celebrate his seventeenth birthday and enlist in the navy, hoping for duty aboard a submarine.

The navy turned him down again, this time for a perforated eardrum he had suffered in a brawl. He was devastated, he said, but not defeated. He looked for an angle, and he found one when he learned the Marine Corps was looking for Japanese interpreters. He told a recruiter, "I read, write and speak Japanese like a native." That was a lie, of course, but it worked. He passed his Marine Corps physical — no mention was made of the perforated eardrum — and was bused to Camp Pendleton for basic training.

He was often ridiculed at boot camp for being so short and looking even younger than his seventeen years. He was a poor shot too, by his own admission. He barely qualified as a marksman, the minimum qualification for a marine. He dismissed the rationale for boot camp's "seven weeks of concentrated harassment," that the hard training saved lives, as an "excuse for sadism." But none of it seems to have bothered him too much or shaken his self-confidence. "I knew that sheer determination would get me through," he wrote. He didn't need to be a good shot, he explained: "In the jungle . . . you shoot fast, from the hip."

He got thirty days leave after basic training before he had to report to language school at Camp Elliot in San Diego. He spent most of the time at a bowling alley in East L.A., an old high school haunt, flirting with Russian girls whose boyfriends were overseas. He was back at the bowling alley one weekend a few weeks after starting language school and got into a fistfight over a girl with "a big Russian" who shattered his jaw. He spent two weeks recovering at Long Beach Naval Hospital and partying in East L.A. on the weekends. The marines kicked him out of language school and trained him to be a mortarman.

He shipped out for Pearl Harbor with a replacement battalion in December 1943. In Hawaii he tried again to pass himself off as an interpreter, this time to the 2nd Marine Division. Again he was rejected, but he was allowed to join a scout and observer company in his regiment's intelligence section. He spent another five months training on the Big Island, mostly in staged beach assaults and reconnaissance missions. He became close friends with another scout, Private First Class Lloyd Hurley from West Virginia, and suffered, he wrote, his first experience of overt racism in the Corps at the hands of a "redneck" sergeant from Oklahoma. He would later blame the decision not to give him a Medal of Honor or a promotion on the bigotry of what he called "the Old Corps." In the years before World War II, "Blacks, Browns or Yellows" felt unwelcome, and Gabaldon wrote that that sentiment still lingered in the hearts and minds of veteran officers. He exempted from the complaint his commanding officer, Captain John Schwabe, a veteran of Guadalcanal and Tarawa, whom he considered a fair, sympathetic, and capable officer.

Sometime in May 1944 the division was loaded aboard transport ships and left Hawaii without fanfare. They just "quietly slip[ped] out of our berths," Gabaldon remembered, in a convoy bound for a destination they were not told in advance.

On June 11, 1944, five days after the Allied landings in Normandy, the second largest naval armada ever assembled set out from Eniwetok, an atoll in the Marshall Islands: 535 aircraft carriers, battleships, destroyers, cruisers, transport ships, and landing craft, carrying an invasion force of seventy thousand men. Their destination was Saipan, one of four islands in the Marianas archipelago (Tinian, Roto, and Guam were the others) targeted for invasion as part of

Operation Forager, the American offensive against the Japanese-held Marianas and Palau Islands. Admiral Spruance still commanded the Fifth Fleet, and Vice Admiral Richmond Kelly Turner commanded the amphibious landing force. Major General Holland "Howlin' Mad" Smith, his nickname a nod to a legendary temper, had been given command of all ground forces on Saipan, army and marine, and told to take the island in three days. On June 9 he told the reporter Robert Sherrod, "A week from today, there will be a lot of dead Marines."

On June 13 the Fifth Fleet's guns began pounding Saipan and Tinian. Air squadrons from a fast carrier task force commanded by Admiral Marc "Pete" Mitscher (and subsequently commanded by John S. McCain Sr.) had been periodically bombing Saipan for months, and intensely so in the days before the fleet arrived.

Saipan's topography favored the defenders. It's a large island, thirteen miles long with a varying width of three to five miles. It is volcanic, with hills, ravines, swamps, heavily forested mountains, and jagged cliff faces, unlike typically flat and sandy coral islands. Saipan's two ridgelines run the length of its interior on either side of a central valley with thick fields of sugarcane. It has four prominent peaks; the highest, Mount Tapotchau, in the center of the island, rises fifteen hundred feet. Limestone caves are hidden everywhere.

Since the first American air raid in February, Japan had been sending men and matériel to the Marianas. Twenty-five thousand Japanese soldiers defended Saipan, commanded by Lieutenant General Yoshitsugu Saito. There were over six thousand Imperial Japanese Navy sailors on the island as well. Admiral Chuichi Nagumo, who lost four carriers at the Battle of Midway, had been dispatched to Saipan to command the small craft fleet there. Saipan had one airfield and another, smaller airstrip under construction. The Japanese had artillery batteries positioned in the hills and ridges to cover the beaches and an armored regiment with forty-eight tanks.

Japan had occupied Saipan since the end of World War I, and it was the first American invasion target with a large civilian population. More than twenty-three thousand Japanese, Okinawan, and Korean civilians were living on the island in 1944. Both sides recognized the Battle for the Marianas would likely prove a turning point in the war. The Japanese high command had expected the initial strike farther south, at Guam. But surprised or not, General Saito was prepared to give his life, and the lives of every other Japanese on Saipan, military and civilian, rather than surrender the island.

The naval and aerial bombardment that began the offensive continued almost uninterrupted for forty-eight hours. Battleships, destroyers, and heavy cruisers fired nearly two hundred thousand shells of various calibers. It was an unprecedented bombardment that had Japanese soldiers hunkered down in caves writing of it in their diaries with awe.

Admiral Turner gave the order "Land the landing force" at 5:42 on the morning of June 15. At seven o'clock eight thousand marines from the 2nd and 4th divisions began climbing down cargo nets to three hundred armored amphibious landing vehicles (LVTs). Shortly after eight o'clock the LVTs, accompanied by twenty-four light gunboats, started racing toward eight landing sites along a four-mile stretch of the island's southwest coast. Ahead of them, battleships, destroyers, gunboats, and carrier bombers hit the island with a rolling bombardment while carrier fighters strafed the beaches and the trenches behind them.

As soon as the first LVTs crossed the barrier reef, Japanese artillery and mortar batteries started shelling them, using red flags that had been placed in the water to mark distances. Twenty amtracs in the first wave were destroyed. Some of the landing ships ferrying tanks (LST) got hung up on the reef. The first marines came ashore at 8:45 and met a hail of fire from machine guns and rifles as shells and mortars rained down on them from the hills and land mines sent men and machines hurtling into the air.

The 2nd Marines were hit hardest. Some battalions came ashore well north of their assigned landing zones, causing traffic bottlenecks and presenting densely crowded targets to Japanese gunners, who held their fire until the beaches were crammed with marines. Commanders trying to organize their battalions in the chaos were among the first casualties. Despite the heavy casualties, the intensity of the fire they faced, and the chaotic scene they encountered, at least the assault battalions hadn't had to wade ashore under fire, as they had at Tarawa. They landed on the beaches, and the beaches were bad enough. And the marines kept coming. An hour after the first landing, all eight thousand marines in the initial assault were fighting, wounded, or dead on the crowded beaches. By day's end twenty thousand had come ashore.

As the morning wore on the detritus of combat accumulated on the beaches: parts of destroyed vehicles and other machinery, abandoned weaponry, shell craters, and body parts. John Chapin, who as a young marine officer had fought on Saipan and later wrote a brief history of the battle, described the scene: "Jap and Marine bodies lying in mangled and grotesque positions; blasted and burnt-out pillboxes; the burning wrecks of LVTs that had been knocked out by Jap high velocity fire; the acrid smell of high explosives; the shattered trees; and the churned-up sand littered with discarded equipment."

The dead and wounded too were aggregating. Many of the latter would succumb to their wounds when the crowded, confused, and dangerous conditions on the beaches prevented their evacuation. The marines suffered nearly two thousand casualties that first day. Japanese casualties were mounting faster, though. Marines who landed later in the morning had to wade through dead bodies, Japanese and American. Guy Gabaldon would always remember the smell that assaulted him as he approached the beach: "The Jap bodies were already starting to rot. . . . If I were to live a thousand years I would never get over that sweet stink."

The marines advanced relentlessly but slowly. Well-placed Japanese artillery and mortar batteries had stopped amtracs from bringing men to the woods behind the beaches. By nightfall most of the invasion force was still on the beaches, still braving shellfire, machine guns, and snipers, and hadn't secured its first-day objectives. The Japanese made repeated small-scale attacks through the night, especially against the 2nd Division's left flank. They launched a massive counterattack against the entire beachhead at three o'clock in the morning on June 16. It continued in waves for three hours. Finally the weary marines repulsed the last attack as the first rays of sun illuminated beaches littered with some seven hundred Japanese dead.

Private Gabaldon hit the beach late that morning and described it as "a mad house . . . bullets were kicking up the sand . . . and dead Marines were all over the area. . . . It was almost every man for himself until late that afternoon when we established our first lines. It took us almost eight hours to gain the first mile and that was under extremely heavy opposition."

Captain Schwabe hustled the company across a beach road next to the airstrip and ordered them to dig in. Gabaldon stumbled upon a marine, no older than eighteen, with a bullet hole in his head lying dead on the road "in a grotesque position," and he froze. He wondered to himself what he was doing there. He should have been back at his neighborhood bowling alley doing the things eighteen-year-olds normally did. He couldn't explain why the sight of one dead marine among hundreds affected him so, but it practically paralyzed him. "I just stood there," he remembered, "in the middle of the cross fire, the Japs ahead, and our boys on the beach behind me."

Lloyd Hurley pulled him into a foxhole and told him, "Get your ass in gear and start shooting." Gabaldon and the rest of his unit remained in their foxholes along the airstrip, exchanging fire through the night and into the next morning. Schwabe had ordered them to stay there until he determined where they would set up their observation post. But after a quick breakfast of "canned scrambled eggs and beach sand," Gabaldon, who seemed to have quickly acclimated to combat after his horror, decided to leave their lines and venture into "no man's land to see what it's all about."

He reached a trench filled with Japanese killed during the shelling that preceded the landings. Crawling carefully around the trench, he approached from behind three Japanese soldiers who were still alive and watching the Americans. He ordered them in Japanese to raise their hands. One soldier swung his rifle around and Gabaldon shot him. "My first Jap," he records. "I feel nothing, neither pride in killing him nor fear that I will be killed." The other two raised their hands. He assured them in Japanese they wouldn't be harmed if they obeyed him, and marched them back to his command post. He expected to be commended for his audacity and possibly rewarded with the interpreter's job he still hoped to land. Instead an angry Schwabe threatened to have him court-martialed if he ever pulled a stunt like that again. "Don't you ever go off on your own again," the officer demanded. "Understand?"

That afternoon a Japanese soldier in the same trench, pretending to be dead, suddenly came alive and bayoneted a sergeant in the Scouts. Gabaldon remembered him as the "type of Marine you see in the movies. He came into the Command Post holding his guts in . . . [and] had a smile on his face as if nothing had happened." The sergeant was evacuated to a hospital ship, where he died from his wound.

The Japanese launched another large counterattack that night, June 16, including a tank assault. It lasted until dawn, "a madhouse of noise, tracers and flashing lights," as one marine described it. Dozens of crippled tanks, most of them Japanese, burned through the night and were still smoking when the sun came up. "We shot at everything that moved," Gabaldon remembered, "and God help the Marine who got out of his foxhole."

But Gabaldon, for reasons he never convincingly explained, decided to get out of his. He took a carbine off a dead marine, left his heavier M-1 behind, stuffed some ammo clips in his pockets, and without telling anyone what he was doing, crawled off into the darkness. Later he said he was looking to avenge the attack on Pearl Harbor that resulted in his friends being sent to internment camps. He also said he thought if he brought back more Japanese prisoners for interrogation, he might be reconsidered as an interpreter. Whatever his motive, even if it were nothing more than the glory-seeking his critics accused him of, there is no denying what he accomplished. He approached a dugout where he recognized the smell of Japanese food cooking and waited there until dawn. He could hear Japanese soldiers inside reassure each other that the Imperial Japanese Navy would soon reach Saipan with supplies and reinforcements. When the sun started to rise, he tossed a couple of fragmentation grenades into the dugout, then a smoke grenade, and single-handedly took prisoner the dozen enemy soldiers who came out of the bunker to find a single marine pointing a weapon at them. He threatened to kill them if they didn't surrender. Then he ordered them to strip and ran all twelve of them back to his command post, shouting, "Don't shoot! Don't fire! These are prisoners."

Though Captain Schwabe was likely vexed by Gabaldon's rank insubordination, he valued its results. The two prisoners interrogated the day before and the twelve captured that day provided useful intelligence. So he decided to authorize his enterprising subordinate's freelancing. It would likely get Gabaldon killed, but it was obvious he was going to do it anyway. He was just a "lone wolf sort of guy," Schwabe recognized. He would be the 2nd Regiment's lone wolf from then on, bringing in

as many prisoners as he could get to surrender using his bravado, cunning, and
broken Japanese for as long as he wanted to
and as long as he stayed alive.

The two days after D-Day saw 2nd and
4th Division marines advance by close-
quarter fighting from their beachheads
toward their objectives. Their progress
continued slowly and they were still well
behind schedule, but they were inching
ahead against determined Japanese resistance. The army's 27th Infantry Division
had followed the marines ashore on the
16th. One army regiment supported the 4th
Division's right flank, and by the end of
D-Day+2, the 4th had reached Saipan's
operational airfield and forced the Japanese
to abandon it, which had been one of its
D-Day objectives. The 2nd Division fought
its way north toward the town of Garapan.
That same day Admiral Nagumo's gunboats
hove into view behind the beachhead and
attempted an attack from the rear. U.S.
Navy gunboats and marine artillery destroyed the little fleet in detail.

On June 18 the Americans on Saipan
awoke to a puzzling and worrying sight. The
powerful American fleet that had brought
them there and pounded Saipan for days
and carried their supplies, ammunition, and

reinforcements had disappeared from view. Admiral Spruance had ordered it to more secure positions as Admiral Mitscher's task force broke off and rushed six hundred miles west to meet an Imperial Japanese Navy fleet that had been spotted coming through the San Bernardino Strait.

The conversation Gabaldon overheard the night he waited outside the Japanese bunker hadn't been the false bravado or wishful thinking of a besieged enemy. Knowing American control of the Marianas would bring the home islands within range of American B-29s and determined to prevent it, the Japanese had launched Operation A-Go and dispatched an immense fleet for a final showdown with the American Fifth Fleet, using land-based as well as carrier-based aircraft to compensate for the greater number of American carrier planes.

The Battle of the Philippine Sea began the following day, June 19, and lasted into the early morning hours of the 21st. It was the greatest carrier battle of the war. The clashing fleets were the largest assembled in a single battle. It began with an eight-hour air battle involving over a thousand aircraft. The American aviators who fought in it called it "the Great Marianas Turkey Shoot." The Japanese fleet discovered there were not as many land-based planes available for its support as expected; for weeks Mitscher's aviators had been bombing Japanese planes on runways in the Marianas and Palau and on the island of Truk.

Japan lost three carriers in the Battle of the Philippine Sea, two sunk by American submarines and another by American aviators. It also lost nearly four hundred sea- and land-based aircraft and managed to destroy only twenty-six American planes. The smashing defeat effectively ceded control of the Marianas. There would be no relief for Saito's army on Saipan. Nor could much of anything be done for Japanese garrisons on Guam and Tinian. The Imperial Japanese Navy would not continue as an effective fighting force much longer. It had one last epic battle to fight, at Leyte Gulf, and then it would cease, for practical purposes, to pose any serious impediment to the conquest of the Japanese Empire. The American fleet reappeared off Saipan, returning with its nearly inexhaustible cargo of supplies and ammunition for the invasion force and the supporting fire of its big guns and carrier planes. But despite this irreversible turn in the fortunes of war, there was still hard fighting ahead on Saipan, and on Tinian and Guam as well.

General Saito, aware that there would be no reinforcement of his outnumbered army, set up his lines east to west with Mount Tapotchau in the center, in the rugged, hilly terrain of the island's interior. There his soldiers, hiding in caves during the day and attacking at night, would make the Americans pay dearly for every mile gained in landscapes named for the sacrifices their conquest demanded: a line of hills remembered as Purple Heart Ridge, an open field called Death Valley, a small mountain cove dubbed Hell's Pocket.

By the end of the first week on Saipan the two marine divisions, the 2nd pushing north along the west coast and the 4th having cut across the island to the east coast, had suffered more than six thousand casualties. General Holland Smith had them form the flanks of an east-west front with an army infantry regiment in the center, and on June 22 they started a long, slow slog north in the teeth of fierce resistance. The Americans cleared out the defenders cave by cave with flamethrowers and grenades after artillery had pounded the positions. They repulsed counterattacks at night. Dug-in Japanese on

397

Mount Tapotchau and Purple Heart Ridge had clear fields of fire to the narrow, open expanse below, Death Valley, which the Americans had to traverse to reach them.

Smith ordered the rest of the army's 27th Division to clear out remaining Japanese resistance in the southeast corner of the island. Progress was excruciatingly slow on both fronts, so much so that Smith relieved the 27th's commanding general, Major General Ralph Smith, on June 24. The advance north had been almost completely bogged down by then, though the marine divisions on the flanks had gained much more ground than the army infantry in the center. The front had become U-shaped. Whether or not it was justified, the relief of an army general in the field by a Marine Corps general engendered considerable and enduring animosity in the offended service.

The entire line resumed its advance on the 25th. Five days of bitterly hard fighting later, all three divisions were advancing in a relatively straight line. The marines in the 4th Division on the right were fighting in cane fields. The soldiers in the 27th had killed the last defender in Hell's Pocket, pushed through the last of the resistance in Death Valley, and taken the last rise on Purple Heart Ridge. The 2nd Division had reached the outskirts of Garapan on its left, as navy guns reduced the town to rubble and most of its inhabitants fled to the hills, and reached Mount Tipo Pale and Mount Tapotchau on its right. Meanwhile the 2nd Regiment's lone wolf was still busy freelancing.

Gabaldon said it became a game, to see how many he could bring in. He thought he could set some kind of record. One night he approached a large cave and called to the soldiers inside in what he described as a condescending form of speech, believing it would either enrage them or demoralize them. The first soldier who came out was enraged, and Gabaldon killed him. Nine others came out with their hands up after he warned them he had a hundred marines with him. He loaded them all in an ox cart and had them wave their white skivvies overhead as they approached the marines' lines while he walked behind them, pointing his carbine at their backs. He started bringing in larger and larger groups. When some of the marines started a pool, and Hurley bet Gabaldon would take fifty prisoners, he brought in fifty-two. He went out each night, almost always on his own, and he almost always returned with prisoners. It was foolish, and he knew it. "I must have seen too many John Wayne movies," he admitted. But he was addicted to the thrill. "I couldn't stop. I was hooked."

He spent a long night in the hills near Mount Tapotchau pinned down by American artillery firing at a nearby concentration of Japanese. In the morning he picked his way through the enemy dead, collecting a few souvenirs and tins of crabmeat, some rock candy, and two bottles of sake. He was an avid looter, accumulating a store of Japanese watches, swords, medals, and other paraphernalia, even diaries, and supplies of lemon soda, Kirin beer, rock candy, and crabmeat. He once returned to the observation post with a phonograph, some 78s, and two canteens filled with sake. Another time he blew the safe of a bank that had been leveled by artillery, and he and a pal made off with a bag full of yen, which they eventually threw away. His prize possession was a Japanese officer's .32 caliber pistol, which he wore in a shoulder holster for the duration of the campaign. He decorated himself with captured Japanese medals and wore aviator shades and a baseball cap with the brim turned up. In photographs he looks like a movie character, eager and friendly.

He had a lot of close calls. Once he was caught for hours in a ferocious cross fire, crouched behind a boulder with a Catholic priest, as marines were falling on his right and left. He was nearly killed again by friendly fire one night when sentries shot at him after failing to acknowledge his signal. Returning from another mission he commandeered a truck and loaded fifteen naked prisoners into it. When an officer tried to take the truck away from him, Gabaldon refused to relinquish it, complaining he could get killed trying to walk fifteen Japanese through a battalion at night. When the officer demanded to know who he was, Gabaldon didn't give his name, answering only that he was a scout and interpreter. The officer told him to get out of there, that they already had "the best interpreter on the Island, his name's Gabaldon."

Some nights he couldn't talk the enemy into surrendering; he would kill them then. He stood behind a boulder and shouted at the Japanese in one cave that they were surrounded. When two soldiers rushed out with bayonets fixed, Gabaldon shot them dead. Then he threw four grenades into the cave, followed by a satchel charge. Before the smoke cleared, he ran into the cave and sprayed rounds in every direction. He counted seven dead inside, two of them civilians, both women.

When he recounts these and other incidents in his book, he often uses the most disparaging language to refer to the Japanese he killed. They're stupid and sneaky, cruel and disreputable. When he killed them, he was sending them to their "dishonorable ancestors." In one instance he calls them vermin. He writes that he never got used to killing, yet he recalls his kills either matter-of-factly or boastfully. He kept a careful body count and boasted often that he killed thirty-three soldiers on Saipan. He proudly recalled taking careful aim and killing three Japanese so he could appropriate the Harley-Davidson they were riding. On a mission in Garapan he called on two "Imperial Marines" coming out of a building to surrender. They drew their swords, and he "fired off fifteen rounds, point blank." One man was killed instantly, "but the other joker was squirming." Gabaldon approached him and asked if there were other Japanese around. "I had shot his left arm off and he had a few holes in his gut, but the stupid sonavabitch swung out with his saber and I was forced to send him to Valhalla with a round in his temple." He includes a reporter's account of the incident in his book: "E.L.A. GETS TWO JAPS IN SAIPAN ACTION." He mentions another wounded Japanese soldier he had to finish off, "going in for the kill my style, from up close."

It's hard to know how much of the swagger is intended to make his book a good read and how much reflects the real Gabaldon. There are clearly other sides to his personality. He wrote affectingly of a family of Japanese civilians held captive in a bunker with two Japanese soldiers, when marines arrived and tossed grenades into it. The mother died, the father was badly wounded, and an eight-year-old girl convulsed in death spasms as Gabaldon and the other marines worked frantically to save her. "This was a scene I hadn't bargained for," he wrote. He encountered a Japanese soldier badly burned by a flamethrower and stumbling around senselessly, and rather than kill him treated him compassionately. Instead of shooting an escaping prisoner, he ran the man down and became angry when another marine shot him.

Contrary to the callousness and bravado that pervade his reminiscences and attitudes toward the enemy, which he attributed to his impoverished, rough-and-tumble childhood, Gabaldon often displayed a convincing empathy when he talked Japanese soldiers into surrendering. He used threats too, of course, and he maintained he was always

the very picture of a cool, confident con-
queror in the presence of his prisoners. But
he often seemed almost to plead with them
to surrender. He told them he understood
the demands of Bushido, but they had
fought bravely and honorably until fighting
had become impossible and their families
deserved to have them home. He told them
his "shogun," General Holland Smith,
admired them as honorable warriors and
would treat them honorably. They would
not be harmed, he insisted, but fed, clothed,
and shown respect, and would be returned
unharmed to their families after the war. If
they refused his offer of good treatment they
could be certain he and the hundred or so
marines surrounding their cave would kill
them. But it need not come to that, and he
hoped it wouldn't. It was an effective
combination of bravado, despair, and sympathy, all the more impressive considering
in most instances Gabaldon claims he had
to kill one or two before the others would
surrender. But out they came with their
hands up, singly, then by the dozens, then
scores, then hundreds of them, naked, waving their skivvies, marching off to the
stockade with the man who came to be
called "the Pied Piper of Saipan."

The battle of Saipan began drawing to a close in the first week of July, but not without a few last spasms of horrific violence and bloodletting. The ratio of dead and wounded was 9 to 1, to the Americans' advantage. The majority of Saito's army was dead, sacrificed along with his tanks in the many failed frontal counterattacks. Only seven thousand were still able to fight. They were being pushed farther and farther north, until their backs were to the sea, and they were running desperately low on ammunition, food, and water. The seriously wounded were killing themselves now. The marines occupied Garapan on the Fourth of July. Gabaldon claimed he and a buddy were the first to enter the city, days before it fell.

General Smith issued orders for the 4th Division and the 27th to pivot west around the 2nd Division north of Garapan. He planned to relieve the 2nd once the 4th and 27th reached the west coast and use it in reserve in the invasion of Tinian on July 24. On July 5 General Saito and Admiral Nagumo met in Saito's last command post, a cave north of the coastal village of Tanapag, in an area the Americans had heavily bombarded and nicknamed Paradise Valley. Saito, tired and wounded, held a ceremonial dinner with his senior commanders, then dispatched runners to deliver to his scattered forces his final orders for one last mass frontal assault. The communiqué acknowledged they were doomed. "There is only death," it read. "However in death there is life. We must utilize this opportunity to exalt true Japanese manhood. I will advance with those who remain to deliver still another blow to the American Devils and leave my bones on Saipan as a bulwark of the Pacific."

With that, Saito cut his wrists and an aide shot him in the temple. Nagumo and his chief of staff also took their own lives that night, reportedly committing ritual seppuku.

A final banzai charge was not a surprise to the Americans, who could hear preparations being made before it was launched and waited anxiously for it. It seemed every pitched battle on Saipan had ended with a suicide attack. This one would be different in two respects. First, it would be larger than any previous charge, the largest of the war, involving nearly all Japanese soldiers still capable of fighting and many who couldn't, as well as civilians who had been

406

convinced by propaganda that Americans would murder them in the most gruesome ways imaginable. Second, the Japanese believed the emperor had ordered the charge, which conferred a special distinction. It would be a *gyokusai* attack, a fight to the last man. *Gyokusai* translates literally as "shattered jade." It is better to die with honor, like "shattered jade," than live in shame.

The attack's ostensible objective was to sweep through the American lines and retake Tanapag and Garapan. But the true purpose was to die and take as many Americans with them as possible. It began in the early morning of July 7, when several thousand Japanese swarmed from their cover, crying "Tenno Haika! Banzai!" (Long live the emperor! Ten thousand ages!), and rushed at the American lines. They carried rifles, swords, grenades, and knives fastened onto bamboo poles. Many of the walking wounded who joined the attack — and some were barely able to walk — were armed with only rocks and their fists. American artillery tore into them, and when they got too close, the gunners shortened their fuses and fired shells into the ground in front of them. Machine gunners swept their guns right to left, cutting down hundreds, thousands. And still they came. Mortar crews fired round after round until they ran out of shells. And still wave followed wave, breaking through the American lines in several places, overwhelming and nearly destroying two battalions in the 27th and one marine artillery battalion. The Americans put up a valiant and determined resistance. In one infantry battalion, the 105th, three soldiers would receive the Medal of Honor for their heroism that day, all of them posthumously. The fighting was soon hand to hand, with knives and fists. Some veterans who had fought on Tarawa and in other campaigns remembered it as the most desperate fighting of the war.

The attack finally slowed and then expired around eight o'clock in the evening, about a thousand yards south of Tanapag. Over four thousand Japanese had been killed. There weren't enough left alive to continue. The Americans suffered over a thousand dead and wounded but quickly recovered the ground they lost. There were Japanese survivors hiding in caves who were still capable of putting up some resistance. Presumably they planned to die defending the last few miles of Saipan. Many of them would, as would many civilians, convinced that the American barbarians would roast and eat their children if they were taken alive.

Gabaldon tried to save as many lives, American and Japanese, as he could. He reported taking over a hundred prisoners two days before the *gyokusai* charge. He had spent the previous night behind enemy lines, where he remained for the duration of the attack, hiding near the cliffs at Marpi Point at the northern end of the island. He watched wounded Japanese coming back from the attack throw themselves into the sea. He watched others disappear into the caves in the cliffs, along with thousands of civilians.

On the morning of July 8 he took two prisoners on the head of what would thereafter be known as Suicide Cliff. He pointed to the armada standing offshore and said it would soon train all its big guns on the caves. They would surely be killed, he told them. Why die when they had a chance "to surrender under honorable conditions"? He convinced one of them to carry his appeal to his fellow *gyokusai* survivors at the bottom of the cliff. Later he wrote that while he waited for their answer, he wondered who the real prisoner was. There were hundreds, maybe thousands of Japanese there, who had but hours ago been trying to kill every American they could, at the cost of their own lives. They could take his life in a flash if they wanted it. He was still pondering his predicament when the Japanese soldier returned with twelve others, all carrying rifles.

Gabaldon didn't know if they were giving up or if he was now their prisoner. They didn't point their weapons at him, but they didn't lay them down either, and he wasn't in a position to order them to do so. This time he couldn't convince anyone that there were a hundred marines hiding somewhere on the open expanse of the cliff top. *"Dozo o suwari nasai"* (Please sit down), he invited them and offered them cigarettes. He told them he was his shogun's emissary. "General Smith admires your valor and has ordered our troops to offer safe haven to all the survivors of your intrepid Gyokusai attack yesterday. . . . You will be taken to Hawaii where you will be kept together in honorable quarters until the end of the war. The General's word is honorable."

Their commanding officer, a first lieutenant, reached for one of Gabaldon's cigarettes and asked if his wounded would receive treatment in a hospital. Gabaldon assured him they would. The officer gazed at the American fleet for a moment, then

410

turned to Gabaldon and announced, *"So da yo! Horyo ni naru!"* (So be it. I become your prisoner.) With that, he stood up, and leaving four of his soldiers with Gabaldon, went to summon the others from the caves. He returned with fifty more soldiers. Gabaldon was still apprehensive. "They do not look like defeated men," he reported. "They are proud and serious — as if they haven't really made up their minds." The Japanese officer informed him there were many more wounded below, soldiers and civilians, and they needed urgent treatment. He insisted the worst wounded be given medicine and water immediately. Gabaldon explained that he hadn't enough of either commodity to meet their needs, but all would be provided once they reached American lines. He asked the lieutenant to bring up all his people. Some minutes later a seemingly endless train of soldiers and civilians, hundreds of them, some grievously wounded, emerged from their caves and began working their way up the cliff.

When they reached the top they expected to find a large party of Americans. Instead all they saw was one small Chicano kid from East L.A. in a white T-shirt, wearing aviator sunglasses, a baseball cap with the brim turned up, and a pistol in a shoulder harness busily separating soldiers, civilians, and wounded into separate groups and silently wondering how the hell he was going to get all these prisoners to the rear by himself. It wasn't long before his prisoners became restive, but then they spotted a group of puzzled marines on a nearby hill staring at them. Gabaldon had one of the Japanese wave his skivvies on a stick. The marines hopped in a jeep and drove to them, while another group came running. Soon afterward the party of marines brought in the first of Gabaldon's prisoners to the command post. Eight hundred more followed. They brought the last bunch in at ten o'clock that night, after which Gabaldon ate a K ration and went to bed.

He awoke the next morning to excited congratulations from his lieutenant. Hurley told him he had heard Captain Schwabe was going to recommend him for a Medal of Honor. Gabaldon replied he'd believe it when he saw it, and then he and Hurley headed back to the cliffs to see if they could convince any more to surrender.

While many of the surviving Japanese were resigned to surrendering, and some even desperate to, there were others still intent on killing and dying. Many marines had approached caves and bunkers and tried to coax them out; they were killed for their compassion. More often grenades and flamethrowers were used to settle the question, or bulldozers closed up entrances and left the inhabitants to die a slow death. Japanese who wouldn't surrender broke the fuse on their grenades and clutched them to their chest. Others simply swam out to sea until they could swim no farther, while some marines took potshots at them for sport. Many jumped from Suicide Cliff onto the rocks below, where they died slowly and painfully. To the horror of the Americans, many of the suicides were civilians, entire families of civilians, hundreds of them.

The Americans tried to save some of them, and did. Others couldn't be persuaded. Gabaldon recalled one mother running toward the cliff with an infant in her arms. He pleaded with her not to jump and asked permission to shoot her in the legs, which an officer refused to grant, and then watched as she threw first her child and then herself over the edge. While the suicides were occurring, General Smith declared Saipan officially "secured." Many hardened veterans of the Pacific were haunted by their memory of Suicide Cliff more than any other experience in the war.

■ ■ ■ ■

Two weeks later Gabaldon landed with the rest of the division on Tinian. He claimed he was officially credited with taking 183 prisoners there, "a record in itself," he wrote, "but to me anti-climactic." The Battle of Tinian lasted a week and claimed two thousand American casualties, a seventh of the fourteen thousand dead and wounded on Saipan. Gabaldon was back on Saipan in August, helping mop up isolated bands of diehard Japanese still hiding in the mountains and jungles. He heard more rumors that he would receive the Medal of Honor, and his superiors assured him he was going to be promoted. Not long after returning to Saipan, he was caught in an ambush and wounded in his wrist and side by machine-gun fire. Just before he left Saipan, he was awarded the Silver Star and was clearly disappointed it wasn't a Medal of Honor, as were, he claims, his immediate superiors. Then someone stole his war souvenirs.

He lived a colorful and peripatetic life after the war. He went back to school, married and divorced, and ran a seafood and bush-flying business in Mexico, where he met his second wife, Ohana, whose father was Japanese. He claimed he recruited a battalion of volunteers to fight Castro in 1961 but was stopped by Attorney General Robert Kennedy, who denounced him as a vigilante. He tried to lead a group of freedom fighters in Nicaragua, he said. He ran unsuccessfully for Congress as a Republican in 1964. He had five sons and three daughters.

In 1957 he was surprised to find himself the subject of an episode of the television show *This Is Your Life.* Captain Schwabe was there, along with two others of his officers, to testify to his courage, enterprise, and humanity. Hurley appeared on the show too; so did Lane and Lyle Nakano, whom he hadn't seen in years. He was overjoyed to be reunited with them. Three years later Paramount Studios released *Hell to Eternity,* a film based on his exploits on Saipan. In the movie Gabaldon became an Italian surname, and blue-eyed, six-foot-two Jeffrey Hunter played him. Gabaldon served as a technical advisor on the film and appeared to have enjoyed the experience. But he wanted it known that, unlike in the movie, where his character often has a sidekick on his missions, in reality he was always alone.

After the movie his Silver Star was up-graded to a Navy Cross, the second highest decoration a marine can receive. That was nice, but he still felt shortchanged. He believed he had earned a Medal of Honor, and so did his immediate superiors. He had captured over fifteen hundred Japanese and killed thirty-three by himself, and you didn't have to take his word for it, he insisted, his officers would vouch for the numbers. He believed only racism could explain why he did not receive the decoration he deserved. In his later years he said he felt happy and blessed. But you could tell it still bothered him.

In 1980 he moved with his family to Saipan, where he owned a couple of small businesses, worked with the police for a time, and ran a program to keep kids off drugs. He resented the influence Japan had on the island, which he attributed to orga-nized criminal networks. He resented too that the memorial on Saipan for Japanese war dead was more impressive than any tribute to the Americans who sacrificed so much there, and he campaigned for a memorial that would do justice to their memory.

He went home to California in 1995 and eventually retired to Florida to be near some of his children. He died there in 2006. He never received the Medal of Honor. There are many who feel that is an injustice; others feel differently. His Navy Cross citation commends his "extreme courage and initiative" on Saipan. No one would argue with that. Perhaps the best summary of Gabaldon's actions on Saipan is the one that the lone wolf from East L.A. himself gave to an interviewer not long before he died: "I fought my war the way I wanted to, when I wanted to and where I wanted to."

No one could argue with that either.

Sergeant First Class Chester D. "Pete" Salter Jr. upon his return from Korea in 1951.

CHAPTER NINE: DUTY

Chester "Pete" Salter fought hand to hand to get off a hill in Korea, and was wounded fighting to take the hill back and retrieve the body of the man who had saved his life.

Most of them were inexperienced, poorly trained, ill-equipped, and fresh from the comforts of occupation duty in Japan. But green or not, every soldier in the 19th Infantry Regiment would have known he had walked into a disaster as soon as he reached the Eighth Army's front lines on the southern bank of the Kum River.

On July 12, 1950, the U.S. Eighth Army in Korea comprised the 24th Infantry Division, which, at that time, consisted of just three understrength regiments: the 21st, the 34th, and the 19th. The bloodied remnants of the decimated 21st passed through the 19th's ranks to take up a blocking position in the rear. The whipped and demoralized 34th held the line to the left of the 19th. On the other side of the river were two of North Korea's best divisions, and they had armor, the feared Soviet T-34s, which couldn't be stopped by any weapons the thin American line then possessed.

There wasn't much fighting that first day. The 19th didn't lose a man to hostile fire as it took its place on the right of the line. But one soldier, Corporal John Carlyle Smith from Lowell, North Carolina, twenty-seven years old, died from a heart attack. In a few days hundreds of names would appear with his on the 19th Infantry's casualty list.

The Eighth Army was deployed to Korea piecemeal. Given the speed with which the three invading columns of the North Korean People's Army, the Choson Inmin'gun, had overwhelmed the unprepared, outnumbered, and less armed forces of the Republic of Korea, this was hardly ideal. It was, however, a necessity. On June 26, when President Harry S. Truman authorized General Douglas MacArthur to send American troops to Korea, the 24th Division, like the other three divisions occupying Japan, was understrength and scattered around the home islands of Japan. It would take time to consolidate, reinforce, and organize its transport to Pusan. MacArthur directed the division's commanding general, Major General William Dean, to send a small force at once to Pusan with orders to deploy as far north as possible and delay for as long as possible the North Korean advance. A Guadalcanal veteran, Lieutenant Colonel Charles B. "Brad" Smith, commanding officer of the 1st Battalion of the 21st Infantry Regiment, got the call.

Task Force Smith consisted of two reinforced but still understrength rifle companies, a heavy weapons platoon, and a number of headquarters and communication personnel, about five hundred soldiers in all, each equipped with 120 rounds of ammunition and two days' worth of C rations. About a third of the officers had combat experience, as did about half of the noncommissioned officers. In the ranks, though, very few had fought in World War II, maybe less than a sixth, typical in the postwar army. They left for Pusan by airlift the morning of July 1 with a parting instruction from MacArthur, the general of the army and supreme commander of the newly authorized United Nations Command, to confront the advancing enemy "with an arrogant show of force." The following night the first elements of the 34th Infantry Regiment left for Pusan by ship, and the night after that the rest of the 21st Infantry deployed. Both regiments had two rather than the regulation three battalions, and their mobility, firepower, and training were far from combat-ready due to massive postwar defense budget cuts.

From Pusan the task force traveled by train to the city of Taejon, where Smith conferred with Brigadier General John Church, who had arrived in South Korea several days earlier with a party of officers from MacArthur's headquarters to assess the situation. He told Smith to take his force to a place several miles north of Osan, near the town of Sowan on the Osan-Seoul Highway, to support South Korean troops that had been driven from the capital and were in danger of annihilation. Smith would have a single field artillery battery to support his mission.

On July 5, in the Battle of Osan, Task Force Smith managed to hold up a North Korean column for several hours before being enveloped and decimated. That was a commendable achievement considering they were seriously outnumbered and had no way of stopping the T-34s. About 40 percent of the task force was killed, wounded, or missing. The rest worked their way down to the 34th's lines fifteen miles to the south or scattered into the hills.

Two days later the 34th, having fallen back prematurely from its initial positions, set up a new defensive line in the town of Chonon, which also quickly collapsed. Most of the regiment bugged out in a disorderly retreat south. Many of the wounded were executed by North Koreans, and many others shot while trying to surrender. The regiment's commanding officer, Colonel Robert Smith, was killed while trying to stop a T-34 with a 2.36-inch bazooka.

On July 10 Colonel Dick Stephens tried to hold a ridge about twenty miles northeast of Taejon with the 3rd Battalion, 21st Regiment, and what was left of Brad Smith's 1st Battalion task force. General Dean asked Stephens to delay the North Koreans for four days, while he set up his defensive line along the bend of the Kum River above Taejon. Stephens could give him only two days before two North Korean divisions enveloped his lines. Many of his men fought valiantly and well under the circumstances, and their retreat to the river was orderly. Since the Battle of Osan, the 21st had lost over half its soldiers. Including support personnel, the regiment had about eleven hundred men still able-bodied, but they looked anything but combat-effective as they slogged past the newly arrived 19th Regiment.

Major General Walton "Johnny" Walker, veteran of both world wars and a corps commander in Patton's Third Army, arrived in Pusan on July 13 to assume command of the Eighth Army, which still amounted to not much more than the three under-strength regiments of the 24th Division that were manning the thin line along the Kum River. Walker established his headquarters at Taegu, just east of the Naktong River. He had wanted to be closer to the front, at Tae-jon, the important transportation hub where Dean and the 24th's HQ were presently located. But Taejon was a confused, chaotic place, overcrowded with refugees pouring south in front of the Inmin'gun columns, and communications were hard to maintain there.

More to the point, the city was certain to fall, as Walker and Dean both realized. *When* was the critical question. Walker pressed Dean to hold off the North Koreans as long as he could to give him enough time to set up a defensive perimeter along the Naktong that could hold while the Eighth Army built up strength. Taejon was snug behind a wide bend of the Kum that served as a moat around three sides of the city. To hold the city you had to hold the river, so Dean ordered all the bridges blown after the last, weary soldiers of the 21st Infantry crossed to the south bank on July 12, and the 19th Regiment, untested and no doubt a little scared, took its place in the line.

The 19th Infantry Regiment, nicknamed "the Rock of Chickamauga" for its famous stand in that bloody Civil War battle, had started arriving in Pusan on July 4. Most of the regiment had been stationed in Japan. They had had no time in country to train or prepare before they were rushed to the front. The regiment had brought twenty-two hundred men in total to Korea, including headquarters staff and communications and support personnel. As the only regiment in the division that hadn't been chewed up already, the 19th was expected to hold the longest stretch of the river, nearly thirty critical miles, with 3rd Battalion, 34th Infantry holding the left flank. So long a front with so few troops to defend it necessitated wide gaps in the line. The 19th's commanding officer, Colonel Guy Meloy, put his 1st Battalion and two rifle companies in the 2nd Battalion, E and G, on the line. He held the rest of the 2nd in reserve. He had six artillery batteries supporting him.

On July 14 the left of the line started to come under pressure. The night before one of the 34th's companies, K, had been withdrawn to Taejon because it had barely a handful of men fit to fight. In the morning North Korean tanks gathered along the north bank and, with artillery and mortar batteries, began shelling L Company. American air strikes failed to drive them off. A couple miles downriver boats were spotted ferrying small numbers of enemy soldiers across the river. L Company's commander, having lost communication with the battalion, spooked and pulled the company off the line and back to battalion headquarters. I Company was left to hold the left of the line alone that day, with no one to its left and the 19th regiment two miles to its west. That afternoon North Koreans breached the line and attacked and overran an artillery battalion three miles south of the river. That night I Company received orders to withdraw and rejoin the regiment. The 19th's left flank was now completely exposed and Indians were in the fort.

In the morning Colonel Meloy sent the rest of 2nd Battalion to shore up his left flank, keeping only one rifle company in reserve. All day the tense 19th line could see the North Koreans readying for a massive attack across the river. They repulsed small probing attacks several times during the day, while hearing reports of more and more North Koreans coming across in the west.

At three o'clock on the morning of July 16, a North Korean plane dropped a flare over the river, giving the signal to attack. North Korean artillery, tanks, mortars, machine guns, and rifles fired an opening salvo the intensity of which even the regiment's veterans had not experienced. As the regiment stood the barrage, the North Koreans plunged into the Kum to wade and swim across. For a critical period they were invisible when a howitzer stopped firing flares to illuminate the crossings. By the time it resumed, hundreds were already across, driving through the thousand-yard gap between E and C companies, turning west and hitting C with everything they had. In the east the enemy was crossing in even greater numbers. By daybreak they were swarming across everywhere and attacking 1st Battalion's command post.

Meloy organized a counterattack, using just about every able-bodied soldier in the regiment, including cooks and clerks, and succeeded in pushing back the North Korean advance through the center of the line. Dean had asked Meloy to hold on until nightfall and then withdraw to a position closer to Taejon. But with the enemy infiltrated behind them and, for some unexplained reason, very little to no air support, that was an exceedingly difficult request to fulfill. By late morning the North Koreans had set up a roadblock on the highway three miles behind the line, trying to trap the 1st Battalion at the river. Meloy personally led an unsuccessful attempt to clear it and was severely wounded. Most of the regiment was in combat for the first time. They had been fighting desperately for seven hours and were still crouched down in withering fire from their front, while enemy soldiers were swarming around their flanks and blocking their retreat. There weren't enough men to hold the line and clear out the enemy behind them. By noon the temperature had reached 100 degrees Fahrenheit. They had little water and nothing to eat. Their ammunition was running low. But they had to keep fighting all afternoon. They had no other choice.

When word of the deteriorating situation reached Dean in Taejon around one o'clock, he ordered the regiment to withdraw and said he would send a force to clear the roadblock. Second Battalion's commander tried and failed to open the road, and his men, those who weren't killed and wounded in the attempt, were now pinned down. No one from Taejon managed to clear it either. With the road now closed to them, the regiment's survivors took to the hills, leaving vehicles and artillery behind. Some of the wounded were left behind too, along with the hundreds dead. A chaplain, Franciscan priest Father Herman Felhoelter, remained behind with a group of thirty wounded men after the soldiers serving as stretcher bearers became too exhausted to continue. When they reached the top of the ridge, the men looked back to see North Koreans surround Father Felhoelter and his charges. One of them shot the priest in the back of the head, while the others killed all the wounded.

The 19th suffered catastrophic losses on July 16. Well over three hundred men were killed in action; hundreds of others were wounded or taken prisoner; thirty-four officers were killed or missing. C Company had the worst of it; its casualty rate was a shocking 70 percent. Only two companies, E and G, were in decent shape.

The regiment reorganized and reequipped in the town of Yongdong, twenty miles southeast of Taejon, where the division's command post was located. Few soldiers would have felt capable of anything beyond rest and mourning their dead, but they would have to fight again very soon. The Battle for Kum River was over. The Battle for Taejon was about to start, and General Dean had only three broken regiments to fight it with.

Dean didn't expect to hold on to Taejon for long. He thought they could put up enough of a fight to keep the North Koreans outside the city until July 19. General Walker asked him for a day beyond that to get enough forces into position to stop the enemy at the Naktong. Elements of the 1st Cavalry Division and other units were already arriving in country. So Dean and his battered division held on until July 20, when the enemy swarmed the defenders and infiltrated into the city and T-34s patrolled its streets. It was every man for himself as the survivors again took to the hills, heading this time for the Naktong, where they hoped they would find an American line that could hold.

In the afternoon of July 18 Dean ordered the regiment's 2nd Battalion, which was in far better shape than the decimated 1st Battalion, to Taejon. It arrived the next day around noon and was immediately rushed to the Nonsan road west of the city at the Kapchon River, where Dean was watching the enemy envelop a company in the 34th Regiment. The 2nd Battalion's commander, Colonel Thomas McGrail, positioned three companies to cover both sides of the road. E Company was south of the road on the left; F Company dug in on the right, on a hill north of the road, where it confronted the North Koreans that had flanked L Company of the 34th. A mile to their right 1st Battalion, 34th Infantry was positioned along the Seoul highway a mile in front of Taejon's airstrip and was under heavy fire. Its commanding officer wanted to retreat and recommended the entire regiment be withdrawn that night. He was ordered to hold.

The soldiers of F Company fought to hold their ground all afternoon. That night they could hear North Koreans on their right moving through the gap that separated the 19th and 34th Infantry positions. At three o'clock on the morning of July 20, enemy infantry and armor rolled down both sides of the highway, infiltrated 1st Battalion, 34th Infantry, and reached the airfield and the outskirts of the city.

On the Nonsan road companies E and F

431

had been fighting for hours. By daylight F Company had fallen back a few hundred yards but was still fighting. E Company, "Easy," was holding fast but taking heavy casualties. Colonel McGrail, believing the enemy was already in the city and their road back blocked, abandoned his command post and ordered both companies to withdraw. The 2nd Battalion had suffered 203 casualties, 30 percent of its strength. F Company had lost ten men killed in action. Easy Company lost seventeen. The battalion escaped into the hills south of the road, breaking into small bands, some in pairs and even individually. A twenty-year-old private first class in Easy's heavy weapons platoon, Ed Svach, remembered Taejon as his second worst fight in the war: "We were told to put our personal effects in a box that was to be buried and were given the option of surrendering. But we didn't want to surrender. We'd already seen the bodies of guys who had been shot in the head with their hands tied behind their backs. We figured we had better odds trying to fight our way through."

Most men made their way back to Yongdong over the next two days. A few would trek for many days in the direction of Pusan, 130 miles to the southeast.

There were no more American forces blocking the western approaches to the city. Taejon's situation was hopeless. Dean made plans to abandon the city that afternoon, and he remained there to the end. He even hunted a T-34 himself with a weapon that had finally been supplied that could actually kill one, the 3.5-inch bazooka.

With the retreat from Taejon, the 24th Division had been pushed a hundred miles to the southeast in two and a half weeks of war. The green, unprepared soldiers who filled its ranks had in some instances given a good account of themselves under the circumstances. In other instances, not so much. Few if any had expected to fight a war when they enlisted. They were thrown into combat without any clear idea of how to achieve their mission or, in some instances, of exactly what that mission was. They had lost most of their vehicles and a lot of their artillery and suffered shortages in just about everything: armor, anti-armor, ammunition, communications equipment, rations, and water. Even uniforms were hard to come by. They were often new to the units they fought in, as were their officers. Some second and first lieutenants were nearly as green as the men they commanded, and a disproportionately high number of them were killed in those first weeks, as were many noncommissioned officers. In sum, the 24th Division had not been combat-ready when it was unexpectedly sent to war. It held on as best as it could, narrowly escaped annihilation, and delayed the enemy's advance just long enough for the Eighth Army and retreating Republic of Korea (ROK) forces to set up a defensible line along the Naktong River and stop the enemy from driving them into the sea.

The North Koreans set up roadblocks on the main routes out of Taejon, forcing most of the retreating Americans into the mountains. Dean himself, traveling with a small party of officers and wounded, was forced off the road a few miles south of the city. Climbing a mountain in the dark that night, Dean left the party to fetch water for the wounded. He lost his footing and fell into a ravine unseen, was knocked unconscious, and broke his shoulder. When he came to he was alone. For thirty-six days he wandered the mountains trying to make his way to the American lines. For a few days he traveled in the company of First Lieutenant Stanley Tabor, who had also become separated from his unit, E Company in the 19th Infantry. At one point they were discovered by North Korean soldiers, but Dean managed to escape through a rice paddy. Tabor was wounded and died in a prison camp three months later. Dean stayed at large until August 25, when he was betrayed by South Koreans, captured, and taken north, where he remained a prisoner for the duration of the war.

On July 23 General Church replaced the missing-in-action Bill Dean as commanding general of the 24th Infantry Division. That same day air reconnaissance discovered a North Korean column attempting to pivot east around the Eighth Army's left flank in a drive on Pusan. Walker told Church the exhausted 24th would have to plug the gap. "I am sorry I have to do this," he apologized. The 24th had been off the line for only a day, when the newly arrived 1st Cavalry relieved them at Yongdong. They had yet to be resupplied or receive replacements. Church instructed Colonel Ned Moore, the wounded Meloy's replacement, to deploy the 19th to positions near the city of Chinju, a little more than fifty miles west of Pusan. They arrived on July 25, just as the North Koreans took Yongdong from the 1st Cavalry, and the front moved south again. Five days earlier a troop transport had docked in Okinawa carrying four hundred fresh recruits for the 29th Regiment, 2nd Division. They were quickly armed and equipped, assigned to companies, and reloaded on ships for Pusan.

Hardly any of the new recruits had any combat experience or instruction other than basic training, which they had only recently completed at Fort Riley, Kansas. They had expected to receive six weeks of additional training in Japan. When the misfortunes of war necessitated their immediate transport to the Eighth Army in Korea, they were told they would receive ten days of training there before being moved into the line. Instead, after they arrived in Pusan on July 24, they were assigned to the depleted 19th Regiment and moved the next morning to Chinju.

That day Colonel Moore received word that North Korean soldiers were entering the mountain-pass village of Hadong, thirty miles west of Chinju. He ordered Lieutenant Colonel Harold Moore and 3rd Battalion, 29th Infantry to drive the enemy from the town and secure the approach to Chinju. They made camp the following night in a village three miles east of Hadong and went into combat the next morning. It was over by midafternoon, and it was a debacle. The North Koreans were waiting.

They infiltrated the gaps between company positions, targeted company officers, and generally sowed panic and confusion among the raw recruits, who broke and ran back in the direction whence they came, suffering hundreds of casualties. The 3rd Battalion, 29th Regiment existed no more. The battalion was disbanded and its survivors parceled out to different units, many of them to the 19th Infantry.

The Inmin'gun launched an advance east along a wide front the following day. An enemy column with armor poured through the pass at Hadong and on the morning of July 29 smashed into the 19th's lines six miles west of Chinju. Pusan was now in peril. Were the North Koreans to reach the port they would cut off the entire Eighth Army from resupply and reinforcement. Two days earlier MacArthur had met with Walker at the Eighth Army commander's headquarters in Taegu and told him there would be "no Dunkirk." As North Korean tanks were rumbling toward Chinju, General Walker issued his famous "stand or die" order: "There will be no more retreating, withdrawal or readjustment of the lines. . . . There is no line behind us to which we can retreat. . . . If some of us must die, we will die fighting together. . . . We are going to hold this line."

On the morning of July 30 two 19th Infantry companies, Easy and Fox, were forced to pull back several miles. The Battle for Chinju was over twenty-four hours later. The North Koreans took the city, and the 2nd Battalion retreated across the Nam River, accompanied by hordes of refugees. The regiment's losses were staggering: seventy-five killed in action and hundreds wounded in two days of fighting. Walker ordered all Eighth Army and ROK units to begin to pull back and cross the Naktong, blow the bridges, and prepare for a last stand. The enemy waited a day before advancing on Masan, the last city west of the Naktong River and the North's penultimate objective. If it took Masan, the North Koreans could drive directly on Pusan. On August 2, at the Battle of the Notch, the 19th redeemed itself. It repulsed several North Korean attacks on a mountain pass outside Masan. The victory ended the offensive against the Eighth Army's southern flank. American lines would now consolidate behind the Naktong, while more troops and supplies arrived daily at the port that so many Americans had already died to protect.

The 19th Infantry had received some

replacements and new equipment and, finally, some tanks before the Battle of the Notch. More men had just arrived at Pusan. One of them, assigned to Easy Company, should have arrived with the earlier replacements. He had been unavoidably detained, however, and missed the boat to Okinawa. All things considered, he probably didn't regret his tardiness, though he would have wished its cause had been more benign.

Corporal Chester Day "Pete" Salter Jr. was hitchhiking from his family's home in Pleasant Valley, Iowa, to Fort Riley, Kansas. His furlough after completing basic training was over, and he had to rejoin his unit, a replacement battalion bound for Korea. They were leaving for the West Coast in a few days, and from there to Japan and on to Korea by sea. The three men who had just picked him up seemed friendly. One of them had gotten out of the front passenger seat when they pulled over and given it to him. The driver was quiet, but the two men in the back engaged Salter in conversation. They said they had friends at Fort Riley. They were obviously veterans.

One of them hit him hard on the back of his head with something made of metal, a sap or a length of pipe or a pistol butt. They took his wallet as he struggled to stay conscious. When one of the men in the back instructed the driver to turn off at the next road so they could "finish him," Salter was alert enough to open the door and roll out when the car slowed for the turn. He ran into a cornfield and hid until they drove away. Then he made his way to the nearest farmhouse and collapsed.

Two days passed before Fort Riley received word of what had happened. The army had already declared Salter absent without leave. He was hospitalized for three weeks, and his battalion sailed without him. His fellow replacements had already been assigned to their new units, and some of them had just reached Chinju, by the time Salter boarded an airplane flight, his first, for the coast. From there he flew to Okinawa, then on to Pusan by transport ship with a large group of replacements.

Salter was born and raised in Iowa, the first of three children to an upper-middle-class family. His father was a good man, firm but not severe, unpretentious, hardworking, and generous. He raised his children to be respectful and respectable people. His mother had been the more impatient parent, sharper in her criticism

440

and more sparing in her affection. When Pete grew to be a handful, a little rebellious, his mother thought instruction at a military academy would correct the deficiencies in his character that taxed her patience. He was sent to Shattuck Military Academy in Faribault, Minnesota, for three years of secondary education. There he learned something of martial discipline, though not so much that it noticeably affected his behavior. He was a good-looking kid, athletic, and popular with both sexes. He smoked, drank, fought, and broke a few other rules. He wasn't much of a delinquent, just a little willful and given to misadventure for the fun of it. One of his friends at Shattuck, Marlon Brando, perhaps anticipating some of the roles he would play early in his film career, was the more determined rebel. There had been some trouble at a high school in Omaha, which is why he found himself unhappily enrolled at a military academy in Minnesota. He wasn't there long, Salter remembered. Shattuck too eventually expelled him.

World War II was raging, and like most boys his age Salter wanted to fight. At the end of his junior year he tried to join the Marine Corps. Since he was only seventeen, he needed his parents' permission. His

441

father agreed, and then quietly saw to it that his son shipped out as a sailor. Salter spent the last year of the war aboard a troop transport ship in the Pacific theater. He mustered out eighteen months later, an electrician's mate third class.

Back in the States, he finished his last year of high school at a Catholic boys' academy in his hometown and was nearing the end of his first year at Iowa State when an army recruiter offered him a chance for a more distinguished military career. With the prospect of an officer's commission and the warning that a war with the Soviet Union could not be far off, Pete Salter joined the U.S. Army. Since he had reached his majority, he no longer needed his parents' consent.

He started basic training at the end of April 1950. The North Koreans crossed the 38th parallel two months later. A month after that Salter was on his way to war with a lump on the back of his head and the promise of a commission forgotten. In deference to his previous service and his military-style education, the army had made him a corporal and sent him to E Company, 2nd Battalion, 19th Infantry Regiment. Easy had already had a hard war by the time Salter joined it, but its hardest time was yet to come.

The Pusan Perimeter was a rectangular box of mountainous terrain one hundred miles long north to south along the Naktong's east bank and fifty miles wide, with the highest mountains in the north and the Sea of Japan in the south. It gave the Americans a conventional front line behind a natural barrier they knew how to defend, unlike the constantly flanked, collapsing, shifting front and cross-country scrambling of the past few weeks. They also had for the first time a numerical advantage over the enemy. Walker believed his divisions, especially the 24th, were woefully in need of rehabilitation, but he had a combined troop strength within the perimeter of over 140,000 men. Combat troops numbered around ninety-two thousand. More than half the United Nations forces were ROKs, who had the hardest war of all thus far. They had inflicted more casualties than the Americans and suffered ten times more. The North Koreans had approximately seventy thousand combat troops at the front at the beginning of August. The American Fifth Air Force had complete air supremacy, and the U.S. Seventh Fleet completely secured supply lines to Japan. With men and matériel now flooding into Pusan, the U.S. Armed Forces rounding up able-bodied soldiers worldwide to throw into the fight, and the enemy's heavy casualties and depleted supplies, time wasn't on North Korea's side. Nevertheless the six-week battle of the Pusan Perimeter would be a near-run thing.

Walker had eight divisions defending the perimeter at the beginning of August. Five depleted ROK divisions protected his northern flank. The 25th U.S. Infantry Division protected the extreme southwestern flank south of the river. The 1st Provisional Marine Brigade had arrived in country on August 3 and was sent to the 25th Division around Masan. Unlike most of the army divisions in Korea, the great majority of the marine brigade were combat veterans. The 1st Cavalry and the beat-up 24th Division protected the rest. The 24th's sector ran along forty miles of riverfront that seriously stretched the understrength, exhausted division. Walker planned to bring newly arrived regiments of the 2nd Division to the front to relieve the 24th. The entire UN line was thinly stretched and had significant gaps. Much would rely on Walker's being able to move his forces quickly to shore up the vulnerable places in his line when the enemy pressed them.

After its victory at Masan, the 19th Regiment had crossed the Naktong and was held in reserve while it rested and reequipped. Corporal Salter reported to Easy just after the 2nd Battalion arrived in the rear. That night, at a bend in the Naktong just north of its confluence with the Nam, soldiers from North Korea's 4th Division, which had sent the 24th reeling at Taejon, stripped, hoisted their weapons and packs above their heads, and waded across the river to punch a sizable salient hole in the perimeter. It was the start of the Battle of the Naktong Bulge. The 34th was the first regiment hit. At midmorning General Church ordered the 19th into the fight.

The tide was with the attackers, who had caught the defenders by surprise and would move many more men, artillery, and tanks across the river over the next two days. Americans put up a pretty stout defense and counterpunched effectively. The 34th managed briefly to keep the North Koreans from taking a critical road junction, but they were only slowing and not repulsing the attack. On Salter's first day in combat Easy helped trap hundreds of enemy soldiers in a village a mile east of the river. He killed men for the first time. Years later he would still marvel at how the North Koreans and then

445

the Chinese would expose themselves in the front ranks of wave attacks as if they wanted to die.

The next day, August 7, the counterattacks started to run out of gas. The full-strength 9th Infantry, 2nd Division was rushed to the front and recovered some of the lost ground. The North Koreans took it back the next day, and by nightfall the entire North Korean division was across the river. On August 10 the 19th's 2nd battalion was hit so hard, its casualties so heavy, that there were only one hundred men still capable of fighting in all three rifle companies. Twenty-three men were killed in action, and many more were wounded. Four of the dead were from Easy, which was the most intact of the three companies. Salter was still alive and physically unharmed his fifth day in Korea. He wasn't as young as most recruits; he was twenty-three and a veteran of World War II. Still he must have been stunned by the ferocity and confusion of his first experience in ground combat. He kept his head, though. He watched how Easy's veterans behaved and tried to act like them. They were getting used to days like this.

The very next day General Church ordered a counterattack by four regiments: the 9th, 19th, 34th, and 21st. It failed completely, and losses continued to be heavy. Successive counterattacks were launched over the next week, but none succeeded in driving the North Koreans back across the river. The Americans were putting up a stubborn defense and inflicting heavier casualties on the enemy than they were suffering. But the fresh, full-strength 9th Regiment was now as battered and bleeding as the gasping, weary, shot-up regiments of the 24th Division. Finally the marines were pulled from the southern flank and brought into the fight. On August 17, following an artillery barrage and air strike, they attacked the North Koreans at the strongest point of the salient and by the middle of the next day had them in full flight.

That was hardly the end of the Battle for the Pusan Perimeter. There was a second Battle of the Naktong Bulge, and fighting in various sectors of the front continued uninterrupted for six weeks. Though it would be bled white at the perimeter, the Inmin'gun stayed the aggressor. Its numerical disadvantage worsened daily, although it conscripted thousands of South Koreans and threw them into the meat grinder. Its supply lines stretched for hundreds of miles. The defense of the perimeter was aided considerably by American airpower, but Walker had also proven to be a master of improvised defense; his North Korean counterparts were inept tacticians in comparison. They probed the perimeter in uncoordinated, relatively small assaults. With acute timing Walker shuffled his units wherever they were most needed to plug gaps in the line, inflicting heavy casualties on the enemy and draining the vitality out of the offensive while his army grew stronger every day. The ROK divisions had regrouped. Great Britain had committed the 27th Commonwealth Brigade. A regimental combat team from Hawaii had arrived, as had four tank battalions.

By September the tide of war was poised to turn, waiting for just one bold move to throw the North off the initiative and onto the defensive. MacArthur made that move on September 15, when he launched Operation Chromite. In one of the most daring amphibious landings in history, X Corps, consisting of the storied 1st Marine Division and the 7th Infantry Division, stormed ashore at Inchon, the Yellow Sea port southwest of Seoul, and easily overran its North Korean defenders. Racing east it cut all the North's major supply lines before turning south. Walker waited twenty-four hours for word of the landing to reach the North Koreans besieging the Pusan Perimeter before giving the order for the Eighth Army to break out and advance north. After six weeks of bloody stalemate, Easy was on the march again, and this time the odds were on its side. Salter was a veteran now, accepted by the company's surviving original members. As they reached the outskirts of the city they had been forced to abandon, he would have laughed along with them as they sang a ditty written for the occasion.

The last time we saw Taejon, it was not
    bright and gay,
Now we're going back to Taejon, to blow
    the goddamn place away!

The best soldier in the company, the one they all looked up to, veterans and new guys, enlisted and officer alike, was Corporal Mitchell Red Cloud Jr. Like Salter, he was a veteran of the previous war in a different service. He too had dropped out of high school to enlist in the marines. But his father had given his consent, and Red Cloud had served with distinction with Evan Carlson's Raiders during their legendary "long patrol" on Guadalcanal. A qualified sharpshooter, he saw action in dozens of battles before a bout of malaria sent him back to the States. He returned to the Pacific in time to fight on Okinawa, where a Japanese bullet earned him an honorable discharge.

He had returned home to the Winnebago (now Ho-Chunk) reservation in Jackson County, Wisconsin, the latest in a long line of family warriors. Both his parents claimed descent from famous chiefs. His mother's ancestor had been decorated for bravery by George Washington. His father had served in the army in World War I. They raised Mitchell, their oldest child, in the traditions of his people. He learned to hunt with a bow and arrow as well as a shotgun. He was taught the value of hard work, to respect his elders, to be honest and brave, and to help others. He was a quiet boy growing up, but after the excitement of war, life back home seemed too quiet and familiar. In 1948 his brother was killed in an accident while serving in the peacetime army. Mitchell decided to keep the family name on the army's roster. He enlisted and was soon on his way back to Okinawa.

He was an easygoing fellow, quick with a joke, well liked and respected. He didn't treat new guys with the disdain other veterans showed them; he was friendly and free with advice. Everyone called him "Chief," naturally. Salter, like everyone else, looked up to Red Cloud. He observed how he behaved under fire and tried to follow his example.

Caught between the anvil of X Corps and the Eighth Army's hammer, the Inmin'gun was nearly finished as an effective fighting force a week after the breakout at the perimeter. Elements of the Eighth Army linked up with X Corps on September 26. Seoul was liberated the next day. Only twenty-five thousand North Koreans escaped envelopment and managed to straggle back to their country. MacArthur initially ordered his armies to halt their advance at the 38th parallel, but with total victory in sight and on the principle of hot pursuit, Truman gave MacArthur permission to continue his advance into the enemy's country with two conditions: that no significant Chinese or Soviet presence was discovered in the North, and that only ROK troops advance to the far north, where the Yalu River formed the border between Korea and China.

The first ROK units entered North Korea on October 1. The 19th Infantry crossed the parallel eight days later and helped capture Pyongyang, the North Korean capital. Between the breakout at the perimeter and its entry into North Korea, the regiment had not lost a single soldier killed in action. They had been the easiest three weeks of the war, and it was hard to suppress the feeling among the men that the whole damn thing would soon be over. In the last week of October the regiment was spread out in the hills north of the Chongchon River, just fifty miles south of the Yalu, where it started picking up signs that there may be more trouble coming than anticipated.

China had issued vague warnings not to cross the parallel, but in their conference on Wake Island, MacArthur convinced Truman that Chairman Mao Zedong was bluffing. The supreme commander wanted to bring his armies home in time for Christmas, and on October 24 he instructed his commanders to advance north as rapidly as possible. The next day, as the first ROK troops reached the Yalu and X Corps began withdrawing from the front to prepare for another amphibious landing on the peninsula's east coast, an advance unit of the Eighth Army captured a Chinese prisoner. Over the next week ROK and Eighth Army soldiers reported stiffening resistance in the northern extremes of the allied advance from what appeared to be Chinese soldiers reinforcing the beleaguered North Koreans. Just north of the Yalu, undetected by American reconnaissance flights, the Chinese had positioned a quarter of a million soldiers. Over the next ten days five divisions would slip into the mountains of North Korea. Easy Company would be among the first to fight them.

Salter had been in Korea less than three months. His swift introduction to combat had been a trial, and he had now been in enough fights to be proud of the combat infantry badge he wore. He hadn't panicked even in those first desperate hours of fighting. He had done his job as well as the next guy. Now the enemy was in disarray. The army's breakneck advance north had been pretty damn exciting, and casualties had been few. All the talk was that they would be home for Christmas, and Salter had come through it without a scratch. For Easy's oldest veterans, the ones who had survived Kum River and Taejon, Christmas couldn't come soon enough. They were running a little short of ammunition. C rations were running low too. They were constantly hungry and had grown to hate rice. "You would, too," Salter later insisted, "if you had to mix it with coffee grounds to give it some flavor."

Most of all, "the goddamn cold" was starting to get them, Salter remembered. An early winter was coming, with its sharp blasts of Siberian winds. Although Salter came from the upper Midwest and had experienced harsh winters before, the cold in Korea seemed of a different magnitude. Much of his discomfort was attributable to the summer uniform and unlined boots he still wore. Even his sleeping bag was made for summer. For the rest of his life he would remember that cold as if it were the most malevolent force in the universe.

By November 4 Salter and the rest of Easy Company had become good and tired of the war. That night the regiment ran into Chinese soldiers, sizable numbers of them, and had a rough time of it, 1st Battalion especially. War is always chaotic, even when it's going well. Now things were getting seriously confused. They didn't know how many Chinese were hiding in the hills they patrolled. They never saw them during the day, after they had gone to ground, pulling white tarps over themselves to melt into the snow cover.

MacArthur and Walker still didn't believe China was in the fight to stay, mistaking these first engagements for volunteers coming to aid their exhausted fellow communists or as just an elaborate bluff by Mao to spook the Americans into backing off the border. A huge Chinese force had kicked the hell out of a 1st Cavalry regiment near Usan on November 1. The next day, on the other side of the Taebaek Mountains from the Eighth Army, the 7th Marines, 1st Marine Division encountered an entire Chinese division, including tanks, and whipped it. Still MacArthur and Walker weren't convinced China had really committed to the war. The thing was nearly over. Why would they want to jump into the losing end of it? Nevertheless they thought it wise to pull the Eighth Army back across the Chongchon River to regroup and prepare for a new offensive planned for Thanksgiving. Their supply lines were stretched thin, and the forces north of the river were becoming disorganized. Walker gave the order to fall back and directed the 19th Infantry to remain in the north to protect the bridgeheads around Anju.

That's where Easy was the night of November 4, when a Chinese force hit the 1st Battalion and knocked it back to the river. The 3rd Battalion had tried and failed to retake the ground. Easy too ran into some

Chinese that night and engaged in a pretty hot firefight, their second in as many days, but they didn't lose anyone. They were all tired and on edge the next day as 2nd Battalion tried to restore their lines. Companies were scattered and communications had deteriorated. Easy patrolled the hills, trying to make contact with Fox Company, but with no success before it bedded down for the night.

Something about the unusual quiet the night of November 5 spooked Easy's commanding officer, Captain Walter Conway, and he ordered the men to dig in to the left of G Company on a little hill five miles north of the river, designated Hill 123. Normally Conway would have chosen a higher elevation, but he didn't know how close the Chinese were or how many of them were out there. His men could run into them any minute. The last two nights the Chinese "were in, on the flanks of, and behind the company position," he reported. A full moon illuminated the darkness that night. He told the men to dig in quietly: "We don't want to draw any more mortar fire." "And stay on the lookout," he warned. "They're here, somewhere."

As usual Conway had Red Cloud guard the perimeter. The guy had a sixth sense for enemy movement and could be counted on to give the alert in time and hold his position while the rest of the men got into theirs. Private Svach remembered how his friend claimed he always knew when an attack was imminent. "It's like hunting those Wisconsin deer," Red Cloud told him. "I can smell 'em coming." He knew the enemy. He knew they liked to swing around and attack from behind after first staging a noisy assault on the front. He didn't sleep. He was ready for them.

Salter didn't sleep either, and not just because he liked to keep an eye on Red Cloud for reassurance. He was too cold to sleep. Most of the men just scraped out a shallow depression in the frozen earth and tried to get what rest they could. Salter decided to dig the biggest hole he could, all night long, just to stay warm. They were all low on ammunition. The company sergeants circulated among them, asking, "How much you got?," and the answers were disappointing: "I got two clips and a bandolier." "I got three clips and a couple grenades." "I got one bandolier, no clips." They could already hear shooting in the distance.

A five-mile gap separated them from the predominantly Canadian 27th Commonwealth Infantry Brigade, which had also been assigned to protect the Chongchon bridgeheads. Second Battalion was supposed to patrol the gap constantly to prevent the enemy from driving between the two forces. But that proved a practical impossibility. A mountain ridge ran through the gap that made it pretty much a no-man's-land.

That's where most of the Chinese came from that night, swarming down the mountains between the Canadians and the 2nd Battalion. They drove in from the right too, between the 2nd and 1st Battalion positions. They hit all three forces in a coordinated attack all along the bridgehead line. Before they hit Easy and G companies on Hill 123, they set up a roadblock to cut off their retreat. Then they came up both sides of the hill, following the communications wire that led to Easy's command post. They completely enveloped both companies and caught most of the men in their sleeping bags. They shot them where they lay.

Red Cloud was the first to see them, and he shouted a warning from his position below the command post and opened up with his Browning automatic rifle. He fired magazine after magazine into the onslaught. The soldier feeding him his ammunition was killed in the first minutes of the battle.

Red Cloud too was hit early, in the chest, but he kept firing and gave Conway a little time to try to organize some kind of defense. They were overrun by a battalion-size force of Chinese. Svach, who had been in every tough fight the regiment had, remembered it simply as "the worst night of my life."

Salter was still awake, still digging his hole, when the night exploded with gunfire and Chinese buglers sounded the attack. Scrambling out of his foxhole, he saw tracers streaking everywhere and illumination rounds casting an eerie light on the slaughter below. He saw Chinese soldiers shoot men who had thrown their arms up in surrender. All was confusion and terror. The men couldn't tell if they were firing at the enemy or at each other. No one knew what to do, and it was deteriorating into an every-man-for-himself fight, except for Red Cloud and another Browning automatic man, Private First Class Joseph Balboni. They were keeping the enemy in a cross fire and opening a draw for those who were still alive to follow down the hill.

On the rare occasions later in his life when Salter talked about that night, he did so with economy and no bravado. "I wanted to bug out. I just couldn't figure out how," he admitted. He jumped back in his foxhole for a minute or two and began a brief, intense negotiation with God, promising to live an exemplary life if He would just get him the hell off this hill.

A medic reached Red Cloud to dress his wounds. He didn't think they were fatal and left Red Cloud to treat other wounded. He came back after Red Cloud had been hit again, this time more seriously, and told him he had to get off the hill or he would die there. Red Cloud refused the advice, got to his feet, rested his Browning in the crotch of a tree, and resumed firing. He and Balboni knew they would die where they fought. Red Cloud would receive the Medal of Honor, Balboni the Distinguished Service Cross. The official account said Red Cloud wrapped his arm around the tree to stay upright. Salter remembered it differently. He and another man crawled down to Red Cloud, who asked their help to keep him upright. Salter got a web belt and wrapped it around Red Cloud and the tree. Then Salter thanked him and started down the draw. He could hear the bark of Red Cloud's Browning all the way down.

A lot of men had to fight hand to hand to get off the hill. Salter did too. When his rifle jammed, all he had for a weapon was his trench knife. Before he got very far, he saw three Chinese approach another Easy man's foxhole. He rushed the first Chinese and strangled him to death, took the dead man's weapon and shot the second soldier. The soldier in the foxhole shot the third. Moments after both men made it down the hill, Red Cloud's gun went silent, and Chinese flooded down the draw, chasing after the survivors. But by that time, around three o'clock on the morning of November 6, four Quad 4s, armored vehicles with .50 caliber machine guns, had shown up at the base of the hill, opened up on the enemy, and cut down scores of them.

After the Battle for Hill 123, Svach believed no more than twenty of Easy's original members were still alive and fit for service. Among the company's dead were First Lieutenant Leslie Kirkpatrick, a West Pointer, and Second Lieutenant John Horony, a World War II veteran. Five of the company's sergeants had been killed and two of its medics. It had been a long, long war for Easy Company, though not a man in it had been in Korea longer than four months. Not a man had been ready for what he would experience. Not a man had been adequately armed and equipped for the war. Not a man had imagined what he would be called on to do and what he could endure.

And now most of them were dead or wounded or missing, and the survivors were suddenly at war with the most populous nation on earth.

As the Chinese began withdrawing, an officer who had arrived with the Quad 4s ordered Salter and the other survivors to take back the hill. "With what?" they yelled. "We haven't got any ammunition." But they knew they had to go back up; they could hear wounded crying out. So up they went. Salter had barely started when he was concussed by a mortar round and hit with shrapnel. Those who got to the top unhurt counted around five hundred Chinese dead, many of them lying in front of the bodies of Mitchell Red Cloud and Joseph Balboni.

Walker got the rest of his army back across the Chongchon, and Mao briefly accommodated Walker and MacArthur's optimism that the Chinese weren't in the war to stay. The Chinese divisions in Korea seemed to disappear after that first week of November. The Eighth Army regrouped, and on Thanksgiving Walker ordered the offensive to the Yalu that would get them all home for Christmas. But the Chinese were waiting for them, armies of them. American and ROK forces west of the Taebaeks were knocked back past Pyongyang, past Seoul, finally halting their retreat and holding near Osan, where Task Force Smith had made its seven-hour stand. On the other side of the mountains, 1st Division Marines were trapped at the Chosin Reservoir, where they would begin their legendary fighting retreat to the sea. General Walker was himself killed in an automobile accident in Pyongyang two days before Christmas. General Matthew Ridgway assumed command of the Eighth Army, and under his leadership the army would fight its way back to the 38th parallel by April, where the fighting would stalemate until a cease-fire was agreed to in 1953.

Salter was taken first to a field hospital and eventually transported to Japan to convalesce. He rejoined Easy in time for China's New Year's Offensive, and he fought in more desperate battles in that cruel and chaotic first year of war. The company would lose many more men. Salter was promoted to sergeant first class and received the Silver Star for his heroism on Hill 123. In a firefight south of the Han River in February, he volunteered to flank and lob a grenade at an enemy machine-gun nest that had his squad pinned down. His lieutenant told him he'd write him up for a Medal of Honor if he did. "I decided against doing it," he recalled. "I wouldn't even have brought it up if I'd known it would be that dangerous." When that same lieutenant was later wounded, Salter took command of the squad.

He was home in time for Christmas 1952. He lived a good and happy life, but he never forgot the terrible responsibility he and other green kids had been given in an unexpected war, and what it had cost them to do it.

Wild Weasels Leo Thorsness and Harry Johnson in regulation mustaches and bush hats with their F-105 "Thud."

CHAPTER TEN:
VALOR

Leo Thorsness, a Vietnam War pilot and POW, fought MiGs, missiles, and artillery to protect the lives of his wingmen.

When Operation Rolling Thunder began in March 1965, North Vietnam's air defenses were rudimentary and vulnerable to destruction from the air. Luckily for Hanoi, the U.S. government had no intention of authorizing anything so provocative. The "program of measured and limited air action . . . against selected military targets in the DRV [Democratic Republic of Vietnam]" authorized by presidential memorandum on February 13, 1965, would prove to be so gradual and selective that it gave the North Vietnamese and their Soviet and Chinese sponsors the time they needed to create the most sophisticated, lethal air defenses U.S. air power had ever faced.

The longest bombing campaign in American military history began with strikes on minor military targets in the Vietnamese panhandle north of the Demilitarized Zone and south of the 19th parallel. Rolling Thunder's initial strategic objective was to discourage North Vietnam's further support of the communist insurgency in South Vietnam using tactics that were more likely to encourage them. It is not just in hindsight that the campaign's limitations and gradual escalation appear absurd. Starting a month after the campaign began, when President Lyndon Johnson ordered the first pause in the bombing, some of its advocates were conceding privately that it wasn't yielding the kind of response they had expected from Hanoi. Henceforth they would shift its objective to interdicting and destroying North Vietnamese support for the Viet Cong, while authorizing more targets north of the 19th parallel and escalating the commitment of American ground forces. Thirty-five hundred marines sent to secure the airfield at Da Nang at the start of the air campaign would become the first combat troops in Vietnam when Rolling Thunder's lack of success persuaded Washington to fight a ground war.

The recognition that Rolling Thunder wasn't achieving its objective never seemed to prompt the revelation among its advocates that perhaps it had been a stupid idea to begin with. That conclusion appeared reserved for the men who flew the missions. They recognized the folly and realized the dangers posed by rules of engagement that seemed perversely designed to lower the risk of enemy casualties by increasing the risk to American pilots. Even now, a half-century later, recalling those restrictions can summon up old resentments better left buried.

The targets, timing of strikes, and number of sorties were decided in Washington and approved by civilian authorities in the White House. For almost two years final decisions were made almost exclusively by civilian authorities, many of them in meetings of the famous Tuesday Lunch in the Johnson White House. Those meetings, after Johnson's election in late 1964, were usually limited to the president, the secretary of defense, the secretary of state, the national security advisor, and, for some reason, the White House press secretary. It wasn't until late 1967 that a military representative, the chairman of the Joint Chiefs of Staff, was regularly invited to join their council.

Targets were selected and restrictions imposed not to win a war by crippling the enemy's ability to wage it but to persuade

Hanoi to negotiate a political settlement and to avoid upsetting the Soviets and Chinese. As Defense Secretary Robert McNamara put it, Rolling Thunder should present only "a credible threat of *future* destruction [and make] it politically easy for the DRV to enter negotiations." The result, according to the Air Force historian Wayne Thompson, was "an air campaign that did a lot of bombing in a way calculated not to threaten the enemy regime's survival." Or, as James Stockdale described it, "We were making gestures with our airplanes."

The initial rules of engagement for Rolling Thunder excluded almost everything in a thirty-mile-wide zone around Hanoi and a ten-mile zone around Haiphong. The latter restriction meant critical war supplies coming into Haiphong Harbor were protected. Nothing within thirty miles of Vietnam's northern border with China could be targeted. Power plants were originally off limits, as were North Vietnamese air bases. American pilots sometimes flew right past airfields where enemy MiGs were parked. They could shoot down a MiG that was shooting at them, but they couldn't hit one on the ground. The day before my last combat mission in October 1967, I dropped my CBUs, cluster bombs, on the runway at

Phúc Yên airfield north of Hanoi, destroying two parked MiGs in the process. It was my proudest accomplishment of the war to date, and I got an Air Medal for it. It was also the first time the MiG base was attacked in the nearly twenty months Rolling Thunder had been under way.

The same weird logic governed U.S. rules regarding the enemy's surface-to-air missile (SAM) sites. If a SAM site was shooting at them and if it was located outside a restricted zone, pilots could destroy it. Otherwise, it was off limits. There was a concern that the Soviets, who supplied most of the missiles, might have had advisors present at some of the sites. They did, of course, especially early in the war, when our intelligence believed Russians probably manned every SAM site in the North.

Sometimes rationales for forbearance were even more *Alice in Wonderland*–like. The first North Vietnamese SAM sites were spotted by a U2 spy plane early in April 1965. The U.S. Air Force and Navy petitioned Washington for permission to strike them. Washington refused: the sites were in the restricted zone around Hanoi. Even as more SAM sites were installed, Assistant Secretary of Defense John McNaughton convinced McNamara that refraining from

471

bombing them would send "a signal to Hanoi not to use them." In a meeting in Saigon, McNaughton brushed aside the concerns of the air force fleet commander, Lieutenant General Joseph Moore, saying, "You don't think the North Vietnamese are going to use them! Putting them in is just a political ploy by the Russians to appease Hanoi." Navy flyers once counted 111 missiles on railcars near Hanoi. They were denied permission to destroy them, provoking one of the aviators to complain, "We had to fight all 111 of them one at a time." I, too, observed Soviet ships come into Haiphong Harbor and off-load SAMs. I saw them transported to firing sites and put into place, and I couldn't do a damn thing about them.

Even when SAM batteries were operational and firing at Americans, to no one's surprise, the Vietnamese and their Russian advisors made sure to locate them within the restricted zones around Hanoi and Haiphong, where the Americans couldn't hit them without special permission. My squadron lost an aviator to a SAM near Haiphong one day. None of us saw a chute open. Another pilot dropped his bombs on the location where he thought the missile had launched. He was grounded when the squadron returned to the ship because his target hadn't been on Washington's list.

At the beginning of Rolling Thunder, North Vietnamese air defense relied almost entirely on anti-aircraft artillery (AAA), and many of those were comparatively small caliber. It's believed the North had about fifteen hundred anti-aircraft guns at the start of 1965, most of them of the 37 mm and 57 mm variety. By the start of the following year, it had five thousand guns, many of them radar-guided 85 mm and 100 mm. By 1967 the routes Thunder pilots flew were bristling with AAA: seven thousand guns, U.S. intelligence estimated. Although the SAM threat and, to a lesser extent, MiGs, preoccupied mission planners and pilots, anti-aircraft fire was responsible for most of the U.S. aircraft losses during Rolling Thunder.

The SAMs' principal utility was forcing American pilots to fly low to avoid them, into the waiting embrace of North Vietnamese anti-aircraft gunners. Not long before my own encounter with a SAM, my squadron lost a guy near Haiphong. None of us saw him eject, but our squadron's commanding officer, Commander Bryan Compton, possibly the bravest man I have known, was determined to find out what happened to him. He kept circling the area at extremely low altitudes, searching for some sign of him, as we got our closest look ever at the enemy's AAA. It was something. We took a terrific pounding from flak. I was scared to death, and the memory of it is still one of my most vivid of the war. Compton, just as cool as you like, made eight passes before finally breaking off the search. Before we left the area, we wanted to take out the SAM site that had shot down our friend, but because it was within ten miles of the city we weren't allowed to touch it.

Around five thousand SAMs were launched during Rolling Thunder, and they brought down 101 aircraft. As pilots adjusted tactics to the threat and electronic jamming capability improved, the SAMs' success rate declined correspondingly. But that's not to say the threat didn't warrant the attention given it. I knew more than a few guys who were among the unlucky 101. I happened to be one of them. More to the point, SAMs were an essential component of a sophisticated triple-threat air defense system supplied by the Soviets and Chinese that was quickly set up, integrated, and as formidable as any seen before. And it was the gradual escalation of Rolling Thunder and the foolish assumptions of its architects that made that possible.

North Vietnamese SA-2 surface-to-air missile sites proliferated rapidly after the first were sighted in April 1965, while the enemy acquired more and deadlier anti-aircraft artillery than any Allied pilots had braved over Germany. North Vietnam had about fifty MiG-17s at the start of Rolling Thunder. Slower than American fighters, they were maneuverable and effective at the disruptive hit-and-run tactics their pilots were trained to perform. By 1966 the first MiG-21s, supersonic and armed with heat-seeking Atoll missiles, had started to arrive in country and gave Hanoi more than a hundred aircraft capable of intercepting American planes. An advanced early-warning radar system with over two hundred facilities tracked U.S. aircraft incoming from Thailand, Laos, and the Tonkin Gulf and coordinated counterattacks from guns, missiles, and MiGs.

In his memoir *Fighter Pilot,* the legendary World War II and Vietnam War ace Brigadier General Robin Olds, who led the single most effective raid against Vietnamese MiGs of the war, described the experience of aerial combat over North Vietnam: "Missiles streaked past, flak blackened the sky, tracers laced patterns across my canopy, and then, capping the day, MiGs would suddenly appear — small, sleek sharks, cutting and slashing, braving their own flak, firing missiles, guns, harassing, pecking."

It was dangerous work, often for objectives of little or no strategic value. Worthwhile or not, they cost many good men their lives. In my A-4 squadron alone, thirty-eight aviators were killed or captured over Rolling Thunder's three years. In 1967 we lost one third of our guys. With so many more valuable targets off-limits, pilots were asked to hit the same things over and over again. I flew my first combat mission campaign in June 1967, more than two years into Rolling Thunder. The night before, I had gone to my squadron's intelligence center to punch out information about my target. Out came a picture of a military barracks in Vinh, with some details about the target's recent history. It had already been hit twenty-seven times. Hardly any structures were still standing; it was basically a rubble heap. There was a bridge a half mile away that the North Vietnamese Army used. It had never been touched. It wasn't on the list.

Some targets were hit again and again not because Washington wanted to make the rubble bounce but because they proved remarkably resilient. The most memorable of these was the famous "Dragon's Jaw," the Thanh Hoa Bridge over the Red River.

The first of many strikes on the Thanh Hoa Bridge was led by my friend Robbie Risner on April 3, 1965. Seventy-nine aircraft were involved, including forty-six F-105s, some armed with guided missiles and the others carrying bombs, that were assigned to strike the target. The missiles practically bounced off the bridge's superstructure; in the words of one pilot, it was like firing "BB pellets at a Sherman tank." Thirty-two missiles were fired at the bridge, and over a hundred 750-pound bombs were dropped that day. Some bombs hit the bridge and some didn't, but no bomb or missile did more than char it and stop traffic for a few hours. Two planes were lost to anti-aircraft fire and the pilots captured. Risner's F-105 was hit by flak and burning while he continued to direct the strike until it was completed. There were many future missions to knock down the Dragon's Jaw before Rolling Thunder stopped in 1968. Thousands of tons of ordnance were dropped and fired at it. All failed. The bridge became an icon to the North Vietnamese, a memorial to their unyielding resistance. It became a symbol to a lot of Americans too, many of them pilots who got to know the damn thing too well, a symbol of a war that was becoming a lost cause. The bridge was finally destroyed in 1972. Americans were using laser-guided munitions then, and they brought it down in the first strike after bombing resumed in the North. The Vietnamese rebuilt it the next year.

In the forty months between the first raid in 1965 and the last strike in 1968, Vietnam's air defenses shot down 104 pilots in the vicinity of the Thanh Hoa Bridge. I was destined to become friends with and be inspired by quite a few of them: Jim Stockdale, Jerry Denton, Paul Galanti, Jerry Coffee, Howie Rutledge, and, of course, Colonel James Robinson Risner, who was shot down a few miles from the bridge in September 1965. He had been an ace in the Korean War, as well as an outstanding wing commander in Vietnam. A couple weeks after the first raid on the Dragon he was the subject of a *Time* magazine cover story. The head of the prison camp system greeted him personally when he arrived in Hanoi. "Ah, Colonel Risner," said the man the American prisoners called "the Cat," smiling at his newest inmate, "we've been waiting for you."

The first dogfight of the Vietnam War occurred in the second massive air raid on the Thanh Hoa Bridge, the day after the first strike. Four MiG-17s dropped from the clouds and dove on a formation of F-105s. They shot down two before breaking off the attack and returned to a base that was excluded from Washington's approved target list. Two air force pilots, Captain James Magnusson and Major Frank Bennett, were killed.

On July 24, 1965, four F-4C Phantom fighter escorts were targeted by two SA-2s, the first surface-to-air missiles launched by the North Vietnamese or, more likely, by Russians acting on their behalf. All four Phantoms were damaged, and one was destroyed. Its pilot, forty-one-year-old Captain Richard "Pop" Keirn, ejected safely and was taken prisoner. His backseater, Captain Roscoe Fobair, who was on his last mission and scheduled to go home the next day, was killed. It would be Keirn's second time as a prisoner of war. He had been shot down over Germany in World War II.

A lively debate within the administration concluded with President Johnson ordering retaliatory strikes on the two offending

SAM sites. Three days later more than a hundred aircraft — air force, navy, and marine — took wing to execute the president's order, and flew into a trap. One target turned out to be a dummy site, and the other was unoccupied when the bombers arrived. Anti-artillery guns were waiting instead. They shot down four F-105s and so badly damaged another that it crashed while trying to land and destroyed the plane escorting it in the process. Three pilots were killed, two captured, and one rescued.

Now that the missile batteries Americans had known about for months were operational, something had to be done to address the threat they posed. That something was Project Weasel, "Wild Weasel," as it quickly came to be known. Wild Weasels were dedicated SAM killers assigned to every Rolling Thunder mission. The first Weasel aircraft were F-100F Super Sabres, two-seat fighters specially equipped to track SAMs. Their pilots were among the air force's elite, and most of the backseaters, the electronic weapons officers (EWOs), had been weapons specialists on B-52 crews. Their training began in October 1965 at Eglin Air Force Base in Florida's panhandle. The first Weasels were all volunteers, which seemed only fair given the nearly suicidal nature of their earliest missions.

In the first missions, code-named "Iron Hand," Weasels would fly ahead of the strike force. Weasels were always "first in, last out," staying on station until the last bomber had delivered its payload and was headed home, which could mean fifteen minutes or longer in the high-threat areas. That's a long, long time when somebody's shooting at you, and somebody was always shooting at Weasels.

They were hunter-killers. Weasels would bait the enemy into firing missiles at them. Camouflaged SAM sites were hard to spot through the thick jungle canopy that covered much of North Vietnam. To find them you had to get their crews to turn on their acquisition radar. To get them to do that you had to give them a target to acquire. So the Weasels, paired with F-105D bombers, would fly ahead of the strike force, get themselves noticed, or "painted," by SAM radar and usually shot at by SAM crews, shoot back, and call in the F-105Ds for the kill. One of the first Weasel EWOs, Air Force Captain Jack Donovan, gave them their motto when, after he arrived at Eglin and heard the tactics for killing SAMs, he exclaimed, "You've gotta be shitting me!"

The first five Weasel crews arrived at the

Royal Thai Air Force Base at Korat, Thailand, in November 1965, after five weeks of rushed training. They flew their first mission the next month, paired with supersonic F-105D fighter-bombers. The Sabres were supposed to find the SAMs and then strafe the sites with their 20 mm cannon while the F-105Ds bombed it. The first confirmed SAM kill was credited to captains Al Lamb and Jack Donovan on December 22. By the summer of 1966 the Weasels could claim nine SAM sites destroyed. Despite its successes, Weasel I ended that summer; its casualty rate of 50 percent was unsustainable. For all their fine qualities and the valor and skill of their crews, Sabres weren't the right aircraft for the job; they weren't fast enough and couldn't keep up with the F-105s. Weasel II was launched with F-4s as the SAM hunters, but they weren't right for the job either. So in the summer of 1966 training for Weasel III commenced, with F-105s, a two-seat version of the fighter-bombers, claiming the honor.

The F-105 Thunderchief was already the air force's workhorse in Vietnam, flying three-quarters of Rolling Thunder sorties and suffering the highest casualties. By the end of the war 334 Thunderchiefs, over 40 percent of the air force's F-105 inventory, had been lost. The pilots who flew them loved them and called them the Thud. There are various explanations for the nickname: that it was named for the sound it made when it landed or when it crashed in a jungle, and that "Thud" was just a funny diminutive of "Thunderchief." The etymology of warplane nicknames is an inexact science. We do know Thuds were very fast, could take a beating, and packed a big punch. Originally designed to deliver a single nuclear bomb from a fuselage bomb bay at low altitudes and high speed, it could carry a lot of ordnance: six-thousand-pound bombs under its wings. It was a lot faster than the Sabre, even faster than the F-4s that flew fighter cover for them, and more agile, but not that agile. A big plane with little wings, it sacrificed maneuverability for firepower. But Thuds weren't made for aerial combat. They were built for speed and punch, and only the top pilots got to fly them.

Thuds were in a few dogfights in Vietnam, some by choice and others by necessity. But the F-4 was the designated MiG killer, responsible for destroying 107 of the 137 MiG-17s and MiG-21s shot down in the war. Some Thud pilots went looking for MiGs after they unloaded their bombs, but that wasn't advisable. F-105s had the speed advantage over MiGs, although less of one with the MiG-21. MiGs were a hell of a lot more maneuverable, and they tended not to be found when they didn't want to be. They liked to hit and run. I didn't see many MiGs until my last few missions in Vietnam. When I did see some, the F-4s kept them from bothering us. They were sleek, hard to spot, and quick. They darted in and usually got right back out after one pass. Thud pilots did manage to shoot down twenty-seven MiGs during the war, and they got all but three of them with the Gatling. But MiGs shot down nearly an equivalent number of Thuds. The Phantoms were better suited for the work, and the MiG pilots knew it. When they were out hunting, they were hunting Thuds.

Rolling Thunder's planners had divided North Vietnam into six mission sectors, called route packages or PAKs. Three were assigned to the navy carriers at Yankee Station. The three northern and western PAKs belonged to the air force, one of which it shared with the marines at Da Nang. The navy's routes brought pilots in over the Gulf; their targets, especially in the early months of Rolling Thunder, were usually in coastal areas. The air force pilots flew out of the Thai bases. PAK VI was the most dangerous route they flew; it was the most northern and closest to Hanoi, and it boasted the most formidable air defenses. There were two ways in: one took them out over the Tonkin Gulf, where they would come around and attack from the east; the other, more popular route had them come in from the west, flying over the center of a mountain ridge north of the Red River. Stray to the south or north of "Thud Ridge," and there was hell to pay from anti-aircraft and SAM batteries. But until later in the war, when the Vietnamese managed to haul some AAA up the mountains, staying over the middle of the ridge was the safest way in, even though it got its nickname for the Thuds that were lost over it.

A strike package could consist of anywhere from thirty to over seventy aircraft, including fighter-bombers, fighter escorts, electronic jamming aircraft, Weasels, command-and-control aircraft, and search-and-rescue planes. Each Thud formation, including Weasels, had a dedicated KC-135 fuel tanker that flew a pattern over Laos roughly halfway to the target, where the Thuds would take on fuel before entering North Vietnamese airspace and again on their way home from the mission. Once over the target, the bombers would descend to between three thousand and one thousand feet and drop their payload. As soon as they did, they were free to head home.

Modified for Weasel missions, F-105Fs and, in 1967, the updated F-105Gs were loaded with the new radar honing and launch-detection electronics, carried Shrike missiles under their wings that honed in on SAM radar, and, like all Thuds, had a 20 mm Gatling gun in the nose. The Shrike had a range of seven miles. The North Vietnamese SA-2 surface-to-air missiles had a seventeen-mile range. That was part of the thrill for the Weasels. The enemy almost always got to shoot first.

Training for the new Wild Weasels was moved from Eglin to Nellis Air Force Base outside Las Vegas. They deployed in May 1966, this time to the air base at Takhli, Thailand, and went into action almost immediately. By the end of August five of the first eleven F-105F Weasels in country had been shot down. That year 126 Thuds were lost, although obviously not all of them were Weasels.

A full combat tour for a pilot in the Vietnam War was one hundred missions. Thud pilots at Takhli and Korat usually flew sixteen missions a month, so it took them a little more than six months to complete a tour, which they had roughly a 60 percent chance of doing. A Defense Department study claimed Rolling Thunder lost one plane for every forty sorties. The Thud pilots had a saying: "By your sixty-sixth mission, you'll have been shot down twice and picked up once." If you were a Weasel, your chances of returning from one hundred missions were poorer.

Not everyone has the temperament to live with those kinds of odds. Every group of Weasels would have one or two who couldn't hack it after the first or second mission. Those who could handle it found a way to put the future and everything in it out of their mind — their family, their ambitions, everything. It's not that you didn't think about your loved ones or life back in the States, but you had to try to not put yourself in the picture. Otherwise you started wondering whether you *would be* in the picture again, ever.

People have different ways of coping under that kind of strain. Some guys rely on dark humor, others on false bravado. Most Thud pilots were heavy smokers in those days and joked that the optimistic among them were the ones who thought they would die of lung cancer. Quite a few found relief in rowdy off-duty habits. Whatever gets you through the night, as the song goes. But however differentiated their psychological defense mechanisms might be, combat pilots tended to imitate the same style. The air force pilots at Korat and Takhli wore Australian bush hats, grew their mustaches, and were somewhat unruly in their recreation.

That doesn't quite describe my friend Leo Thorsness, a man of gracious manners and steady temperament. He is from the upper Midwest and possesses the friendliness and equanimity common to people of that region. He certainly wore the hat and the mustache, and when I first got to know him, I could see he was tough. I can't picture him being too wild, though. He would not have found that to be a necessary quality for the job. He had what he needed: the skills, guts, and mental toughness to do a hard job in extreme circumstances. And he was faithful to his country, to the men he served with, to the call of duty — Leo had fidelity in spades.

He was born in 1932, the youngest of Emil and Bernice Thorsness's three children, and raised on a farm outside Walnut

Grove, Minnesota. His family had always worked the land. It was the Great Depression, and the Thorsnesses scraped out a modest living from the soil. They grew their own food and made good use of everything they possessed. They were raised to work hard. His father hired himself out as a farmhand to earn extra income. When they were old enough, Leo and his brother John baled alfalfa for neighboring farmers. They were poor, though Leo said he didn't realize it until he was older. "We defeated the Depression one day at a time," he remembered. They had everything they needed, never went hungry, and never lost their land. "We were a typical family."

A popular, good-looking kid, he played sports, did well in school, and liked to hunt and fish. He was an Eagle Scout. He had ambitions: he wanted to go to college, though he hadn't quite figured out how he would earn the money to pay for it. His brother had enlisted in the army and was serving in Korea in that first, awful year of the war, when Leo enrolled at South Dakota State, just across the border from Minnesota. His first day there, while waiting in line to register, he spotted Gaylee Anderson, another freshman and "the cutest girl there." He got behind her in line and started a conversation with her that has never finished.

By the end of 1950, with the example of his brother in mind and a plan to return to school four years later on the GI Bill, Leo quit South Dakota State and enlisted in the air force. He was nineteen. Two years later the air force, in need of pilots for the war, initiated the Aviation Cadet Program. Leo applied, and in January 1953 attended officer training school at Lackland Air Force Base in San Antonio, Texas, then learned to fly at Goodfellow Air Force Base in San Angelo, Texas. While he was at Goodfellow, he got some advice from a veteran aviator that he never forgot. "There are old pilots and there are bold pilots," the older man told him, "but no old, bold pilots."

During his Christmas leave in 1953, he and Gaylee were married. Their daughter, Dawn, was born the following year, after Leo had received his second lieutenant's commission and pilot's wings.

He was trained to fly the big B-36 strategic bombers but ended up flying F-84s and the F-100 fighter-bombers before transitioning to the F-105. He was stationed at the big American air base in Spangdahlem, Germany, from 1959 to 1963. While there Leo took night classes to complete his college degree in between "seventy-two-hour tours sitting at the end of the runway with a nuclear bomb in an F-105 bomb bay." By the time he was rotated back to the States he was only six months shy of a degree; the air force let him finish at the University of Omaha, then assigned him to Nellis Air Force Base in Nevada, where F-105 drivers trained. He lived in Los Angeles and pursued a master's degree at the University of Southern California, while commuting to Vegas once a month to fly enough hours to stay qualified as an F-105 pilot.

He did more than stay qualified; he earned top marks in flying hours and gunnery and bombing scores. After earning his master's degree in defense systems management he moved his family to Vegas. He knew he would have to go to Southeast Asia soon. Rolling Thunder was well into its second year, and the air force had lost a lot of men and aircraft. It was his turn, and he was ready for it — as ready as you can be. He assumed he would fly Thuds in the big strike force packages. It was dangerous work. He knew that; he knew the casualty rates. He'd heard reports of the North's lethal air defenses. What he didn't want to do was become a Wild Weasel. That would just tempt fate too much. There are no "old, bold pilots," he remembered. He was more than willing to do his duty, with all its attendant risks, but he wanted to have a decent chance to get home to his family. The "first in, last out" live-bait missions of the Wild Weasels looked a little too much like suicide runs. But even if they were — especially if they were — you needed the best pilots to fly them because only the best stood a decent chance of surviving them. Unfortunately for Leo, he was one of the best pilots.

On his first day back at Nellis, his operations officer congratulated him. His orders for Southeast Asia had come in and had obviously taken account of his experience and high marks as an F-105 driver. "You are now a Wild Weasel," he told Leo. His training began at Nellis that summer, where he was introduced to his backseater, Harry Johnson, another farm boy from the Midwest with skills and ambition. Captains Thorsness and Johnson finished their training at George Air Force Base that fall and received orders to report to the 355th Tactical Fighter Wing at Takhli Royal Thai Air Force Base. They were among the first F-105 Weasels; five crews had arrived at Takhli before them, and all five were shot down in less than two months. Informed that Leo was a Weasel, the sergeant assigning living quarters joked, "You won't be around long enough to need a hooch." Yet despite the odds, Leo and Harry would fly every combat mission together. They would go home together, too, eventually.

They studied the tactics their five unfortunate predecessors had used and changed them, hoping to improve their odds. They flew their missions at higher altitudes, but there really wasn't a lot anyone could do to make Weasel missions safer. When a SAM launched, the Weasels would "take it down." They shook them off in steep dives at high speeds right past the SAM, descending to within AAA range, and pulled out of it sharply as, ideally, the less maneuverable missile slammed into the ground. Then they could turn on the SAM site, no longer hidden as dust and debris stirred up by the fired missile marked the target, and destroy it with Shrikes and CBUs. It was wild, furious work, and Leo and Harry's first and most important discovery was that they could handle the job.

No combat pilot likes to admit to having doubts about that, and the regulation élan of the combat pilot is intended to dispel doubts and fears, or at least mask them. But the truth is you don't really know if you can do it until you've done it. There are worse ways to fight a war, of course. Air combat is fought in brief bursts, and then it's home to ship or base for a hot meal and a good night's rest. But it's a pretty terrifying experience while you're up there, when the odds are against you and minutes seem like hours. Experienced one hundred times, if you make it to a hundred, takes some nerve.

Leo and Harry could do it, and do it well. An account of Leo's heroism published in *Airman Magazine* a couple years after the war includes a brief description of his combat experience: "He had been challenged by MiGs and counted 53 SAMs fired at him. He had experienced 'white knuckles' in the target area when he squeezed his stick nearly in two. And he knew the singular sensation of a flour-dry mouth in combat, when gum stuck to his teeth and to the roof of his mouth."

You won't detect fear in cockpit recordings, when Harry calls out approaching MiGs or SAMs, and Leo responds "Yep" or "Got it." But no one goes through an experience that intense and deadly without being really scared. The question you cannot answer for certain before you experience it is whether you can concentrate on your job and do it while you're terrified.

The ones others look up to, who become leaders, aren't the ones who scare the least; they're the highest functioning among the terrified.

Leo was that kind of pilot, highly skilled no matter how great the strain. In the spring of 1967, promoted to major and well past his sixty-sixth mission, when by Wild Weasel standards he should have been shot down twice and picked up once, he became head Weasel. He was their leader, the guy the other Weasels looked up to, whose instruction they'd take without quarrel or truculence, whose judgment they trusted most. He had something else too, the quality most admired in the profession of arms: he was valorous.

Valor isn't just a synonym for courage, at least it isn't to combat veterans, for whom courage is a more common virtue than it is in the general population. It's a higher, more exalted quality than being brave. It is the supreme martial virtue. Every citation for the nation's highest decoration for valor, the Medal of Honor, has begun by praising the recipient for his gallantry and intrepidity. They are well-chosen words. Gallantry denotes the kind of courage that is directed exclusively or mostly for the benefit of others, a selfless courage. Intrepidity is the kind of daring that appears resolute and fearless, even if it isn't. Valor, the amalgam of the two qualities, seems a fair definition for such a princely virtue: a self-sacrificing, resolute daring. But words may not convey its full value. It is not a concept that is usually considered in the abstract by its witnesses. It is known when it is seen. And that is usually just a glimpse.

This is what valor looked like on the afternoon of April 19, 1967, in the confused and treacherous skies above the Democratic Republic of Vietnam, when Leo Thorsness, according to the strike force commander Colonel Jack Broughton, fought "most of North Vietnam all by himself."

Leo and Harry were more than five months into their tour. They had flown eighty-eight missions and survived plenty of close calls. They were getting close to the number that would be their ticket home, but they didn't want to say that out loud or even think about it too much; they didn't want to jinx it. They had recently adapted their tactics and had started splitting their four-plane formations into two elements, which let them attack two SAM sites simultaneously when it was too late for the SAM operators to adjust. However, this meant each element had less firepower and, more important, fewer eyes scanning for SAMs and MiGs.

Their target on April 19 was the Xuan Mai army barracks in the Red River delta, about forty miles southwest of Hanoi. They flew in about ten minutes ahead of the strike force and were followed by four F-4s looking for MiGs. The group call sign for the four Weasels, three F-105Fs, and a single-seat F-105D was "Kingfish." Twenty-five miles from the target, Leo rocked his wings to give the single to split in two. Leo and Harry in Kingfish 1, and their wingmen, Major Tom Madison, and the EWO Major Tom Sterling, in Kingfish 2 flew south of the target. Kingfish 3, with Captain Jerry Hoblit and his backseater, Tom Wilson, and Kingfish 4 would come in from the north. As soon as they entered Vietnamese airspace, Harry heard the crackle in his headphones that indicated they were being tracked by SAM and AAA radar. He told Leo, "It's going to be a busy day."

By the time Kingfish split, Leo counted four blips on his radar screen. Four SAMs, at least, were tracking them. Pilots were calling out flak and MiG alerts on different radio channels. Harry heard a familiar rattle in his headphones and saw a long, black, telephone pole–shaped S-2 arcing toward them. He called out "Valid launch," and then "Multiple launches," as two more were fired. "By this time, every cell in one's body is focused," Leo told *Air Force Magazine* years later.

Just the radio chatter by itself was enough to consume you. . . . Listening to Harry, Harry listening to me, listening for my wingmen, listening for the tail end of the strike flights so we know when we can 'get out of Dodge.' While staying on top of all that going on, we are looking for more SAM sites, keeping our [position] clear of MiGs, jinking to avoid flak, monitoring the aircraft, setting bomb/Shrike/gun switches for the next run, and nursing our fuel so as to cover the last strike flight.

Leo shook off one missile after a steep dive, then turned in the direction of one of the SAM sites and fired one of his two Shrikes at it. He couldn't see the target, but almost instantly the site's radar signal disappeared from their screen just as another, stronger signal drew their attention. They turned north and saw another SAM site. Kingfish 1 and 2 flew low and fast over a ring of anti-aircraft artillery. Harry dropped their cluster bombs directly on target, destroying it. Then they fired their last Shrike at yet another SAM site that had painted them. A second later Kingfish 2 was hit by flak.

Madison radioed that the hit was serious and his "engine overheat" alert was blinking. Leo told him to put the Thud in afterburner, head toward the hills in the west, where they would have a chance of evading capture if they had to eject, and keep transmitting. He would track them on his radio's emergency channel. As Harry continued calling out missile launches, their automatic direction finder homed in on Kingfish 2's transmission, and Leo listened as Madison complained he was getting more cockpit warning lights. Then he heard the shrill distress signal that indicated a man had ejected and his chute had opened, then a second one indicating the other one had punched out too.

Unbeknownst to Leo and Tom at the time, the other Weasels, Kingfish 3 and 4, had left the area. Two MiGs had attacked them, and when the Thuds had tried to outrun them, Kingfish 4's afterburner had failed to ignite. Hoblit in Kingfish 3 had to fight off the MiGs while escorting his crippled wingmen out of harm's way. Kingfish 1 was the only Weasel left, and their situation was about to get a lot worse.

Leo spotted his wingmen's chutes about two miles to the west, flew toward them, circled overhead, and radioed their co-ordinates to the strike force's airborne command post. The two men appeared to be descending near a village and were within fifteen miles of a SAM battery, which could complicate a rescue mission. MiGs were in the vicinity too, and a moment later Harry alerted him to the MiG-17 flying beneath them that appeared ready to dive and strafe the helpless men. Leo dropped to three thousand feet, flying at more than 500 mph, came in behind the MiG, fired a burst from his Gatling gun, and missed. He flew beneath the MiG, came around to the left and got in behind it again, fired another burst, and shot off its left wing just as Harry said, "We got MiGs on our ass." Leo looked back and saw them about a thousand feet back. They were in the enemy's gun sights when he turned sharply to the right and punched it. The MiGs fired and missed, and Leo outran them.

Low on fuel, they headed to the fuel tanker flying its orbit over southern Laos after Leo confirmed that two search-and-rescue planes, propeller-driven, thick-skinned, low-flying A1-E Skyraiders, Sandys

1 and 2, were circling the downed flyers until the rescue helicopters arrived. Once they refueled, Leo and Harry could return to Takhli, having taken out two, possibly three missile sites, shot down one MiG, and done what they could for Madison and Sterling. The strike force had done its work. Most of the planes had already refueled and were heading home. Leo and Harry had fired both their Shrikes and were low on 20 mm ammunition. They had only five hundred rounds left. And they knew if they went back to fly cover for the rescue, they would do so alone. They had a quick discussion, then turned east and crossed back into enemy airspace as SAM radar quickly acquired them again.

Leo tried to get Madison on the radio but heard only a faint, garbled transmission in reply. As they flew at about eight thousand feet over the site of the bailout, the Sandys circling beneath them, Harry called out the first MiG at eight o'clock. Leo saw the second at eleven o'clock and then several more MiGs in a classic wagon wheel formation orbiting the site. He dropped to two thousand feet, turned off his oxygen, and fired the last of his ammunition at a MiG that had unwittingly flown into their gun sight, probably destroying it, although he couldn't be sure; his gun camera had run out of film by this point. Harry called out four MiGs on their tail, and Leo, out of ammunition now, turned his plane into the MiGs and got a couple of them to shoot at him instead of the A-1s and chase him one more time as he punched it, dropped to as low as fifty feet, and shook off his pursuers in the hills to the north, "twisting and turning through the mountains skimming the trees," he recalled.

Starting to run low on fuel again, they radioed the tanker for another rendezvous when Sandy 1's pilot announced that one of the MiGs had hit Sandy 2 and it was "going in," crashing. The rescue helos had been scared away. The evacuation of the downed Weasel crew had failed, and now a Sandy pilot was lost too. Leo told the pilot to drop to just above treetop level, too low for the MiGs, he hoped. Then Leo and Harry flew back to the scene, planning to entice more MiGs into chasing them while Sandy 1 made its escape. They reached the area about the same time as a flight of four F-105Ds arrived and engaged the MiGs in a dogfight. After fifty minutes of murder and mayhem in the skies, fighting single-handed combat against SAMs, MiGs, 85 mm antiaircraft guns, and, for all they knew, small arms fire as they flashed by at treetop level with MiGs on their tail, Kingfish 1 was finally free to go home.

They were almost out of gas and talking to the tanker pilot waiting for them in the skies above southern Laos, when one of the F-105D pilots that had come to the Sandys' aid radioed Leo in distress. Leo knew he was in distress because the pilot called him by his first name, not his call signal. "Leo, I'm not with the rest of the flight, and I don't know where I am. I've only got six hundred pounds [of fuel]. What should I do?" It isn't any more unusual to get lost in the confusion of a battle above ground than it is to do so on the ground. In some ways it's easier. You're covering vast distances in seconds. Jinking SAMs and dodging AAA, chasing MiGs, being chased by them, flying supersonic, diving, pulling up, rolling, listening to all the noise on the radio — it's a surprise pilots aren't chronically lost. But it must be about the loneliest feeling anyone has ever experienced. "I never felt so sorry for anyone," Leo said of the lost F-105D pilot.

He got the tanker pilot back on the radio, explained the situation, and told him to fly north, toward the lost F-105D: "You have six minutes to rendezvous . . . or he ejects."

The tanker replied, "Roger, Kingfish, we'll do our best."

That took care of the lost pilot, but Leo and Harry didn't have enough fuel to get home. They thought that if they climbed high enough and glided as they descended they might have barely enough to get to Udorn, the Thai air base nearest the border with Laos. If they didn't, Leo thought, he could get them across the Mekong and over friendly territory before they had to eject. He climbed the Thud to thirty-five thousand feet. Seventy miles north of the Mekong their fuel gauge registered empty. Leo put it in idle and glided at 300 mph. Luck was on their side. They had just enough to reach the runway at Udorn. "Just after we touched down the engine shut off." When they rolled to a stop, Harry nonchalantly remarked, "That was a full day's work."

The full day had lasted an afternoon, less than an hour of it spent in combat. But it had been one crowded hour of conspicuous gallantry and intrepidity, "above and beyond the call of duty," in the familiar stipulation of Medal of Honor citations. Leo received the Medal of Honor for his valor that day, and Harry the Air Force Cross. It would be six years before it was made official, though, and President Richard Nixon draped the blue-ribbon decoration around Leo's neck.

On the afternoon of April 30, eleven days after they "took on most of North Vietnam" by themselves, Leo and Harry flew their second mission of the day. They shouldn't have had to fly again, but one of the Weasels scheduled to fly reported a mechanical problem, and Leo's plane took its place. They weren't expecting a particularly rough trip, though Leo still felt a little uneasy about it. It would be their ninety-third mission. Just seven more to go.

Seventy miles west of Hanoi their air-to-air warning signal shrieked. The F-4s were behind them trolling for MiGs. Leo and Harry flew right over two MiGs lurking behind a mountain. One of them pulled its nose up and fired an Atoll missile "right up the tailpipe," as Leo described the hit. They ejected at almost 700 mph, and when Leo hit the slipstream his legs flailed sideways at ninety degrees, shredding the cartilage in his knees. His chute caught on a tree limb and it took him time to get down. It didn't matter, though. He couldn't have gotten away; he couldn't walk. His captors beat him when he tried to explain that, so he fashioned bamboo splints and did the best he could until he collapsed, unconscious.

He spent the night in a large bamboo hut. Harry was already there when he arrived. They tortured them the next morning for information. That night they took them to Hao Lo, "the Hanoi Hilton." That was the last they saw of each other for a long while, until the day they flew home six years later.

Harsh treatment was the norm in those days, and Leo had more than his share of it. One stretch early in his captivity was particularly brutal. They broke his back. Eventually they broke his will too, as they broke most of the POWs. But he bounced back. He was a tough resistor. After he refused to bow to a guard he did a long stretch of solitary and spent time in a punishment camp the prisoners called Skid Row. I met him when we were moved into the same big cell with dozens of other POWs later in the war, after Ho Chi Minh died and treatment improved. The others knew who Leo was when he got there. Though there hadn't been an official notice of his Medal of Honor because the air force didn't want the news to get him singled out for torture, word had circulated among the POWs that he been recommended for it, as had the story of how he earned it. Valor like his is hard to keep secret from men who have need of it.

Sergeant Mary Rhoads and the other survivors of the 14th Quartermaster Detachment are welcomed home in western Pennsylvania.

CHAPTER ELEVEN: WOUNDS

Mary Rhoads was an army reservist whose life was forever changed by an Iraqi Scud missile attack in the 1990–91 Persian Gulf War.

Military service was a tradition in the families of the men and women who joined the Army Reserve's 14th Quartermaster Detachment. They came from communities and circumstances that yield more volunteers for the military than do other parts of our society. They lived in a part of Pennsylvania where so many young people were in the military that "whenever a disaster happens anywhere in the world," a local reporter observed, "people around here hold their breath." They are likely to know some of the casualties.

Specialist John August Boliver Jr., twenty-seven, had not grown up, like most of them, in the hills and fading steel towns of western

Pennsylvania. He was a Louisville, Kentucky, native, the son and grandson of military veterans. His wife, Paula, was a local girl. They met at the Baptist Nursing Home in Mt. Lebanon, where they both worked. They had been married three years, settled in Monongahela, and had two children, Matthew and Melissa. They celebrated Melissa's first birthday just before he left. His first letter home and the notification officer who told Paula he was dead arrived on the same day.

Sergeant Joseph Phillip Bongiorni, twenty, from Hickory, Pennsylvania, was an engineering major and honor student at West Virginia University. Joey wanted to be a soldier "ever since he was a little boy," his mother, Rita, told the *New York Times*. His mom and dad made him promise to go to college before he joined the regular army, but they let him join the Reserves when he was a junior at Fort Cherry High School. He was eager to go when he was called up and not happy about having to serve far from the front.

Specialist Frank Scott Keough, twenty-two, from North Huntington, was the fourth of Art and Barbara Keough's eight children. He was loud, funny, friendly, and smart, with an IQ of 137, his dad proudly remembered. He had served a four-year enlistment in the regular army. He wanted to be a math teacher and joined the Army Reserve to earn money for college.

Specialist Anthony Erik Madison, twenty-seven, had been a standout on the Monessen High School football team, playing both sides of the ball, but an indifferent student. His parents divorced and his mom died during his junior year. He joined the army not long after graduation, returned home after his three-year enlistment was up, and got married. He had two kids, a son and a daughter, but had a hard time finding work. Steel mill jobs had disappeared in Monessen, as they had everywhere in western Pennsylvania. His dad, Norman, suggested he join the Reserves to earn some money. He would later blame himself for Tony's death. When Tony's son, Anthony Jr., grew up he joined the army and served three tours in Iraq.

Specialist Thomas Gerald Stone, twenty, was from Jamestown, New York. He too had a hard time earning a living and joined the Reserves for the extra money. He hadn't expected to go overseas. Recently he had moved his wife and baby daughter, Cassandra Renee, to Austin, Texas, where he had found work. He transferred from an artillery battalion to the 14th Quartermaster Detachment in the 99th Army Reserve Command, which he correctly assumed would be posted well to the rear.

Sergeant John Thomas Boxler, forty-four, was the old man in the unit. He had served two tours in Vietnam and was the father of two teenagers, John Jr. and Rebecca. He had lost his job with Bethlehem Steel fourteen years earlier but found work as a mechanic for the U.S. Postal Service in his hometown, Johnstown. Everybody liked him. As more than one neighbor remarked, he was a salt-of-the-earth type, active in the community, a volunteer firefighter. He loved the army. His wife, Elaine, said he was excited to be called up.

Corporal Steven Eric Atherton, twenty-six, grew up in Templeton, Pennsylvania, the youngest of six boys. He loved to hunt and fish in the fields and streams near his boyhood home. He operated a forklift at a lumber company. He enlisted in the army after high school and married his wife, Brenda, after his enlistment was finished and he had joined the Reserves. They had been married about a year when they had their first child, a baby boy, Aaron, who was six months old when Steve left.

Private First Class Richard Wolverton,

twenty-two, from Latrobe, followed a similar path. He enlisted in the army after high school and joined the Reserves when his four years were up, partly to supplement his income at a local truck dealership, but also because "he kind of enjoyed the military life," his mother said. He met his wife, Marlene, in Germany when he was stationed there. They had been married only eight months when he left. She wouldn't let the two uniformed men at her door deliver their sad news, telling them, "Stop. I don't want to hear it."

Sergeant Alan Brent Craver, thirty-two, was from Penn Hills. He joined the Reserves in 1983, when he was still enrolled at Penn State University. He had a degree in environmental resources management, a job in his field he enjoyed, and a steady girlfriend he was thinking about proposing to. His brother said he was just getting his life "to the point where he wanted it to be." He had recently reenlisted in the 14th because he believed the work the unit did, water purification, was socially responsible. He wasn't thrilled about deploying overseas but told his family, "I gave my word and I need to follow through."

Specialist Steven Julius Siko, twenty-five, followed a couple of friends into the Reserves. He had enlisted in the regular army right out of high school, got married and divorced, and was the father of a five-year-old son, Jake. He had recently been made a supervisor at the foam manufacturing company where he worked. A couple of days after he was notified of his only child's death, Steve's father, Julius, received a letter from him. He wrote that the war was going well and he expected to be home in July. They would go trout fishing when he got back.

Sergeant Frank James Walls, twenty, grew up in New Bethlehem, a well-liked kid. He played varsity football in high school and trumpet in the band and read scripture at his Presbyterian church. He had just joined the Reserves the summer before, after finishing a two-year enlistment in the regular army, including a year spent in Korea. In the fall he enrolled at Indiana University of Pennsylvania but hoped to transfer to the University of Pittsburgh, where he wanted to study civil engineering.

Specialist Christine Mayes, twenty-two, was from the coal town of Rochester Mills. Her story broke a lot of hearts. She had been a shy child. She served in the regular army after high school, was stationed in Germany, and, according to friends and family, had come home all grown up and outgoing. She was working as a cook and taking classes part time at the Punxsutawney campus of Indiana University of Pennsylvania. She joined the Reserves in October to help pay for college and help out her family, who were going through a difficult financial time. The weekend before she deployed to Saudi Arabia, her boyfriend, David Fairbanks, asked her to marry him. She said yes and left her engagement ring behind, afraid she would lose it in the desert. They were to be married when she returned that summer. She wasn't worried, she told her mother. She liked the army, and the unit was going to be far from the front lines.

Specialist Beverly Sue Clark, twenty-three, was also from Indiana County. She had joined the Reserves out of high school. She worked as a security guard and as a secretary at a local window and door manufacturer. She too was planning to enroll at IUP. She wanted to be a teacher. She was popular and athletic and loved to ski. Her best friend in the 14th Quartermaster Detachment, headquartered in Greensburg, Pennsylvania, was Mary Rhoads, a meter maid in California Borough, Pennsylvania. Mary was the soldier seen in the CNN broadcast of the

Scud attack, cradling in her arms the dead body of her best friend, Beverly.

Mary Alice David was born and raised in Canonsburg, Pennsylvania, the sixth of nine children born to David and Ruth David, who had married over their families' objections three days after they had fallen in love at first sight. David was a steel worker and Ruth a homemaker. Like most western Pennsylvania families, the Davids had a long tradition of military service. David was a veteran of World War II. Three of Mary's brothers had served in the military. Her oldest brother, Johnny, had done two tours in Vietnam. Her brothers Chuck and Jimmy had served in the air force and navy, respectively, during the Vietnam era.

Mary joined the Army Reserve in 1974, during the summer between her junior and senior years at Canon-McMillan Senior High, south of Pittsburgh. She didn't have clear plans for her life after graduation, and she thought a part-time job in the army would let her follow in the family tradition and bring home much needed extra income. Her dad had died of heart disease two years earlier. She joined C Company, 429th Engineer Battalion, based in nearby Washington, Pennsylvania, where she was the only woman in the unit. Three years later she transferred to Company D in Greensburg, where there were other women on the roster.

After high school she found work in a nursing home for retired Catholic nuns. In 1979 she transferred from the engineering company to the 1004th General Supply Company, also based at the Army Reserve Center in Greensburg. She was married that same year. But the marriage failed, and she divorced in 1983, the year her daughter and only child, Samantha, was born.

Mary and Beverly Clark became friends when Beverly joined the 1004th in 1985. They hit it off right away. Mary, ten years in the Reserves by then, took the younger woman under her wing. They were road buddies. They volunteered for an eighteen-month tour at Fort Meade in Maryland and for a summer duty assignment in Canada. They enjoyed each other's company. They made each other laugh. When Mary transferred to the 14th Quartermaster Detachment at Greensburg in 1988, Bev followed her. At Greensburg the two friends became a trio when Specialist Kellie George joined the unit. They were close, and thought they always would be. They would watch each other's kids grow up. Mary's daughter, Samantha, called Beverly "Aunt Bev" and always pestered Mary to pass the phone to Beverly when she called home.

It was at Fort Meade where a federal employee, Reed Rhoads, caught Mary's eye and she asked him out. He was a fellow reservist and a western Pennsylvania native, having grown up in California Borough, about a half-hour drive from Canonsburg. They married in 1989, and Reed adopted Samantha. That same year Mary started work as a meter maid in California Borough. Scott Beveridge, a reporter for a local paper, the *Observer-Reporter,* met Rhoads when she was writing parking tickets. Her manner was so friendly and engaging that a motorist smiled when she handed him his ticket. Beveridge told her every town should have someone like her in that job. She could have told him that some people weren't as charmed by her manner; some folks gave her a hard time when she gave them a ticket, especially some of the younger ones. But she took it in stride. She liked being friendly. Life was good.

In the predawn hours of Friday, August 2, 1990, four Iraqi Republican Guard divisions spearheaded an invasion of Iraq's oil-rich neighbor, the Emirate of Kuwait. Saddam Hussein had been threatening trouble for months, but the Kuwaitis were still caught by surprise. The conquest was nearly complete the following day. After a weekend spent considering his response, President George H. W. Bush declared in an impromptu Sunday afternoon statement on the South Lawn of the White House, "This aggression will not stand." He dispatched Secretary of Defense Richard Cheney to King Fahd of Saudi Arabia with an offer of military assistance, setting in motion a gathering force that would ultimately bring the armed representatives of thirty-four countries and over half a million Americans to the Arabian desert for the purpose of liberating Kuwait from Iraqi rule. They would need clean water.

Five months of Desert Shield preceded the six-week Desert Storm. On August 8 Iraq announced it had formally annexed Kuwait as its nineteenth province. That same day the first F-15 Eagle fighters from Langley Air Force Base in Virginia landed at the big air base in Dhahran, Saudi Arabia, and immediately began flying combat air patrols along the Saudi-Kuwaiti border. The first boots of the 82nd Airborne Division's ready brigade stepped onto the tarmac at Dhahran the next day, and two carrier battle groups steamed into the Gulf.

These were the very tip of what Rick Atkinson, in his superb history of the war, called "an expeditionary masterpiece rivaling the invasion of Normandy."

On August 12 Air Force Staff Sergeant John Francis Campisi of West Covina, California, sat with his maintenance unit's gear piled on a darkened runway at Dhahran and smoked a cigarette. He was hit and killed by a van driven by another airman, becoming the first American casualty of the Gulf War. Predictions varied about how many dead and wounded the United States would suffer in the war. Most were wildly off the mark. The Pentagon expected somewhere between twenty thousand and thirty thousand. One military analyst reckoned the United States would lose 160 to 170 killed in action every day of the war. Saddam's army was estimated to be the fourth largest in the world and was believed capable of putting up a tough fight. It was widely assumed a lot of Americans would have to die to eject it from Kuwait.

That turned out not be the case. The U.S. Armed Forces were immeasurably better war fighters, better armed and equipped, and better led than the armed forces of the Republic of Iraq. The ratio of combat casualties suffered by each country, roughly one hundred Iraqis for every American killed in action or wounded, would bear that out. None of the prognosticators realized just how much of a war you could fight from the air over a desert battleground where the enemy parked his tanks and artillery in the glaring sun and sheltered his soldiers in sand berms. Nor did they appreciate just how determined Desert Storm's commander, General H. Norman Schwarzkopf Jr., was to use the immense force he assembled to keep casualties low. When the blow was finally struck, the fight would be decisive and over as rapidly as possible, with the loss of coalition lives kept to a minimum.

Yet during the weeks and months of Desert Shield, Americans watching the build-up in Saudi Arabia on their televisions heard again and again how daunting the task would be, how prepared the nation must be to lose many valiant sons and daughters. That's as it should be, of course, even if few of the talking heads enjoining our sober reflection had any real idea what they were talking about. When Americans and their elected leaders contemplate sending soldiers to war, they ought to appreciate the costs that will be borne on their behalf, though the only people who can appreciate them fully are the soldiers themselves and the families who bury them and tend to their wounds.

For the sake of expelling Saddam's army from Kuwait and restoring stability to a region that produces great quantities of a critically important resource, hundreds of thousands of Americans were going into harm's way. Given the nature of that war — a long air campaign followed by a short ground war and Iraq's quick capitulation — casualties were far fewer than the most optimistic analyst had expected. But there were casualties: 149 killed in action, a comparable number of noncombat deaths, such as Sergeant Campisi's, and eight hundred or so wounded. Three hundred graves over which three hundred families wept and prayed. Many thousands of survivors wept too and bore their own wounds, seen and unseen. It helps none of them to know it could have been worse.

A force as immense as the one General Schwarzkopf required necessitated the activation of Reserve and National Guard forces in very large numbers. The post-Vietnam, all-volunteer force depended on the Army Reserve to a greater extent than at any other time in history. Critical combat support functions were entrusted to the Reserves, from military police to fuel tank-ers and water purification units. The army couldn't go to war without them. President Bush authorized the first call-up two weeks after the first American soldiers arrived in Saudi Arabia. When he made the decision in November to double the size of U.S. forces in Saudi Arabia, he increased the Reserve and Guard call-ups correspondingly and extended their active duty tour to 180 days.

Members of the Reserves deployed to the Gulf numbered 217,000. Half of them would serve in Kuwait, and the rest would stay behind the front lines in Saudi Arabia. But the nature of this conflict, and the tactics Saddam used in response to the pounding his army and capital took during the air campaign, meant that no matter how deep in the rear echelon you belonged, you could suddenly, unexpectedly discover the battle had come to you.

The most powerful air assault in the history of warfare began at 2:38 on the morning of January 17, 1991, when eight Apache helicopters destroyed Iraqi radar sites near the Saudi border. A moment later U.S. warships in the Persian Gulf launched the first barrage of Tomahawk cruise missiles against Iraqi air defenses in and near Baghdad. They were followed by warplanes of every description using the latest stealth technology and carrying laser-guided munitions in the first of over one hundred thousand sorties that would quickly establish near total coalition air supremacy, devastate Iraqi command and control, and relentlessly pound the Iraqi Army in advance of the ground war. The six-week air campaign began five days after Congress authorized the use of force and twenty-four hours after the UN Security Council deadline for Iraq to withdraw from Kuwait had expired. But moon phase rather than political events determined the timing of H-Hour. The vast airborne armada would deal out death and destruction for the first time on the darkest night of the month.

The shock and awe of the unprecedented campaign stunned Iraqis in its first hours. But it did not incapacitate the decision making of the mass murderer and reckless gambler who had ruled Iraq through violence and terror for twelve years. Saddam's first gambit in response to Desert Storm's launch had American commanders scrambling to counter it and divert coalition warplanes from their mission to destroy the enemy's command and control and pulverize his armed forces.

Five hours after the first shot was fired,

Saddam declared on state radio, "The mother of all battles has begun." The next day he ordered eight Scud missiles fired in the direction of Tel Aviv. He had threatened such an attack in advance of Desert Storm, and American war planners, not to mention the Israelis, had worried he was serious, and worse, that the missiles would carry chemical weapons. An attack on Israel could serve as a blow to coalition unity. Were Israel to respond, which Saddam devoutly hoped it would, it could rally support for Saddam in the Arab streets, which in turn could imperil the Saudis' and other Arab states' continued participation in the coalition. And the State of Israel had not survived for over forty years by turning the other cheek when attacked.

Complicating matters was the less than warm relationship President Bush and Secretary of State Jim Baker had with Israel's prime minister Yitzhak Shamir. Secretary Cheney made the first call, to Israeli defense minister Moshe Arens, who described the location and damage of the attacks. The Israeli Army initially believed at least one of the Scuds had carried a chemical warhead. But initial reports were wrong. Saddam had considered arming them with chemical weapons, but he feared the Israelis would respond with a nuclear attack on Baghdad, which would have made the coalition's continued unity rather beside the point. They might not have liked each other, but Bush and Shamir wouldn't talk past each other in a critical hour for both countries. Shamir made clear his intention to defend his people from the Scuds if the coalition couldn't, and Bush made clear the importance of keeping the coalition focused on destroying their mutual enemy. He pleaded for Israel's patience, promised to redirect air assets to seek and destroy Iraqi missile sites, and offered to strengthen Israel's air defense assistance with Patriot antiballistic missile batteries. Demonstrating wisdom and a forbearance many countries would have found impossible, Israel refrained from retaliation.

Scuds were not the most accurate weapons to begin with, yet to extend their range, the Iraqis reduced warhead weights and added bigger fuel tanks, which made the missiles even more unstable, inaccurate, and unpredictable. Many broke up in flight, and no one, Iraqi, American, or Israeli, knew with much confidence where they would strike and what damage they would do. No one knows for certain either the total number of Scuds fired by the Iraqis because so many of them broke up in flight or fell harmlessly in the Persian Gulf and Saudi desert. An air force analysis put the number at eighty-six, forty of them directed against Israel and forty-six fired at targets in Saudi Arabia. Most of the Scud attacks targeting Saudi Arabia also did less damage than feared.

The Scuds fired at Israel largely targeted the Tel Aviv metropolitan area. No Israelis were killed in the first attack. In all, two Israelis were killed directly by Scud attacks over the course of the war, although other fatalities were attributed indirectly to them, including heart attack victims and people who suffocated by wearing their gas masks incorrectly. Scores more were injured, and Israelis lived in terror that the more desperate Saddam became, the more likely he would be to attack them with chemical weapons.

With warheads permanently attached to the missiles and traveling at around 4,000 mph, Scuds had a high-velocity impact. Like Londoners reacting to the German V-2s, which the Scud is descended from, Israelis experienced helplessness, terror, and panic as they hurried to put on gas masks and take shelter.

Allaying that somewhat were the approximately fifteen hundred air strikes against suspected Scud launch sites, which represented a substantial daily diversion of air assets. Within a week of the first Scud launches, 40 percent of all coalition sorties flown and a considerable commitment of intelligence resources were employed in the search for and destruction of Scuds. Coalition aircrews would claim they destroyed eighty or more mobile launchers over the course of the war, but the number is almost certainly exaggerated. Most of the sorties failed to find their prey, which usually did their work at night and were hard to find. Others destroyed objects they mistook for launchers. The minimal success of the strikes was a source of frustration to the pilots flying them, the coalition commanders, and the watching Israelis.

Of greater reassurance were the Patriot batteries, which appeared at first to provide surprisingly effective missile defense, although twelve Scuds would hit Israel before the first Patriot battery in the country was operational. There was palpable relief in Israel and among coalition commanders and American political leaders when, the day after the first Scud attack on Israel, Schwarzkopf announced that a Patriot battery had claimed its first Scud kill, destroying a missile targeted at Dhahran. Even better, the successful intercept had been captured on tape, which was broadcast over and over again on the news.

Only after the war would the people of Israel and the United States discover what the Patriot battery operators had realized early on, that the Scud killers were considerably less effective than they first appeared and the army claimed. Only seventeen of the twenty-eight missiles fired at Israel after the Patriots arrived were engaged. The other ten struck underpopulated areas that weren't covered by the batteries and did little damage. Of those seventeen, the army credits the Patriots with seven successful intercepts at most, but is highly confident of only three.

About half the Scuds fired at Saudi Arabia targeted the air base at Dhahran. Most of the rest were fired at Riyadh, where the coalition headquarters were located. The U.S. Army said as many as 70 percent of those Scuds might have been successfully intercepted but could claim only 40 percent with high confidence, and even that number, eighteen or so Scuds out of forty-six, might be somewhat exaggerated.

Nevertheless just one of the Scuds aimed at Riyadh caused a fatality, and just one of the more than twenty fired at Dhahran claimed lives. But they were more lives than were lost in any other single engagement of the war, and they were American lives. Patriots didn't just fail to destroy that one very lethal Scud, which missed the air base (assuming that was its intended target) by several miles; they failed even to track it.

In January President Bush authorized the call-up of one million reservists and national guardsmen for up to two years. The sixty-nine soldiers of the 14th Quartermaster Detachment had started hearing scuttlebutt back in November that they would eventually deploy to the Gulf. Their order to mobilize came on January 15, 1991, the day before Desert Storm commenced. They arrived at Fort Lee, Virginia, three days later and spent the following thirty days drilling and training for their job: water purification and distribution. They left for Saudi Arabia on February 18 and arrived at the air base the next day. They were quartered temporarily in a large corrugated metal warehouse in Al Khobar, a suburb several miles from Dhahran. When all their equipment arrived they would split up and deploy to different field support locations.

There were a few Vietnam War veterans in the detachment, although most of the unit had not been to war, and if truth be told, they had not expected they would be. More than a few of them were scared when they received their deployment orders. The air campaign that unfolded while they drilled at Fort Lee had calmed some nerves, although no one knew how hairy it would get when the ground campaign began. Of course, they wouldn't be on the front lines, although to do their jobs they would have to be closer than two hundred miles behind the front in Al Khobar. Some soldiers had premonitions, as soldiers off to war often do. Beverly Clark told her friend Mary Rhoads she had a bad feeling about the whole thing. She also mentioned her apprehension in the journal she kept. Soldiers' families have premonitions too, especially the mothers. Just before she passed away from pancreatic cancer in November, Rhoads's mother had told her that something terrible would happen but that Rhoads would be okay. Whatever fears disturbed them, none of the reservists resented their call-up. They hadn't seen the war coming, but that didn't make any difference. They had signed up, taken the government's money, and accepted the risks. They had to go, and they would do so without complaint, or at least with no more than soldiers' usual reflexive grumbling about bad luck and the idiots in their chain of command.

Eleven of the reservists in the 14th who deployed to Saudi Arabia were women. The Persian Gulf War occasioned the largest single deployment of women to a combat zone in American military history. Forty-one thousand officers and enlisted — one out of every five women in uniform — deployed. They were pilots, aircrew, doctors, dentists, nurses, military police, truck drivers, communications technicians, intelligence analysts, security experts, administrative clerks, and water purification specialists deployed to a society built on tribalism, Islamic fundamentalism, and primitive notions of gender inequality. Thirteen of them would be killed, four from enemy fire. Twenty-one were wounded in action and two taken prisoner. They did just about everything the men did, including flying missions and accepting other assignments that blurred the lines separating women from combat roles. But this was a war where lines were readily blurred. Even the idea of a front line seemed an anachronism in a war where so much of the fighting was in the air and where missiles were fired at targets located far to the rear, even at a country that wasn't a belligerent. The metaphor "a line in the sand" has come to mean a statement of resolve, but it originally indicated something impermanent, something that disappears in the first breeze. That is an apt metaphor for the Persian Gulf War, where the front was, literally and figuratively, a line in the sand. Even two hundred miles in the rear, the front could suddenly encompass you.

A common and underappreciated complaint of soldiers at war is the boredom that attends so much of it. It is boredom punctuated regularly by the most terrifying exhilaration, but boredom most of the time, oppressive, enervating boredom. For people in a can-do profession with can-do mentalities, boredom is more of a sacrifice than most civilians appreciate. It's not that you'd rather be getting shot at, but you don't want to be sitting idle with your mind drifting to places it shouldn't and the senses your safety relies on getting duller by the minute.

For people of an active disposition, the Gulf War, irrespective of its high-tech thrills, its stunning successes and surprising brevity, could have been stultifying to soldiers who weren't involved in the fighting. Mary Rhoads was bored to tears sitting in that big warehouse, and she hated being bored. Even though they had been in country for only a few days, even after the ground war started on February 24, she was so bored it drove her crazy. She just wasn't the type to enjoy sitting around and shooting the breeze in between guard duty rotations. She had to keep herself busy. Some soldiers sat on their bunks, slept, wrote letters, read, played cards. Rhoads liked to run errands.

She had spent seventeen years in the Army Reserve, half her life. She looked at the kids in the unit as *her* kids, saw herself as the mother hen. To relieve the boredom, she would take one of the buses to the PX at Dhahran or visit a friend she knew in a supply unit. She was a scrounger. She picked up stuff they liked to eat, things to read, games to play, anything that might shorten the days until they were sent forward to do the job they had come to do. She had purchased a Trivial Pursuit game, among other diversions, and it was instantly a favorite entertainment in the barracks. She still felt closest to Clark. They both brought teddy bears with them to war; Clark's was white and Rhoads's brown. One night they were both on guard duty on the warehouse roof when Bev noticed a mist forming in the desert. "Look," she pointed, "the angel of death." Rhoads would remember that through all the years that followed, wondering if her friend had had another premonition.

People had started to relax about the Scuds. The number of launches had declined to an average of one a day, when earlier they had numbered a dozen or more. Their unpredictability was still unsettling, but more and more Scuds were dismissed as the sideshow they were. People made fun of them. Fears that Saddam would arm them with chemical warheads had dissipated; few people clutched at their gas masks anticipating the next warning siren. The Saudi government typically downplayed the damage they did. Israel still threatened eventual retaliation, but the attacks there had dwindled to a few and were doing little damage. The Patriot batteries still seemed to reassure people there was an effective countermeasure to a capricious weapon that, despite its ultimate pointlessness, could, if you were unlucky, kill you.

Rather than the lingering Scud threat, on the second day of the ground war people were paying more attention to the American armored columns crossing the Kuwaiti border and plunging into Iraq and to the thousands of Iraqi soldiers emerging from their bunkers, blinking in the bright sunshine, shell-shocked after six weeks of inces-

535

sant bombardment, and surrendering by the thousands. People were more worried about and perplexed by the oil well fires the Iraqis had started, the first of almost seven hundred. They might have felt otherwise if they had known there was a bug in the Patriot's software.

The Israelis noticed it first and told the Americans that after eight hours of continuous operation, the Patriot's targeting was unreliable. Patriots had been developed initially as a defense against Soviet bombers and cruise missiles that traveled at twice the speed of sound. They were mobile to avoid detection, designed to be shut down and moved every day, not continuously operated as a static defense against missiles that reached Mach 5.

The Patriot's "range gate" is the device in its radar that tracks incoming missiles by calculating the area where they should be based on their velocity and the last time radar detected them. But the Patriot's timing drops a microsecond for every second of operation, a tiny error that wouldn't matter if the Patriots were used for their original purpose and operated accordingly. When the system is turned off, its clock resets automatically and the error is corrected. But the Patriots in Saudi Arabia weren't shut down and moved every day. Alpha, one of the batteries protecting the area around Dhahran, had been operating continuously for over four days and had accumulated a timing error of a third of a second. A Scud travels a little over a mile a second. Alpha's tracking was off by more than a third of a mile, a distance outside its range gate.

The Iraqis fired four Scuds the night of February 25. Three of them appeared to break up in the atmosphere. The missile fired at 8:32 p.m. was detected by satellite and its position relayed to Patriot crews in Saudi Arabia. Three batteries tracked it on their radarscopes but didn't launch their missiles because the Scud was outside their respective sectors. Two batteries, Alpha and Bravo, protected the air base at Dhahran. Bravo was shut down for maintenance that night. Alpha's crew had been alerted to the Scud traveling in their direction, but their screen was blank. They checked to make sure their equipment was operating properly and were satisfied that it was. Still they saw nothing. They didn't know their range gate had miscalculated the missile's whereabouts. No one knew a Scud was plunging to earth at five times the speed of sound above the big metal warehouse where 127 reservists were living.

Rhoads had made plans with friends in the 475th Quartermaster Group, who were also quartered in Al Khobar, to eat dinner at the air base in Dhahran. She wanted to relieve the monotony of sitting in that warehouse before suffering the monotony of guard duty later that night. Steve Siko, Frank Keough, Beverly Clark, and a few others were engrossed in a game of Trivial Pursuit while Rhoads was getting ready to leave. She asked Clark to come along but got a firm no in response. Before she left, Clark asked her for the answer to one of the game's questions. Rhoads didn't know the answer. "You know, for a sergeant, you're not very smart," Clark cracked.

Ten minutes later, driving down the highway toward Dhahran, Rhoads heard the siren. They pulled off the road and watched as the Scud slammed into the barracks and detonated, creating a red and orange inferno that engulfed twisted beams, flying shrapnel, the modest possessions and mementos of the dead, and their charred bodies. Twenty-eight people were killed and ninety-nine wounded, grievously wounded in many cases. Among the dead were thirteen reservists in the 14th Quartermaster Detachment, including Keough, Siko, and Clark. Forty-three of the reservists wounded in the attack were from the 14th, which meant the detachment had suffered in a single attack a casualty rate higher than 80 percent, about as high a rate as any recorded. They had been in Saudi Arabia only six days.

Rhoads and her companions raced back to the base. They had to climb a fence to get into the compound, where all was bedlam. Fire trucks and ambulances had raced to the scene, sirens wailing. Black-hawks descended from the dark heavens to airlift the most seriously wounded. Scores of Saudi civilians crowded around, trans-fixed by the sights and sounds of the disas-ter: girders bent by the heat groaning as they yielded, aluminum walls clanging as they fell, M-16 rounds cooking off, the shouts of rescuers, the agonized cries of the injured, the pitiful wailing of the survivors.

Rhoads tried to enter the burning build-ing, but one of the rescuers stopped her. "My friends are in there," she repeated over and over again. "You don't want to go in there," he warned her. When the ambulances pulled away, she ran to the other side and entered the building there. The smell of burned flesh, of death, filled her nostrils. She thought they were all dead. A moment later she tripped over a girder, wrenching her knee. A soldier in a transportation unit pulled her back outside and told her to stay there. That was where she saw the bodies. The Vietnam veterans in the unit who survived the attack had retrieved them and lined them up side by side. She recognized Clark right away. She limped over to her friend, embraced her lifeless form, and shrieked at the treacherous night, while a news camera recorded her agony.

Everyone who wasn't badly hurt was quartered that night in a large, convention center–like meeting space, where television sets replayed the disaster on what seemed a continuous loop. Rhoads called her husband to let him know she was alive and reported to a sergeant back at the Reserve center in Greensburg. Then she and a few others, impatient and wanting to help, commandeered a van and drove first to the warehouse, then to different hospitals to locate the wounded, and then to the morgue to identify the dead. Rhoads identified the bodies of Tony Madison, Frank Keough, and Beverly Clark.

Back home the 99th Army Reserve Command had set up a casualty assistance center in Greensburg. Chaplains and counselors and support personnel from various federal agencies were flown in to help families, who, two days after the attack, were still waiting to learn if their loved ones were among the casualties. They gathered at the armory in Greensburg and were keeping vigil in a room above the hall where the 99th's commanding officer, Major General James Baylor, was holding a news conference they hadn't been permitted to attend. Baylor informed the media that all but nine of the dead had been identified. He also said the only Patriot battery protecting Al Khobar had been down for maintenance and that even if it had been operational it wouldn't have prevented the tragedy because the Scud was disintegrating and falling end over end when it struck the barracks. None of that was true, but Baylor hadn't intentionally misled reporters; he was only repeating what Riyadh had told him.

Baylor made another mistake that day. The families were quite understandably agitated that they still hadn't been informed if their loved ones had been killed or wounded, and the atmosphere inside the armory was, in the words of an eyewitness, "indescribable tension, frustration, anxiety and stress." Since most of the families were present at the armory, Baylor directed a chaplain to begin the sad task of notifying the families of the dead right there rather than dispatch notification teams to their homes. In a subsequent review of the decision, one of the chaplains present recalled the trauma that ensued: "The notified families' reaction sent panic through other family members sitting in the assembly hall. A second family was called out to talk with the notification officer. Their reaction further destabilized an already disrupted situation."

In all, three families were notified of their loss in this manner, crying out in anguish at the news, while the other families sat gripped by terror waiting for the messenger of death to signal to them. The last was Beverly Clark's family. Her shattered mother wailed, "She was my baby." Finally a chaplain convinced the army to halt the dreadful proceedings. The families were escorted home, where they waited to be notified in the appropriate manner: the dark sedan rolling to a slow stop in front of their house, two men in green removing their caps on their doorsteps before they unburdened themselves of terrible news and offered the president's condolences.

The survivors waited in a tent city in the desert for ten days, unfairly stricken with guilt for not being among the dead, and then finally they too were escorted home.

They arrived first to a solemn welcome at Fort Lee, and then the next day to a tearful and relieved homecoming at the little airport in Latrobe, where a news photographer snapped a picture of Rhoads hurrying toward the open arms of her husband and daughter. She was happy to be home, of course. They all were. But they would not easily recover from the wounds they bore. They had returned too late for the funerals or the big memorial service the governor and secretary of the army had attended, where the letter of condolence from President Bush was read. But there would be a memorial service every year on the anniversary, February 25, and an appropriate monument raised to the fallen. Rhoads would bring a white teddy bear with her to the memorials.

She returned to her job with her leg in a big white brace. She was eager to get going; she wanted her life back. Something was wrong, though. She had frequent nightmares; she lost her temper. She used to shrug off the kids who hassled her and called her names for giving them a parking ticket; now she got into it with them, right in their faces, daring them. She wasn't herself. She froze once while directing traffic when she heard an emergency vehicle's siren. Then she started getting really sick.

Chronic vaginal bleeding resulted in a hysterectomy. She had her gall bladder removed and her appendix. Stomach ailments, headaches, sinus troubles, and serious difficulty breathing brought her to Walter Reed Army Medical Center in Bethesda, Maryland, then the hospital in Brownsville, Pennsylvania, the VA hospital in Pittsburgh, then back to Walter Reed and again to Pittsburgh. Doctors discovered precancerous cells in her esophagus. She developed liver disease. And she suffered such terrible acid reflux it necessitated a Nissen wrap, a procedure named for the doctor who invented it, in which the upper part of the stomach is wrapped around the lower part of the esophagus and stitched in place.

These and other ailments were attributed to the mysterious malady that afflicted many Desert Storm veterans, called Persian Gulf War syndrome. None of the doctors Rhoads saw in Bethesda or Pittsburgh could figure out what was making her so sick. She was becoming almost completely incapacitated. She worried the doctors were using her as a guinea pig, unable to diagnose the cause of her illnesses, offering no cure and giving little hope. Her sister, Kathy, beat on doors for help: the VA, the army, local officials, anyone she could reach. She was a tireless advocate. Scott Beveridge and another local reporter, Connie Gore, took a genuine interest in her case and wrote about her often. Her local congressman, Frank Mascara, and his aide, Pam Snyder, got involved and pushed the VA to recognize that whatever its cause, Gulf War syndrome was real, and it was destroying the lives of people who had risked everything to serve their country and who deserved their government's attention to their service-related illness. Their persistent appeals on her behalf resulted in a full disability pension, one of the first awarded to a sufferer of Gulf War syndrome. She gave testimony to the Senate Veterans Affairs Committee in 1991 and traveled to Washington in 1995, while very ill, to testify to President Bill Clinton's Advisory Commission on Gulf War Illnesses. Congressman Mascara began his statement in a hearing at the House Veterans Committee by invoking her as the poster child for Gulf War syndrome.

When word got around about his successful intervention on Rhoads's behalf, Mascara's office was swarmed with calls from veterans around the country, who like Rhoads were plagued by numerous illnesses since coming home from the Gulf. No one has yet to establish a cause or causes of the disorder that appears to weaken the immune system, making its victims susceptible to multiple illnesses. There are many theories — fumes from the oil well fires, reactions to inoculations, Iraq's undetected use of chemical weapons, Scud warheads carrying biological agents, combat stress — but none have been proven. Whatever its cause, thousands of Gulf War veterans suffer chronic and multiple illnesses attributed to it. According to a congressionally mandated advisory committee of independent scientists, at least a quarter of the seven hundred thousand Gulf War veterans suffer from a disorder that "fundamentally differs from trauma and stress-related syndromes described after other wars." Beveridge's newspaper conducted a survey among the 14th's surviving members and found that seventeen of them had ailments that could be linked to Gulf War syndrome.

After her testimony to President Clinton's advisory commission, Rhoads dropped out of public view. Beveridge wrote that he had received "anonymous hate mail" attacking Rhoads for publicizing her suffering and condemning the deployment of women to war theaters. It appears she heard some of the same criticism. She might have been estranged, for a brief time anyway, from a few others in her unit. When asked, she said the 14th was like a family, and like all families, they have their squabbles and then make up. "We love each other," she maintains.

She volunteers at a care facility that treats veterans but spends most of her time these days caring for her husband, who is also in ill health. Her own health continues to be precarious. She has had mini strokes and two small heart attacks in the past ten years. She lost a lot of weight and has persistent breathing difficulty. She admits to having a rough time emotionally during the first three months of every year, the months when the 14th had been mobilized for war. She still has survivor's guilt. She still misses Bev Clark. But she possesses a naturally cheerful personality, which seems irrepressible even in the most trying of circumstances. "I'm still on my feet," she laughs, "which is a good thing." Her daughter is trying to have children, and she's excited about becoming a grandmother.

She was not able to attend the past two memorial services for the eleven men and two women in the 14th Quartermaster Detachment who gave their lives for their country. Her husband was too ill. But she intends to go next year, no matter what. She'll greet old friends and shed tears for absent ones. She'll carry old wounds earned in service to her country and a white teddy bear for her friend.

Combat medic Specialist Monica Lin Brown stands a post at FOB Salerno in Eastern Afghanistan.

Chapter Twelve:
The Job

Monica Lin Brown, a frontline medic in Afghanistan, risked her life to save others in an ambush.

"You've been treated like a superstar, really. And you're just a kid," the reporter observed.

"Yeah, I'm just a child," the soldier agreed.

Monica Lin Brown was decorated for "extraordinary heroism," which she plays down as her training taking over. "Robot mode," she calls it. There isn't a trace of false modesty in her self-effacement. Throughout all of it — the *60 Minutes* interview, the *Washington Post* story, the visit with the president — her humility appears as genuine as her courage. An observer gets the sense it is the source of her courage rather than a separate virtue. She calls it "duty," one of the "Seven Army Values" she was trained to uphold. But it is humility that makes the duty binding, that holds the "job" above self. It is humility, as much as training and courage, that compels combat medics and corpsmen to do their job, to run toward danger rather than take cover. It is humility that makes them heroes.

"Doc" is a hard-earned title of respect in the military, an expression of the trust a medic or corpsman has earned from soldiers who have come to believe Doc will be there for them in the very worst circumstances. To a scared and bleeding soldier, Doc might be an agent of deliverance who will get him home, if not intact at least alive. Or Doc might be the last human face a dying soldier sees. Neither job can be refused. Imagine soldiers on the beaches of Normandy or marines at Okinawa taking temporary shelter from a curtain of fire in a shell crater or behind the hulk of an armored vehicle. Maybe they try to return fire from their position, or maybe they just need a minute to steel themselves to their duty in the knowledge they are likely to die. They hear the cries of a wounded soldier. Maybe they go to him or at least try to, but the fire is just too hot to brave right then. Maybe all they can do is join the chorus of "Medic!" or "Corpsman up!" Only Doc answers, no matter what. Only Doc must go and do what can be done: stanch the bleeding, relieve the pain, hold their hand. That's the job.

There aren't many jobs that are more important, more dangerous, or more critical to the morale of a platoon. Medic, or 68W, is the second largest occupation in the army, right after infantry rifleman. Soldiers place immense value on having a medic or a corpsman they can count on and will take risks to protect him. And they hold few soldiers in greater contempt than the medic who doesn't do his job, whom they cannot count on. What is often observed about soldiers in battle is more true for medics and corpsmen than others: their greatest fear is not of being killed or wounded by the enemy, but of being unreliable under fire.

Seventy-five medics and corpsmen have received the Medal of Honor, most posthumously. Over two hundred have been killed in Iraq and Afghanistan. The most decorated American in World War I was not Sergeant Alvin York, as is popularly believed, but Private First Class Charles Denver Barger, a stretcher bearer. In addition to the Medal of Honor and more than twenty other decorations, Barger earned a Purple Heart with nine oak clusters, signifying that he was wounded on nine separate occasions. His Medal of Honor citation reads in part, "Learning that two daylight patrols had been caught out in No Man's Land and were unable to return, Pfc. Barger and another stretcher bearer, upon their own initiative, made two trips 500 yards beyond their lines, under constant machine gun fire, and rescued two wounded officers."

Not many soldiers in France would have expected to survive a five-hundred-yard excursion into no-man's-land. Only a medic would have tried it twice. The accounts of the sacrifices medics and corpsmen have made to answer their summons are gripping to read and some of the most astonishing examples of battlefield heroism.

Specialist Edgar Lee McWethy from Denver, a combat medic in the 1st Cavalry Division, was wounded four times coming to the aid of soldiers caught in a North Vietnamese ambush in Binh Dinh Province in June 1967. After crossing a "fire-swept" field to dress his platoon leader's wounds, McWethy was wounded in the head and knocked down as he tried to reach other wounded men. He got up and continued to make his way to the wounded but was brought down again by a wound to the leg.

He was wounded a third time as he crawled toward another bleeding rifleman. "Weakened and in extreme pain, [he] gave the wounded man artificial respiration but suffered a fourth and final wound."

Medics usually carry a rifle along with their aid bag. They have received combat and weapons training and are expected to fight when taking lives takes priority over saving them. Staff Sergeant David Bleak, a high school dropout from rural Idaho, was serving as the medic on a patrol into Chinese-held territory in Korea, when the patrol suddenly encountered an intense barrage of fire from entrenched Chinese. Bleak treated the wounded before rushing toward the enemy trench and killing five Chinese, four of them with his bare hands.

Since they are usually the only medical professional on the scene, and in earlier wars often the only one a wounded man was likely to see for quite some time, medics were sometimes expected to undertake responsibilities well beyond those they were trained to perform. In World War II a twenty-three-year-old corpsman aboard the submarine USS *Seadragon*, Pharmacist's Mate Wheeler Lipes, was ordered by his skipper to perform an emergency appendectomy on a sailor. Before Lipes deployed, a prescient navy surgeon had him assist in operations at the base hospital, including several appendectomies, to prepare him for such an eventuality. But onboard the submarine Lipes didn't have surgical instruments, equipment to deliver anesthesia, intravenous fluid, or an operating table. Instead he used kitchen cutlery sterilized with torpedo alcohol and placed the patient on the wardroom table. The skipper dove the boat to 120 feet to escape the ocean swells. Lipes covered the patient's mouth with a mask made from a tea strainer covered in gauze, had an assistant drip ether onto it, and then cut through the stomach muscles. He located the nearly ruptured appendix, removed it, careful not to puncture it and kill the patient, sprinkled ground-up sulfa tablets on the area to disinfect it, and sewed the wound closed.

Doctors at the navy's Bureau of Medicine and Surgery were apoplectic when they learned a corpsman had performed surgery, but what choice did the corpsman — or the patient — have?

When Lipes left the navy, he received letters of commendation praising his bravery in combat actions, but none mentioned the appendectomy. "Not that the incident in itself was so important," he conceded. "It was my job to do anything I could to preserve life and, really, I didn't deserve special credit or recognition for doing that."

The vocabulary of the medic and corpsman is identical in most instances to the language of civilian medical professionals. Considering the conditions in which they work, familiar terms such as *health care specialist,* the army's official title for a combat medic, *primary care providers,* and *patients* sound almost as if they're meant to be ironic, as does the army's posted job description for a health care specialist:

- Administer emergency medical treatment to battlefield casualties.
- Assist with outpatient and inpatient care and treatment.
- Prepare blood samples for laboratory analysis.
- Prepare patients, operating rooms, equipment and supplies for surgery.

Among the skills the army considers "helpful" to a combat medic are the desire to help others, an attention to detail, and an "ability to communicate effectively and work under stressful conditions."

Consider the reality behind the anodyne descriptions. Health care professionals wearing body armor and a vest with a full combat load of ammunition, carrying an M-4 rifle and possibly a 9 mm Beretta, lugging at least forty pounds of medical gear in addition to other equipment might have to run hundreds of yards under fire to the aid of a wounded soldier. They examine the patient quickly to ascertain the location and severity of the wound or wounds. If there is more than one wounded, they do rapid triage. They instantly decide on a course of treatment to stabilize the patient and give him the best chance of staying alive long enough to be airlifted to a hospital. They might have to apply a tourniquet to stop massive hemorrhaging or insert a chest tube to drain air from the space around the lungs or perform a tracheotomy to let the patient breathe. They could be under fire the entire time. The enemy might specifically target them because their death would demoralize the platoon. But they can't lose their focus on the patient, on the life-and-death decisions they must quickly make and execute. You can see why an ability to "work under stressful conditions" would be helpful.

Modern combat medics are highly trained paramedics who carry an astonishingly varied inventory of medical equipment into battle. They are perhaps the biggest reason the mortality rate for wounded soldiers has greatly declined in America's wars in this century. In World War II a soldier had a less than 75 percent chance of surviving his wounds. In Vietnam the rate improved to a little better than 80 percent. Today more than 90 percent of soldiers wounded in Afghanistan survive — this in an age when the weapons of war have never been more accurate or lethal.

Since most soldiers who succumb to their wounds do so before they reach the hospital, it stands to reason that the higher survival rates are mostly attributable to major improvements in the training, skills, and equipment of the combat medic, as well as better body and vehicle armor. Those improvements were initiated after the *Blackhawk Down* disaster in Mogadishu, Somalia, in 1993, when fourteen soldiers died from their wounds for lack of adequate care and equipment.

It's an exaggeration, but only a slight one, to claim medics are now equipped better than entire field hospitals were in twentieth-century wars. They certainly bring to the battlefield considerably more resources than the equipment medics in past wars carried, which wasn't much more than a first aid kit and morphine. Today medics select the equipment they will carry into battle based on the length and kind of mission they are going on. A typical aid pack includes a set of surgical instruments, IV fluids, tubing and needle sets, catheters of various sizes to use as chest tubes and in tracheotomies, a nasopharyngeal airway or nasal trumpet to open a patient's nasal passage, tourniquets, pressure bandages, dressings for sucking chest wounds, burn dressings, coagulant agents, assorted gauze bandages, ace bandages, splints, morphine, a drug to counter the morphine, antibiotics, antinausea medicine, drugs to counter severe allergic reactions, syringes, alcohol, iodine, tape, scissors, stethoscopes, blood pressure cuffs, thermometers, gloves, surgical sponges, and various other items.

That medics can competently use all this is a tribute to the training they receive today. The army puts about seventy-five hundred prospective medics a year through advanced individual training (AIT), a demanding, sixteen-week course of instruction at Fort Sam Houston outside San Antonio, Texas. The first part of the AIT is essentially an emergency medical technician course, at the end of which students are required to pass the national EMT test. The rest of the training is in combat medicine. In a change from practice in previous decades, most instructors are now veteran medics, not nurses who may have had experience in field hospitals but not in combat. Much of the training focuses on controlling bleeding, the most critical element of trauma care. Students are taught how to apply a tourniquet in under sixty seconds and how to stop hemorrhages in areas of the body where a tourniquet can't be used. They're also taught how to clear airways, seal a sucking chest wound, and treat other trauma. They're taught how to triage mass casualties, how to treat casualties on patrol, how to serve as the sole medical professional on a forward operating base, and how to provide rudimentary medical care to local communities.

The course culminates in twelve days of field exercises at nearby Camp Bullis, where the extreme noise, heat, excitement, terror, and fatigue of battle are replicated as authentically as possible. To graduate, students must prove their competence in a trauma lane test, where they are timed and graded as they successively treat four life-threatening wounds: massive hemorrhaging caused by loss of limb, a blocked airway, a chest wound, and a hemorrhage without using a tourniquet. And they have to demonstrate their proficiency in these tasks while under live fire.

On average nearly a third of students wash out of the training; in some years the fail rate has exceeded 40 percent. Those who survive the course are judged to be proficient in making complex medical evaluations and performing emergency trauma care while under extreme duress for up to seventy-two hours at a stretch. Most of them will have a chance to prove it in real combat. During the wars in Iraq and Afghanistan more than two-thirds of new medics could expect to deploy to one or the other conflict within six months of completing their AIT.

Private First Class Monica Lin Brown didn't deploy immediately to Afghanistan after she finished her AIT; she went to airborne school first. There is a great deal of improbability in Brown's story. How could there not be? It's the story of a slightly built, seventeen-year-old girl, who had an unsettled childhood, a self-described "girly girl" who was afraid of heights and got sick at the sight of blood, who learned to jump out of airplanes and stop a massive hemorrhage as a combat medic. She would also save two lives at great risk to her own and help change official army policy that insisted she did not belong there. It's a story as irresistible as it is improbable.

Monica Lin Brown was thirteen on September 11, 2001. Unlike many soldiers who enlisted in the military in reaction to that atrocity, joining the army didn't occur to her then. It did occur to her brother Justin, who was a year older, but he had always seen himself as a soldier, even in his early childhood, playing with his GI Joes. As a teenager he studied and absorbed the "Seven Army Values" and the "Warrior Ethos." He was impatient for the day when his childhood dream became a reality.

Brother and sister were best friends, but Monica didn't expect their closeness to influence her career decisions. At thirteen she didn't have a firm idea of what she might do with her life, just that she wanted a more normal, stable life than the itinerant, disrupted childhood she had suffered.

Her parents had divorced when she was three after her father was convicted of drug possession and distribution and sentenced to prison. She wouldn't see her dad again until she was thirteen, and she would never have much of a relationship with him. Her mom worked night shifts as a nurse in a succession of hospitals. The family was constantly relocating. The bond between

Monica and Justin grew stronger with each new school and community they had to navigate as they relied on each other for the sense of security and stability their mother was unable to provide. They helped each other adjust. They looked out for each other, and for their baby brother, Kristofer.

After their mother was injured in a car accident, their maternal grandmother moved in with them and tried to compensate for their mother's limitations as a parent. Still theirs continued to be an unsettled and unsettling adolescence. The family moved constantly. That kind of rootlessness can breed resentment and insecurity in children, even if at times it seems like a big adventure. It also instills self-reliance and resilience, and children who might have resented their nomadic childhood can grow up to be adults at ease with changes and disruptions that others find disquieting. It is not an ideal way to grow up, to say the least. But it does provide some advantages, even if those advantages are not apparent to the constantly uprooted child. If it does nothing else, a nomadic childhood can certainly help prepare you for the demands of a military career.

The high school in tiny Kopperl, Texas, about an hour's drive from Waco, was Monica's eighth school in eleven years. She and Justin might have disliked having to start over so often, but they were good at it. They were used to making friends quickly. They were both good athletes. Monica played on the volleyball and softball teams and made the cheerleading squad. Her favorite pastime, the one she was best at, is the simplest and most solitary of sports: running. "Running is like meditation to me," she says. "I can just think without anyone talking to me." She was the best runner on Kopperl's cross-country team. She was a good student too. The day after she turned seventeen and a year and a half ahead of schedule, she graduated from Brazos River Charter School in nearby Nemo, Texas, her ninth and final school, in May 2005, the same year as Justin.

After graduation Monica and Justin went to live with their paternal grandmother, Katy Brown, in Lake Jackson, Texas, near Houston, where Monica had been born. She planned to go to college when she worked out how to pay for it. The idea of becoming an X-ray technician had lately appealed to her. An aunt worked in the field, and it seemed like interesting work that provided a good living and stability. Health care was important and honorable work, and radiology was an area of health care that didn't involve the sight of blood. She found a training program and was waiting to turn eighteen before applying. She hadn't figured out how to pay for it yet, but she was working on it.

Justin had already talked to army recruiters and had put in his papers. He was going to stop by the recruiting office one afternoon in November 2005, and Monica decided she would keep him company. Justin introduced her to the recruiters. One of them asked her about her own career plans. She mentioned the X-ray tech program, and the recruiter did what any recruiter would have done: he told her she wouldn't have to pay tuition if she were an X-ray tech in the army. He also offered her a signing bonus and promised her the adventure of her life, which would almost certainly include deployment to exotic locations in Iraq or Afghanistan.

As it turned out, the army's X-ray technician training program was filled for the year. But she was intrigued, so when the recruiter suggested she consider the army's health care specialist training program instead, she was receptive. She signed the papers, but because she was seventeen, she needed her guardian's permission. Their grandmother told them she was proud of them both and gave Monica her blessing. If Justin was joining the army, she reasoned, she had to let Monica go too. Justin "was older," she explained years later to a reporter for the *Washington Post,* "but [Monica] was always the caretaker, always the boss."

The army wouldn't let them remain together; with few exceptions, siblings are not allowed to serve in the same unit. Additionally Monica, being female, was prohibited by a 1994 Defense Department policy from serving in frontline combat units. Justin would be an infantry rifleman and would almost certainly be going to war. Monica might be a qualified combat medic, she might deploy to the same theater as her brother, but she wouldn't be allowed to fight. There was a rule against that, a good rule, many people believed, people who didn't think women could ever be "qualified" to serve in combat because training couldn't replace what nature had withheld. The prohibition had become more controversial as lines between combat and combat support blurred in Iraq and Afghanistan and more and more women in uniform were doing their jobs while being shot at, but it was still the rule.

Justin did his basic training at Fort Ben-

ning, Georgia. Monica went to Fort Leonard Wood in Missouri. Two duffel bags
containing her uniforms and other gear
were thrust at her when she arrived, and
her first concern was, "Oh my God, am I
going to be able to carry all this stuff?" She
managed to, and, with growing confidence
and satisfaction, she managed to get through
nine weeks of marching, drilling, endurance
training, marksmanship qualifying, live-fire
exercises, and combat skills development.

Her AIT at Sam Houston was harder. She
vomited the first time she saw a tracheotomy
performed. But she got through AIT too
and acquired the skills she needed to treat
all kinds of wounds in all kinds of high-
stress situations. She passed her trauma lane
test with flying colors.

She had always loved a challenge, and she
liked almost all of AIT, her occasional
nausea notwithstanding. One of her instructors at Sam Houston, a sergeant from the
82nd Airborne Division, had a self-assured,
vibrant personality, and Monica wanted to
be like her, wanted the kind of confidence
and dynamism you got from being really
challenged and exceeding your own expecta-
tions. So she went to Fort Bragg in North
Carolina, home of the 82nd Airborne, after
she finished her AIT. She learned to jump

out of airplanes and helicopters with a weapon, body armor, and her aid bag and got "into the best shape in her life." She became a paratrooper, and had the maroon beret and shoulder patch to prove it. And in January 2007 Private First Class Monica Lin Brown, a 68 Whiskey in the 782nd Brigade Support Battalion, 82nd Airborne Division, was on her way to Afghanistan.

A little over 11 percent of the roughly 2.5 million Americans deployed to the wars in Iraq and Afghanistan have been women. Almost three hundred thousand female soldiers, marines, airmen, and sailors in active, Reserve, and National Guard units have served in one or the other conflict, many of them in both, and many of them on more than one tour.

On October 6, 2013, Army Captain Jennifer Moreno, a twenty-five-year-old nurse from San Diego, assigned to a Special Operations support team and on her first deployment to Afghanistan, was killed in a suicide bombing and multiple improvised explosive device (IED) ambush in the Zhari district west of Kandahar. As we write this, she was the latest of 159 American women in uniform to die in Iraq or Afghanistan. In comparison, eight women in military service died in eight years of war in Vietnam, only one of them from hostile fire. The prohibition against women in frontline combat units was lifted in January 2013, yet all but seven of the forty-nine women lost in Afghanistan and all 110 lost in Iraq were killed before the ban was lifted. Over eight hundred women have been wounded in Iraq or Afghanistan, the vast majority of them before the policy change. Many hundreds of women received the Combat Action Badge before 2013. Many have lost a limb or limbs. Many have been badly burned. Many suffered traumatic brain injuries. Posttraumatic stress seems to afflict roughly similar percentages of returning male and female soldiers; in one study a higher percentage of women veterans reported suffering emotional distress, although the overwhelming number of veterans who have committed suicide were male. The majority of female soldiers who died in Iraq or Afghanistan were twenty-five or younger, many were mothers, and most of them were killed by hostile fire. They were killed by IEDs or rocket-propelled grenades (RPGs), mortars, grenades, or small arms fire, or in suicide bombings. Many of them were health care professionals. Some were military police. Some flew helicopters. Some drove trucks. Others served in bomb-disposal units and some in gun crews. Whatever their mission, wherever they were posted, they died in combat because, as they and Brown and countless other veterans have pointed out, there were no front lines in Iraq and Afghanistan. Every forward operating base, camp, outpost, firebase, airfield, hospital, aid station, roadside clinic, every village and city, every patrol, convoy, and meeting with locals could be the target of enemy attacks, some planned and others just opportunistic.

Jenny Moreno was a bright, popular kid with an infectious smile and a close-knit family, who loved being a nurse and was proud of being selected to work with Special Forces. The exclusion of women from ground combat units had been dropped before she came to the aid of a wounded Ranger and was killed by an IED. But many of the women killed before her died in similar situations. Something besides the circumstances of their death unites them. They shared patriotism and courage, of course, but this too: most of them were where they belonged, doing what they were trained to do. It cost them everything to be there, and until recently their government officially thought they shouldn't have been there. But they were there. They died there, and they were as much a credit to their service, to their country, and to themselves as was any man there.

Private Monica Brown reported to the hospital at Forward Operating Base Salerno in Khost Province, Afghanistan, on February 7, 2007. Salerno is situated on three hundred flat acres in the shadow of the jagged mountain peaks along Afghanistan's border with Pakistan. In 2007 it was one of the biggest and oldest FOBs in Afghanistan, a small city of canvas and plywood with a population of three thousand, and a major hub of coalition operations. It had an airstrip, helo pads, airplane hangars, well-staffed medical facilities, a big chow tent, decent food in ample quantities, a good-sized, well-equipped gymnasium, a PX, a chapel, a movie theater (with a large-screen TV and DVD player), a café, and a restored mosque. Taliban and al Qaeda attacked it so often with rockets and mortars its harassed inhabitants nicknamed it "Rocket City." A few days before Brown arrived there, a suicide bomber had killed himself and a dozen others at Salerno's front gate.

Brown helped medical staff treat trauma patients, both soldiers and local civilians.

The first patient she worked on was a local male with a gunshot wound. "That's when the switch flipped," she recalled, "and . . . everything changed over from training to me really liking the job."

In March she was temporarily detailed to an isolated outpost with the 4th Squadron, 73rd Cavalry Regiment in rugged, volatile Paktika Province. The squadron needed a female medic to provide basic medical care to Afghan women in the villages they patrolled. Female medics and corpsmen were often temporarily assigned to combat units to treat Afghans in their homes or in clinics the army set up to help build local relationships crucial to a successful counterinsurgency. Male medical personnel aren't permitted to examine Afghan women in the extremely patriarchal society, especially in the remote, poorest locations where the Taliban is strongest. Female soldiers often helped in home searches and interrogations too. They shared the same risks and hardships male soldiers faced on the missions, the same threat of ambush, the same threat of death or injury from enemy fire or IEDs. They ate the same food, slept on the same stony ground, felt the same fears.

Brown arrived in the advent of spring, when the snow was starting to melt in the

Toba Kakar Mountains, the apricot trees were beginning to bloom, and the Taliban were launching another offensive. It was a dangerous place to be, and it got more dangerous every day Brown was there. Taliban and Haqqani network fighters are plentiful there. Paktika's rugged terrain offers abundant hiding places and hard-to-detect routes into the country from Pakistan. One of the important tribes in the province, the Sulaimankhel, was hostile and a reliable source of recruits for the Haqqani. Suicide bombings were common.

Living conditions in the outpost were pretty primitive. Soldiers were crowded together in tents behind Hesco barriers — wire mesh containers filled with dirt that served as the walls of the command observation post. They were without power or running water. They ate MREs (meals ready to eat) or local dishes Afghan soldiers and interpreters sometimes provided. The aid tent where Brown worked was only forty square feet. And she was the only woman there. She loved it, she told the *Washington Post*.

Brown wasn't there very long when she started going on patrols as a line medic with Delta and Charlie troops. That wasn't in her job description or consistent with official policy, but nobody bothered about that, not out there. Medics were in scarce supply at the outpost, and as someone in Charlie Troop commented afterward, she was one of the best there. They went looking for Taliban, weapons caches, and bomb makers for three, four, and five days at a time, returned for a day's rest and resupply, and went back out again. She loved that too, hunting bad guys, sleeping under the stars. She carried her own weight, she later insisted to the *60 Minutes* reporter Lara Logan. "I expected to be treated like one of the guys. So, that's how I got treated."

She hadn't run into any serious trouble yet. No IEDs, no ambushes, no firefights. She had been on patrol almost constantly for several weeks, and she still did not know for certain if she could do the job. She had not had to keep someone alive while someone else was trying to kill her.

On the afternoon of April 25, 2007, she had been out two days on a patrol with 2nd Platoon from Charlie Troop. The platoon's medic had gone on leave, and Brown was the best of the available replacements. They had received a tip there might be a couple members of a bomb-making cell and some weapons in a little village in the Jani Khel district. It would be their last stop of the day before spending the night at an Afghan National Army camp. They searched a dry well before entering the village and searching a few homes. If there were Taliban there they had been warned in advance and made their escape. The streets were empty, but the Afghans they encountered in their homes were noticeably hostile. Their welcome worn out the moment they appeared, the soldiers were as happy to vacate the area as its inhabitants were to see them leave.

They traveled in a column of four up-armored Humvees and an Afghan Army Ford pickup truck. Approximately a hundred meters separated each vehicle from the next, a distance considered prudent in hostile country, where, in the words of the army manual for convoy tactics, you want "to reduce the number of vehicles in the kill zone," in the event you are attacked or drive over a mine. As the sun started to set, the convoy took another precaution a couple of miles outside the village: they pulled off the road into an adjacent *wadi,* a dry riverbed. As a general rule, you are less likely to encounter an IED if you drive off-road. The Taliban believe ours is a road-bound army. They are right for the most part, and it is a liability in the asymmetrical wars the army has fought this century. But soldiers adjust their tactics to the threat, and when a *wadi* or open field can get them to where they need to be, they'll take it.

The platoon commander, Lieutenant Martin Robbins, was in the lead Humvee. Staff Sergeant Aaron Best was Robbins's gunner. Brown was in the third Humvee with platoon sergeant Jose Santos. A hundred meters behind her, in the last Humvee, were Sergeant Zachary Tellier and specialists Jack Bodani, Stanson Smith, and Larry Spray. The first three Humvees and the pickup had turned into the *wadi* and were rolling. The last Humvee started to ease over the bank when its left rear tire struck a pressure-plate mine. The explosion nearly blew a man out of the gun turret. It ignited the fuel tank and the extra fuel cans stored in the rear, creating a fireball that engulfed the Humvee. All four men inside were wounded.

Bodani and Tellier escaped the Humvee with minor burns and lacerations, although Bodani remembered thinking that his entire crew was lost. Smith and Spray were still inside, seriously hurt and disoriented. Tellier pulled Smith out of the burning vehicle and then managed to extricate Spray, whose boot had caught on something. Smith was bleeding profusely from a forehead wound, and Spray was seriously burned. Tellier suffered more burns pulling them out of the Humvee, but he was still able to function, as was Bodani.

Brown had not heard the explosion. She had been looking at the slanting rays of the setting sun paint the western slope of the distant mountain range, when her gunner shouted, "Two-One is hit!" and their Humvee slammed to a stop. She looked out the window and saw only smoke and fire and a tire bouncing across the field. As she opened the Humvee's door the column came under intense fire from at least two machine guns, and small arms fire ricocheted off the vehicles. The driver yelled for her to shut the door as bullets struck their Humvee. Then Sergeant Santos turned to her and said, "Doc, let's go," before he jumped out of the vehicle. She grabbed her aid bag and weapon and followed him.

They could hear bullets fired about a hundred yards away impacting all around them as they ran a couple hundred yards in the open to where the burning Humvee was hung up on the lip of the *wadi*. Santos saw injured men rolling in the dirt, trying to put out the flames burning their uniforms. Brown doesn't remember thinking about the danger that she would be killed as she ran, but only wondering what kind of shape the casualties would be in when she reached them and if she would be able to do her job and keep them all alive until the medevac bird arrived. She was afraid of failing, she admitted to *60 Minutes,* of being responsible for the survival of other soldiers.

With all five men out of the Humvee, she did quick triage. Initially she thought Smith was in the worst shape. He was in shock, bleeding heavily from the cut on his head, and his face appeared badly burned. Best, the gunner on the lead Humvee, saw Smith and remembers telling himself, "He's dead." Spray was actually the most severely injured, having been the longest inside the Humvee and sustaining burns over much of his body. Both men appeared to have life-threatening wounds, and their situation was obviously untenable as insurgent gunfire intensified. Brown and Bodani grabbed Smith by his body armor and hauled him fifteen yards deeper into the ditch while Tellier helped move Spray.

No sooner had they repositioned than Brown heard the whistle of mortar rounds being fired at them. She yelled "Incoming!," threw her body over Spray, and told Bodani to "cover up" Smith. Fifteen or more mortars followed in quick succession and shook the ground around them. Then ordnance inside the burning Humvee started cooking off, sending their own 60 mm mortar rounds, as well as grenades and .50 caliber ammunition, flying in every direction through the open doors of the Humvee. They were caught in a cross fire between enemy fire from two or more locations and friendly fire from the burning Humvee. Shrapnel streaked through the air and tore up the earth as Brown repeatedly shielded her patient with her body.

All who witnessed Brown's actions that day hailed her as a model of composure and concentration as she tended to her patients amid the noise and desperation of combat. She didn't look up as she worked, wasn't unnerved by enemy fire concentrated on their position, didn't even appear distracted by it. "Rounds were literally missing her by inches," Bodani recalled. Best would later tell the *Washington Post* that he'd seen a lot of grown men who didn't have the courage and weren't able to handle themselves under fire like she did. Brown, he insisted, "never missed a beat."

The three operational Humvees maneuvered into a defensive crescent in front of the wounded and started laying down suppressive fire. Lieutenant Robbins had his

Humvee positioned closest to Brown and her patients, trying to shield them from the heavy incoming. A year later he recounted the scene for the *Washington Post:* "I was surprised I didn't get killed, and she had been over there for ten, fifteen minutes longer. There was small arms fire coming in from two different machine-gun positions, mortars falling . . . a burning Humvee with sixteen mortar rounds in it, chunks of aluminum the size of softballs flying all around. It was about as hairy as it gets."

Somehow Santos managed to drive the Ford pickup through the shower of small arms and mortar fire, stopping close to where Brown was trying to protect her patients. While the platoon returned fire, he helped her drag Smith and Spray the short distance to the truck and lift them into the back. She jumped in with them and again positioned herself between the wounded men and incoming fire, which kept coming until Santos got them out of range. She put pressure on Smith's head wound, held Spray's hand, and told them both they would be okay. As soon as they sped off, a mortar round exploded near the spot where they had been, and shrapnel ripped through the air she had breathed a moment before.

When they reached relative safety about

three hundred yards to the rear, they called in the medevac helicopter. Brown directed the less wounded to assist her as she got IVs started for Smith and Spray and began dressing their wounds. At one point small arms fire started to get a little close for comfort, and Santos worked the .50 caliber on the truck, while Brown shielded her patients from the flying brass shells and any incoming that might reach them. Smith was losing consciousness as Brown bandaged his head wound and burns and gave him something for the pain. She ran out of gauze trying to wrap all of Spray's burns before pulling a hypothermia blanket around him. Another three-quarters of an hour, what seemed to her an eternity, passed as she stabilized her patients and got them ready for medevac. Then the helo finally arrived and flew the wounded to a base hospital.

The shooting had stopped and the insurgents were moving out by the time the helicopter lifted off, almost two hours after the fight had started. It was dark as Brown walked in strange solitude through tall grass toward the Humvees with her nearly empty aid bag, her ears still ringing from the noise that had finally subsided. She was suddenly stunned by all that had happened and realized the extreme peril she had been in.

She worried whether she had done all right by Smith and Spray. "All this stuff was just . . . rushing to me," she told *60 Minutes.* "It was a hard thing to think about." That's when she threw up.

Her fellow soldiers threw their arms around her and thanked her. Robbins wrote her up for a medal, and brigade signed off on it. He wrote Tellier up for one too, for rescuing Spray and Smith from the Humvee. Spray and Smith were eventually flown to the States to recover. The other three wounded soon returned to the field. Sergeant Zach Tellier, a brave and exceptional soldier, was killed five months later in another firefight.

Private Brown stayed where she belonged after her first firefight, in the field with fellow combat soldiers, for a few more days until word of her performance under fire drew attention to the fact that she was a woman. She was ordered back to FOB Salerno. She didn't want to leave, nor did the soldiers in Troop C want their doc to leave. "Of all the medics we've had with us throughout the year," Bodani observed, "she was the one I trusted the most."

But there were no more firefights or patrols for her; she remained at Salerno for the rest of her tour. She still wasn't out of harm's way, of course. No one serving there is ever completely out of danger. "You go out on missions. Whether it be humanitarian aid or . . . searching for the Taliban," Brown explained. "You go out there and you do your job. And you don't know what's gonna happen. Anything could happen."

It took a while, but at Bagram Air Base in March the following year she received her Silver Star from the vice president of the United States, Dick Cheney. The army brought her brother Justin to the ceremony. It was only their second reunion since they had enlisted, and she cried when she saw him. She had wanted the soldiers who called her "Doc" to be there, but they had already rotated home. "I wouldn't be here today if not for them," she insisted.

In April she was summoned to a NATO summit in Bucharest, where she and twenty-four other Afghanistan veterans from NATO member states were acknowledged and thanked for their service, and where she met her commander in chief and fellow Texan, President George W. Bush. That's when the press got interested in her story, when the *Washington Post* and *60 Minutes* came calling. She went home for a month's R&R in May, visited Larry Spray in the hospital, and almost cried when Spray's mother thanked her for saving him. She rode in the back of a convertible in a parade that Lake Jackson organized for her, wearing her uniform and looking a little uncomfortable waving to the cheering crowd. You could see she was touched. But nothing had meant more to her — not the medal or the meeting with the president or the national media interviews or the parade — than the fact that she had been tried in combat and not found wanting by the men she served with. No recognition or tribute made her prouder than the simple respect paid her by the soldiers who called her "Doc."

Brown was only the second woman to receive a Silver Star since World War II. Not everyone in Charlie Troop thought she had done anything more that day than the other soldiers in 2nd Platoon had. She did her job in a firefight; they all had. And she was the first to agree. "Everything I had done during the attack was just rote memory," she allowed. "Kudos to my chain of command for that. I know with training like I was given, any medic would have done the same in my position."

60 Minutes asked to interview Stanson Smith, but he declined, noting that he opposed allowing women to serve in combat units. Not one of the soldiers she served with faulted her performance as their doc. On the contrary, the very fact that they called her Doc is an expression of their trust in her. She had only done her job, they maintained, same as a man would have. But as Best added, she had "done a very, very good job." That is a soldier's tribute, the only recognition she wanted. She didn't really care about the Silver Star or all the attention. "If I could take back the entire day I would," she told *60 Minutes*.

Maybe lifting the prohibition against their service in ground combat is a better tribute to Private Brown and to all women who served our country in difficult circumstances with skill and humility. Brown might want to take back the events that won her public acclaim, but the men she served with wouldn't have wanted her to be anywhere else that day. She had earned the right to stay where she belonged, answering the call "Doc, let's go," saving lives, and doing what she proved she could do: her job.

Navy SEAL Mikey Monsoor on patrol in the treacherous streets of Ramadi.

CHAPTER THIRTEEN:
ABOVE AND BEYOND

Michael Monsoor, a Navy SEAL in Iraq, would not let his brothers be killed.

On May 9, 2006, Petty Officer Second Class Michael Anthony Monsoor was in another firefight. He had been in a few by then. He was the machine gunner for Delta Platoon, and for the past month he and his brothers from SEAL Team 3 had been operating in the most dangerous city on earth, Ramadi, the capital of Iraq's Anbar Province. Mikey, as his family and fellow SEALs called him, would be in Ramadi for six months and in thirty-five firefights, by one count. That number is most likely low; as anyone who fought in Ramadi in the summer of 2006 would tell you, you were pretty much guaranteed contact with the enemy almost anytime you were "outside the wire." On 75 percent of Delta Platoon's missions, the SEALs ended up in a firefight.

Monsoor would receive a Bronze Star for his actions in eleven separate operations in Ramadi from April to September. According to the citation, "Petty Officer Monsoor exposed himself to heavy enemy fire while shielding his teammates with suppressive fire." That's the machine gunner's job. And Monsoor was good at it. "He aggressively stabilized each chaotic situation with focused determination and uncanny tactical awareness."

Delta Platoon was operating in Ramadi's most dangerous neighborhood, the Ma'Laab district, on May 9, providing sniper overwatch protection for an Iraqi Army counterinsurgency operation, when insurgents started lighting them up. A SEAL was shot through the legs and lay in the street unable to move on his own. Monsoor made his way over to the wounded man, firing his MK-48 as he went. He dragged his comrade with one arm and with the other kept firing his weapon as bullets "kicked up the concrete at their feet." He got the man to safety, helped load him in a vehicle for evacuation, and went back to the fight. "I thought he was the toughest member of my platoon," recalled the skipper, Lieutenant Commander Seth Stone.

Stone and the SEAL task unit commander, Lieutenant Commander John Willink, recommended Monsoor for the Silver Star for rescuing the wounded frogman, which the navy would award him months later. He never mentioned it to his family, not the incident or the Silver Star he had earned. The Monsoors were a close-knit family. They knew Mikey was serving in the most dangerous place in Iraq, but he didn't like to worry them with details. When he called home, he kept things light and general. His parents learned about the Silver Star from one of their son's fellow SEALs when they were all attending the funeral of another SEAL.

Later, when it would seem all the more appropriate and poignant, Mikey's Aunt Patty received a photograph from the SEAL her nephew had rescued. It was of a tattoo he had gotten, showing Mikey holding his machine gun and wearing wings like his patron saint, Michael the Archangel. Part of the prayer to St. Michael was inked, too, which was fitting, considering Mikey was a devout Catholic: "St. Michael the Archangel, defend us in battle. Be our protection against the wickedness and snares of the devil."

These were still early days in Ramadi. There

was plenty of fighting in the streets in the spring of 2006, but the Battle of Ramadi, or, as it is sometimes called, the Second Battle of Ramadi, did not really get under way until mid-June, after the 1st Brigade Combat Team, 1st Armored Division, "the Ready First," had arrived, under the leadership of a smart, determined, unpretentious West Pointer, Colonel Sean MacFarland.

MacFarland had been given overall command of the joint operation to tame Ramadi, then the center of the Sunni insurgency and al Qaeda in Iraq operations. He had roughly fifty-five hundred Americans and twenty-three hundred soldiers from two Iraqi brigades with which to accomplish the mission. The American forces under his command included two armored battalions, one mechanized army infantry battalion, the 3rd Battalion, 8th Marine Infantry, and a battalion from the storied 506th Infantry Regiment of the 101st Airborne, the "Band of Brothers" regiment chronicled by the historian Stephen Ambrose in his book of the same name. It also included a Navy SEAL task unit with thirty-two SEALs from Team 3.

MacFarland and the 1st Brigade Combat Team relieved Colonel John Gronski's 2nd Brigade Combat Team of the Pennsylvania

National Guard when U.S. commanders in Baghdad decided to take back Ramadi from the insurgents. At the time, coalition forces in the area operated out of major bases located on the city's western and eastern outskirts, Camps Ramadi and Corregidor, respectively, and a few strongholds along the main road through the city, Route Michigan. Most of the marines were camped at Hurricane Point just east of Camp Ramadi, and a marine company garrisoned an outpost near the Government Center. There were a few areas of the city where coalition forces held disputed control, but insurgents owned most of the city. When MacFarland arrived at Camp Ramadi on May 22 and paid his first visit to the city he had come to liberate, he had to run from his vehicle into the office building where the Iraqi governor of Anbar waited to meet him, so severe was the threat from insurgent snipers.

I Marine Expeditionary Force was responsible for Anbar, and the Battle of Fallujah two years before had been a mostly marine operation. In 2004 insurgents in Fallujah had killed four private security contractors with the American firm Blackwater who had made the mistake of driving through the city on their way to somewhere else. The charred remains of two of the Americans had been strung from a bridge over the Euphrates River and displayed to television cameras, arousing a furor back home and demands for retaliation. In April, over the objections of the Expeditionary Force commander, Lieutenant General James Conway, and the 1st Marine Division's Major General James Mattis, Washington and Baghdad ordered the marines to take the city of Fallujah.

Generals Conway and Mattis argued that taking the insurgent stronghold would drain resources from counterinsurgency operations elsewhere and unavoidably require razing the city. They also believed Ramadi was a bigger problem. They preferred to find and kill the people responsible for the atrocity rather than make the massive commitment in men and resources it would take to pacify and garrison Fallujah. Washington overruled them, and Operation Phantom Fury was launched the night of April 4. Conway made one request when he received his orders: Don't stop us once we start. That request too would be denied.

The marines had cordoned off the city and made good progress clearing out insurgents one neighborhood at a time when the television station al Jazeera broadcast video purporting to show heavy civilian casualties in the city. There had undoubtedly been civilian casualties, but the marines had gone to great lengths to minimize them, and Arab media greatly exaggerated the extent of the suffering. Nevertheless the Iraqi Governing Council put pressure on American authorities in Baghdad, and on April 9, five days after the operation had started, Paul Bremer, the American viceroy in Iraq, ordered a unilateral cease-fire. Insurgent attacks in the city continued and marines fought back, but by the end of the month the Americans were ordered to withdraw and turn over the city's security to an Iraqi Army brigade.

What had looked to be a mounting catastrophe for al Qaeda in Iraq became a military and propaganda victory. Fallujah became AQI's primary base of operations, a sanctuary almost entirely under their control and from where they planned and organized attacks on targets elsewhere in Iraq. By the fall of 2004 the situation had become intolerable. A second Battle of Fallujah was ordered, a joint operation led by the marines and including three U.S. Army battalions, as well as Iraqi and British soldiers, and using air, armor, and artillery to make short work of enemy strongholds. The bloodiest battle of the war to date began on November

7. It would kill more than a thousand insurgents and about a hundred Americans. The insurgents fought tenaciously, and sporadic fighting continued well into December. But major fighting was over within two weeks. Much of the city was wrecked. Two-thirds of its buildings were damaged or completely destroyed. And many of the insurgents who escaped death in Fallujah fled to Ramadi.

The first Battle of Ramadi had played out while the press's attention was mostly focused on the interrupted first Battle of Fallujah. The 2nd Battalion, 4th Marines had suffered more casualties battling insurgents in Ramadi in the spring of 2004 than any battalion in the war to date. Twelve marines were killed in one day alone. But in four days of fighting the marines succeeded in killing hundreds of insurgents, driving the rest into hiding and halting the insurgency's momentum in the city. But once Fallujah was taken in November and December, Ramadi, thirty miles to the west, became the center of the insurgency. Al Qaeda in Iraq and its sadistic leader, Abu Musab al-Zarqawi, would eventually declare it the capital of the Islamic State of Iraq. Insurgents overwhelmed Ramadi police and other local authorities and claimed most of the city as their sanctuary. They planted IEDs everywhere. They contested most patrols by U.S. and Iraqi forces, which in 2005 and part of 2006 still operated out of three main bases except for the brave company of marines garrisoned in the isolated outpost near the Government Center. Al Qaeda was ascendant in the Sunni insurgent movement throughout Anbar and was challenging Sunni tribal sheiks for control of the province.

The 2nd Brigade, stitched together from National Guard units in a dozen states, was a force suitable for garrisoning a pacified city, training civilian authorities, and other nation-building exercises. But a brigade of mostly part-time soldiers, some of them approaching middle age, is obviously not ideal for contesting a major insurgent stronghold. They did fine under the circumstances, with less armor, equipment, and experience than MacFarland's 1st Brigade would bring to Ramadi. During their year there they fought hard, losing over eighty soldiers and marines to hundreds of IEDs and rocket attacks and firefights. They secured the main road, Route Michigan, and manned checkpoints into and out of the city. But they could never take back the city from the insurgents. They held their own. No more could have been expected from them. And they managed to clear some neighborhoods. But most of Ramadi, and practically all the city center, remained a no-go zone for coalition forces. By the end of 2005 Ramadi was in fact as well as declaration the capital of the Sunni insurgency as the enemy occupied neighborhoods within mortar and rocket range of the main U.S. bases.

The situation could not be allowed to continue. Ramadi was too important, the key to winning Anbar Province. There were other coalition forces in Anbar in the same situation, operating from mostly secure bases, subjected to mortar and rocket attacks, patrolling cities teeming with insurgents, contending with IEDs, rocket-propelled grenades, snipers, and hit-and-run ambushes. In addition to being the capital and the largest city in the province, Ramadi sat astride the major rail line and numerous roads and was a gathering place for foreign fighters entering the country from Syria. It was the bellwether. "If Ramadi fell," General Mattis explained, "the whole province goes to hell." Take it back, and the rest of Anbar would likely follow.

In 2005 and throughout 2006 it appeared that the opposite was happening. Ramadi, and with it all the province save Fallujah, looked increasingly to be slipping beyond the reach of the central government's authority and possibly beyond pacifying by force, at least at a cost acceptable to Washington and Baghdad. Most press reports described the situation going from bad to worse to hopeless throughout 2006 and into 2007. A few observers glimpsed the reality. Starting in the summer of 2006, when the Ready First assumed responsibility for Ramadi, the tide began turning very slowly, barely perceptibly. The pace quickened with the Anbar Awakening, when Sunni tribal leaders started turning against the foreign jihadis in the fall of that year. But no one in the press could be blamed for missing the signs of the turnaround when many people in the U.S. intelligence community, who possessed more knowledge of the situation, believed Ramadi and most of Anbar were probably beyond recovering.

In September 2006 an assessment by the marines' chief intelligence officer in Iraq, the highly respected Colonel Pete Devlin, was leaked to the *Washington Post,* and an updated assessment was leaked to the same reporters in November. "The U.S. military is no longer able to defeat a bloody insurgency in western Iraq," the report bluntly asserted, "cr counter Al Qaeda's rising popularity there." That certainly appeared true to many observers, including most Bush administration officials. In his memoirs President Bush would recall 2006 as the bleakest time in the war and the lowest point of his presidency. Mounting casualties in Ramadi and elsewhere in Anbar, vicious sectarian fighting in Baghdad, and three years of occupation mistakes by American civilian and military authorities in Baghdad and Washington, which were by then obvious to almost everyone, made it seem all Iraq was a hopeless cause.

That wasn't the case, and, thankfully, no policy steps were then taken that would have made it a self-fulfilling prophecy. On the contrary, it was in this bleak and discouraging moment that President Bush made the hardest and best decisions of his presidency. He replaced Secretary of Defense Donald Rumsfeld, ordered increased troop levels for Iraq, and authorized General David Petraeus to conduct the counterinsurgency that eventually snatched success from the jaws of defeat.

Colonel MacFarland, and the force he had the honor to command, launched a counterinsurgency in Ramadi in June 2006 using tactics that would be the hallmark of the "surge" the following year. They stuck it out through a long, hot, hard summer and fall, when hard-won gains were modest and mostly unnoticed and casualties mounted. Anbar tribal leaders, disgusted and angered by the viciousness of al Qaeda and the imposition of its customs on local traditions, rebelled and made common cause with the Americans, a development partly orchestrated by one of the most enterprising soldiers in the U.S. Army, Captain Travis Patriquin, sometimes called "Lawrence of Anbar," who was killed in Ramadi by an IED in December 2006. What began in Ramadi wasn't merely the pacification of one city or even an entire province. Ramadi is where the rescue of the American effort in Iraq began.

By the spring of 2007, as U.S. forces surged in Iraq and the marines at Ramadi had their tours extended three months, what had appeared lost was well on the way to recovery. It began with the decision to fight, which was first evident in the decision to send the Ready First to Ramadi with instructions to take the city back without destroying it. Americans from every service carried out that tough assignment — army, marine, navy, and air force. They were infantry, armor, artillery, engineers, intelligence, and Special Forces. Their cooperation and mutual respect set a high standard that joint operations don't always meet. They were all a credit and invaluable to the country that had sent them there.

The first SEAL task unit in Ramadi arrived in October 2005. They were from the East Coast–based SEAL Team 2 and tasked mostly with training Iraqi Army scouts in Camp Ramadi. The SEALs camped on the Euphrates River outside the wire of Camp Ramadi in an old guardhouse that had once housed Saddam Hussein's bodyguards. They called it Shark Base, apparently because of its proximity to the river. The accommodations were too small for the SEAL detachment, and what the camp lacked in amenities it also lacked in security. The SEALs' first job in Ramadi was to improve both with the help of navy Seabees. Then they started training Iraqis, which was a learning experience for both trainers and trainees, as each worked to overcome cultural differences that made the job harder than it needed to be.

The hairiest part of the job was running patrols in the city with the Iraqis. At first they went out only at night. Night vision equipment and the SEALs' experience fighting in the dark gave them an unmatchable advantage, and insurgents rarely challenged them — although, as many SEALs later remarked, you don't need night vision to detonate IEDs, which remained a problem day and night.

Eventually, as they learned the city better, they started patrolling during the day, teaching the Iraqis how to clear buildings and other tactics of urban counterinsurgency, and regularly running into resistance. They started in some of the quieter neighborhoods before venturing deeper into what they called "Indian country." When intelligence started giving them valuable target leads, the SEALs set up and executed assaults. But throughout their deployment the first SEAL task unit's primary mission remained training Iraqis to take and hold their cities.

The second Ramadi SEAL task unit relieved their predecessors in early April 2006, six weeks or so before MacFarland and the Ready First arrived in Ramadi. The new task unit, two full platoons, was from San Diego–based SEAL Team 3, the task unit commanded by Lieutenant Commander Willink. It was the start of Willink's second rotation in Iraq. It was the very first combat rotation for the heavy weapons guy in Delta platoon, Petty Officer Monsoor, who was considered one of the most dependable SEALs in the unit.

Michael Anthony Monsoor was born in 1981 in Long Beach, California, the third of George and Sally Monsoor's four children, and raised in Garden Grove in Orange County. He suffered from asthma as a child and trained himself to become an athlete and overcome his condition. He was a typical athletic, outdoorsy kid from southern California, tough but fun-loving and good-natured. He surfed, snowboarded, spearfished, played tight end for his high school football team, and rode a motorcycle. After he joined the navy, he drove a Corvette.

The Monsoors were devout Catholics, and Mike was a practicing Catholic all his life, regularly worshipping God at Mass and turning to the solace of the confessional at home and overseas. He was said to have attended Mass before every mission. The SEALs' chaplain, Father Paul Halladay, remembered Monsoor asking him to hear his confession just after he arrived in Ramadi.

He came from a tradition of military service. His dad was a Marine Corps veteran of the Vietnam War. His brother, Jim, had also served in the Corps, and Mike felt pulled from childhood to military service. He was drawn to the navy, though, and not to any billet. He wanted to join the most selective outfit in the navy, some would argue in all the armed services. He wanted to be a frogman, one of the Sea Air Land commandos, who trace their lineage to the navy combat demolition units in World War II. They are elite warriors, whose toughness, weapons and tactical skills, and legendary perseverance are formed in what is arguably the toughest training in the military, BUD/S (Basic Underwater Demolition/SEAL) in Coronado, California. It's a six-month trial of the outer limits of human endurance and rigorous instruction in the frogman's special skills and tactics. Each new class has about two hundred candidates. On average, 150 of them drop out of the program by the end of the third week, the notorious "Hell Week," five and a half days of brutally difficult, sleep-deprived training. Candidates can quit when they "ring the bell," sounding a bell three times to signal their inability to continue. Those who succeed will have proven their physical stamina, mental toughness, leadership, and ability to work as a team as much as can be outside of combat. They will receive the SEAL trident insignia to wear on their uniforms and ample opportunity to prove themselves loyal to the SEAL creed, which reads in part:

In the absence of orders I will take charge, lead my teammates and accomplish the mission. I lead by example in all situations.

I will never quit. I persevere and thrive on adversity. My Nation expects me to be physically harder and mentally stronger than my enemies. If knocked down, I will get back up, every time. I will draw on every remaining ounce of strength to protect my teammates and to accomplish our mission. I am never out of the fight.

We demand discipline. We expect innovation. The lives of my teammates and the success of our mission depend on me — my technical skill, tactical proficiency, and attention to detail. My training is never complete.

We train for war and fight to win. I stand ready to bring the full spectrum of combat power to bear in order to achieve my mission and the goals established by my country. The execution of my duties will be swift and violent when required yet guided by the very principles that I serve to defend.

Brave men have fought and died build-

ing the proud tradition and feared reputation that I am bound to uphold. In the worst
of conditions, the legacy of my teammates
steadies my resolve and silently guides
my every deed. I will not fail.

Monsoor graduated from high school in
1999 and enlisted in the navy two years
later. After basic training at the Naval Station Great Lakes, he went to BUD/S. He
broke his heel during Hell Week but tried to
stick it out. He described to his younger
brother, Joe, the excruciating pain he experienced running hard in the sand, telling
himself, "Don't pass out. I can't pass out."
But he couldn't go on, and he rang the bell.
The navy sent him to the Naval Air Station
in Sigonella, Italy, for two years. His mother
visited him there and remembers him constantly "working out, running and swim-
ming," hoping for another crack at qualifying as a frogman.

He graduated BUD/S in September 2004,
at the top of his class. The Monsoors remember his graduation as their proudest
moment — not only Mikey's but the family's. He completed advanced SEAL training
in the spring of 2005, before being assigned
to Delta Platoon, SEAL Team 3. He went
to war for the first time a year later, at the

age of twenty-five. Just before he deployed he took a last trip with his brother Joe, driving him to his university in North Dakota. "He knew what he believed in and would stand by what he believed in," Joe remembered. "He couldn't be corrupted." He assured his family he would be okay. He trusted himself and his teammates to come through whatever dangers they faced. Most of them would.

The task unit initially thought they would be based in Baghdad, helping to train the Iraqi Special Operations Force headquartered there. They found out they were going to Ramadi only a few weeks before they deployed. They came ready for combat. By then the decision had been made to take the city from the insurgents, although ways and means had yet to be decided. The SEALs knew a big fight was coming, and their primary mission would change from training to operational. They didn't know when exactly that transition would occur, but whenever it did, they would be ready for the perils of operating in Iraq's most dangerous city.

The departing SEAL team stayed in Ramadi a few weeks to give their relief the lay of the land and introduce them to the Iraqi scouts they would be training. For their first six weeks in Ramadi, Monsoor and his teammates focused on close-quarter fighting and fire and maneuver drills at Camp Ramadi. Later, when trainers and trainees were familiar with each other, patrols in the city resumed.

Early on, Lieutenant Willink made a decision to send one platoon, Delta, to support the 1st Battalion of the 506th, which had arrived in Ramadi in advance of MacFarland's brigade. They were based on the eastern edge of town at Camp Corregidor, a smaller and less secure base than Ramadi and a pretty miserable place. It was situated a few hundred yards from one of the city's most dangerous neighborhoods. The 506th had quickly gotten used to dodging regular mortar, RPGs, and small arms fire. Enemy snipers often took potshots at the camp from the minarets of mosques in the city, although they never hit anyone from that distance. Radar gave only a few seconds' warning before an incoming mortar round hit. Soldiers wore their body armor and helmets to and from the toilet. So did the SEALs. In their spare time SEAL snipers would climb up Corregidor's observation towers and pick off insurgents planting IEDs nearby. The accommodations were far more spartan at Corregidor than at Camp Ramadi. Frogmen and grunts grew close in their shared danger and discomfort. They would come to respect each other as warriors, too, when the hard fighting got under way in June.

Until then Delta Platoon spent most of its time training soldiers from one of the Iraqi Army's oldest and most prestigious brigades, which had recently arrived in Ramadi and was camped just across Route Michigan from Corregidor. SEALs and scouts got along well. The scouts whom Delta Platoon trained seemed more experienced and quicker learners than other Iraqi soldiers they had encountered. As they crossed an open field on one of their first patrols together, they were pinned down by sniper fire. The Iraqis reacted exactly as they had been trained to react: aggressively. The men nearest the shooter laid down cover fire, while the scouts behind leapfrogged them, drawing steadily closer to the enemy until they drove him off.

In the beginning they stuck to patrolling a couple of the comparatively quiet neighborhoods, first at night and then with growing confidence in day patrols. By May they were pushing deeper into "real Indian country," including the Ma'Laab, where they took fire on every patrol, often operating with larger U.S. Army units, including elements of the 506th. "The deeper we went, the stiffer the resistance became," a Delta Platoon lieutenant remembered. They were getting themselves and the Iraqis they trained ready for the decisive battles to come. "Some of the Iraqi units felt the enemy was ten feet tall." But with their aggressive responses to the enemy, the SEALs "convinced our scouts . . . that we could beat these guys."

Monsoor walked just behind the platoon's point man on patrol, where the machine gunner is positioned to put out cover fire in the event the patrol is attacked, as it frequently was. He also served as one of the platoon's communicators. On patrols where he served as both machine gunner and communicator, he carried a hundred pounds of gear into combat, in temperatures in excess of 120 degrees Fahrenheit, while wearing body armor. He never complained. Everyone in the platoon remembered that about him. He didn't seem bothered. He was always alert, usually quiet on the job, but not in a way that made him seem stressed or tightly wound. He was one of those guys who appear easygoing not because they are lackadaisical or acting cool but because they are quietly self-assured and competent. That was the impression he made on his friend, the platoon skipper, Lieutenant Stone, who called him "a fantastic warrior." "He was always there, 110 percent and all business, yet in a nice way," another officer in the platoon remembered. "When Mike was around, things seemed to go better, easier."

MacFarland was a counterinsurgency veteran when he got to Ramadi, having served in Tal Afar in northern Iraq under a master of counterinsurgency operations, Colonel H. R. McMaster. And he brought with him a number of veterans from the northern Iraq campaign. There was little doubt MacFarland would avoid a full assault on Ramadi, like the one in Fallujah. First, Ramadi was a lot larger than Fallujah, too large for the force he had to be everywhere at once. Second, that kind of assault often turns into a "destroy the village to save it" affair — counterproductive, to say the least, to the civil and economic progress necessary to preserve gains toward a stable peace.

In a counterinsurgency's "take, hold, and build" strategy, you liberate territory piece by piece, getting civil institutions such as a capable police force up and running as you go. You also cause far fewer noncombatant casualties. "My intent," MacFarland later told a reporter, was "to take this city back without destroying it." His plan was to establish secure areas throughout the city, which American and Iraqi soldiers would garrison and slowly expand, initiating reconstruction projects and strengthening civil institutions as security improved.

MacFarland's first move was swiftly setting up four combat outposts (COPs) deep in insurgent strongholds in neighborhoods under al Qaeda control. These were complicated, daringly confrontational, all-hands-on-deck operations, using marine and army infantry, armor, air assets, engineers, construction, and, in a volunteer capacity, the SEALs. Once the COPs were established, they were manned by Americans and Iraqi soldiers, and the neighborhoods where they were located were cleared of insurgents a block at a time.

Willink's task unit had been sent to Ramadi to train Iraqi soldiers and engage with local tribes. Both tasks were useful to MacFarland in the long term, but not particularly relevant to his immediate intention to plant his forces in enemy territory. The SEALs could be a great asset, but they were not MacFarland's to command. Instead Willink asked MacFarland how the SEALs could help. And MacFarland, Willink recalled, "basically wanted one thing from me; he wanted me to kill insurgents."

Thus it was decided that the SEALs would provide operational security. They would still train and work with the Iraqis and hunt and kill the targets assigned them. But now the SEALs would also work with conventional forces securing areas in advance of the engineers rushing in to set up defensible combat outposts. They would also provide overwatch security from Ramadi rooftops as conventional forces cleared the neighborhoods around the COPs building by building.

SEAL snipers were MacFarland's favorite asset for intimidating the enemy. One of them, Chief Petty Officer Chris Kyle, was so feared and notorious the insurgents called him "the devil of Ramadi." He was reported to have killed two insurgents on a motorcycle with one round and to have killed another at more than a mile's distance. Kyle served four tours in Iraq and fought in many of the major battles of the war, including the 2003 invasion, the Battle for Fallujah, in Ramadi, and in the fight to pacify Sadr City in 2008. That violent 2006 summer in Ramadi would be his fiercest and longest battle, where he would claim more than ninety of his 160 confirmed kills.

He went home in September, shaken up by the losses the SEALs suffered, and returned in 2008 for his fourth and final tour. In 2013, retired from the navy and back home in Texas, he was murdered by a disturbed marine veteran he was trying to help.

Two welcome developments occurred just before the operation launched. First, the butcher Zarqawi was killed. More immediately useful for MacFarland's purposes was the Ramadi insurgents' misreading of his intentions. The Ready First had more than 150 M-1 Abrams tanks and Bradley Fighting Vehicles, as well as hundreds of armored Humvees, enough armor to make it look to insurgents as if the brigade was readying for a Fallujah-style assault. As MacFarland began setting up a security cordon around Ramadi in advance of setting up the outposts, many insurgents, and thousands of noncombatants, decided discretion was the better part of valor and left Ramadi before the assault began, likely planning to return and lay claim to the rubble. Those who remained, and a good many did, were caught by surprise when the infidels were suddenly in fortified outposts in their backyards.

The Battle for Ramadi got under way on June 17, 2006, with the establishment of two combat outposts, Iron and Spear, in the southeast and southwest of the city. The construction of COP Eagle's Nest near Corregidor started the next day, and COP Falcon, in one of the most dangerous places in the city, followed the next week. Dick Couch, the author of a fascinating study of the battle, *The Sheriff of Ramadi,* wrote a detailed description of the outposts' construction (jokingly named "COP in a box" by the men who built them), which we summarize here.

The day before the operation launched, final briefings were held, and the armor, vehicles, and materials to be used were staged. The SEAL teams, who did their own night reconnaissance of the sites a few days prior, were inserted before dawn with a small contingent of conventional forces, including interpreters and Iraqi scouts. They carried enough ammunition and supplies to last them several days. When they got to the site, they claimed the building to use as the COP, paying off and brusquely evicting the families living there. Then they set up their shooting positions on the upper floors and rooftops.

The Dagger teams (IED clearance specialists) were next, with armored vehicles designed to detonate mines. If the SEALs had managed to clear the site and get in position undetected, the noisy Dagger teams would alert insurgents something big was happening. Once the Daggers had finished, the armor (Abrams tanks and Bradleys) rolled in and set up a security perimeter around the site encompassing a block or more. They were immediately followed by at least a company of infantry, who provided additional security. Then came the occupants of the new COP, a company-size or larger unit that usually included several infantry platoons, a mortar platoon, an engineering platoon, a headquarters element, and tanks.

Once the outpost occupants arrived, the SEALs switched to an "area denial mission," repositioning to buildings on the outer perimeter to protect routes into the site. Couch described the mechanics of sniper overwatch in Ramadi, which again we summarize. A suitable building was chosen and entered either relatively politely or forcibly, depending on whether or not its occupants were hostile. Friend or foe, they were paid for their trouble and not permitted to leave. Iraqi scouts guarded the families on the lower floor while the SEALs set up their shooting positions on the upper floors and the roof. Inside positions were preferable as they were usually less vulnerable than rooftops. If the windows and roofs didn't offer good angles or protection, the SEALs blew shooting holes in the walls and paid the residents for the damage.

The construction work began once the SEAL snipers were in place. Convoys of army engineers and navy Seabees in full combat armor rolled down the streets, carrying concrete barriers, sandbags, concertina wire, and other building materials, to a site ringed by armor, where soldiers and marines and Iraqi scouts cleared buildings inside the perimeter and F-18s and drones circled overhead. If insurgents hadn't yet contested the foray into their territory, they usually wanted to start when the convoy alerted them to the purpose of the operation. By then, though, it was too late. They usually managed to snipe at the convoys and fire RPGs at the site, but in that first week, by the time they realized what was happening, the coalition presence in their midst was too strong to repel. Thirteen more COPs and several Iraqi police stations were established in every contested area of the city over the summer and fall of 2006. The enemy got better at contesting the operations as they became more familiar with them, but they never stopped an outpost from being established wherever MacFarland determined he needed one. They had to settle for making life miserable for the inhabitants of the outposts, who lived under regular assault from rockets, mortars, and small arms fire.

As the insurgents became more familiar with SEAL overwatch teams, they got better at assaulting them too. In the beginning, as those first COPs were built, SEAL snipers may have seemed invincible to the insurgents. But the smarter insurgents, the ones who learned from watching others die, became tougher adversaries as the summer wore on. They learned how to locate the positions of the overwatch teams and, knowing the area better than the SEALs did, move unseen by snipers. "The overwatch often became nothing more than an elevated, covered position from which to engage the insurgents in a sustained gun battle," Couch explained.

As MacFarland's forces pushed deeper and deeper into Ramadi, the summer became long, hard, and very violent. Elsewhere in Iraq U.S. forces consolidated on big bases and reduced their casualties, but the Ready First was doing the opposite. The decision to surge forces to Iraq and authorize General Petraeus to conduct a counterinsurgency hadn't been made yet, but MacFarland was running one in Ramadi, scattering his forces and Iraqi soldiers and police throughout the enemy's territory, taking the fight to the enemy and staying there, tactics that can be and were costly. Baghdad didn't second-guess him, though, at least not enough to make him change course, and he had the support of his superior, Lieutenant General Richard Zilmer, who had assumed command of I Marine Expeditionary Force in June.

Some journalists who reported from Ramadi that summer rather than from Baghdad could see the counterinsurgency's progress or at least understand its strategy. But most of the press thought Ramadi was a vicious, hopeless slaughterhouse, where an enterprising colonel and his brigade were doing the best they could to hold off the inevitable. That point of view appeared to be reinforced by the Devlin Report when it was leaked in September. When it was updated and leaked again in November, opinions about Ramadi hadn't changed much, even though the battle, while not over, was nearly won.

But winning or losing, there was no denying it was a bloody summer and fall in Ramadi. The killing increased as more outposts were built and American and Iraqi soldiers pushed insurgents out of the areas surrounding them. Roadside IEDs were the biggest killers, as they were everywhere else in Iraq. There were hundreds of them in Ramadi. MacFarland was nearly killed by an IED that detonated under his armored vehicle on Route Michigan as he was returning from visiting the wounded. But death came by other means as well. In the first week of July the marines succeeded in capturing the Ramadi General Hospital, which the insurgents had used as living quarters. When the marines searched the hospital, they found bombs planted everywhere and the severed heads of Iraqi soldiers who had been wounded and captured by al Qaeda.

On July 24 insurgents staged a counterattack against various targets, but chiefly centered on the Government Center. Zarqawi's successor, Abu Ayyub al-Musri, was reported to have been in Ramadi for the assault. The attacks were repulsed, and a hundred or more insurgents killed in the process, but it was hard, costly fighting, with many coalition wounded. As the Government Center would likely continue to be a focus of insurgent attention, MacFarland ordered the buildings surrounding it razed and a public park built in their place.

On the morning of August 2, SEALs in Charlie Platoon provided sniper overwatch for Iraqi soldiers and a U.S. Army tank unit clearing neighborhoods near COP Falcon in south central Ramadi. Of all the areas where COPs had been established, the Ma'Laab district, where Falcon was located, was considered the most dangerous. Intelligence reports the day before identified two al Qaeda cells based in the area. They soon made their presence known, waiting for the armor to pass them before opening up from rooftops and windows on the infantry who followed.

The SEALs had arrived at the scene in Bradleys before the shooting started. Chris Kyle, his platoon's machine gunner, Petty Officer Ryan Job from Issaquah, Washington, and another SEAL sniper took up positions on the roof of a four-story apartment building. No sooner had they settled in than they started taking a lot of fire. A round struck Job's M-60 and shrapnel ripped into his face, destroying one eye and severing the optic nerves of the other. Kyle and Charlie's skipper, Lieutenant Leif Babin, rushed to Job's aid and called in a Bradley to evacuate him. As Kyle helped the wounded man, who was choking on his blood, sit up, Petty Officer Marc Lee, a twenty-eight-year-old SEAL from the Columbia River Gorge in Oregon, reached the roof and started firing his machine gun to cover the evacuation. Kyle and Babin helped Job downstairs and into the Bradley, which sped him to the hospital at Camp Ramadi.

After Job was extracted, Charlie Platoon and their Iraqi scouts, exhausted and low on ammunition, headed back to COP Falcon, about five hundred yards from the scene of the fighting. The army patrol continued to fight a running battle as more insurgents poured into the area. After a brief rest and rearming, Babin ordered the SEALs into the Bradleys and back to the fight.

They reached a building thick with insurgents about a block from where Job had been hit. An M-1 let rip with cannon and machine-gun fire, knocking down part of a wall. The Bradleys dropped their ramps and the SEALs sprinted into the building as sheets of machine-gun fire followed them. They secured the ground floor, and with Lee on the point, started ascending a stairwell. Lee noticed fire coming through an open window. He approached it and fired a burst from his machine gun, and was just turning to alert the SEALs behind him when a round struck him in the head and severed his spine. Again that day Charlie Platoon had to fight desperately to get a wounded SEAL off the battlefield. Babin was wounded too, but continued to direct the platoon. After the SEALs left and the exhausted army patrol withdrew to Falcon, M-1s and F-18s blew the place to hell.

Lee was dead when he arrived at the hospital, the first SEAL to die in Iraq. His brothers in SEAL Team 3 were deeply shaken by the loss. They renamed Shark Base Camp Marc Lee and mourned as they fought.

Job was blinded but survived. He spent time in a series of military hospitals. He got married, climbed Mt. Rainier, and moved to Arizona. He got his bachelor's degree and was working on his master's and expecting his first child when he went into the hospital for reconstructive surgery in September 2009 and died from postsurgical complications. His death was unexpected and indescribably unfair.

The fighting in Ramadi got no easier after the August 2 firefight, but later that month insurgents made what would be their biggest strategic mistake, not just in Ramadi but for the entire insurgency. They killed a local sheik who had encouraged his tribesmen to join the ranks of the local police. Then they hid his body so his tribe could not bury him within twenty-four hours, as Islam requires. That was considered a worse offense than his murder. On September 9, with funding from the United States, fifty sheiks from twenty Anbar tribes, some of whom had at one time been allied with al Qaeda, announced the formation of an anti-insurgent council called the Anbar Awakening. It was led by the first sheik in Anbar to turn against al Qaeda, Abdul Sattar Abu Risha, whose father and three brothers had been killed by AQI. It might not have looked like it at the time, but the outcome of the Battle for Ramadi and Anbar was determined on September 9, although it would require months more of hard fighting and many more casualties to secure.

Delta Platoon's last operation in Ramadi, a sniper overwatch mission, began in the predawn hours of September 29. The SEAL task unit was nearing the end of their six-month rotation in Iraq. They were scheduled to start making their way back to Coronado in less than two weeks, and most of their gear was already packed and staged for redeployment. Mikey Monsoor was making plans to attend an October Minot State

University football game in North Dakota to watch his younger brother play. He had called home a few days before, typically cheerful and discreet about the war.

Two squads from Delta Platoon and a contingent of Iraqi scouts set out on foot from Corregidor for a rail line on the southern outskirts of the city, where marines were going to string razor wire that day. Delta's skipper, Lieutenant Stone, commanded one squad; a lieutenant j.g. was in charge of the other. They seized two buildings about a block apart. The scouts secured the ground floor, while the SEALs got in position on the rooftops. They punched shooting holes in a low stucco wall on the ledge of the roof. By three o'clock everyone was in position with good fields of fire, waiting for daybreak.

"As soon as it became light," the lieutenant in charge of Monsoor's squad told Dick Couch, "we knew it was going to be a day of fighting."

The insurgents focused most of their attention that day on the SEAL teams rather than the more exposed marine platoon stringing the wire. Early on, each SEAL squad killed insurgents scouting their position. A loudspeaker in the minaret of a nearby mosque blared a summons for mujahideen to join the battle. Neighborhood residents blocked off streets in the area, and insurgents armed with AK-47s started taking potshots at the SEAL positions before speeding off in cars and small trucks. About noon Monsoor's squad took their first RPG round, which exploded on the roof, causing no more damage than a shower of dust and debris. By then small arms fire on both locations was constant, but still mostly ineffective. The SEALs knew the attacks would continue all day but felt secure that their overwatch wasn't in real jeopardy. Insurgents tried to maneuver closer to the SEALs, dodging in and out of the surrounding buildings. The snipers shot them or drove them back whenever they broke cover.

Bullets peppered the stucco wall on the roof's ledge that shielded the snipers. Monsoor's lieutenant had him move to a hidden position behind the wall, near the only exit to the floors below. He was kneeling with his MK-48 between the lieutenant to his right and another sniper to his left, who were in prone shooting positions. A single insurgent slipped under their guns unseen by the SEALs or the scouts on the lower floors. He threw a fragmentation grenade toward the roof. It managed to clear the stucco wall and hit Monsoor in the chest, then bounced off him and rolled on the ground between him and the other two SEALs. Monsoor had a split second to make a decision. The grenade's fuse was too short to toss it back over the wall. He could dive for the stairway and likely escape without life-threatening wounds, but the two men beside him would not have time to scramble to their feet and hurl themselves toward the stairs; they would probably be killed. So he shouted, "Grenade!," threw himself on it, and absorbed its blast.

The two SEALs whose lives he had just saved were severely wounded. Both had taken shrapnel in their legs, and neither could walk. A fourth SEAL, farthest from the grenade, was also wounded, but not as seriously. Four Iraqi scouts on the roof panicked at the site of three wounded SEALs, and three of them fled down the stairs. One scout stayed on the roof, but he was in shock. Monsoor was still alive. The least injured SEAL pulled him away from the wall and examined his wound. Then he picked up Monsoor's machine gun and started returning fire. Monsoor's communications equipment had been destroyed in the blast, and the lieutenant had to crawl to the Iraqi who was frozen in shock and use his radio to call Stone for help. Then he coaxed the other Iraqis back onto the roof as insurgents continued to press the attack.

Stone and the SEALs in the other overwatch team arrived minutes later, having battled insurgents every step of the two-hundred-yard sprint to reach their wounded brothers. Stone had already called in casualty evacuation vehicles. When he saw Monsoor and learned what he had done, he remembered thinking that it made tragic sense. It was "in keeping with the man I knew," he said. The arriving SEALs quickly secured the perimeter and set up cover fire for the evacuation as two Bradley vehicles from Eagle's Nest tore through Ramadi's streets to retrieve the wounded. As the SEALs loaded Monsoor into one of them they knew he was breathing his last. And they knew what he had done.

He "had the best chance of avoiding harm altogether," the lieutenant whose life he saved told Couch, "but he never took his eye off that grenade. His only movement was down toward it."

The evacuation team reached Camp Ramadi, where Father Halladay, Monsoor's confessor, was waiting to give him the Church's last rites. Monsoor expired a few minutes later in the late afternoon of September 29, the day Catholics call the Feast of St. Michael the Archangel.

The Iraqi scouts who had panicked but then returned to the fight kept a picture of Monsoor in their lockers. Three SEALs limped together to the pulpit of a San Diego church where his memorial service was held. They thanked him and the Monsoor family for their lives. Lieutenant Willink recalled how devastated the team was by his loss and described the trembling voice of the SEAL who had told him that Monsoor wouldn't make it. Every SEAL on the West Coast, including Ryan Job, is said to have attended the service. They formed two columns on either side of his coffin as it was moved from the hearse to his gravesite in Fort Rosecrans National Cemetery. Each man took the gold trident insignia he wore on his uniform and slapped it into the coffin lid, the sound of each slap reverberating across the cemetery.

A year and a half later, on April 8, 2008, three U.S. senators, one of whom would be elected the next commander in chief, left the presidential campaign trail with the media circus in tow and returned briefly to the Senate. General Petraeus and the American ambassador to Iraq, the very capable Ryan Crocker, were testifying that day on the progress of the surge before the Senate Armed Services Committee and the Foreign Relations Committee. Each of the presidential aspirants had different positions on Iraq to defend. Senators Barack Obama and Hillary Clinton would use their questions to make their points, and I would make mine. Not one of us would say anything unexpected or particularly enlightening. Nor did we mention the more genuine and moving event that the hearings would overshadow in the press.

At the other end of Pennsylvania Avenue, President Bush was losing his fight to hold back tears as he recalled the ultimate sacrifice Petty Officer Michael Anthony Monsoor had made. "Greater love hath no man than this," the president quoted from scripture, "that a man lay down his life for his friends." Monsoor's parents sat stoically through the Medal of Honor ceremony at the White House, holding hands, while his siblings and brother SEALs brushed tears from their eyes.

General Petraeus testified that day that the progress of the surge was real but fragile and reversible. He might have added for everyone's benefit that it had been achieved at a great and terrible cost, as all wars demand from victor and vanquished alike.

AFTERWORD

Private David Thompson (let's call him Davey, as his contemporaries likely did) served with the 9th New York Volunteers. He fought at Antietam and left an eyewitness account of the terrible contest. Historians have relied on him for descriptions of the battle and for insights into the minds of the soldiers who strove and suffered and died there. We think he is quoted so often because he is a pleasure to read, much like our first soldier, Joseph Plumb Martin. As it did Martin, war seems to have made Davey Thompson a philosopher, and like the best philosophers, his ideas are presented with honesty and humor and very little sentimentality.

He scoffed at newspapers that exaggerated the zeal of Union soldiers. "The truth is, when bullets are whacking against tree-trunks and solid shot are cracking skulls like egg-shells, the consuming passion in the breast of the average man is to get out of the way," he wrote. Then he added this existential gem, his most quoted observation: "Between the physical fear of going forward and the moral fear of turning back, there is a predicament of exceptional awkwardness."

Davey's formulation is, of course, the central conundrum of combat. That the moral fear prevails more often than not is the soldier's most impressive feat. But like Davey, we should be careful not to let our admiration for the triumph of a soldier's sense of obligation over his instinct for self-preservation cause us to sentimentalize the war that occasioned his heroism. It is disrespectful to sentimentalize war, to make it seem glorious and romantic. When we do, we devalue the sacrifices made in it.

War is wretched beyond description. Only a fool sentimentalizes its cruel realities. When nations seek to resolve their differences by force of arms, a million tragedies ensue. The lives of a nation's best patriots are sacrificed. Innocent people suffer and die. Commerce is disrupted; economies are damaged; strategic interests shielded by years of patient statecraft are endangered as the exigencies of war and diplomacy conflict. Not the valor with which it is fought nor the nobility of the cause it serves can glorify war. Whatever gains are secured, it is mostly loss that veterans remember. And they remember it until the end of their days.

We tried not to sentimentalize the soldiers whose stories we chose for this book, or their wars. They have earned our admiration without embellishing what they did or the cause they served. Our obligation to honor their sacrifices was honestly incurred and should be honestly discharged. They should not be forgotten. But they should be remembered for who they really were: ordinary people, possessing the virtues and vices common to our nature, placed in extraordinary circumstances, who did something exceptional. They risked their comfort, their health, their future for people they would never meet and who might or might not appreciate what they did.

Some were recognized and honored for their service; others were not. Soldiers are rarely compensated for their sacrifices as well as they ought to be. Every story of a veteran waiting months to see a doctor at the local VA hospital reminds us of that. And how can we repay the dead? The feebleness of our gratitude isn't improved by glorifying sacrifices that were not made for glory. Rather we owe veterans, the living and the dead, a country that remains worthy of their sacrifice. And we owe them our respect for the truth of what they did.

If war has any glory, it is a hard-pressed, bloody, awful glory that no one who hasn't experienced it can ever completely understand. It is the glory of knowing you withstood the cruelty and madness of war to do your duty to the country that sent you there, and you were not found wanting by the soldiers who stood next to you. All else, as the poet said of beauty, "drifts away like the waters."

American soldiers have been at war since the second year of this century. Their long campaign is now nearing its end. But peace, no matter how long it endures, is always temporary. There will be other wars, probably not for a while and hopefully not for a long time. But America will send soldiers into battle again. Though the world is growing smaller all the time and nations are becoming interdependent, peace will always be vulnerable to human folly and iniquity. We should pray that when the day comes, the cause will be just and necessary and the field well chosen. Pray too that we remember that the sacrifices made by the few for the many are always terrible and nearly unbearable and that we cannot repay the dead.

Davey Thompson wrote, "Before the sunlight faded, I walked over the narrow field. All around lay the Confederate dead . . . clad in 'butternut.' . . . As I looked down on the poor pinched faces . . . all enmity died out. There was no 'secession' in those rigid forms nor in those fixed eyes staring at the sky. Clearly it was not their war."

ACKNOWLEDGMENTS

This book and five previous books were conceived and produced with the guidance of our publisher, Jonathan Karp, whose discernment, encouragement, and patience have been our principal support in these amateur endeavors. We are indebted to him beyond our means of repayment.

We are indebted too to his Simon & Schuster associates, who made this book much better than it would have been without their help: Nicholas Greene for his smart and extraordinarily fast editing of a tardy manuscript; Megan Hogan for her many assists and considerations; our friends Cary Goldstein and Larry Hughes for their typically excellent efforts to bring attention to the book; and Richard Rhorer and Elina Vaysbeyn for helping us find readers for it. Our thanks also to Irene Kheradi, Gina Di-Mascia, Ffej Caplan, Jackie Seow, Christopher Lin, Joy O'Meara, and George Turianski, and to Jonathan Evans and Judith Hoover for their skillful copyediting.

As always, Philippa Brophy, agent and friend, offered good advice and skillfully represented our interests.

We are very grateful to Mary Rhoads for her help with chapter 11 and for the sacrifices she made for our country. And thanks to Scott Beveridge for making the introductions.

Dr. Philip Mead, historian and expert on Joseph Plumb Martin, helped importantly with the chapter on the remarkable patriot. Thank you, also, to Jim Buchanan for his help on the Battle of Antietam.

Thank you, of course, to Roxanne Coady, discerning reader and even better friend, for her advice and encouragement.

Finally, to our wives, Cindy and Diane, and our children, thank you always for everything.

SELECTED BIBLIOGRAPHY

Chapter One

Boatner, Mark M., III (1994). *Encyclopedia of the American Revolution.* Mechanicsburg, PA: Stackpole Books.

Keegan, John (1995). *Fields of Battle: The Wars for North America.* New York: Random House.

Martin, James Kirby, and Mark Edward Lender (2006). *A Respectable Army: The Military Origins of the Republic 1763–1789.* 2nd edition. Wheeling, IL: Harlan Davidson.

Martin, James Kirby, ed. (2008). *Ordinary Courage: The Revolutionary War Adventures of Joseph Plumb Martin.* 3rd edition. Malden, MA: Blackwell.

McCullough, David (2005). *1776.* New York: Simon & Schuster.

McGuire, Thomas J. (2007). *The Philadelphia Campaign.* Vol. 2. Mechanicsburg,

PA: Stackpole Books.

Middlekauff, Robert (2005). *The Glorious Cause.* New York: Oxford University Press.

Royster, Charles (1979). *A Revolutionary People at War: The Continental Army and American Character, 1775–1783.* Chapel Hill: University of North Carolina Press.

Young, Alfred, Gary B. Nash, and Ray Raphael, eds. (2011). *Revolutionary Founders: Rebels, Radicals, and Reformers in the Making of the Nation.* New York: Knopf.

Chapter Two

Altoff, Gerard (1996). *Amongst My Best Men: African-Americans and the War of 1812.* Put-in-Bay, OH: Perry Group.

Altoff, Gerard (1999). *Oliver Hazard Perry and the Battle of Lake Erie.* Put-in-Bay, OH: Perry Group.

Barnes, James (1897). *Yankee Ships and Yankee Sailors: Tales of 1812.* New York: Macmillan.

Bolster, Jeffrey (1997). *Black Jacks: African American Seamen in the Age of Sail.* Cambridge, MA: Harvard University Press.

Fitz-Enz, David G. (2001). *The Final Invasion: Plattsburgh, the War of 1812's Most*

Decisive Battle. New York: Cooper Square Press.

Hitsman, MacKay (1965). *The Incredible War of 1812.* Toronto: University of Toronto Press.

Nell, William Cooper (1851). *Services of Colored Americans in the Wars of 1776 and 1812.* New York: Prentiss & Sawyer.

Wilson, Joseph (1994). *The Black Phalanx: African American Soldiers in the War of Independence, the War of 1812, and the Civil War.* New York: Da Capo Press.

Chapter Three

Chamberlain, Samuel E. (1996). *My Confession: Recollections of a Rogue.* Edited by William H. Goetzmann. Austin: Texas State Historical Society.

Dishman, Christopher D. (2010). *A Perfect Gibraltar: The Battle for Monterrey, Mexico 1846.* Norman: University of Oklahoma Press.

Doubleday, Abner (1998). *My Life in the Old Army: Reminiscences of Abner Doubleday.* Edited by Joseph E. Chance. Fort Worth: Texas Christian University Press.

Eisenhower, John S. D. (1989). *So Far from God: The U.S. War with Mexico, 1846–1848.* New York: Random House.

Groom, Winston (2011). *Kearney's March: The Epic Creation of the American West, 1846–1847*. New York: Knopf.

Lavender, David (2003). *Climax at Buena Vista: The Decisive Battle of the Mexican-American War*. Philadelphia: University of Pennsylvania Press.

McCaffrey, James M. (1992). *Army of Manifest Destiny: The American Soldier in the Mexican War, 1846–1848*. New York: New York University Press.

Chapter Four

Buchanan, Jim. (July 21, 2010). " 'It was a pitiable sight . . . this great caravan of pilgrims': Oliver Wendell Holmes' Hunt for the Captain." *Walking the West Woods*. http://walkingthewestwoods.blogspot.com/2010/07/it-was-pitiable-sightthis-great-caravan.html.

Faust, Drew Gilpin (2012). *This Republic of Suffering: Death and the American Civil War*. New York: Knopf.

Holmes, Oliver Wendell, Sr. (1864). *Soundings from the Atlantic*. Boston: Ticknor and Fields.

Howe, Mark de Wolfe, ed. (2000). *Touched with Fire: Civil War Letters and Diary of Oliver Wendell Holmes (The North's Civil War)*.

New York: Fordham University Press.

Keegan, John (2009). *The American Civil War: A Military History.* New York: Knopf.

McPherson, James M. (2002). *Antietam: The Battle That Changed the Course of the War.* New York: Oxford University Press.

Miller, Richard F. (2005). *Harvard's Civil War: The History of the Twentieth Massachusetts Volunteer Infantry.* Lebanon, NH: University Press of New England.

Novick, Sheldon M. (1989). *Honorable Justice: The Life of Oliver Wendell Holmes.* Boston: Little, Brown.

Shi, David E. (1995). *Facing Facts: Realism in American Thought and Culture 1850–1920.* New York: Oxford University Press.

Chapter Five

Cashin, Herschel V. (1993). *Under Fire: With the Tenth U.S. Cavalry.* Niwot: University Press of Colorado.

Egan, Timothy (June 6, 1998). "The American Century's Opening Shot." *New York Times.*

Johnson, Edward A. ([1899] 2004). *History of Negro Soldiers in the Spanish-American War, and Other Items of Interest.* Raleigh, NC: Project Gutenberg eBook.

Jones, Virgil Carrington (1971). *Roosevelt's*

Rough Riders. Garden City, NY: Double-
day.
Nalty, Bernard C. (1986). *Strength for the
Fight: A History of Black Americans in the
Military.* New York: Free Press.
Roosevelt, Theodore (2004). *The Rough Rid-
ers: An Autobiography.* New York: Penguin.
Schubert, Frank N. (1997). *Black Valor:
Buffalo Soldiers and the Medal of Honor,
1870–1898.* Lanham, MD: Rowman &
Littlefield.
Steward, T. G. (1904). *The Colored Regulars
in the United States Army.* Philadelphia:
AME Book Concern.

Chapter Six

"American Soldiers in the Philippines Write
Home about the War." History Matters:
The U.S. Survey Course on the Web.
http://historymatters.gmu.edu/d/58/.
Jones, Gregg (2012). *Honor in the Dust:
Theodore Roosevelt, War in the Philippines,
and the Rise and Fall of America's Imperial
Dream.* New York: New American Library.
Miller, Stuart Creighton (1982). *Benevolent
Assimilation: The American Conquest of the
Philippines 1899–1903.* New Haven, CT:
Yale University Press.
Nebrida, Victor (1997). "The Balangiga

Massacre: Getting Even." Los Angeles: Philippine History Group of Los Angeles.

Schott, Joseph L. (1964). *The Ordeal of Samar.* Indianapolis, IN: Bobbs-Merrill.

Chapter Seven

Axelrod, Alan (2007). *Miracle at Belleau Wood: The Birth of the Modern U.S. Marine Corps.* Guilford, CT: Lyon Press.

Clark, George B. (2010). *Battle History of the United States Marines Corps, 1775–1945.* Jefferson, NC: McFarland.

Keegan, John (1976). *The Face of Battle.* New York: Viking.

Keegan, John (1999). *The First World War.* New York: Knopf.

Kindsvatter, Peter (2003). *American Soldiers: Ground Combat in the World Wars, Korea and Vietnam.* Lawrence: University Press of Kansas.

Mackin, Elton (June 29, 1973). Oral interview with Carl D. Klopfenstein, professor of history at Heidelberg College, Norfolk, OH. Transcript at Rutherford B. Hayes Presidential Library, Fremont, OH.

Mackin, Elton (1993). *Suddenly We Didn't Want to Die: Memoirs of a World War One Marine.* Novato, CA: Presidio Press.

Persico, Joseph E. (2004). *Eleventh Month,*

Eleventh Day, Eleventh Hour: Armistice Day, 1918. World War I and Its Violent Climax. New York: Random House.

Zieger, Robert (2000). *America's Great War: World War I and the American Experience.* Lanham, MD: Rowman & Littlefield.

Chapter Eight

Chapin, John C. (1994). *Breaching the Marianas: The Battle for Saipan.* Marines in World War II Commemorative Series. Washington, DC: U.S. Marine Corps History & Museum.

Gabaldon, Guy (1990). *Saipan: Suicide Island.* Self-published.

Goldberg, Harold J. (2007). *D-Day in the Pacific: The Battle of Saipan.* Bloomington: Indiana University Press.

"Guy Gabaldon: An Interview and Discussion" (1998). *War Times Journal.* http://www.wtj.com/articles/gabaldon/.

Moore, David (2002). "The Battle of Saipan: The Final Curtain." The Battle of Saipan. http://www.battleofsaipan.com.

Sherrod, Robert L. (1983). *Tarawa: The Story of a Battle.* New York: Bantam Books.

Wukovits, John (2006). *One Square Mile of Hell: The Battle for Tarawa.* New York: New American Library.

Chapter Nine

Appleman, Roy E. (1961). *South to the Naktong, North to the Yalu: United States Army in the Korean War.* Washington, DC: Center of Military History, U.S. Army.

Boose, Daniel (2005). *U.S. Army Forces in the Korean War 1950–1953.* Oxford: Osprey.

Fehrenbach, T. R. (1963). *This Kind of War: A Study in Unpreparedness.* New York: Macmillan.

Korean War Project. http://www.koreanwar .org/.

Maihafer, Harry J. (1993). *From the Hudson to the Yalu: West Point '49 in the Korean War.* College Station: Texas A&M University Press.

McCain, John S. (2004). *Why Courage Matters: The Way to a Braver Life.* New York: Random House.

Chapter Ten

Bell, Kenneth H. (2000). *100 Missions North: A Fighter Pilot's Story of the Vietnam War.* Paducah, KY: Turner.

Correll, John T. (March 2005). "Rolling Thunder." *Air Force Magazine.*

Correll, John T. (June 2005). "Full Day." *Air*

Force Magazine.

Frisbee, John L. (April 1985). "Wild, Wild Weasel." *Air Force Magazine.*

Grant, Rebecca (February 2013). "The Crucible of Vietnam." *Air Force Magazine.*

Lewis, Adrian R. (2006). *The American Culture of War: A History of U.S. Military Force from World War II to Operation Enduring Freedom.* New York: Routledge.

Moymer, William M. (2003). *Airpower in Three Wars (WWII, Korea, Vietnam).* Maxwell AFB, AL: Air University Press.

Nastasi, Mike (2002). "The Wild Weasels: Daredevils of the Sky." Military History Online. http://www.militaryhistoryonline.com/vietnam/airpower/wildweasel.aspx.

Posey, Carl (February 2009). "Thuds, the Ridge, and 100 Missions North." *Air & Space Magazine.*

Reardon, John. "King of the Wild Weasels." Redbubble. http://www.redbubble.com/people/warwolf/writing/3709578-the-king-of-the-wild-weasels.

"Rendezvous with a Rattlesnake." (December 1974). *Airman Magazine.*

Rochester, Stuart I., and Frederick Kiley (1998). *Honor Bound: The History of American Prisoners of War in Southeast Asia, 1961–1973.* Washington, DC: Historical

Office of the Secretary of Defense.

Thompson, Wayne (2000). *To Hanoi and Back: The U.S. Air Force and North Vietnam, 1966–1973.* Washington, DC: Smithsonian.

Thorsness, Leo (2008). *Surviving Hell: A POW's Journey.* New York: Encounter Books.

Chapter Eleven

Apple, R. W. Jr. (February 26, 1991). "War in the Gulf: Scud Attack. Scud Missile Hits a U.S. Barracks, Kills 27." *New York Times.*

Atkinson, Rick (1993). *Crusade: The Untold Story of the Persian Gulf War.* New York: Houghton Mifflin.

Beveridge, Scott (February 23, 1995). "Rhoads Reliving Worst Nightmare." *Observer-Reporter* (Washington and Green Counties, PA).

Beveridge, Scott (October 20, 1995). "Woman Testifies of Persian Gulf Perils." *Observer-Reporter* (Washington and Greene Counties, PA).

Beveridge, Scott (February 29, 2011). "Some Good out of War." Travel with a Beveridge. http://scottbeveridge.blogspot.com/2011_02_01_archive.html.

Blood, Michael (July 17, 1991). "Vets Detail Stress Family Problems from Gulf Service." Associated Press.

Brooks, Mary (March 11, 1991). "Honoring Fallen Son Soldier's Death Leaves Pain, Pride." *Orlando (FL) Sentinel*.

Ciotti, Paul (May 12, 1991). "The Scud That Hit Greensburg: For One Pennsylvania Community, the Gulf War Has Not Ended." *Los Angeles Times*.

"Fallen Comrades." (February 28, 1991). *Newsweek*.

Fuoco, Michael A. (March 1, 1991). "Scud Death Toll Rises to 13 from Greensburg Army Unit." *Pittsburgh Post-Gazette*.

Gonzales, David, and E. R. Shipp (March 15, 1991). "So Few Died but How It Hurt Those Back Home: 11 Stories." *New York Times*.

"The Greensburg Disaster: The Story of the 14th Quartermaster Disaster" (Summer 1991). *Military Chaplains' Review*.

Marodi, Randi Ross (February 27, 1991). "Reservist from California Escapes Missile Attack." *Observer-Reporter* (Washington and Green Counties, PA).

Presidential Advisory Committee on Gulf War Illnesses Final Report (December 1996). Washington, DC: U.S. Government Printing Office.

Terry, Don (February 28, 1991). "War in the Gulf: The Families. Scud's Lethal Hit Takes First 3 Female Soldiers." *New York Times.*

Terry, Don, Sam Howe Verhovek, and Mary B. W. Tabor (March 4, 1991). "After the War: The Fires of Patriotism and Cold Necessity Put 13 in Harm's Way." *New York Times.*

Urban, Jim (February 24, 1992). "Reservists Fight Memories of Scud Attack." *Deseret News* (Salt Lake City).

Vigoda, Ralph (December 23, 2002). "In Western Pa., Families Attest to the Price of War." *Philadelphia Inquirer.*

Weigand, Ginny (February 2, 1992). "A Pa. Town Mends Slowly a Year after Scud Attack, Bitterness, Pain." *Philadelphia Inquirer.*

Chapter Twelve

Clare, Micah E. (March 24, 2008). "Face of Defense: Woman Soldier Receives Silver Star." American Forces Press Service.

Littleton, Mark R., and Charles Wright (2005). *Doc: Heroic Stories of Medics, Corpsmen, and Surgeons in Combat.* St. Paul, MN: Zenith.

McGaugh, Scott (2011). *Battlefield Angels:*

Saving Lives under Enemy Fire from Valley Forge to Afghanistan. Oxford: Osprey.

Price, Jay (May 9, 2008). "A Silver Star for Her Mettle." *Chicago Tribune.*

"Private Monica Brown and the Silver Star" (November 26, 2008). Lara Logan interview with Monica Lin Brown. *60 Minutes.* CBS.

"Real Hero: Sgt. Monica Brown" (January 27, 2009). Live Leak. http://www.liveleak .com/view?i=4db_1233100944.

"Silver Star" (March 21, 2008). Katie Couric interview with Monica Lin Brown. *Eye to Eye.* CBS.

Tan, Michelle (September 18, 2011). "Wars Have Changed Combat Medic Training." *Military Times.*

Tyson, Ann Scott (May 1, 2008). "Woman Gains Silver Star and Removal from Combat." *Washington Post.*

Chapter Thirteen

Couch, Dick (2008). *The Sheriff of Ramadi: Navy Seals and the Winning of al-Anbar.* Annapolis, MD: Naval Institute Press.

Deane, Anthony E. (January–February 2010). "Providing Security Force Assistance in an Economy of Force Battle." *Military Review.*

Filkens, Dexter (June 27, 2006). "U.S. and Iraq Take Ramadi a Neighborhood at a Time." *New York Times.*

Fumento, Michael (November 21, 2006). "Return to Ramadi." *Weekly Standard* (Washington, DC).

Fumento, Michael (April 21, 2008). "A Debt That Can Never Be Repaid." *Weekly Standard* (Washington, DC).

Linzer, Dafna, and Thomas E. Ricks (November 28, 2006). "Anbar Picture Grows Clearer, and Bleaker." *Washington Post.*

Lubin, Andrew (April 2008). "Ramadi from the Caliphate to Capitalism." *Proceedings Magazine* (U.S. Naval Institute).

Luttrell, Marcus, and James D. Hornfischer (2012). *Service: A Navy Seal at War.* Boston: Little, Brown.

Michaels, Jim (August 28, 2006). "In Ramadi, the Force Isn't Huge but the Task Is." *USA Today.*

Michaels, Jim (2010). *A Chance in Hell: The Men Who Triumphed Over Iraq's Deadliest City and Turned the Tide of War.* New York: St. Martin's Press.

"Monsoor, Michael Anthony, Petty Officer Second Class (SEAL)" (n.p.). April 5, 1981–September 29, 2006. U.S. Navy biography.

"Navy SEAL Dies Saving Comrades" (October 14, 2006). Associated Press.

Neville, Leigh (2008). *Special Operations Forces in Iraq.* Oxford: Osprey.

Perry, Tony (April 1, 2008). "Giving One Life to Save Three." *Los Angeles Times.*

Reyes, David (October 8, 2006). "Petty Officer 2nd Class Michael A. Monsoor, 25, Garden Grove, California: Navy SEAL Killed in Combat in Ramadi." *Los Angeles Times.*

Roggio, Bill (November 28, 2006). "Anbar, the *Washington Post,* and the Devlin Report." *The Long War Journal.*

Schogol, Jeff (April 1, 2008). "SEAL to Receive Medal of Honor on April 8." *Stars and Stripes.*

Schogol, Jeff (June 14, 2008). "Mike Was a Giver." *Stars and Stripes.*

Tyson, Ann Scott (April 1, 2008). "SEAL Killed in Iraq to Get Medal of Honor." *Washington Post.*

Afterword

Thompson, David L. (1883). "With Burnside at Antietam." In *Battles and Leaders of the Civil War.* Vol. 2. New York: Century.

PHOTO CREDITS

Scott Beveridge, *Observer-Reporter:* 508

AP Photo/Rafiq Maqbool: 550

Courtesy of the Monsoor family and the U.S. Navy: 588

ABOUT THE AUTHORS

Senator John McCain served in the U.S. Navy from 1954 until 1981. He was elected to the U.S. House of Representatives from Arizona in 1982 and to the U.S. Senate in 1986. He was the Republican Party's nominee for president in the 2008 election. He is currently serving his fifth term in the Senate.

Mark Salter is the author, with John McCain, of several books, including *Faith of My Fathers.* He served on Senator McCain's staff for eighteen years.